Readings
in the Philosophy
of Religion

Readings
in the Philosophy
of Religion

edited by
Kelly James Clark

broadview press

Canadian Cataloguing in Publication Data

Main entry under title:
Readings in the philosophy of religion

Includes bibliographical references.
ISBN 1-55111-246-9

1. Religion – Philosophy.   I. Clark, Kelly James, 1956-   .

BL51.C42 2000   210   C99-932225-7

The publisher has made every attempt to locate the authors of the copyrighted material or their heirs and assigns, and would be grateful for information that would allow correction of any errors or omissions in subsequent editions of the work.

broadview press, ltd.
is an independent, international publishing house, incorporated in 1985

North America
Post Office Box 1243, Peterborough, Ontario, Canada K9J 7H5
3576 California Road, Orchard Park, New York, USA 14127
TEL: (705) 743-8990; FAX (705) 743-8353; E-MAIL: customerservice@broadviewpress.com

United Kingdom and Europe
Turpin Distribution Services, Ltd.,
Blackhorse Rd., Letchworth, Hertfordshire, SO6 EHN
TEL: (1462) 672555; FAX: (1462) 480947; E-MAIL: turpin@rsc.org

Australia
St. Clair Press, Post Office Box 287, Rozelle, NSW 2039
TEL: (612) 818-1942; FAX: (612) 418-1923

www.broadviewpress.com

Broadview Press gratefully acknowledges the support of the Ministry of Canadian Heritage through the Book Publishing Industry Development program.

Printed in Canada

To Nicholas Wolsterstorff
friend and philosopher (in that order)

Contents

Part Six
ASIAN PHILOSOPHY OF RELIGION
Introduction: Asian Philosophy of Religion   359

Introduction

The Renaissance in the Philosophy of Religion

During the past thirty years, there has been a remarkable renaissance in philosophy of religion. Due to the influence of Alvin Plantinga, J.L. Mackie, William Alston, Antony Flew, George Mavrodes, Ludwig Wittgenstein (or Wittgensteinians), Nicholas Wolterstorff, Robert and Marilyn Adams, Norman Kretzmann and Eleonore Stump (to name a few), philosophy of religion has grown into many areas. The theistic arguments have been dusted off, developed and criticized; new forms of arguments for the existence of God have sprung up. The daunting deductive argument from evil has been shown to be unsound while new versions of the problem of evil as well as new theodicies have been introduced. Philosophers of religion have given up their defensive stance and have pushed ahead with distinctively religious projects in such areas as God and morality, God and human knowledge, and the nature of God; philosophers are using their technical and intuitive abilities to discuss distinctively religious questions such as "Why pray?" and "Is there a hell?" And increasing recognition of non-theistic religions has forced discussion of, for example, religious pluralism and Buddhist philosophy of religion.

The rebirth of philosophy of religion is especially noteworthy given the reigning anti-religious philosophies. In the heyday of logical positivism, for example, religious belief was reduced to emotive utterances or unimportant nonsense. Religious claims were considered beyond the pale of intelligibility. This rejection of religious belief as nonsensical was not rooted in a deep awareness of divine transcendence; rather it was rooted in intellectual imperialism: to a prior and restrictive commitment to the "world of science."

Logical positivism has been shown for the will-o-the-wisp that it was: prejudice masquerading as cool and detached reason. Logical positivism died a well-deserved death but its facile dismissal of religious belief continues to hold sway in philosophical circles. After all, hasn't Hume shown the arbitrariness of religious hypotheses to account for the design of the universe? Didn't Nietzsche, Freud and Marx reveal the ignoble sources of religious belief? Hasn't the problem of evil demonstrated the impossibility of an omniscient, omnipotent, wholly good being, given the fact of evil?

For most ordinary believers around the world, news of the demise of the divine would have come as a shock. Blissfully unaware of the latest views on this or that, ordinary religious believers struggle to accept and maintain their religious beliefs as they have for millennia. Professional philosophical reflection has grown more and more distant from ordinary people's believing experience and it has gotten increasingly technical and inaccessible to even the most well-educated laypersons.

This collection of essays is an attempt to take seriously the experience of non-professional philosophical religious believers (and unbelievers). The essays have been tried out on undergraduate students for over a decade. Those that students have found to be esoteric, pedantic or incomprehensible have been eliminated. Those that students have found to be disconnected from their own lived experience have been removed. The essays that have survived are potent in terms of both clarity and existential import. Not every essay will appeal to every student, of course, and some are more difficult than others. Nonetheless, for those who are interested in critical reflection on the most fundamental religious concerns, there is ample opportunity here in these essays. And who does not want to know what kind of God, if any at all, exists?

This collection contains essays from both historical and contemporary sources. A good place to start—even where one disagrees—is with Thomas Aquinas (as well as other medievals). Few have reflected on the divine so well and so thoroughly as Thomas Aquinas. The bulk of the essays are from the past twenty years or so and demonstrate the remarkable fertility of recent philosophy of religion.

In conclusion I would like to thank my secretary, Donna Kruithof, for her characteristically kind and generous assistance. I would also like to thank my student assistants, Danielle VandeZande and Jill Forcier, for their invaluable help. And, finally, I'd like to express my gratitude for the inspiration and encouragement of Nicholas Wolsterstorff, to whom this book is dedicated.

Sources

Aquinas. "The Five Ways." From *Summa Theologica*. ©1920-42 Burns & Oates Ltd. (London). Reprinted by permission of Burns & Oates, Ltd.

Leibniz. "On the Ultimate Origination of Things." Public domain.

J.L. Mackie. "Cosmological Arguments." *The Miracles of Theism*. Oxford: Oxford University Press, 1982. Reprinted by permission of Oxford University Press.

William Lane Craig. "The Kalaam Version of the Cosmological Argument." *The Existence of God and the Beginning of the Universe*. ©1979 Here's Life (San Bernardino, CA). Used by permission of the author.

William Paley. "The Watch and the Watchmaker." Public domain.

David Hume. "Critique of the Argument from Design." Used by permission of James Fieser.

Richard Dawkins. "The Blind Watchmaker." *The Blind Watchmaker: Why the Evidence of Evolution Reveals a Universe Without Design*. Copyright ©1996, 1987, 1986 Richard Dawkins. Reprinted by permission of W.W. Norton & Company, Inc.

Michael Denton. "The Puzzle of Perfection." From *Evolution A Theory in Crisis*. Bethesda, Maryland: Adler and Adler Publishing, 1985. ©1985 Michael Denton. Used by permission of the author.

Robin Collins. "The Fine-Tuning Argument." *Reason for the Hope Within*. Ed. Michael Murray. ©1999 Wm B. Eerdmans Publishing Company (Grand Rapids, Michigan). Reprinted by permission of the publisher; all rights reserved.

Plato. "Euthyphro." Public domain.

Robert Merrihew Adams. "Moral Arguments for Theistic Belief." *Rationality and Religious Belief*. Ed. C.F. Delaney. ©1977 University of Notre Dame Press. Used by permission of the publisher.

Linda Zagzebski. "The Virtues of God and the Foundations of Ethics" *Faith and Philosophy* 15:4 (October 1998): 538-53. Reprinted with permission of the editor.

William P. Alston. "Perceiving God." *Journal of Philosophy* LXXXIII (11 November 1986): 655-65. Reprinted by permission.

Alvin Plantinga. "The Self-Refutation of Naturalism." *Warrant and Proper Function.* ©1993 Alvin Plantinga. Reprinted by permission of Oxford University Press, Inc.

Richard Swinburne. "A Cumulative Case for the Existence of God." *Philosophers Who Believe.* Ed. Kelly James Clark. ©1993 InterVarsity Press (Downers Grove, IL). Reprinted by permission of InterVarsity Press.

J.L. Mackie. "The Balance of Probabilities." *The Miracle of Theism.* ©1982 Oxford University Press (New York). Reprinted by permission of Oxford University Press.

Alvin Plantinga. "Arguing for God." *Perspectives in Philosophy.* Ed. Michael Boylan. (Orlando, FL: Harcourt Brace & Company,1993). ©1993 by Alvin Plantinga. Reprinted by permission of the author.

William Wainwright. "The Nature of Reason." *Reason and the Christian Religion.* Ed. Alan Padgett. ©1994 Oxford University Press (New York). Reprinted by permission of Oxford University Press.

W.K. Clifford. "The Ethics of Belief." Public domain.

Anthony Flew. "The Presumption of Atheism." *The Presumption of Atheism* (New York: Barnes & Noble, 1976). ©1976 Antony Flew. Reprinted by permission of the author.

Norman Malcolm. "The Groundlessness of Belief." *Reason and Religion.* Ed. Stuart C. Brown. ©1977 Cornell University Press (Ithaca, NY). Used by permission of Cornell University Press.

Kai Nielsen. "Religion and Groundless Believing." *Autonomy of Religious Belief: A Critical Inquiry.* Ed. Frederick J. Crosson. ©1981 University of Notre Dame Press. Used by permission.

Blaise Pascal. "The Wager." Trans.W.F. Trotter. 1660. Public domain.

William James. "The Will to Believe." Used by permission of James Fieser.

Kelly James Clark. "Without Evidence or Argument." *Five Apologetical Views* (Grand Rapids, Michigan: Zondervan Publishing House, 2000). Reprinted by permission of the publisher.

Philip Quinn. "On Finding the Foundations of Theism." *Faith and Philosophy* 2 (October 1985): 468-86. Reprinted with permission of the editor.

David Hume. "God and Evil." Used by permission of James Fieser.

John Hick. "The Soul-Making Theodicy." *Evil and The God of Love.* ©1996 Harper and Row (New York). Used by permission of the author.

Marilyn McCord Adams. "Horrendous Evils and the Goodness of God." *Proceedings of the Aristotelian Society.* Suppl. V.63 (1989). ©1989 Aristotelian Society. Reprinted by courtesy of the editor.

William Rowe. "The Problem of Evil and Some Varieties of Atheism," *American Philosophical Quarterly,* 16 (1979): 335-341. Reprinted by permission of the editor.

Daniel Howard-Snyder. "Rowe's Argument from Particular Horrors." Used by permission of the author.

Karl Marx. "The Opium of the Masses." The first selection was published in the *DeutschFranzösische Jahrbücher* 1844 (translation located on World Wide Web at URL <http://english-www.hss.cmu.edu/marx/1844-intro.hegel.txt>. The second selection is from *On Religion* with Frederick Engels. ©1964, Schocken Books (New York). Public domain.

Friedrich Nietzsche. "Religion as Resentment." *A Genealogy of Morals*. Trans. William A. Haussmann (New York: Macmillan, 1924). Public domain.

Sigmund Freud. "The Future of an Illusion." *The Future of an Illusion*. Trans. William Robson-Scott (New York: Liveright Publishing Company, 1928). Public domain.

"A Humanist Manifesto." *The New Humanist* VI:3 (May/June 1933):1-5. Public domain.

Johan Scotus Eriugena. "Divine Impassibility," *Periphyseon: On the Division of Nature*. Trans. Myra L. Uhlfelder. ©1976 Bobbs-Merrill (Indianapolis, IN).

Nicholas Wolterstorff. "Suffering Love." *Philosophy and the Christian Faith*. Ed. Thomas V. Morris. ©1988 University of Notre Dame Press. Used by permission.

Thomas Aquinas. "Whether it is Becoming to Pray?" *Summa Theologica*. ©1920-42 Burns & Oates Ltd. (England). Reprinted by permission of Burns & Oates, Ltd.

Eleonore Stump. "Petitionary Prayer." *American Philosophical Quarterly* 16:2 (April 1979): 81-91. Reprinted by permission of the editor.

Stephen Davis. "Universalism, Hell and the Fate of the Ignorant," *Modern Theology* 6 (January 1990): 173-186. Used by permission of Blackwell Publishers.

Marilyn McCord Adams. "The Problem of Hell: A Problem of Evil for Christians." *Reasoned Faith*. Ed. Eleonore Stump. ©1993 Cornell University Press (Ithaca, NY). Used by permission of Cornell University Press.

John Hick. "The Philosophy of Religious Pluralism," *An Interpretation of Religion*. (New Haven, Connecticut: Yale University Press, 1989). ©1989 by John Hick. Used by permission of the author.

Peter van Inwagen. "Non Est Hick," *God, Knowledge and Mystery*. ©1995 Cornell University Press (Ithaca, NY). Used by permission of Cornell University Press.

Patricia Altenbernd Johnson. "Feminist Christian Philosophy." *Faith and Philosophy*, 9:3 (July 1992): 320-34. Used by permission of the Editor.

"The Upanishads." *Upanishads*. Trans. Eknath Easwaran. ©1987 The Blue Mountain Center of Meditation. Reprinted by permission.

"The Life of Buddha." *The Experience of Buddhism*, John Strong (Belmont, CA: Wadsworth Publishing Company, 1995). Reprinted by permission of the publisher.

Bimal K. Matilal. "Mysticism and Reality: Ineffability." *Journal of Indian Philosophy*, 3 (1995): 217-52. Reprinted with kind permission from Kluwer Academic Publishers.

Edward Conze. "Buddhist Philosophy and Its European Parallels," *Philosophy East and West* 13: 1 (January 1963): 9-23. ©1963 by University Of Hawaii Press. Reprinted by permission of the publisher.

Lao-Tzu. "Tao-Te Ching." Trans. Charles Muller. World Wide Web URL <http://www.human.toyogakuenu.ac.jp/~acmuller/contao/laotzu.htm>. Reprinted with kind permission of the translator.

T'ang Chün-I. "Spiritual Values in Taoism." *Philosophy and Culture East and West: East-West Philosophy in Practical Perspective*. Ed. Charles A. Moore (Honolulu: University of Hawaii Press, 1962, repr. 1968). Used by permission of the publisher.

Part One

Arguments for the Existence of God

Introduction

❦

Arguments
for the Existence of God

Introduction. Attempts to prove the existence of God (or the gods or a deity or an ultimate divine reality) are as ancient as philosophy itself. In Western philosophy, the best-developed theistic argument was offered by Aristotle in the fourth century B.C. So compelling was Aristotle's argument that Thomas Aquinas, the great Christian philosopher, reaffirmed it in 1300 A. D. Variations on Aristotle's argument were developed into the so-called cosmological argument. The cosmological argument begins with the existence of the universe itself and asks for an explanation of the universe. Although the argument typically (in modern times) begins from the general fact of the existence of the universe, versions of the cosmological argument are also based on motion and change.

The cosmological argument belongs to a broader class of arguments that are called *a posteriori*. *A posteriori* arguments rely on premises that are known or knowable through experience. The *a posteriori* premises in cosmological arguments include the claims that some things are in motion, that things change, and that the universe exists. Other prominent *a posteriori* arguments are based on the design of the universe, alleged religious experiences, and our sense of right and wrong. *A priori* arguments, on the other hand, are based on premises that are known or knowable independently of experience. The most significant *a priori* argument for the existence of God is the ontological argument. This argument attempts to establish the existence of God by way of the definition or essence of God.

Proofs for the existence of God are part of the project of natural theology. *Natural theology* is the attempt to prove the existence of God without reference to information gained from reputed divine revelation. Natural theology relies not on revelation but on reason and experience to establish the existence of God. The grand tradition of natural theology attempted to prove the existence of God from premises that are universally known. *Classical natural theology* is the attempt to prove the existence of God on the basis of premises that all rational creatures are obliged to accept. If one could make an easy inference to the existence of God on the basis of universally acceptable (and, reputedly, obvious) premises, then belief in God would be required by reason.

The project of classical natural theology was a failure for two reasons. The first is, I believe, the most important. First, there are few universally acceptable premises, at least in matters of fundamental human concern. Rational people, we have learned, rationally disagree. In areas of deep human concern—ethics, for example, politics, and human nature—reasonable people simply judge fundamental truths differently from other reasonable people. The attempt to justify *any* philosophical argument to everyone's rational satisfaction is a snare and a delusion. The second problem is not unrelated to the first. All of the arguments for the existence of God employ key premises whose truth values are difficult, upon reflection, to decide. Although *a posteriori* arguments are rooted in experience, they almost always rely on a controversial metaphysical claim which is distant from experienceable reality, difficult to grasp and resistant to a simple determination of its truth. All of this is not to say, of course, that the premises involved are not true or false; all that follows is that not everyone will see their truth or falsity in any easy way. Rational people—I'll say it again—rationally disagree.[1]

Let us turn to a brief introduction of the proofs and disproofs that are presented in each section.

The cosmological argument. We begin with Thomas Aquinas's famous (or infamous!) Five Ways or five proofs of the existence of God. The first three proofs are, roughly, cosmological arguments. The first of these relies upon the indisputable fact of motion and the second upon the fact of change (from potency to act—say, from cold but potentially hot to actually hot). Both, in turn, depend upon the claim that an infinite regress of movers or changers is impossible. There must be, according to these arguments, a first mover or changer. The third way is intuitively more difficult. It is based on possibility (something that exists but might not have, or doesn't exist but might have) and necessity (something that cannot fail to exist). The assumption that everything is merely possible, according to Aquinas, leads to the absurd conclusion that nothing exists now. But, of course, something does exist now, so our assumption must have been false—not everything is merely possible or, in other words, a necessary being (God?) exists. The fourth way is based on gradations of goodness. And the fifth way, typically called the teleological argument, is based on the simple fact that things work towards ends. These things that attain their ends, but are stupid, must be guided or directed toward that end by something outside of themselves, and this guide or director is God. In our day most people believe that Aquinas's arguments rely on an outdated Aristotelian science (Ways 1, 2 and 5) or are simply fallacious (Way 3).

Leibniz's version of the cosmological argument has supporters even today. This argument is simple:

---

[1] I have stated this as if the crux of the matter for theistic proofs is that there is legitimate disagreement about the truths of the premises. It should be recognized, of course, that some philosophers believe that the crucial premises in all theistic arguments are false.

1. The universe exists.
2. There is a sufficient explanation of the existence of everything.
3. God is the sufficient explanation of the existence of the universe.

Leibniz's argument depends upon the controversial principle of sufficient reason: for every positive fact or truth there is a sufficient reason for its existence or its truth. The principle of sufficient reason does not deny that some things are self-explanatory—they bear their own explanation, so to speak, within themselves. God, of course, is just such a self-explanatory being—he carries his existence within his own nature.

As you might imagine with philosophers, and will discover as you work through this textbook, Leibniz's argument has been roundly criticized. For every philosophical claim there is an equal and opposite criticism. One critic is J.L. Mackie, a recently deceased Oxford philosopher, who offers two objections to the cosmological argument.

A new version of the cosmological argument is based on an older, Arabic argument called the Kalaam argument. William Lane Craig argues that an actual infinity is impossible. Since an eternally existing universe would be an actual infinity, an eternal universe is impossible; therefore, the universe had a beginning in time. He contends that God is the only adequate explanation of the beginning of the universe (although I omit his arguments in support of the existence of God).

The argument from design. The argument from design is probably the most intuitively appealing of all the arguments for the existence of God. Many people are taken with the wonder and beauty of the world, or some feature of it, and contend that it simply could not have occurred by accident or unintentionally. This may be simply formalized as follows:

1. The world is designed.
2. Design implies a designer.
3. Hence, the world has a designer.

Critics of the argument attack either or both of the premises.

This section begins with William Paley's famous argument from design, which had the misfortune of being published twenty-five years after David Hume's powerful critique of arguments from design! Paley's argument begins with the famous analogy of stumbling upon a watch in the wilderness. Rejecting a variety of possible explanations, Paley contends that the only reasonable explanation of the existence and design of the watch is that it had a watchmaker. Paley completes the analogy by demonstrating that the universe resembles a watch in relevant respects. The portion of his book that I have chosen focuses (no pun intended) on the eye. The watch-like character of such parts of the universe implies, according to Paley, that the universe was designed.

Hume's famous critique of the argument from design was published posthumously. Some people consider this work the definitive critique of all natural theology. After carefully presenting the argument, Hume notes its essential reliance on analogy—the universe is *like* a machine. First, Hume demonstrates that even if we accept the analogy, we are not led by reason to affirm the existence of God. Second, Hume offers reasons to reject the analogy—there are relevant disanalogies between the universe and machines. And, finally, Hume suggests that given sufficient time and limited possibilities, the apparent design of the universe would come into existence (without the necessity of divine forethought).

Hume merely suggested that the universe, with all of its remarkable but merely apparent design, could have arisen by chance. But it was not until Darwin that a mechanism was offered to account for "design." As a young student Darwin was deeply impressed with the arguments of Paley. His subsequent research, however, led him to reject the notion of a supernatural designer in favor of a purely natural explanation of "design"—natural selection. There is a watchmaker, contends Richard Dawkins, a contemporary defender of Darwin, but the watchmaker is blind.

Just when some thought the final death-knell had sounded for the argument from design, it has resurfaced in two guises. Michael Denton contends that the design of microscopic cells is so magnificent as to be beyond the reach of chance. Contemporary microbiology sees into a machine-like world that could only have appeared as an undifferentiated blob to the technologically-impaired Darwin. Had Darwin seen into this microscopic world, Denton argues, he would not have been so confident in his rejection of Paley's argument.

The so-called "fine-tuning" argument takes a step back from the design of parts of the universe—like the eye, the wing or the cell—and asks what conditions are necessary for the existence of (human) life at all. Physical constants, such as the law of gravity and the initial explosive forces of the big bang, are precisely fine-tuned for the existence of life. Even the slightest of variations of such constants (and there are many of them) would not have permitted the existence of life. The evidence of fine-tuning suggests, so Robin Collins argues, the existence of a being who intended to create a world which permitted the existence of human agents capable of responding to him.

Moral arguments. Moral arguments for the existence of God are both simple and initially appealing:

1. Right and wrong are objective properties.
2. The best explanation for the existence of objective moral properties is their agreement or disagreement with the will of God.
3. Hence, there is a God.

As early as Plato, this "divine command" theory of morality was critiqued. In his dialogue, "Euthyphro," Plato asked the following questions: Are good things good because the gods will them? Or do the gods will them because they are good? If the former is true, that things are good simply because God wills them, then morality seems arbitrary (God could have willed just anything). But if the latter is true, and God wills things because they are good, then God seems irrelevant to morality (he simply recognizes an independent standard and wills it).

Robert Merrihew Adams offers a defense of the divine command theory which attempts to avoid the charge of arbitrariness. He believes that the arbitrariness problem is resolved by locating the source of morality in the will of a loving God who couldn't and, hence, wouldn't will cruelty. Adams also defends a Kantian approach to morality: the theist has a better reason to be moral which provides a practical reason to believe in God.

Linda Zagzebski opposes divine command theories of morality precisely because of their difficulties in adequately overcoming Euthyphro problems. In addition, she believes that morality focuses more properly on emotions than actions. Emotions, construed as essential to motivations, are the central evaluative property of virtues which are the locus of good actions. Zagzebski's divine motivation theory endorses the view that morality is rooted in the divine, but shifts the locus of morality from the divine will to the divine emotions. In taking this approach, Zagzebski needs to defend the view, against her own tradition's objections, that God indeed has emotions. Zagzebski concludes her essay with a discussion of what she takes to be the advantages of her theory over divine command theories such as those endorsed by Robert Adams.

Religious experience. Arguments for the existence of God based on alleged religious experiences have recently received new life. Perhaps the most important contemporary defender of religious experience is William Alston, who favorably compares religious experience with sensory experience. We routinely take sensory experience to provide reliable information about an empirical reality independent of our minds; likewise Alston contends that religious experience provides reliable information about a divine reality independent of our minds. Alston's strategy is to anticipate and respond to objections to his claim that religious experience relevantly resembles ordinary sensory experience.

The self-refutation of naturalism. Can evolutionary naturalism provide the resources to enable us to trust the reliability of our cognitive faculties? Plantinga's intriguing essay develops the nagging thought, called Darwin's doubt, that evolutionary naturalism can account only for the *survival value* of our beliefs and not the truth of our beliefs. Starting with the undeveloped worries of prominent naturalists, Plantinga develops a sophisticated probabilistic argument against the reliability of our cognitive faculties given the hypotheses of naturalism and evolution. If, given those hypotheses, our cognitive faculties can't be trusted, then they can't be trusted in defense of naturalism and evolution. Theism, of the Christian-Jewish-Moslem variety, however, has the resources to adequately account for the reliability of our cognitive faculties. While the theist can consistently maintain the reliability of her cognitive faculties, the naturalist-evolutionist can do so only on pain of irrationality.

In this and the preceding two sections I have included some of the recent, novel defenses of religious belief without the usual instant "refutation" by a non-theist critic. I have done so for two reasons. First, I want to leave the reader with the (correct) impression that recent philosophy of religion has demonstrated the rich fertility of the project of theistic arguments. Second, I have allotted an entire section to critiques of God, which critiques themselves shall go uncriticized. There have been and will continue to be criticisms of moral arguments, arguments from religious experience and Plantinga's critique of naturalism. And these arguments will be revised in light of legitimate criticism, new arguments will be developed, and new criticisms will be offered.

The balance of probabilities. We have considered various individual arguments for the existence of God. That is, we have considered diverse phenomena—the sheer existence of the universe, the alleged design of the universe, morality, religious experience and the reliability of our cognitive faculties—separately as evidence for the existence of God. One of the most prominent recent developments in theistic arguments involves considering all of this apparently disparate evidence conjointly rather than singly. Relying on developments in the probabilistic analysis of, for example, scientific theories, these new sorts of arguments ask the following question: what is the best explanation of all of the relevant data taken together? Defenders of these so-called "cumulative case arguments" contend that God is the best explanation of, for example, the sheer existence of the universe, the alleged design of the universe, morality, religious experience and the reliability of our cognitive faculties.

Richard Swinburne is perhaps the best-known defender of cumulative case arguments for the existence of God. He contends that all of the traditional arguments provide *some* evidence for God's existence but that, when they are taken together (cumulatively), they make it more probable than not that God exists.

J.L. Mackie, no friend of theism as we have seen, argues that the evidence, when taken cumulatively, makes it overall unlikely that God exists. There are, he contends, adequate naturalistic explanations for all of the phenomena that the theist takes as evidence. Likewise there is the significant improbability of God's existence given the fact of evil. So, given all of the available evidence, it is unlikely that God exists.

Alvin Plantinga offers up quite a few theistic arguments. While admitting that the project of classical natural theology was a failure, Plantinga contends that, nonetheless, the existence and design of the universe do constitute some reason to believe in God. Likewise, other sorts of reasons are available: the success of our cognitive equipment, for example, as well as the phenomena of music and love. In addition, Plantinga offers a rebuttal to Mackie's claim that the existence of God is impossible or unlikely given the fact of evil. Finally, Plantinga briefly defends his famous thesis that belief in God is rational even without the support of an argument.

Conclusion. As noted, we are faced with the remarkable fact of rational disagreement. Brilliant thinkers, with no obvious cognitive defects (but, perhaps, with religious axes to grind), disagree concerning the most fundamental of human questions: Does God exist?

When it comes to theistic arguments, why do apparently rational people disagree? William Wainwright contends that believing involves not only the intellect but the will and the passions. Wainwright contrasts the Lockean view of reason (which opposes the influence of the will and the passions on right reason) with the view of Jonathan Edwards (which both admits and affirms that reason cannot function, in some cases, without the influence of the will). Wainwright comes out on the side of Edwards and defends the significance of this view for the assessment of theistic arguments.

Both Wainwright and Plantinga nudge us toward our next section: What makes belief in God rational? I leave it to the reader to consider whether or not theistic arguments have been defended to such an extent as to establish the rationality of religious belief. I will leave to another section the discussion of whether or not theistic arguments are essential for rational religious belief.

Chapter 1

~~~~

The Cosmological Argument

The Five Ways

Thomas Aquinas *

Claim. The existence of God can be proved in five ways.

The argument from motion. The first and more manifest way is the argument from motion. It is certain, and evident to our senses, that in the world some things are in motion. Now whatever is in motion is put in motion by another, for nothing can be in motion except it is in potentiality to that towards which it is in motion; whereas a thing moves inasmuch as it is in act. For motion is nothing else than the reduction of something from potentiality to actuality. But nothing can be reduced from potentiality to actuality, except by something in a state of actuality. Thus that which is actually hot, as fire, makes wood, which is potentially hot, to be actually hot, and thereby moves and changes it. Now it is not possible that the same thing should be at once in actuality and potentiality in the same respect, but only in different respects. For what is actually hot cannot simultaneously be potentially hot; but it is simultaneously potentially cold. It is therefore impossible that in the same respect and in the same way a thing should be both mover and moved, i.e., that it should move itself. Therefore, whatever is in motion must be put in motion by another. If that by which it is put in motion be itself put in motion, then this also must needs be put in motion by another, and that by another again. But this cannot go on to infinity, because then there would be no first mover, and, consequently, no other mover; seeing that subsequent movers move only inasmuch as they are put in motion by the first mover; as the staff moves only because it is put in motion by the hand. Therefore it is necessary to arrive at a first mover, put in motion by no other; and this everyone understands to be God.

Argument from the nature of efficient causes. The second way is from the nature of the efficient cause. In the world of sense we find there is an order of efficient causes. There is no case known (neither is it, indeed, possible) in which a thing

---

*Thomas Aquinas (1225-1274), an Italian philosopher-theologian, taught at the University of Paris.

is found to be the efficient cause of itself; for so it would be prior to itself, which is impossible. Now in efficient causes it is not possible to go on to infinity, because in all efficient causes following in order, the first is the cause of the intermediate cause, and the intermediate is the cause of the ultimate cause, whether the intermediate cause be several, or only one. Now to take away the cause is to take away the effect. Therefore, if there be no first cause among efficient causes, there will be no ultimate, nor any intermediate cause. But if in efficient causes it is possible to go on to infinity, there will be no first efficient cause, neither will there be an ultimate effect, nor any intermediate efficient causes; all of which is plainly false. Therefore it is necessary to admit a first efficient cause, to which everyone gives the name of God.

Argument from possibility. The third way is taken from possibility and necessity, and runs thus. We find in nature things that are possible to be and not to be, since they are found to be generated, and to corrupt, and consequently, they are possible to be and not to be. But it is impossible for these always to exist, for that which is possible not to be at some time is not. Therefore, if everything is possible not to be, then at one time there could have been nothing in existence. Now if this were true, even now there would be nothing in existence, because that which does not exist only begins to exist by something already existing. Therefore, if at one time nothing was in existence, it would have been impossible for anything to have begun to exist; and thus even now nothing would be in existence—which is absurd. Therefore, not all beings are merely possible, but there must exist something the existence of which is necessary. But every necessary thing either has its necessity caused by another, or not. Now it is impossible to go on to infinity in necessary things which have their necessity caused by another, as has been already proved in regard to efficient causes. Therefore we cannot but postulate the existence of some being having of itself its own necessity, and not receiving it from another, but rather causing in others their necessity. This all men speak of as God.

The argument from gradation. The fourth way is taken from the gradation to be found in things. Among beings there are some more and some less good, true, noble and the like. But "more" and "less" are predicated of different things, according as they resemble in their different ways something which is the maximum, as a thing is said to be hotter according as it more nearly resembles that which is hottest; so that there is something which is truest, something best, something noblest and, consequently, something which is uttermost being; for those things that are greatest in truth are greatest in being, as it is written in *Metaph.* ii. Now the maximum in any genus is the cause of all in that genus; as fire, which is the maximum heat, is the cause of all hot things. Therefore there must also be something which is to all beings the cause of their being, goodness, and every other perfection; and this we call God.

The teleological argument. The fifth way is taken from the governance of the world. We see that things which lack intelligence, such as natural bodies, act for an end, and this is evident from their acting always, or nearly always, in the same way, so as to obtain the best result. Hence it is plain that not fortuitously, but designedly, do they achieve their end. Now whatever lacks intelligence cannot move towards an end, unless it be directed by some being endowed with knowledge and intelligence; as the arrow is shot to its mark by the archer. Therefore some intelligent being exists by whom all natural things are directed to their end; and this being we call God.

Discussion

1. Which of Aquinas's Five Ways seems, at first glance, the most plausible? Why?
2. Do any of the arguments give you the impression that Aquinas is playing a logical trick? Where do you think the "trick" is located?
3. What exactly would each argument, if cogent, prove about the *nature* of God?
4. Suppose that you, like Aquinas, wished to argue for the existence of God based on the best scientific knowledge (*scientia*) of your day. Where do you think you might start? Are there items of knowledge which you think are best explained by the existence of God?

On the Ultimate Origination of Things

Gottfried Willhelm Leibniz *

The sufficient reason for existence. Besides the world or aggregate of finite things we find a certain Unity which is dominant, not only in the sense in which the soul is dominant in me, or rather in which the self or *I* is dominant in my body, but also in a much more exalted manner. For the dominant Unity of the universe not only rules the world, but also constructs or makes it; and it is higher than the world and, if I may so put it, extramundane; it is thus the ultimate reason of things. Now neither in any one single thing, nor in the whole aggregate and series of things, can there be found the sufficient reason of existence. Let us suppose the book of the elements of geometry to have been eternal, one copy always having been written down from an earlier one; it is evident that, even though a reason can be given for the present book out of a past one, nevertheless out of any number of books taken in order going backwards we shall never come upon a full reason; though we might well always wonder why there should have been such books from all time—why there were books at all, and why they were written in this manner. What is true of the books is true also of the different states of the world; for what follows is in some way copied from what precedes (even though there are certain laws of change). And so, however far you go back to earlier states, you will never find in those states a full reason why there should be any world rather than none, and why it should be such as it is.

What if the world were eternal? Indeed, even if you suppose the world eternal, as you will still be supposing nothing but a succession of states and will not in any of them find a sufficient reason, nor however many states you assume will you advance one step towards giving a reason, it is evident that the reason must be sought elsewhere. For in things which are eternal, though there may be no cause, nevertheless there must be known a reason; which reason in things that are permanent is necessity itself or essence, but in the series of changeable things (if this be supposed to be an eternal succession from an earlier to a later) it will be, as will be presently understood, the prevailing of inclinations, in a sphere where reasons do not necessitate (by an absolute or metaphysical necessity, in which the contrary implies a contradiction), but incline. From this it is evident that even by supposing the world to be eternal we cannot escape the ultimate, extra-mundane reason of things, or God.

The metaphysically necessary being. The reasons of the world then lie in something extra-mundane, different from the chain of states, or series of things, whose

---

*Gottfried Willhelm Leibniz (1646-1716) was a German philosopher, scientist, mathematician and diplomat.

aggregate constitutes the world. And so we must pass from physical or hypothetical necessity, which determines the subsequent things of the world by the earlier, to something which is of absolute or metaphysical necessity, for which itself no reason can be given. For the present world is necessary physically or hypothetically, but not absolutely or metaphysically. In other words, when once it is determined that it shall be such and such, it follows that such and such things will come into being. Since then the ultimate root must be in something which is of metaphysical necessity, and since there is no reason of any existent thing except in an existent thing, it follows that there must exist some one Being of metaphysical necessity, that is, from whose essence existence springs; and so there must exist something different from the plurality of beings, that is the world, which, as we have allowed and have shown, is not of metaphysical necessity.

Discussion

1. Leibniz's argument relies on *the principle of sufficient reason*: for every positive fact there is a sufficient reason why that fact obtains. Do you think this principle is true? What would have to be the case if the principle of sufficient reason were false?

2. The principle of sufficient reason does not claim that we can *know* the explanation of every fact, but it claims that there *is* an adequate explanation of every fact. Do you think there are facts that have no explanation? Try to think of an unexplainable fact.

3. Reflect on Leibniz's claim that if the world (the universe) were eternal, it would still require an extra-mundane explanation of its eternal existence. Does that seem right to you? Why or why not?

Cosmological Arguments
*J. L. Mackie**

Contingency and sufficient reason. Leibniz gives what is essentially the same proof in slightly different forms in different works; we can sum up his line of thought as follows.[1] He assumes the *principle of sufficient reason*, that nothing occurs without a sufficient reason why it is so and not otherwise. There must, then, be a sufficient reason for the world as a whole, a reason why something exists rather than nothing. Each thing in the world is contingent, being causally determined by other things: it would not occur if other things were otherwise. The world as a whole, being a collection of such things, is therefore itself contingent. The series of things and events, with their causes, with causes of those causes, and so on, may stretch back infinitely in time; but, if so, then however far back we go, or if we consider the series as a whole, what we have is still contingent and therefore requires a sufficient reason outside this series. That is, there must be a sufficient reason *for* the world which is *other than* the world. This will have to be a necessary being, which contains its own sufficient reason for existence. Briefly, things must have a sufficient reason for their existence, and this must be found ultimately in a necessary being. There must be something free from the disease of contingency, a disease which affects everything in the world and the world as a whole, even if it is infinite in past time.

This argument, however, is open to criticisms of two sorts, summed up in the questions "How do we know that everything must have a sufficient reason?" and "How can there be a necessary being, one that contains its own sufficient reason?" These challenges are related: if the second question cannot be answered satisfactorily, it will follow that things as a whole cannot have a sufficient reason, not merely that we do not know that they must have one.

Does the cosmological argument assume the ontological argument? Kant's criticism of the Leibnizian argument turns upon this second objection; he claims that the cosmological proof depends upon the already criticized ontological proof.[2] The latter starts from the concept of an absolutely necessary being, an *ens realissimum* [most real being], something whose essence includes existence, and tries to derive from that concept itself alone the fact that there is such a being. The cosmological proof "retains the connection of absolute necessity with the highest reality, but instead of reasoning ... from the highest reality to necessity of existence, it reasons from the previously given unconditioned necessity of some being to the unlimited reality of that being." However, Kant's claim that the cosmological proof "rests" or "depends" on the ontological one, that "the so-called cosmological proof really owes any cogency which it may have to the ontological proof from mere con-

---

*J. L. Mackie (1917-1981) taught at Oxford University.

cepts" is at least misleading. The truth is rather this. The cosmological argument purports to show, from the contingency of the world, in conjunction with the principle of sufficient reason, that there must be something else which is not contingent, which exists necessarily, which is or contains its own sufficient reason. When we ask how there could be such a thing, we are offered the notion of an *ens realissimum* whose essence includes existence....

Does this connection imply that successful criticism of the ontological proof undermines the cosmological one also? That depends on the nature of the successful criticism. If its outcome is that the very concept of something's essence including existence is illegitimate—which would perhaps have been shown by Kant's thesis that existence is not a predicate, or by the quantifier analysis of existence in general, if either of these had been correct and uncontroversial—then at least the final step in the cosmological proof is blocked, and Leibniz must either find some different explanation of how something might exist necessarily and contain its own sufficient reason, or else give up even the first step in his proof, abandoning the search for a sufficient reason of the world as a whole. But if the outcome of the successful criticism of the ontological proof were merely that we cannot validly start from a mere concept and thence derive actual existence—if we allowed that there was nothing illegitimate about the concept of a being whose essence includes existence, and insisted only that whatever a concept contains, it is always a further question whether there is something that instantiates it—then the cosmological proof would be unaffected by this criticism. For it does offer something that purports independently to answer this further question, namely the first step, the claim that the contingency of the world shows that a necessary being is required....

Consequently the cosmological proof is not undermined by the so far established weakness of the ontological, though, since Kant thought he had carried through a criticism of the first sort, it would have been consistent for him to say that the cosmological proof was at least seriously threatened by it, that Leibniz would need to find some other account of how there could be a necessary being.

But perhaps we can still make something like Kant's point, even if we are relying only on a criticism of the second sort. Since it is always a further question whether a concept is instantiated or not, no matter how much it contains, the existence even of a being whose essence included existence would not be self-explanatory: there might have failed to be any such thing. This "might" expresses at least a conceptual possibility; if it is alleged that this being none the less exists by a metaphysical necessity, we are still waiting for an explanation of this kind of necessity. The existence of this being is not logically necessary; it does not exist in all logically possible worlds; in what way, then, does it necessarily exist in this world and satisfy the demand for a sufficient reason?

It might be replied that we understand what it is for something to exist contingently, in that it would not have existed if something else had been otherwise: to exist necessarily is to exist but not contingently in this sense. But then the premiss that the natural world as a whole is contingent is not available: though we have some ground for thinking that each part, or each finite temporal stretch, of the world is contingent in this sense upon something else, we have initially no ground for thinking that the world as a whole would not have existed if something else had been otherwise; inference from the contingency of every part to the contingency *in this sense* of the whole is invalid. Alternatively, we might say that something exists contingently if and only if it might not have existed, and by contrast that something exists necessarily if and only if it exists, but it is not the case that it might not have existed. In this sense we could infer the contingency of the whole from the contingency of every part. But once it is conceded, for reasons just given, that it is not logically impossible that the alleged necessary being might not have existed, we have no understanding of how it could be true of this being that it is not the case that it might not have existed. We have as yet no ground for believing that it is even possible that something should exist necessarily in the sense required.

The principle of sufficient reason. This criticism is reinforced by the other objection, "How do we know that everything must have a sufficient reason?". I see no plausibility in the claim that the principle of sufficient reason is known *a priori* to be true. Leibniz thought that reliance on this principle is implicit in our reasoning both about physics and about human behaviour: for example, Archimedes argued that if, in a symmetrical balance, equal weights are placed on either side, neither will go down, because there is no reason why one side should go down rather than the other; and equally a rational being cannot act without a motive.[3] But what is being used by Archimedes is just the rule that like causes produce like effects. This, and in general the search for, and expectation of, causes and regularities and reasons, do indeed guide inquiry in many fields. But the principles used are not known *a priori*, and Samuel Clarke pointed out a difficulty in applying them even to human behaviour: someone who has a good reason for doing either A or B, but no reason for doing one of these rather than the other, will surely choose one arbitrarily rather than do neither.[4] Even if, as is possible, we have some innate tendency to look for and expect such symmetries and continuities and regularities, this does not give us an *a priori* guarantee that such can always be found. In so far as our reliance on such principles is epistemically justified, it is so *a posteriori*, by the degree of success we have had in interpreting the world with their help. And in any case these principles of causation, symmetry, and so on refer to how the world works; we are extrapolating far beyond their so far fruitful use when we postulate a principle of sufficient reason and apply it to the world as a whole. Even if, within the world, everything seemed to have a sufficient reason, that is, a cause in accordance with some regularity, with like causes producing like effects, this would give us little ground for expecting the world as a whole, or its basic causal laws themselves, to have a sufficient reason of some different sort.

The principle of sufficient reason expresses a demand that things should be intelligible *through and through*. The simple reply to the argument which relies on it is that there is nothing that justifies this demand, and nothing that supports the belief that it is satisfiable even in principle. As we have seen in considering the other main objection to Leibniz's argument, it is difficult to see how there even could be anything that would satisfy it. If we reject this demand, we are not thereby committed to saying that things are utterly unintelligible. The sort of intelligibility that is achieved by successful causal inquiry and scientific explanation is not undermined by its inability to make things intelligible through and through. Any particular explanation starts with premises which state "brute facts", and although the brutally factual starting-points of one explanation may themselves be further explained by another, the latter in turn will have to start with something that it does not explain, *and so on however far we go*. But there is no need to see this as unsatisfactory.

A sufficient reason is also sometimes thought of as a final cause or purpose. Indeed, if we think of each event in the history of the world as having (in principle) been explained by its antecedent causes, but still want a further explanation of the whole sequence of events, we must turn to some other sort of explanation. The two candidates that then come to mind are two kinds of purposive or teleological explanation. Things are as they are, Plato suggested, because it is *better* that they should be so.[5] This can be construed either as implying that (objective) value is in itself creative ... or as meaning that some intelligent being sees what would be better, chooses it, and brings it about. But why must we look for a sufficient reason of either of these sorts? The principle of sufficient reason, thus understood, expresses a demand for some kind of absolute purposiveness. But if we reject this demand, we are not thereby saying that "man and the universe are ultimately meaningless."[6] People will still have the purposes that they have, some of which they can fulfil, even if the question "What is the purpose of the world as a whole?" has no positive answer.

The principle of sufficient reason, then, is more far-reaching than the principle that every occurrence has a preceding sufficient cause: the latter, but not the former, would be satisfied by a series of things or events running back infinitely in time, each determined by earlier ones, but with no further explanation of the series as a whole. Such a series would give us only what Leibniz called "physical" or "hypothetical" necessity, whereas the demand for a sufficient reason for the whole body of contingent things and events and laws calls for something with "absolute" or "metaphysical" necessity. But even the weaker, deterministic, principle is not an *a priori* truth, and indeed it may not be a truth at all; much less can this be claimed for the principle of sufficient reason. Perhaps it just expresses an arbitrary demand; it may be intellectually satisfying to believe that there is, objectively, an explanation for everything together, even if we can only guess at what the explanation might be. But we have no right to assume that the universe will comply with our intellectual preferences. Alternatively, the supposed principle may be an unwarranted extension of the determinist one, which, in so far as it is supported, is supported only empirically, by our success in actually finding causes, and can at most be accepted provisionally, not as an *a priori* truth.

Conclusion. The form of the cosmological argument which relies on the principle of sufficient reason therefore fails completely as a demonstrative proof.

Notes

1. The clearest account is in "On the Ultimate Origination of Things", printed, e.g., in G. W. Leibniz, *Philosophical Writings* (Dent, London, 1934), pp. 32-41.
2. Immanuel Kant, *Critique of Pure Reason*, translated by N. Kemp Smith (Macmillan, London, 1933), *Transcendental Dialectic*, Book II, Chapter III, Section 5.
3. *The Leibniz-Clarke Correspondence*, edited by H. G. Alexander (Manchester University Press, 1956 and 1976), Leibniz's Second Paper.
4. The *Leibniz-Clarke Correspondence*, Clarke's Third and Fifth Replies.
5. Plato, *Phaedo*, 97-9.
6. W.L. Craig, *The Cosmological Argument from Plato to Leibniz* (London: Macmillan, 1980), p. 287.

Discussion

1. If each and every part within the universe were explained, do you think the universe as a whole would nonetheless require an explanation? Why or why not?
2. What is the distinction between *a priori* and *a posteriori*? Mackie claims that the principle of sufficient reason is not justifiable *a priori*, so it must be justified *a posteriori* (which cannot, he contends, be done). If we cannot demonstrate the principle of sufficient reason, *a priori* or *a posteriori*, does that mean that it would not be reasonable for anyone to accept it?
3. What would your life be like if you fully realized the consequences of living in a world which lacked a sufficient reason for its existence?

The Kalaam Version of the Cosmological Argument

William Lane Craig★

Why is there something? "The first question which should rightly be asked," wrote the great German philosopher and mathematician Gottfried Willhelm Leibniz, "is: Why is there something rather than nothing?" Think about that for a moment. Why *does* anything exist at all, rather than nothing? Why does the universe, or matter, or anything at all exist, instead of just empty space?

Many great minds have been puzzled by this problem. For example, in his biography of the renowned philosopher Ludwig Wittgenstein, Norman Malcolm reports,

... He said that he sometimes had a certain experience which could best be described by saying that "when I have it, *I wonder at the existence of the World.* I am then inclined to use such phrases as 'How extraordinary that anything should exist!' or 'How extraordinary that the world should exist!'"[1]

Similarly, the Australian philosopher J.J.C. Smart has said, "... My mind often seems to reel under the immense significance this question has for me. That anything exists at all does seem to me a matter for the deepest awe."[2]

Why *does* something exist instead of nothing? Unless we are prepared to believe that the universe simply popped into existence uncaused out of nothing, then the answer must be: Something exists because there is an eternal, uncaused being for which no further explanation is possible. But who or what is this eternal, uncaused being? Leibniz identified it with God. But many modern philosophers have identified it with the universe itself.

Now this is exactly the position of the atheist, that the universe itself is uncaused and eternal, or, as Russell remarks, "... The universe is just there, and that's all." But this means, of course, that our lives are without ultimate significance, value or purpose, and that we are therefore abandoned to futility and despair. Indeed, Russell himself acknowledges that life can be faced only upon the "firm foundation of unyielding despair."[3]

Are there reasons to believe that the universe is not eternal and uncaused, that there is something more? I think that there are.... I want to ... expound two philosophical arguments for why I believe that the universe had a beginning.

An actual infinite? Here is the first philosophical argument:

1. An actual infinite cannot exist.
2. A beginningless series of events in time is an actual infinite.
3. Therefore, a beginningless series of events in time cannot exist.

★William Lane Craig is an itinerant philosopher who is affiliated with Talbot School of Theology.

Let's first examine step one: *an actual infinite cannot exist.* I need to explain what I mean by an actual infinite. A collection of things is said to be actually infinite only if a part of it is equal to the whole of it. For example, which is greater:

1, 2, 3, ...

or

0, 1, 2, 3, ...?

According to prevailing mathematical thought, they are equivalent because they are both actually infinite. This seems strange because there is an extra number in one series that cannot be found in the other. But this only goes to show that in an actually infinite collection, a part of the collection is equal to the whole of the collection.

For the same reason, mathematicians state that the series of even numbers is the same size as the series of all natural numbers, even though the series of all natural numbers contains all the even numbers plus an infinite number of odd numbers as well:

1, 2, 3, ...
2, 4, 6, ...

So a collection is actually infinite if a part of it equals the whole of it.

Now the concept of an *actual* infinite needs to be sharply distinguished from the concept of a *potential* infinite. A potential infinite is a collection that is increasing without limit but is at all times finite. The concept of potential infinity usually comes into play when we add to or subtract from something without stopping. Thus, a finite distance may be said to contain a potentially infinite number of smaller finite distances. This does not mean that there actually are an infinite number of parts in a finite distance; rather it means that one can keep on dividing endlessly and never reach an "infinitieth" division. Infinity merely serves as the limit to which the process approaches. Thus, a potential infinite is not truly infinite. It is simply indefinite. It is at all points finite but always increasing.

To sharpen the distinction between an actual and a potential infinite, we can draw some comparisons between them. The concept of actual infinity is used in set theory to designate a set which has an actually infinite number of members ... But the concept of potential infinity finds no place in set theory, because the members of a set must be definite, whereas a potential infinite is indefinite and acquires new members as it grows. Thus, set theory has only finite or actually infinite sets.

The proper place for the concept of the potential infinite is found in mathematical analysis, as in infinitesimal calculus. There a process may be said to increase or diminish to infinity, in the sense that that process can be continued endlessly with infinity as its terminus ... The concept of actual infinity does not pertain to these operations because an infinite number of operations is never actually made.

According to the great German mathematician David Hilbert, the chief difference between an actual and a potential infinite is that a potential infinite is always something growing toward a limit of infinity, while an actual infinite is a completed totality with an actually infinite number of things.[4]

A good example contrasting these two types of infinity is the series of past, present and future events. If, as the atheist claims, the universe is eternal, then there have occurred in the past an actually infinite number of events. But from any point in the series of events, the number of future events is potentially infinite. Thus, if we pick 1845, the birth-year of Georg Cantor, who discovered infinite sets, as our point of departure, we can see that past events constitute an actual infinity while future events constitute a potential infinity:

| ...past | 1845 | future... |

This is because the past is realized and complete, whereas the future is never fully actualized, but is always finite and always increasing. In the following discussion, it will be exceedingly important to keep the concepts of actual infinity and potential infinity distinct and not to confuse them.

A second clarification that I must make concerns the word "exist." When I say that an actual infinite cannot exist, I mean "exist in the real world" or "exist outside the mind." I am not in any way questioning the legitimacy of using the concept of actual infinity in the realm of mathematics, which is a realm of thought only. What I am arguing is that an actual infinite cannot exist in the real world of stars and planets and rocks and men.

Absurdities. Let me use a few examples to illustrate the absurdities that would result if an actual infinite could exist in reality. Suppose we have a library which contains an actually infinite number of books. Imagine there are only two colors of books, black and red, and these are placed on the shelves alternately: black, red, black, red and so forth. Now if somebody told us that the number of black books equals the number of red books, we would probably not be too surprised. But would we believe someone who told us that the number of black books equals the number of black books plus red books? For in this latter collection we find all the black books plus an infinite number of red books as well.

Or imagine there are three colors of books, or four or five or a hundred. Would you believe someone who claimed that there are as many books in a single color as there are in the entire collection?

Or imagine that there are an infinite number of colors of books. You might assume that there would be one book per color in the infinite collection. But you would be wrong. According to mathematicians, if the collection is actually infinite, there could be for each of the infinite colors an infinite number of books. So you would have an infinity of infinities. And yet it would still be true that if you took all the books of all the colors and added them together, you wouldn't have any more books than if you had taken just the books of a single color.

Let's continue. Suppose each book had a number printed on its spine. Because the collection is actually infinite, *every possible number* is printed on some book. So we could not add another book to the library, for what number would we assign to it? All the numbers have been used up! Thus, the new book could not have a number. But this is absurd, since objects in reality can be numbered.

If an infinite library could exist, it would be impossible to add another book to it. But this conclusion is obviously false, for all we have to do is tear out a page from each of the first hundred books, add a title page, stick them together and put this new book on the shelf. It would be that easy to add to the library. So the only conclusion left to us is that an actually infinite library could not exist.

But suppose we could add to the library, and I put a book on the shelf. According to mathematicians, the number of books in the collection is the same as before. How can this be? If I put the book on the shelf, there is one more book in the collection; if I take it off the shelf, there is one less. I can see myself add and remove the book. Am I really to believe that when I add the book there are no more books in the collection and when I remove it there are no fewer books? Suppose I add an infinity of books to the collection. Am I seriously to believe that there are no more books in the collection than before? What if I add an infinity of infinities of books to the collection? Is there now not one single book more in the collection than before? I find this hard to believe.

Now let's reverse the process and loan out some of the books. Suppose we loan out book number one. Isn't there now one fewer book in the collection? Let's loan out all the odd-numbered books. We have loaned out an infinite number of books, and yet mathematicians would say there are no fewer books in the collection. When we loaned out all these books, a great number of gaps were left behind on the shelves. Suppose we push all the books together again to close the gaps. All those gaps added together would add up to an infinite distance. But, according to mathematicians, the shelves would still be full, the same as before you loaned any out!

Now suppose we loaned out book numbers 4, 5, 6 ... out to infinity. At a single stroke, the collection would be virtually eliminated, the shelves emptied, and the infinite library reduced to finitude. And yet, we have removed exactly the same number of books this time as when we first loaned out all the odd numbered books! Does anybody believe such a library could exist in reality?

These examples serve to illustrate that an actual infinite cannot exist in the real world. Again I want to underline the fact that what I have argued in no way threatens the theoretical system bequeathed by Cantor to modern mathematics. Indeed, some of the most eager enthusiasts of transfinite mathematics, such as David Hilbert, are only too ready to agree that the concept of actual infinity is an idea only and has no relation to the real world. So we can conclude the first step: an actual infinite cannot exist.

Beginningless series = actual infinity. The second step is: *a beginningless series of events in time is an actual infinite.* By "event" I mean something that happens. Thus, this step is concerned with change and holds that, if the series of past events or changes goes back and back and never had a beginning, then, considered all together, these events constitute an actually infinite collection.

Let me provide an example. Suppose we ask someone where a certain star came from. He replies that it came from an explosion in a star that existed before it. Then we ask, where did *that* star come from? Well, it came from another star before that. And where did that star come from? From another, previous star, and so on and so on. This series of stars would be an example of a beginningless series of events in time.

Now if the universe has existed forever, then the series of all past events taken together constitutes an actual infinite, because every event in the past was preceded by another event. Thus, the series of past events would be infinite. It would not be potentially infinite, for we have seen that the past is complete and actual; only the future can be described as a potential infinite. It seems obvious, therefore, that a beginningless series of events in time is an actual infinite.

But that brings us to our conclusion: *a beginningless series of events in time cannot exist.* We know that an actual infinite cannot exist in reality. Since a beginningless series of events in time is an actual infinite, such a series cannot exist. So the series of all past events must be finite and have a beginning. But the universe *is* the series of all events, so the universe must have had a beginning.

Let me give you a few examples to make the point clear. We know that, if an actual infinite could exist in reality, it would be impossible to add to it. But the series of events in time is being added to every day, or at least, so it appears. If the series were actually infinite, then the number of events that have occurred up to the present moment is no greater than the number of events up to, say, 1789, or any point in the past, no matter how long ago it might be.

Take another example. Suppose Earth and Jupiter have been orbiting the sun from eternity. Suppose that it takes the Earth one year to complete one orbit, and it takes Jupiter three years to complete one orbit. So for every one orbit Jupiter completes, Earth completes three. Here is the question: If they have been orbiting from eternity, which has completed more orbits? The answer is: They are equal. Now this seems absurd, since the longer they went, the farther and farther Jupiter would fall behind. How could they possibly be equal?

Or, finally, suppose we meet a man who claims to have been counting from eternity and now he is finishing: ... -5, -4, -3, -2, -1 -0. Now this is impossible, for we may ask, why didn't he finish counting yesterday or the day before or even the year before? By then an infinity of time had already elapsed, so that he should have finished. The fact is we would never find anyone completing such a task because at any previous point in time he would have already finished. There would never be a point in the past at which we could find him counting at all, for he would have already finished. But if, no matter how far back in time we go, we never find him counting, then it cannot be true that he has been counting from eternity. This illustrates once more that the series of past events could not be without a beginning, for if you could not count numbers from eternity, neither could you have events from eternity.

These examples underline the absurdity of a beginningless series of events in time. Because such a series is an actual infinite, and an actual infinite cannot exist, a beginningless series of events in time cannot exist. This means that the universe began to exist, which is the point that we set out to prove.

The second argument: the impossibility of traversing the infinite. Let's look now at the second philosophical argument for the beginning of the universe. Here it is:

1. The series of events in time is a collection formed by adding one member after another.
2. A collection formed by adding one member after another cannot be actually infinite.
3. Therefore, the series of events in time cannot be actually infinite.

This argument does not debate the existence of an actual infinite. But it does argue that an actual infinite cannot come to exist by adding the members of a collection one after the other.

Let's look at the first step: *The series of events in time is a collection formed by adding one member after another.* This point is pretty obvious. When we consider the collection of all past events, it is clear that those events did not exist simultaneously, but they existed one after another in time. So we have one event, then another after that, then another, and so on. So when we talk about the collection of "all past events," we are talking about a collection that has been formed by adding one member after another.

The second step is the crucial one: *A collection formed by adding one member after another cannot be actually infinite.* Why? Because no matter how many members a person added to the collection, he could always add one more. Therefore he could never arrive at infinity.

Sometimes this is called the impossibility of counting to infinity. No matter how many numbers you count, you could always count one more. You would never arrive at infinity.

Or sometimes this is referred to as the impossibility of traversing the infinite. You could never cross an infinite distance. Imagine a man running up a flight of stairs and every time his foot strikes the top step, another step appears above it. It is clear that the man could run forever, but he would never cross all the steps because you could always add one more step.

Now notice that this impossibility has nothing to do with the amount of time available. The very nature of the infinite requires that it cannot be formed by adding one member after another, regardless of the amount of time available. Thus, an infinite collection could come to exist in the real world only if all the members were created simultaneously. For example, if our library of infinite books were to exist in the real world, it would have to be created instantaneously by God. God would say, "Let there be...!" and the library would come into existence all at once. But forming the library by adding one book at a time would be impossible, because you would never arrive at infinity.

Therefore, our conclusion must be: *The series of events in time cannot be actually infinite.* If there were an infinite number of days prior to today, then today would never arrive. It is impossible to "cross" an infinite number of days to reach today. But, obviously, today has arrived. So we know that prior to today, there cannot have been an infinite number of days. Therefore the number of days is finite, and the universe must have had a beginning.

Contemporary philosophers have shown themselves incapable of refuting this reasoning.[5] Thus, one of them asks: "If an infinite series of events has preceded the present moment, how did we get to the present moment? How could we get to the present moment—where we obviously are now—if the present moment was preceded by an infinite series of events?"[6] Concluding that this difficulty has not been overcome and that the issue is still in dispute, he passes on to another subject, leaving the argument unrefuted. Similarly, another philosopher comments rather weakly, "It is difficult to show exactly what is wrong with this argument," and with that remark moves on without further ado.[7]

Conclusion. So we have two philosophical arguments to prove that the universe had a beginning. First, we argued that an actual infinite cannot exist. Since a beginningless universe would involve an actually infinite number of past events, the universe must have had a beginning. Second, we argued that an actually infinite collection cannot be formed by adding one member after another. Since the series of past events has been formed by adding one event after another, it cannot be infinite, and the universe must have had a beginning. [Which, he argues in the remainder of the book, is God.]

Notes

1. Norman Malcolm, *Ludwig Wittgenstein: A Memoir* (London: Oxford University Press, 1958), p. 70.
2. J.J.C. Smart, "The Existence of God," *Church Quarterly Review* 156 (1955), p. 194.
3. Bertrand Russell and F.C. Copleston, "The Existence of God," in *The Existence of God*, ed. with an Introduction by John Hick, Problems of Philosophy Series (New York: Macmillan and Co., 1964), pp. 174,176.
4. David Hilbert, "On the Infinite," in *Philosophy of Mathematics*, ed. with an Introduction by Paul Benacerraf and Hilary Putnam (Englewood Cliffs, N. J.: Prentice Hall, 1964), pp. 139,141.

5. For an in depth discussion of this, see my book, *The Kalaam Cosmological Argument* (London: Macmillan, 1979; New York: Barnes & Noble, 1979), Appendixes 1 and 2.
6. John Hospers, *An Introduction to Philosophical Analysis,* 2nd ed. (London: Routledge & Kegan Paul, 1967), p. 434.
7. William L. Rowe, *The Cosmological Argument* (Princeton, N.J.: Princeton University Press, 1975), p. 122.

Discussion

1. Has your mind ever reeled at the sheer wonder of the existence of the universe? Why or why not?
2. What makes Craig's argument that an actual infinite cannot really exist *seem* so persuasive? *Is* it persuasive?
3. It is impossible, according to Craig's first argument, for the universe to be an actual infinite. But if there is a God, he surely has existed forever. How could an eternally existent God be a better explanation of the existence of the universe than simply postulating an eternally existent universe?

Chapter 2

~~~~~

The Argument from Design

The Watch and the Watchmaker
*William Paley**

The watch. In crossing a heath, suppose I pitched my foot against a *stone*, and were asked how the stone came to be there, I might possibly answer, that for any thing I knew to the contrary it had lain there for ever; nor would it, perhaps, be very easy to show the absurdity of this answer. But suppose I had found a *watch* upon the ground, and it should be inquired how the watch happened to be in that place, I should hardly think of the answer which I had before given, that for any thing I knew the watch might have always been there. Yet why should not this answer serve for the watch as well as for the stone; why is it not as admissible in the second case as in the first? For this reason, and for no other, namely, that when we come to inspect the watch, we perceive—what we could not discover in the stone—that its several parts are framed and put together for a purpose, *e.g.,* that they are so formed and adjusted as to produce motion, and that motion so regulated as to point out the hour of the day; that if the different parts had been differently shaped from what they are, or placed after any other manner or in any other order than that in which they are placed, either no motion at all would have been carried on in the machine, or none which would have answered the use that is now served by it. To reckon up a few of the plainest of these parts and of their offices, all tending to one result: We see a cylindrical box containing a coiled elastic spring, which, by its endeavor to relax itself, turns round the box. We next observe a flexible chain—artificially wrought for the sake of flexure—communicating the action of the spring from the box to the fusee. We then find a series of wheels, the teeth of which catch in and apply to each other, conducting the motion from the fusee to the balance and from the balance to the pointer, and at the same time, by the size and shape of those wheels, so regulating that motion as to terminate in causing an index, by an equable and measured progression, to pass over a given space in a given time. We take notice that the wheels are made of brass, in order to keep them from rust; the springs of steel, no other metal being so elastic; that over the face of

---

*William Paley (1743-1805) was an English philosopher and theologian.

the watch there is placed a glass, a material employed in no other part of the work, but in the room of which, if there had been any other than a transparent substance, the hour could not be seen without opening the case. This mechanism being observed—it requires indeed an examination of the instrument, and perhaps some previous knowledge of the subject, to perceive and understand it; but being once, as we have said, observed and understood, the inference we think is inevitable, that the watch must have had a maker—that there must have existed, at some time and at some place or other, an artificer or artificers who formed it for the purpose which we find it actually to answer, who comprehended its construction and designed its use.

Anticipated objections. Nor would it, I apprehend, weaken the conclusion, that we had never seen a watch made—that we had never known an artist capable of making one—that we were altogether incapable of executing such a piece of workmanship ourselves, or of understanding in what manner it was performed; all this being no more than what is true of some exquisite remains of ancient art, of some lost arts, and, to the generality of mankind, of the more curious productions of modem manufacture. Does one man in a million know how oval frames are turned? Ignorance of this kind exalts our opinion of the unseen and unknown artist's skill, if he be unseen and unknown, but raises no doubt in our minds of the existence and agency of such an artist, at some former time and in some place or other. Nor can I perceive that it varies at all the inference, whether the question arise concerning a human agent or concerning an agent of a different species, or an agent possessing in some respects a different nature.

Neither, secondly, would it invalidate our conclusion that the watch sometimes went wrong, or that it seldom went exactly right. The purpose of the machinery, the design, and the designer might be evident, and in the case supposed, would be evident, in whatever way we accounted for the irregularity of the movement, or whether we could account for it or not. It is not necessary that a machine be perfect, in order to show with what design it was made: still less necessary, where the only question is whether it were made with any design at all.

Nor, thirdly, would it bring any uncertainty into the argument, if there were a few parts of the watch, concerning which we could not discover or had not yet discovered in what manner they conduced to the general effect; or even some parts, concerning which we could not ascertain whether they conduced to that effect in any manner whatever. For, as to the first branch of the case, if by the loss, or disorder, or decay of the parts in question, the movement of the watch were found in fact to be stopped, or disturbed, or retarded, no doubt would remain in our minds as to the utility or intention of these parts, although we should be unable to investigate the manner according to which, or the connection by which, the ultimate effect depended upon their action or assistance; and the more complex the machine, the more likely is this obscurity to arise. Then, as to the second thing supposed, namely, that there were parts which might be spared without prejudice to the movement of the watch, and that we had proved this by experiment, these superfluous parts, even if we were completely assured that they were such, would not vacate the reasoning which we had instituted concerning other parts. The indication of contrivance remained, with respect to them, nearly as it was before.

Nor, fourthly, would any man in his senses think the existence of the watch with its various machinery accounted for, by being told that it was one out of possible combinations of material forms; that whatever he had found in the place where he found the watch, must have contained some internal configuration or other; and that this configuration might be the structure now exhibited, namely, of the works of a watch, as well as a different structure.

Nor, fifthly, would it yield his inquiry more satisfaction, to be answered that there existed in things a principle of order, which had disposed the parts of the watch into their present form and situation. He never knew a watch made by the principle of order; nor can he even form to himself an idea of what is meant by a principle of order, distinct from the intelligence of the watchmaker.

Sixthly, he would be surprised to hear that the mechanism of the watch was no proof of contrivance, only a motive to induce the mind to think so:

And not less surprised to be informed, that the watch in his hand was nothing more than the result of the laws of *metallic* nature. It is a perversion of language to assign any law as the efficient, operative cause of any thing. A law presupposes an agent; for it is only the mode according to which an agent proceeds: it implies a power; for it is the order according to which that power acts. Without this agent, without this power, which are both distinct from itself, the *law* does nothing, is nothing. The expression, the "law of metallic nature," may sound strange and harsh to a philosophic ear; but it seems quite as justifiable as some others which are more familiar to him, such as "the law of vegetable nature," "the law of animal nature," or, indeed, as "the law of nature" in general, when assigned as the cause of phenomena, in exclusion of agency and power, or when it is substituted into the place of these.

Neither, lastly, would our observer be driven out of his conclusion or from his confidence in its truth, by being told that he knew nothing at all about the matter. He knows enough for his argument; he knows the utility of the end; he knows the subserviency and adaptation of the means to the end. These points being known, his ignorance of other points, his doubts concerning other points, affect not the certainty of his reasoning. The consciousness of knowing little need not beget a distrust of that which he does know....

The eye.... [E]very indication of contrivance, every manifestation of design which existed in the watch, exists in the works of nature, with the difference on the side of nature of being greater and more, and that in a degree which exceeds all computation. I mean, that the contrivances of nature surpass the contrivances of art, in the complexity, subtilty, and curiosity of the mechanism; and still more, if possible, do they go beyond them in number and variety; yet, in a multitude of cases, are not less evidently mechanical, not less evidently contrivances, not less evidently accommodated to their end or suited to their office, than are the most perfect productions of human ingenuity.

I know no better method of introducing so large a subject, than that of comparing a single thing with a single thing: an eye, for example, with a telescope. As far as the examination of the instrument goes, there is precisely the same proof that the eye was made for vision, as there is that the telescope was made for assisting it. They are made upon the same principles; both being adjusted to the laws by which the transmission and refraction of rays of light are regulated. I speak not of the origin of the laws themselves; but such laws being fixed, the construction in both cases is adapted to them. For instance, these laws require, in order to produce the same effect, that the rays of light, in passing from water into the eye, should be refracted by a more convex surface than when it passes out of air into the eye. Accordingly we find that the eye of a fish, in that part of it called the crystalline lens, is much rounder than the eye of terrestrial animals. What plainer manifestation of design can there be than this difference? What could a mathematical instrument maker have done more to show his knowledge of his principle, his application of that knowledge, his suiting his means to his end?...

But this, though much, is not the whole: by different species of animals, the faculty we are describing is possessed in degrees suited to the different range of vision which their mode of life and of procuring their food requires. *Birds*, for instance, in general, procure their food by means of their beak; and the distance between the eye and the point of the beak being small, it becomes necessary that they should have the power of seeing very near objects distinctly. On the other hand, from being often elevated much above the ground, living in the air, and moving through it with great velocity, they require for their safety, as well as for assisting them in descrying their prey, a power of seeing at a great distance—a power of which, in birds of rapine, surprising examples are given. The fact accordingly is, that two peculiarities are found in the eyes of birds, both tending to *facilitate* the change upon which the adjustment of the eye to different distances depends. The one is a bony, yet, in most species, a flexible rim or hoop, surrounding the broadest part of the eye, which confining the action of the muscles to that part, increases the effect of their lateral pressure upon the orb, by which pressure its axis is elongated for the purpose of looking at very near objects. The other is an additional muscle called the marsupium, to draw, on occasion, the crystalline lens *back*, and to fit the same eye for the viewing of very distant objects. By these means, the eyes of birds can pass from one extreme to another of their scale of adjustment, with more ease and readiness than the eyes of other animals.

The eyes of *fishes* also, compared with those of terrestrial animals, exhibit certain distinctions of structure adapted to their state and element. We have already observed upon the figure of the crystalline compensating by its roundness the density of the medium through which their light passes. To which we have to add, that the eyes of fish, in their natural and indolent state, appear to be adjusted to near objects, in this respect differing from the human eye, as well as those of quadrupeds and birds. The ordinary shape of the fish's eye being in a much higher degree convex than that of land animals, a corresponding difference attends its muscular conformation, namely, that it is throughout calculated for *flattening* the eye.

The *iris* also in the eyes of fish does not admit of contraction. This is a great difference, of which the probable reason is, that the diminished light in water is never strong for the retina.

In the *eel*, which has to work its head through sand and gravel, the roughest and harshest substances, there is placed before the eye, and at some distance from it, a transparent, horny, convex case or covering, which, without obstructing the sight, defends the organ. To such an animal could any thing be more wanted or more useful?

Thus, in comparison, the eyes of different kinds of animals, we see in their resemblances and distinctions one general plan laid down, and that plan varied with the varying exigencies to which it is to be applied....

In considering vision as achieved by the means of an image formed at the bottom of the eye, we can never reflect without wonder upon the smallness yet correctness of the picture, the subtilty of the touch, the fineness of the lines. A landscape of five or six square leagues is brought into a space of half an inch diameter, yet the multitude of objects which it contains are all preserved, are all discriminated in their magnitudes, positions, figures, colors. The prospect from Hampstead-hill is compressed into the compass of a sixpence, yet circumstantially represented. A stage-coach, travelling at an ordinary speed for half an hour, passes in the eye only over one-twelfth of an inch, yet is this change of place in the image distinctly perceived throughout its whole progress; for it is only by means of that perception that the motion of the coach itself is made sensible to the eye. If any thing can abate our admiration of the smallness of the visual tablet compared with the extent of vision, it is a reflection which the view of nature leads us every hour to make, namely, that in the hands of the Creator, great and little are nothing.

Sturmius held that the examination of the eye was a cure for atheism. Besides that conformity to optical principles which its internal constitution displays, and which alone amounts to a manifestation of intelligence having been exerted in the structure—besides this, which forms, no doubt, the leading character of the organ, there is to be seen, in every thing belonging to it and about it, an extraordinary degree of care, an anxiety for its preservation, due, it if we may so speak, to its value and its tenderness. It is lodged in a strong, deep, bony socket, composed by the junction of seven different bones, hollowed out at their edges. In some few species, as that of the coatimondi, the orbit is not bony throughout; but whenever this is the case, the upper, which is the deficient part, is supplied by a cartilaginous ligament, a substitution which shows the same care. Within this socket it is embedded in fat, of all animal substances the best adapted both to its repose and motion. It is sheltered by the eyebrows—an arch of hair which, like a thatched penthouse, prevents the sweat and moisture of the forehead from running down into it.

But it is still better protected by its *lid*. Of the superficial parts of the animal frame, I know none which, in it, office and structure, is more deserving of attention than the eyelid. It defends the eye; it wipes it; it closes it in sleep. Are there in any work of art whatever, purposes more evident than those which this organ fulfils; or an apparatus for executing those purposes more intelligible, more appropriate, or more mechanical? If it be overlooked by the observer of nature, it can only be because it is obvious and familiar. This is a tendency to be guarded against. We pass by the plainest instances, while we are exploring those which are rare and curious; by which conduct of the understanding we sometimes neglect the strongest observations, being taken up with others which, though more recondite and scientific, are, as solid arguments, entitled to much less consideration.

In order to keep the eye moist and clean—which qualities are necessary to its brightness and its use—a wash is constantly supplied by a secretion for the purpose; and the superfluous brine is conveyed to the nose through a perforation in the bone as large as a goose-quill. When once the fluid has entered the nose, it spreads itself upon the inside of the nostril, and is evaporated by the current of warm air which in the course of respiration is continually passing over it. Can any pipe or outlet for carrying off the waste liquor from a dye-house or distillery, be more mechanical than this is? It is easily perceived that the eye must want moisture; but could the want of the eye generate the gland which produces the tear, or bore the hole by which it is discharged—a hole through a bone?...

The argument cumulative. Were there no example in the world of contrivance except that of the *eye*, it would be alone sufficient to support the conclusion which we draw from it, as to the necessity of an intelligent Creator. It could never be got rid of, because it could not be accounted for by any other supposition which did not contradict all the principles we possess of knowledge—the principles according to which things do, as often as they can be brought to the test of experience, turn out to be true or false. Its coats and humors, constructed as the lenses of a telescope are constructed, for the refraction of rays of light to a point, which forms the proper action of the organ; the provision in its muscular tendons for turning its pupil to the object, similar to that which is given to the telescope by screws, and upon which power of direction in the eye the exercise of its office as all optical instrument depends; the further provision for its defence, for its constant lubricity and moisture, which we see in its socket and its lids, in its glands for the secretion of the matter of tears, its outlet or communication with the nose for carrying off liquid after the eye is washed with it; these provisions compose altogether an apparatus, a system of parts, a preparation of means, so manifest in their design, so exquisite in their contrivance, so successful in their issue, so precious, and so infinitely beneficial in their use, as, in my opinion, to bear down all doubt that can be raised upon the subject. And what I wish, under the title of the present chapter, to observe, is, that if other parts of nature were inaccessible to our inquiries, or even if other parts of nature presented nothing to our examination but disorder and confusion, the validity of this example would remain the same. If there were but one watch in the world, it would not be less certain that it had a maker. If we had never in our lives seen any but one single kind of hydraulic machine, yet if of that one kind we understood the mechanism and use, we should be as perfectly assured that it proceeded from the hand and thought and skill of a workman, as if we visited a museum of the arts, and saw collected there twenty different kinds of machines for drawing water, or a thousand different kinds for other purposes. Of this point each machine is a proof independently of all the rest. So it is with the evidence of divine agency. The proof is not a conclusion which lies at the end of a chain of reasoning, of which chain each instance of contrivance is only a link, and of which, if one link fail, the whole fails; but it is an argument separately supplied by every separate example. An error in stating an example affects only that example. The argument is cumulative in the fullest sense of that term. The eye proves it without the ear; the ear without the eye. The proof in each example is complete; for when the design of the part, and the conduciveness of its structure to that design is shown, the mind may set itself at rest; no future consideration can detract any thing from the force of the example....

The designer. Contrivance, if established, appears to me to prove every thing which we wish to prove. Among other things, it proves the *personality* of the Deity, as distinguished from what is sometimes called nature, sometimes called a principle which terms, in the mouths of those who use them philosophically, seem to be intended to admit and to express an efficacy, but to exclude and to deny a personal agent. Now, that which can contrive, which can design, must be a person. These capacities constitute personality, for they imply consciousness and thought. They require that which can perceive an end or purpose, as well as the power of providing means and directing them to their end. They require a centre in which perceptions unite, and from which volitions flow; which is mind. The acts of a mind prove the existence of a mind; and in whatever a mind resides, is a person. The seat of intellect is a person. We have no authority to limit the properties of mind to any particular corporeal form, or to any particular circumscription of space. These properties subsist, in created nature, under a great variety of sensible forms. Also, every animated being has its *sensorium*; that is, a certain portion of space, within which perception and volition are exerted. This sphere may be enlarged to an indefinite extent—may comprehend the universe; and being so imagined, may serve to furnish us with as good a notion as we are capable of forming, of the *immensity* of the divine nature, that is, of a Being, infinite, as well in essence as in power, yet nevertheless a person....

Wherever we see marks of contrivance, we are led for its cause to an *intelligent* author. And this transition of the understanding is founded upon uniform experience, We see intelligence constantly contriving; that is, we see intelligence constantly producing effects, marked and distinguished by certain properties—not certain particular properties, but by a kind and class of properties, such as relation to an end, relation of parts to one another and to a common purpose. We see, wherever we are witnesses to the actual formation of things nothing except intelligence producing effects so marked and distinguished. Furnished with this experience, we view the productions of nature. We observe *them* also marked and distinguished in the same manner. We wish to account for their origin. Our experience suggests a cause perfectly adequate to this account. No experience, no single instance or example, can be offered in favor of any other. In this cause, therefore, we ought to rest; in this cause the common-sense of mankind has, in fact, rested, because it agrees with that which in all cases is the foundation of knowledge—the undeviating course of their experience....

Discussion

1. Consider a watch and a rock. Which one does the world more relevantly resemble? How would the conclusion of Paley's argument differ if you were to believe that the universe is more like the rock?
2. Now reconsider the watch and compare it with an eye. Do you find it easy or difficult to resist the inclination to believe that the eye was designed?
3. Are there any adequate, non-supernatural, explanations of the apparent design of things like the human eye?

Critique of the Argument from Design
*David Hume**

Cleanthes. Look round the world: contemplate the whole and every part of it: You will find it to be nothing but one great machine, subdivided into an infinite number of lesser machines, which again admit of subdivisions to a degree beyond what human senses and faculties can trace and explain. All these various machines, and even their most minute parts, are adjusted to each other with an accuracy which ravishes into admiration all men who have ever contemplated them. The curious adapting of means to ends, throughout all nature, resembles exactly, though it much exceeds, the productions of human contrivance; of human designs, thought, wisdom, and intelligence. Since, therefore, the effects resemble each other, we are led to infer, by all the rules of analogy, that the causes also resemble; and that the Author of Nature is somewhat similar to the mind of man, though possessed of much larger faculties, proportioned to the grandeur of the work which he has executed. By this argument *a posteriori*, and by this argument alone, do we prove at once the existence of a Deity, and his similarity to human mind and intelligence....

Philo. What I chiefly scruple in this subject, said Philo, is not so much that all religious arguments are by Cleanthes reduced to experience, as that they appear not to be even the most certain and irrefragable of that inferior kind. That a stone will fall, that fire will burn, that the earth has solidity, we have observed a thousand and a thousand times; and when any new instance of this nature is presented, we draw without hesitation the accustomed inference. The exact similarity of the cases gives us a perfect assurance of a similar event; and a stronger evidence is never desired nor sought after. But wherever you depart, in the least, from the similarity of the cases, you diminish proportionably the evidence; and may at last bring it to a very weak analogy, which is confessedly liable to error and uncertainty....

If we see a house, Cleanthes, we conclude, with the greatest certainty, that it had an architect or builder; because this is precisely that species of effect which we have experienced to proceed from that species of cause. But surely you will not affirm, that the universe bears such a resemblance to a house, that we can with the same certainty infer a similar cause, or that the analogy is here entire and perfect. The dissimilitude is so striking, that the utmost you can here pretend to is a guess, a conjecture, a presumption concerning a similar cause; and how that pretension will be received in the world, I leave you to consider.

Cleanthes. It would surely be very ill received, replied Cleanthes; and I should be deservedly blamed and detested, did I allow, that the proofs of a Deity amounted

---

*David Hume (1711-1776) was a Scottish philosopher best known for his skeptical views.

to no more than a guess or conjecture. But is the whole adjustment of means to ends in a house and in the universe so slight a resemblance? The economy of final causes? The order, proportion, and arrangement of every part? Steps of a stair are plainly contrived, that human legs may use them in mounting; and this inference is certain and infallible. Human legs are also contrived for walking and mounting; and this inference, I allow, is not altogether so certain, because of the dissimilarity which you remark; but does it, therefore, deserve the name only of presumption or conjecture?...

Philo. Experience alone can point out to him the true cause of any phenomenon. Now, according to this method of reasoning ... it follows, (and is, indeed, tacitly allowed by Cleanthes himself,) that order, arrangement, or the adjustment of final causes, is not of itself any proof of design; but only so far as it has been experienced to proceed from that principle. For aught we can know *a priori*, matter may contain the source or spring of order originally within itself, as well as mind does; and there is no more difficulty in conceiving, that the several elements, from an internal unknown cause, may fall into the most exquisite arrangement, than to conceive that their ideas, in the great universal mind, from a like internal unknown cause, fall into that arrangement. The equal possibility of both these suppositions is allowed. But, by experience, we find, (according to Cleanthes), that there is a difference between them. Throw several pieces of steel together, without shape or form; they will never arrange themselves so as to compose a watch. Stone, and mortar, and wood, without an architect, never erect a house. But the ideas in a human mind, we see, by an unknown, inexplicable economy, arrange themselves so as to form the plan of a watch or house. Experience, therefore, proves, that there is an original principle of order in mind, not in matter. From similar effects we infer similar causes. The adjustment of means to ends is alike in the universe, as in a machine of human contrivance. The causes, therefore, must be resembling....

But can you think, Cleanthes, that your usual phlegm and philosophy have been preserved in so wide a step as you have taken, when you compared to the universe houses, ships, furniture, machines, and, from their similarity in some circumstances, inferred a similarity in their causes? Thought, design, intelligence, such as we discover in men and other animals, is no more than one of the springs and principles of the universe, as well as heat or cold, attraction or repulsion, and a hundred others, which fall under daily observation.... But, allowing that we were to take the operations of one part of nature upon another, for the foundation of our judgement concerning the origin of the whole, (which never can be admitted,) yet why select so minute, so weak, so bounded a principle, as the reason and design of animals is found to be upon this planet? What peculiar privilege has this little agitation of the brain which we call thought, that we must thus make it the model of the whole universe? Our partiality in our own favour does indeed present it on all occasions; but sound philosophy ought carefully to guard against so natural an illusion....

But to show you still more inconveniences, continued Philo, in your Anthropomorphism, please to take a new survey of your principles. *Like effects prove like causes.* This is the experimental argument; and this, you say too, is the sole theological argument. Now, it is certain, that the liker the effects are which are seen, and the liker the causes which are inferred, the stronger is the argument. Every departure on either side diminishes the probability, and renders the experiment less conclusive. You cannot doubt of the principle; neither ought you to reject its consequences.

Now, Cleanthes, said Philo, with an air of alacrity and triumph, mark the consequences. First, By this method of reasoning, you renounce all claim to infinity in any of the attributes of the Deity. For, as the cause ought only to be proportioned to the effect, and the effect, so far as it falls under our cognisance, is not infinite; what pretensions have we, upon your suppositions, to ascribe that attribute to the Divine Being?...

Secondly, You have no reason, on your theory, for ascribing perfection to the Deity, even in his finite capacity, or for supposing him free from every error, mistake, or incoherence, in his undertakings. There are many inexplicable difficulties in the works of Nature, which, if we allow a perfect author to be proved *a priori*, are easily solved, and become only seeming difficulties, from the narrow capacity of man, who cannot trace infinite relations. But according to your method of reasoning, these difficulties become all real....

But were this world ever so perfect a production, it must still remain uncertain, whether all the excellences of the work can justly be ascribed to the workman. If we survey a ship, what an exalted idea must we form of the ingenuity of the carpenter who framed so complicated, useful, and beautiful a machine? And what surprise must we feel, when we find him a stupid mechanic, who imitated others, and copied an art, which, through a long succession of ages, after multiplied trials, mistakes, corrections, deliberations, and controversies, had been gradually improving? Many worlds might have been botched and bungled, throughout an eternity, ere this system was struck out; much labour lost, many fruitless trials made; and a slow, but continued improvement carried on during infinite ages in the art of world-making. In such subjects, who can determine, where the truth; nay, who can conjecture where the probability lies, amidst a great number of hypotheses which may be proposed, and a still greater which may be imagined?

And what shadow of an argument, continued Philo, can you produce, from your hypothesis, to prove the unity of the Deity? A great number of men join in building a house or ship, in rearing a city, in framing a commonwealth; why may not several deities combine in contriving and framing a world?

To multiply causes without necessity, is indeed contrary to true philosophy: but this principle applies not to the present case. Were one deity antecedently proved by your theory, who were possessed of every attribute requisite to the production of the universe; it would be needless, I own, (though not absurd,) to suppose any other deity existent. But while it is still a question, Whether all these attributes are united in one subject, or dispersed among several independent beings, by what phenomena in nature can we pretend to decide the controversy? Where we see a body raised in a scale, we are sure that there is in the opposite scale, however concealed from sight, some counterpoising weight equal to it; but it is still allowed to doubt, whether that weight be an aggregate of several distinct bodies, or one uniform united mass. And if the weight requisite very much exceeds any thing which we have ever seen conjoined in any single body, the former supposition becomes still more probable and natural. An intelligent being of such vast power and capacity as is necessary to produce the universe, or, to speak in the language of ancient philosophy, so prodigious an animal exceeds all analogy, and even comprehension....

And why not become a perfect Anthropomorphite? Why not assert the deity or deities to be corporeal, and to have eyes, a nose, mouth, ears, &c.? Epicurus maintained, that no man had ever seen reason but in a human figure; therefore the gods must have a human figure. And this argument, which is deservedly so much ridiculed by Cicero, becomes, according to you, solid and philosophical.

In a word, Cleanthes, a man who follows your hypothesis is able perhaps to assert, or conjecture, that the universe, sometime, arose from something like design: but beyond that position he cannot ascertain one single circumstance; and is left afterwards to fix every point of his theology by the utmost license of fancy and hypothesis....

Discussion

1. Clearly outline the argument from design as offered by Cleanthes in the first paragraph.
2. This argument is an argument from analogy and relies on the principle that *like effects prove like causes*. If it were a good analogy, what would follow about God?
3. Hume suggests that the argument might rely on a bad analogy. In what respects is the universe like and unlike a machine?
4. Hume offers an explanation of the "design" of the universe that does not appeal to God. Can you find it? Is it an equally adequate explanation?

The Blind Watchmaker

*Richard Dawkins**

Paley's genius. The watchmaker of my title is borrowed from a famous treatise by the eighteenth-century theologian William Paley. His *Natural Theology*—or *Evidences of the Existence and Attributes of the Deity Collected from the Appearances of Nature*, published in 1802, is the best-known exposition of the "Argument from Design," always the most influential of the arguments for the existence of a God. It is a book that I greatly admire, for in his own time its author succeeded in doing what I am struggling to do now. He had a point to make, he passionately believed in it, and he spared no effort to ram it home clearly. He had a proper reverence for the complexity of the living world, and he saw that it demands a very special kind of explanation. The only thing he got wrong—admittedly quite a big thing!—was the explanation itself. He gave the traditional religious answer to the riddle, but he articulated it more clearly and convincingly than anybody had before. The true explanation is utterly different, and it had to wait for one of the most revolutionary thinkers of all time, Charles Darwin.

Paley begins *Natural Theology* with a famous passage:

> In crossing a heath, suppose I pitched my foot against a *stone*, and were asked how the stone came to be there; I might possibly answer, that, for anything I knew to the contrary, it had lain there for ever: nor would it perhaps be very easy to show the absurdity of this answer. But suppose I had found a *watch* upon the ground, and it should be inquired how the watch happened to be in that place; I should hardly think of the answer which I had before given, that for anything I knew, the watch might have always been there.

Paley here appreciates the difference between natural physical objects like stones, and designed and manufactured objects like watches. He goes on to expound the precision with which the cogs and springs of a watch are fashioned, and the intricacy with which they are put together. If we found an object such as a watch upon a heath, even if we didn't know how it had come into existence, its own precision and intricacy of design would force us to conclude

> that the watch must have had a maker: that there must have existed, at some time, and at some place or other, an artificer or artificers, who formed it for the purpose which we find it actually to answer; who comprehended its construction, and designed its use.

---

*Richard Dawkins is Charles Simonyi Professor of Public Understanding of Science at Oxford University.

Nobody could reasonably dissent from this conclusion, Paley insists, yet that is just what the atheist, in effect, does when he contemplates the works of nature, for:

> every indication of contrivance, every manifestation of design, which existed in the watch, exists in the works of nature; with the difference, on the side of nature, of being greater or more, and that in a degree which exceeds all computation.

Paley drives his point home with beautiful and reverent descriptions of the dissected machinery of life, beginning with the human eye, a favourite example which Darwin was later to use and which will reappear throughout this book. Paley compares the eye with a designed instrument such as a telescope, and concludes that "there is precisely the same proof that the eye was made for vision, as there is that the telescope was made for assisting it." The eye must have had a designer, just as the telescope had.

Paley's error. Paley's argument is made with passionate sincerity and is informed by the best biological scholarship of his day, but it is wrong, gloriously and utterly wrong. The analogy between telescope and eye, between watch and living organism, is false. All appearances to the contrary, the only watchmaker in nature is the blind forces of physics albeit deployed in a very special way. A true watchmaker has foresight: he designs his cogs and springs, and plans their interconnections, with a future purpose in his mind's eye. Natural selection, the blind, unconscious, automatic process which Darwin discovered, and which we now know is the explanation for the existence and apparently purposeful form of all life, has no purpose in mind. It has no mind and no mind's eye. It does not plan for the future. It has no vision, no foresight, no sight at all. If it can be said to play the role of watchmaker in nature, it is the *blind* watchmaker.

Remarkable complexity. I shall explain all this, and much else besides. But one thing I shall not do is belittle the wonder of the living "watches" that so inspired Paley. On the contrary, I shall try to illustrate my feeling that here Paley could have gone even further. When it comes to feeling awe over living "watches" I yield to nobody. I feel more in common with the Reverend William Paley than I do with the distinguished modern philosopher, a well-known atheist, with whom I once discussed the matter at dinner. I said that I could not imagine being an atheist at any time before 1859, when Darwin's *Origin of Species* was published. "What about Hume?," replied the philosopher. "How did Hume explain the organized complexity of the living world?," I asked. "He didn't," said the philosopher. "Why does it need any special explanation?"

Intellectually fulfilled atheism. Paley knew that it needed a special explanation; Darwin knew it, and I suspect that in his heart of hearts my philosopher companion knew it too. In any case it will be my business to show it here. As for David

Hume himself, it is sometimes said that that great Scottish philosopher disposed of the Argument from Design a century before Darwin. But what Hume did was criticize the logic of using apparent design in nature as *positive* evidence for the existence of a God. He did not offer any *alternative* explanation for apparent design, but left the question open. An atheist before Darwin could have said, following Hume: "I have no explanation for complex biological design. All I know is that God isn't a good explanation, so we must wait and hope that somebody comes up with a better one." I can't help feeling that such a position, though logically sound, would have left one feeling pretty unsatisfied, and that although atheism might have been *logically* tenable before Darwin, Darwin made it possible to be an intellectually fulfilled atheist.

Discussion

1. Dawkins seems to imply that it would have been reasonable, up until the time of Darwin, to believe that God was the explanation of design (even for someone like Hume). Does that seem right?
2. Do you think that Darwinian evolutionary theory is an adequate explanation of, for example, the human eye?
3. If Darwin made it possible to be "an intellectually fulfilled atheist," has he likewise made it impossible to be an intellectually fulfilled *theist*?

The Puzzle of Perfection

Michael Denton *

Perfection and chance. While Darwin was attempting to convince the world of the validity of evolution by natural selection he was admitting privately to friends to moments of doubt over its capacity to generate very complicated adaptations or "organs of extreme perfection" as he described them. In a letter to Asa Gray, the American biologist, written in 1861, just two years after the publication of *The Origin of Species*, he acknowledges these doubts and admits that "The eye to this day gives me a cold shudder."[1]

It is easy to sympathize with Darwin. Such feelings have probably occurred to most biologists at times, for to common sense it does indeed appear absurd to propose that chance could have thrown together devices of such complexity and ingenuity that they appear to represent the very epitome of perfection. There can hardly be a student of human physiology who has not on occasion been struck by the sheer brilliance apparent in the design of so many physiological adaptations. Like, for example, in the elegance manifest in the design of the mammalian kidney which combines so many wonderfully clever adaptations to achieve water and salt homeostasis and the control of blood pressure while at the same time concentrating and eliminating from the body urea, the main end product of nitrogen metabolism....

Aside from any quantitative considerations, it seems, intuitively, impossible that such self-evident brilliance in the execution of design could ever have been the result of chance. For, even if we allow that chance might have occasionally hit on a relatively ingenious adaptive end, it seems inconceivable that it could have reached so many ends of such surpassing "perfection." It is, of course, possible to allude to certain sorts of apparent "imperfections" in life, where an adaptation conveys the impression that nature often makes do in an opportunistic sort of way, moulding the odd lucky accident into something resembling an "imperfect" adaptation....Yet, just as a few missing links are not sufficient to close the gaps of nature, a few imperfect adaptations which give every impression of having been achieved by chance are certainly, amid the general perfection of design in nature, an insufficient basis on which to argue for the all-sufficiency of chance. Such imperfections only serve to highlight the fact that, in general, biological adaptations exhibit, as Darwin confessed: "a perfection of structure and coadaptation which justly excites our admiration."[2]

The intuitive feeling that pure chance could never have achieved the degree of complexity and ingenuity so ubiquitous in nature has been a continuing source of scepticism ever since the publication of the *Origin*; and throughout the past century there has always existed a significant minority of first-rate biologists who have

---

*Michael Denton is a microbiologist in New Zealand.

never been able to bring themselves to accept the validity of Darwinian claims. In fact, the number of biologists who have expressed some degree of disillusionment is practically endless. When Arthur Koestler organized the Alpbach Symposium in 1969 called "Beyond Reductionism," for the express purpose of bringing together biologists critical of orthodox Darwinism, he was able to include in the list of participants many authorities of world stature, such as Swedish neurobiologist Holgar Hyden, zoologists Paul Weiss and W. H. Thorpe, linguist David McNeil and child psychologist Jean Piaget. Koestler had this to say in his opening remarks: ."... [I]nvitations were confined to personalities in academic life with undisputed authority in their respective fields, who nevertheless share that holy discontent."[3]

At the Wistar Institute Symposium in 1966, which brought together mathematicians and biologists of impeccable academic credentials, Sir Peter Medawar acknowledged in his introductory address the existence of a widespread feeling of scepticism over the role of chance in evolution, a feeling in his own words that: ."... something is missing from orthodox theory."[4]

Molecular machines. Perhaps in no other area of modern biology is the challenge posed by the extreme complexity and ingenuity of biological adaptations more apparent than in the fascinating new molecular world of the cell. Viewed down a light microscope at a magnification of some several hundred times, such as would have been possible in Darwin's time, a living cell is a relatively disappointing spectacle appearing only as an ever-changing and apparently disordered pattern of blobs and particles which, under the influence of unseen turbulent forces, are continually tossed haphazardly in all directions. To grasp the reality of life as it has been revealed by molecular biology, we must magnify a cell a thousand million times until it is twenty kilometres in diameter and resembles a giant airship large enough to cover a great city like London or New York. What we would then see would be an object of unparalleled complexity and adaptive design. On the surface of the cell we would see millions of openings, like the port holes of a vast space ship, opening and closing to allow a continual stream of materials to flow in and out. If we were to enter one of these openings we would find ourselves in a world of supreme technology and bewildering complexity. We would see endless highly organized corridors and conduits branching in every direction away from the perimeter of the cell, some leading to the central memory bank in the nucleus and others to assembly plants and processing units. The nucleus itself would be a vast spherical chamber more than a kilometre in diameter, resembling a geodesic dome inside of which we would see, all neatly stacked together in ordered arrays, the miles of coiled chains of the DNA molecules. A huge range of products and raw materials would shuttle along all the manifold conduits in a highly ordered fashion to and from all the various assembly plants in the outer regions of the cell.

We would wonder at the level of control implicit in the movement of so many objects down so many seemingly endless conduits, all in perfect unison. We would see all around us, in every direction we looked, all sorts of robot-like machines. We would notice that the simplest of the functional components of the cell, the protein molecules, were astonishingly, complex pieces of molecular machinery, each one consisting of about three thousand atoms arranged in highly organized 3-D spatial conformation. We would wonder even more as we watched the strangely purposeful activities of these weird molecular machines, particularly when we realized that, despite all our accumulated knowledge of physics and chemistry, the task of designing one such molecular machine—that is one single functional protein molecule—would be completely beyond our capacity at present and will probably not be achieved until at least the beginning of the next century. Yet the life of the cell depends on the integrated activities of thousands, certainly tens, and probably hundreds of thousands of different protein molecules.

We would see that nearly every feature of our own advanced machines had its analogue in the cell: artificial languages and their decoding systems, memory banks for information storage and retrieval, elegant control systems regulating the automated assembly of parts and components, error fail-safe and proof-reading devices utilized for quality control, assembly processes involving the principle of prefabrication and modular construction. In fact, so deep would be the feeling of *déjà-vu*, so persuasive the analogy, that much of the terminology we would use to describe this fascinating molecular reality would be borrowed from the world of late twentieth-century technology.

What we would be witnessing would be an object resembling an immense automated factory, a factory larger than a city and carrying out almost as many unique functions as all the manufacturing activities of man on earth. However, it would be a factory which would have one capacity not equalled in any of our own most advanced machines, for it would be capable of replicating its entire structure within a matter of a few hours. To witness such an act at a magnification of one thousand million times would be an awe-inspiring spectacle.

To gain a more objective grasp of the level of complexity the cell represents, consider the problem of constructing an atomic model. Altogether a typical cell contains about ten million million atoms. Suppose we choose to build an exact replica to a scale one thousand million times that of the cell so that each atom of the model would be the size of a tennis ball. Constructing such a model at the rate of one atom per minute, it would take fifty million years to finish, and the object we would end up with would be the giant factory, described above, some twenty kilometres in diameter, with a volume thousands of times that of the Great Pyramid.

Complexity and time. Copying nature, we could speed up the construction of the model by using small molecules such as amino acids and nucleotides rather than individual atoms. Since individual amino acids and nucleotides are made up of between ten and twenty atoms each, this would enable us to finish the project in less than five million years. We could also speed up the project by mass producing those components in the cell which are present in many copies. Perhaps three-quarters of the cell's mass can be accounted for by such components. But even if we could produce these very quickly we would still be faced with manufacturing a quarter of the cell's mass which consists largely of components which only occur once or twice and which would have to be constructed, therefore, on an individual basis. The complexity of the cell, like that of any complex machine, cannot be reduced to any sort of simple pattern, nor can its manufacture be reduced to a simple set of algorithms or programmes. Working continually day and night it would still be difficult to finish the model in the space of one million years.

In terms of complexity, an individual cell is nothing when compared with a system like the mammalian brain. The human brain consists of about ten thousand million nerve cells. Each nerve cell puts out somewhere in the region of between ten thousand and one hundred thousand connecting fibres by which it makes contact with other nerve cells in the brain. Altogether the total number of connections in the human brain approaches 10^{15} or a thousand million million. Numbers in the order of 10^{15} are of course completely beyond comprehension. Imagine an area about half the size of the USA (one million square miles) covered in a forest of trees containing ten thousand trees per square mile. If each tree contained one hundred thousand leaves the total number of leaves in the forest would be 10^{15}, equivalent to the number of connections in the human brain!

Despite the enormity of the number of connections, the ramifying forest of fibres is not a chaotic random tangle but a highly organized network in which a high proportion of the fibres are unique adaptive communication channels following their own specially ordained pathway through the brain. Even if only one hundredth of the connections in the brain were specifically organized, this would still represent a system containing a much greater number of specific connections than in the entire communications network on Earth. Because of the vast number of unique adaptive connections, to assemble an object remotely resembling the brain would take an eternity even applying the most sophisticated engineering techniques.

Undoubtedly, the complexity of biological systems in terms of the sheer number of unique components is very impressive; and it raises the obvious question: could any sort of purely random process ever have assembled such systems in the time available? As all the complexity of a living system is reducible ultimately to its genetic blueprint, the really crucial question to ask is what is the sum total of all the unique adaptive genetic traits necessary for the specification of a higher organism like a mammal? In effect, how many genes are there in the genomes of higher organisms? And how many unique adaptive features are there in each individual gene?...

Biological design. But it is not just the complexity of living systems which is so profoundly challenging, there is also the incredible ingenuity that is so often manifest in their design. Ingenuity in biological design is particularly striking when it is manifest in solutions to problems analogous to those met in our own technology. Without the existence of the camera and the telescope, much of the ingenuity in the design of the eye would not have been perceived. Although the anatomical com-

ponents of the eye were well known by scientists in the fifteenth century, the ingenuity of its design was not appreciated until the seventeenth century when the basic
optics of image formation were first clearly expressed by Kepler and later by
Descartes. However, it was only in the eighteenth and nineteenth centuries, as the
construction of optical instruments became more complicated, utilizing a movable
iris, a focusing device, and corrections for spherical and chromatic aberration, all
features which have their analogue in the eye, that the ingenuity of the optical system could at last be appreciated fully by Darwin and his contemporaries.

We now know the eye to be a far more sophisticated instrument than it
appeared a hundred years ago. Electro-physiological studies have recently revealed
very intricate connections among the nerve cells of the retina, which enable the eye
to carry out many types of preliminary data processing of visual information before
transmitting it in binary form to the brain. The cleverness of these mechanisms has
again been underlined by their close analogy to the sorts of image intensification
and clarification processes carried out today by computers, such as those used by
NASA, on images transmitted from space. Today it would be more accurate to
think of a television camera if we are looking for an analogy to the eye....

But it is at a molecular level where the analogy between the mechanical and
biological worlds is so striking, that the genius of biological design and the perfection of the goals achieved are most pronounced....

Automated assembly is another feature which has reached its epitome in living
systems. Except for relatively simple pieces of machinery—parts of television sets,
ball bearings, milk bottles—fully automated production has not yet been achieved
in our technology. The cell, however, manufactures all its component structures,
even the most complex, by fully automated assembly techniques, which are perfectly regulated and controlled. Unlike our own pseudo-automated assembly
plants, where external controls are being continually applied, the cell's manufacturing capacity is entirely self-regulated.

Modern technology is constantly striving for increased levels of miniaturization.
Consider the *Viking* biology laboratory which recently landed on Mars. Although only
one cubic foot in volume it could carry out as many chemical operations as a university laboratory, and involved some forty thousand functional components—a genuinely incredible achievement! However, as we have seen, every living cell is a verita-
ble automated factory depending on the functioning of up to one hundred thousand
unique proteins each of which can be considered to be a basic working component
analogous to one of the components in the *Viking* lab. Each protein is itself a very
complex object, a machine very much more sophisticated than any of the components
of the *Viking* biology lab, consisting of several thousand atoms, all of which are specifically orientated in space. For the purpose of this comparison, we will ignore the extra
complexity of each of the cell's working components. A typical cell might have a diameter of 20μ and a volume of roughly 4000cμ: the volume of the biology lab on the
Viking space craft was one cubic foot, or approximately 10^{16}cμ, some 10^{13} times
greater than the volume of a living cell containing an equivalent number of compo-

nents. This comparison does not detract from the genius of our technology; it merely emphasizes the quite fantastic character of the technology realized in living systems....

One of the accomplishments of living systems which is, of course, quite without any analogy in the field of our own technology is their capacity for self-duplication. With the dawn of the age of computers and automation after the Second World War, the theoretical possibility of constructing self-replicating automata was considered seriously by mathematicians and engineers. Von Neumann discussed the problem at great length in his famous book *Theory of Self-Reproducing Automata*,[5] but the practical difficulties of converting the dream into reality have proved too daunting. As Von Neumann pointed out, the construction of any sort of self-replicating automaton would necessitate the solution to three fundamental problems: that of storing information; that of duplicating information; and that of designing an automatic factory which could be programmed from the information store to construct all the other components of the machine as well as duplicating itself. The solution to all three problems is found in living things and their elucidation has been one of the triumphs of modern biology.

So efficient is the mechanism of information storage and so elegant the mechanism of duplication of this remarkable molecule that it is hard to escape the feeling that the DNA molecule may be the one and only perfect solution to the twin problems of information storage and duplication for self-replicating automata.

The solution to the problem of the automatic factory lies in the ribosome. Basically, the ribosome is a collection of some fifty or so large molecules, mainly proteins, which fit tightly together. Altogether the ribosome consists of a highly organized structure of more than one million atoms which can synthesise any protein that it is instructed to make by the DNA, including the particular proteins which comprise its own structure—so the ribosome can construct itself!...

It is astonishing to think that this remarkable piece of machinery, which possesses the ultimate capacity to construct every living thing that ever existed on Earth, from a giant redwood to the human brain, can construct all its own components in a matter of minutes and weigh less than 10^{-16} grams. It is of the order of several thousand million million times smaller than the smallest piece of functional machinery ever constructed by man.

Human intelligence is yet another achievement of life which has not been equalled in our technology, despite the tremendous effort and some significant advances which have been made in the past two decades towards the goal of artificial intelligence—a goal which may still be further away than is often assumed. As David Waltz points out in a recent article in the *Scientific American*, no machines have yet been constructed which can in any significant way mimic the cognitive capacities of the human brain.[6] The most telling criticism of current work in artificial intelligence is that it has not been successful in modelling what is called common sense.... It could turn out that both self-duplication and intelligence cannot be achieved in terms of a non-biological plastics' and metals' technology. Perhaps a fully intelligent machine, i.e., one that could mimic the intelligence of man, requires a structure approaching the complexity of the human brain which could mean, as we have seen above, that the goal may never be reached, for an object of this complexity would require eternity for its assembly in terms of our current engineering capabilities.

Paley revisited. The eerie artefact-like character of life and the analogy with our own advanced machines has an important philosophical consequence, for it provides the means for a powerful reformulation of the old analogical argument to design which has been one of the basic creationist arguments used throughout Western history—going back to Aristotle and presented in its classic form by William Paley in his famous watch-to-watchmaker discourse.

According to Paley, we would never infer in the case of a machine, such as a watch, that its design was due to natural processes such as the wind and rain; rather, we would be obliged to postulate a watchmaker. Living things are similar to machines, exhibiting the same sort of adaptive complexity and we must, therefore, infer by analogy that their design is also the result of intelligent activity.

One of the principal weaknesses of this argument was raised by David Hume, who pointed out that organisms may be only superficially like machines but natural in essence. Only if an object is strikingly analogous to a machine in a very profound sense would the inference to design be valid. Hume's criticism is generally considered to have fatally weakened the basic analogical assumption upon which the inference to design is based, and it is certainly true that neither in the eighteenth century nor at any time during the past two centuries has there been sufficient evidence for believing that living organisms were like machines in any profound sense.

It is only possible to view an unknown object as an artefact if its design exploits well-understood technological principles and its creation can be precisely envisaged. For this reason, stone age man would have had great difficulty in recognizing the products of twentieth-century technology as machines and we ourselves would probably experience the same bewilderment at the artefacts of a technological civilization far in advance of our own.

How would stone age man have judged a motor car or a pocket calculator? Incapable of manufacturing anything other than a crudely shaped flint tool, so primitive that it could hardly be distinguished from a natural piece of rock, the inside of a pocket calculator would seem a purposeless tangle of strings—a random maze of straw trapped inside a leather bag. Even megalithic monuments like Stonehenge or the Pyramids, artefacts which are primitive from our twentieth century standpoint, would cause considerable confusion to a paleolithic man. How would an ancient Egyptian have judged an airplane or a submarine? Only if our ancestors had seen a man in the cockpit of the airplane would they have grasped the incredible, that it was an artefact. It would, of course, be an artefact beyond their comprehension—an artefact of the gods.

It has only been over the past twenty years with the molecular biological revolution and with the advances in cybernetic and computer technology that Hume's criticism has been finally invalidated and the analogy between organisms and machines has at last become convincing. In opening up this extraordinary new world of living technology biochemists have become fellow travellers with science fiction writers, explorers in a world of ultimate technology, wondering incredulously as new miracles of atomic engineering are continually brought to light in the course of their strange adventure into the microcosm of life. In every direction the biochemist gazes, as he journeys through this weird molecular labyrinth, he sees devices and appliances reminiscent of our own twentieth-century world of advanced technology. In the atomic fabric of life we have found a reflection of our own technology. We have seen a world as artificial as our own and as familiar as if we had held up a mirror to our own machines.

Paley was not only right in asserting the existence of an analogy between life and machines, but was also remarkably prophetic in guessing that the technological ingenuity realized in living systems is vastly in excess of anything yet accomplished by man. Paley writes:

> Every indication of contrivance, every manifestation of design which existed in the watch exists in the works of nature with the difference, on the side of nature, being greater and more, and that in a degree which exceeds all computation ... yet in a multitude of cases, are not less evidently mechanical, not less evidently contrivances, than are the most perfect productions of human ingenuity.

The almost irresistible force of the analogy has completely undermined the complacent assumption, prevalent in biological circles over most of the past century, that the design hypothesis can be excluded on the grounds that the notion is fundamentally a metaphysical *a priori* concept and therefore scientifically unsound. On the contrary, the inference to design is a purely *a posteriori* induction based on a ruthlessly consistent application of the logic of analogy. The conclusion may have religious implications, but it does not depend on religious presuppositions.

If we are to assume that living things are machines for the purposes of description, research and analysis, and for the purposes of rational and objective debate ... there can be nothing logically inconsistent, as Paley would have argued, in extending the usefulness of the analogy to include an explanation for their origin. It is interesting to speculate how the theory of natural selection might have fared in the nineteenth century had the analogy between the living and mechanical worlds been as apparent then as it is today. The depth of the machine-organism analogy would have more than satisfied William Paley, and would certainly have provided Darwin's antagonists with powerful ammunition with which to resist the idea of natural selection.

Although the argument for design has been unfashionable in biology for the past century, the feeling that chance is an insufficient means of achieving complex adaptations has continually been expressed by a dissenting minority, and this dissent is undiminished today. As we have seen, the dissenters have not only been drawn from the ranks of fundamentalists, Lamarckists and vitalists such as Bergson and Teilhard de Chardin, but also from very respectable members of the scientific establishment.

It is the sheer universality of perfection, the fact that everywhere we look, to whatever depth we look, we find an elegance and ingenuity of an absolutely transcending quality, which so mitigates against the idea of chance. Is it really credible that random processes could have constructed a reality, the smallest element of which—a functional protein or gene—is complex beyond our own creative capacities, a reality which is the very antithesis of chance, which excels in every sense anything produced by the intelligence of man? Alongside the level of ingenuity and complexity exhibited by the molecular machinery of life, even our most advanced artefacts appear clumsy. We feel humbled, as neolithic man would in the presence of twentieth-century technology.

Conclusion. It would be an illusion to think that what we are aware of at present is any more than a fraction of the full extent of biological design. In practically every field of fundamental biological research ever-increasing levels of design and complexity are being revealed at an ever-accelerating rate. The credibility of natural selection is weakened, therefore, not only by the perfection we have already glimpsed but by the expectation of further as yet undreamt of depths of ingenuity and complexity. To those who still dogmatically advocate that all this new reality is the result of pure chance one can only reply, like Alice, incredulous in the face of the contradictory logic of the Red Queen:

> Alice laughed. "There's no use trying," she said. "One can't believe impossible things." "I dare say you haven't had much practice," said the queen. "When I was your age I did it for half an hour a day. Why sometimes I've believed as many as six impossible things before breakfast."[7]

Notes

1. Darwin, C. (1860) in letter to Asa Gray in *Life and Letters of Charles Darwin* (1888) 3 vols., ed. F. Darwin, John Murray, London, vol 2, p 273.
2. Darwin, C. (1860) *The Origin of Species*, 6th ed. (1962) Collier Books, New York, p 26.
3. Koestler, A. (1969) *Beyond Reductionism*, Hutchinson & Co. Ltd., London, p 2.
4. Medawar, P. (1966) Remarks by chairman in *Mathematical Challenges to the Darwinian Interpretation of Evolution*, Wistar Institute Symposium Monograph, vol 5 xi.
5. Von Neumann, J. (1966) *Theory of Self-Reproducing Automata*, University of Illinois Press, Urbana.
6. Waltz, D.L. (1982) "Artificial Intelligence," *Scientific American*, 247(4), pp 101-122.

7. Carroll, L. (1880) *Alice through the Looking-Glass*, Macmillan and Co., London, p 100.

Discussion

1. If Denton is right, the design argument is alive and well. Do you think he's right? Defend your position.
2. Are cells of living organisms sufficiently machine-like to overcome Hume's criticism that the (parts of) the universe are not like machines?
3. Now do you think Darwinian evolutionary theory is an adequate explanation of the existence of design? Has Denton made it easier to be an intellectually fulfilled theist? Has he made it more difficult to be an intellectually fulfilled atheist?

The Fine-Tuning Argument

Robin Collins ⃰

Introduction. Suppose we went on a mission to Mars, and found a domed structure in which everything was set up just right for life to exist. The temperature, for example, was set around 70° F and the humidity was at 50%; moreover, there was an oxygen recycling system, an energy gathering system, and a whole system for the production of food. Put simply, the domed structure appeared to be a fully functioning biosphere. What conclusion would we draw from finding this structure? Would we draw the conclusion that it just happened to form by chance? Certainly not. Instead, we would unanimously conclude that it was designed by some intelligent being. Why would we draw this conclusion? Because an intelligent designer appears to be the only plausible explanation for the existence of the structure. That is, the only alternative explanation we can think of—that the structure was formed by some natural process—seems extremely unlikely. Of course, it is *possible* that, for example, through some volcanic eruption various metals and other compounds could have formed, and then separated out in just the right way to produce the "biosphere," but such a scenario strikes us as extraordinarily unlikely, thus making this alternative explanation unbelievable.

The universe is analogous to such a "biosphere," according to recent findings in physics. Almost everything about the basic structure of the universe—for example, the fundamental laws and parameters of physics and the initial distribution of matter and energy—is balanced on a razor's edge for life to occur. As the eminent Princeton physicist Freeman Dyson notes, "There are many ... lucky accidents in physics. Without such accidents, water could not exist as liquid, chains of carbon atoms could not form complex organic molecules, and hydrogen atoms could not form breakable bridges between molecules"[1]—in short, life as we know it would be impossible.

Scientists call this extraordinary balancing of the parameters of physics and the initial conditions of the universe the "fine-tuning of the cosmos." It has been extensively discussed by philosophers, theologians, and scientists, especially since the early 1970s, with hundreds of articles and dozens of books written on the topic. Today, it is widely regarded as offering by far the most persuasive current argument for the existence of God. For example, theoretical physicist and popular science writer Paul Davies—whose early writings were not particularly sympathetic to theism—claims that with regard to basic structure of the universe, "the impression of design is overwhelming."[2] Similarly, in response to the life-permitting fine-tuning of the nuclear resonances responsible for the oxygen and carbon synthesis in stars, the famous astrophysicist Sir Fred Hoyle declares that:

⃰Robin Collins is a professor of Philosophy at Messiah College.

I do not believe that any scientists who examined the evidence would fail to draw the inference that the laws of nuclear physics have been deliberately designed with regard to the consequences they produce inside stars. If this is so, then my apparently random quirks have become part of a deep-laid scheme. If not then we are back again at a monstrous sequence of accidents.[3]

The evidence of fine-tuning. A few examples of this fine-tuning are listed below:

1. If the initial explosion of the big bang had differed in strength by as little as 1 part in 10^{60}, the universe would have either quickly collapsed back on itself, or expanded too rapidly for stars to form. In either case, life would be impossible.[4]
2. Calculations indicate that if the strong nuclear force, the force that binds protons and neutrons together in an atom, had been stronger or weaker by as little as 5%, life would be impossible.[5]
3. Calculations by Brandon Carter show that if gravity had been stronger or weaker by 1 part in 10^{40}, then life-sustaining stars like the sun could not exist. This would most likely make life impossible.[6]
4. If the neutron were not about 1.001 times the mass of the proton, all protons would have decayed into neutrons or all neutrons would have decayed into protons, and thus life would not be possible.[7]
5. If the electromagnetic force were slightly stronger or weaker, life would be impossible, for a variety of different reasons.[8]

Imaginatively, one could think of each instance of fine-tuning as a radio dial: unless all the dials are set exactly right, life would be impossible. Or, one could think of the initial conditions of the universe and the fundamental parameters of physics as a dart board that fills the whole galaxy, and the conditions necessary for life to exist as a small one-foot wide target: unless the dart hits the target, life would be impossible. The fact that the dials are perfectly set, or the dart has hit the target, strongly suggests that someone set the dials or aimed the dart, for it seems enormously improbable that such a coincidence could have happened by chance.

Although individual calculations of fine-tuning are only approximate and could be in error, the fact that the universe is fine-tuned for life is almost beyond question because of the large number of independent instances of apparent fine-tuning. As philosopher John Leslie has pointed out, "clues heaped upon clues can constitute weighty evidence despite doubts about each element in the pile."[9] What is controversial, however, is the degree to which the fine-tuning provides evidence for the existence of God. As impressive as the argument from fine-tuning seems to be, atheists have raised several significant objections to it. Consequently, those who are aware of these objections, or have thought of them on their own, often will find the argument unconvincing.... My goal in this chapter, therefore, is to make the fine-tuning argument as strong as possible. This will involve developing the argument in as objective and rigorous way as we can, and then answering the major atheist objections to it. Before launching into this, however, we will need to make a preliminary distinction.

A preliminary distinction. To rigorously develop the fine-tuning argument, we will find it useful to distinguish between what I shall call the *atheistic single-universe hypothesis* and the *atheistic many-universes hypothesis*. According to the atheistic single-universe hypothesis, there is only one universe, and it is ultimately an inexplicable, "brute" fact that the universe exists and is fine-tuned. Many atheists, however, advocate another hypothesis, one which attempts to explain how the seemingly improbable fine-tuning of the universe could be the result of chance. This hypothesis is known as the *atheistic many-worlds hypothesis*, or the *atheistic many-universes hypothesis*. According to this hypothesis, there exists what could be imaginatively thought of as a "universe generator" that produces a very large or infinite number of universes, with each universe having a randomly selected set of initial conditions and values for the parameters of physics. Because this generator produces so many universes, just by chance it will eventually produce one that is fine-tuned for intelligent life to occur.

General principle of reasoning used. We will formulate the fine-tuning argument against the atheistic single-universe hypothesis in terms of what I will call *the prime principle of confirmation*. The prime principle of confirmation is a general principle of reasoning which tells us when some observation counts as evidence in favor of one hypothesis over another. Simply put, the principle says that *whenever we are considering two competing hypotheses, an observation counts as evidence in favor of the hypothesis under which the observation has the highest probability (or is the least improbable)*. (Or, put slightly differently, the principle says that whenever we are considering two competing hypotheses, H_1 and H_2, an observation, O, counts as evidence in favor of H_1 over H_2 if O is more probable under H_1 than it is under H_2.) Moreover, the degree to which the evidence counts in favor of one hypothesis over another is proportional to the degree to which the observation is more probable under the one hypothesis than the other.

For example, the fine-tuning is much, much more probable under theism than under the atheistic single-universe hypothesis, so it counts as strong evidence for theism over this atheistic hypothesis. In the next major subsection, we will present a more formal and elaborated rendition of the fine-tuning argument in terms of the prime principle. First, however, let's look at two illustrations of the principle and then present some support for it.

For our first illustration, suppose that I went hiking in the mountains, and found underneath a certain cliff a group of rocks arranged in a formation that clearly formed the pattern "Welcome to the mountains Robin Collins." One hypothesis is that, by chance, the rocks just happened to be arranged in that pattern—ultimately, perhaps, because of certain initial conditions of the universe. Suppose the only viable alternative hypothesis is that my brother, who was in the mountains before me, arranged the rocks in this way. Most of us would immediately take the arrangements of rocks to be strong evidence in favor of the "brother" hypothesis over the "chance" hypothesis. Why? Because it strikes us as extremely *improbable* that the rocks would be arranged that way by chance, but *not improbable* at all that my brother would place them in that configuration. Thus, by the prime principle of confirmation we would conclude that the arrangement of rocks strongly supports the "brother" hypothesis over the chance hypothesis.

Or consider another case, that of finding the defendant's fingerprints on the murder weapon. Normally, we would take such a finding as strong evidence that the defendant was guilty. Why? Because we judge that it would be *unlikely* for these fingerprints to be on the murder weapon if the defendant was innocent, but *not unlikely* if the defendant was guilty. That is, we would go through the same sort of reasoning as in the above case.

Several things can be said in favor of the prime principle of confirmation. First, many philosophers think that this principle can be derived from what is known as the *probability calculus*, the set of mathematical rules that are typically assumed to govern probability. Second, there does not appear to be any case of recognizably good reasoning that violates this principle. Finally, the principle appears to have a wide range of applicability, undergirding much of our reasoning in science and everyday life, as the examples above illustrate. Indeed, some have even claimed that a slightly more general version of this principle undergirds all scientific reasoning. Because of all these reasons in favor of the principle, we can be very confident in it.

The argument developed. Let us summarize the fine-tuning argument by explicitly listing its two premises and its conclusion:

Premise 1. The existence of the fine-tuning is not improbable under theism.
Premise 2. The existence of the fine-tuning is very improbable under the atheistic single-universe hypothesis.
Conclusion: From premises (1) and (2) and the prime principle of confirmation, it follows that the fine-tuning data provides strong evidence in favor of the design hypothesis over the atheistic single-universe hypothesis.

At this point, we should pause to note two features of this argument. First, the argument does not say that the fine-tuning evidence proves that the universe was designed, or even that it is likely that the universe was designed. In order to justify these sorts of claims, we would have to look at the full range of evidence both for and against the design hypothesis, something we are not doing in this chapter. Rather, the argument merely concludes that the fine-tuning strongly *supports* theism *over* the atheistic single-universe hypothesis.

In this way, the evidence of fine-tuning argument is much like fingerprints found on the gun: although they can provide strong evidence that the defendant committed the murder, one could not conclude merely from them alone that the defendant is guilty; one would also have to look at all the other evidence offered.

Perhaps, for instance, ten reliable witnesses claimed to see the defendant at a party at the time of the shooting. In this case, the fingerprints would still count as significant evidence of guilt, but this evidence would be counterbalanced by the testimony of the witnesses. Similarly the evidence of fine-tuning strongly supports theism over the atheistic single-universe hypothesis, though it does not itself show that, everything considered, theism is the most plausible explanation of the world. Nonetheless, as I argue in the conclusion of this chapter, the evidence of fine-tuning provides a much stronger and more objective argument for theism (over the atheistic single-universe hypothesis) than the strongest atheistic argument does against theism.

The second feature of the argument we should note is that, given the truth of *the prime principle of confirmation*, the conclusion of the argument follows from the premises. Specifically, if the premises of the argument are true, then we are guaranteed that the conclusion is true: that is, the argument is what philosophers call *valid*. Thus, insofar as we can show that the premises of the argument are true, we will have shown that the conclusion is true. Our next task, therefore, is to attempt to show that the premises are true, or at least that we have strong reasons to believe them.

Support for the premises. Premise (1) is easy to support and fairly uncontroversial. The argument in support of it can be simply stated as follows: *since God is an all good being, and it is good for intelligent, conscious beings to exist, it is not surprising or improbable that God would create a world that could support intelligent life.* Thus, the fine-tuning is not improbable under theism, as premise (1) asserts.

Premise (2) may be defended as follows. Upon looking at the data, many people find it very obvious that the fine-tuning is highly improbable under the atheistic single-universe hypothesis. And it is easy to see why when we think of the fine-tuning in terms of the analogies offered earlier. In the dart-board analogy, for example, the initial conditions of the universe and the fundamental parameters of physics are thought of as a dart-board that fills the whole galaxy, and the conditions necessary for life to exist as a small one-foot wide target. Accordingly, from this analogy it seems obvious that it would be highly improbable for the fine-tuning to occur under the atheistic single-universe hypothesis—that is, for the dart to hit the board by chance.

Some objection to the fine-tuning argument. As powerful as the core version of the fine-tuning argument is, several major objections have been raised to it by both atheists and theists. In this section, we will consider these objections in turn.

Objection 1: *More Fundamental Law Objection.* One criticism of the fine-tuning argument is that, as far as we know, there could be a more fundamental law under which the parameters of physics *must* have the values they do. Thus, given such a law, it is not improbable that the known parameters of physics fall within the life-permitting range.

Besides being entirely speculative, the problem with postulating such a law is that it simply moves the improbability of the fine-tuning up one level, to that of the postulated physical law itself. Under this hypothesis, what is improbable is that of all the conceivable fundamental physical laws there could be, the universe just happens to have the one that constrains the parameters of physics in a life-permitting way. Thus, trying to explain the fine-tuning by postulating this sort of fundamental law is like trying to explain why the pattern of rocks below a cliff spell "Welcome to the mountains Robin Collins" by postulating that an earthquake occurred and that all the rocks on the cliff face were arranged in just the right configuration to fall into the pattern in question. Clearly this explanation merely transfers the improbability up one level, since now it seems enormously improbable that of all the possible configurations the rocks could be in on the cliff face, they are in the one which results in the pattern "Welcome to the mountains Robin Collins."

A similar sort of response can be given to the claim that the fine-tuning is not improbable because it might be *logically necessary* for the parameters of physics to have life-permitting values. That is, according to this claim, the parameters of physics must have life-permitting values in the same way $2 + 2$ must equal 4, or the interior angles of a triangle must add up to 180 degrees in Euclidian geometry. Like the "more fundamental law" proposal above, however, this postulate simply transfers the improbability up one level: of all the laws and parameters of physics that conceivably could have been logically necessary, it seems highly improbable that it would be those that are life-permitting.

Objection 2: *Other Forms of Life Objection.* Another objection people commonly raise to the fine-tuning argument is that as far as we know, other forms of life could exist even if the parameters of physics were different. So, it is claimed, the fine-tuning argument ends up presupposing that all forms of intelligent life must be like us. The answer to this objection is that most cases of fine-tuning do not make this presupposition. Consider, for instance, the case of the fine-tuning of the strong nuclear force. If it were slightly larger or smaller, no atoms could exist other than hydrogen. Contrary to what one might see on *Star Trek*, an intelligent life form cannot be composed merely of hydrogen gas: there is simply not enough stable complexity. So, in general the fine-tuning argument merely presupposes that intelligent life requires some degree of stable, reproducible organized complexity. This is certainly a very reasonable assumption.

Objection 3. *Anthropic Principle Objection.* According to the weak version of the so-called *anthropic principle*, if the laws of nature were not fine-tuned, we would not be here to comment on the fact. Some have argued, therefore, that the fine-tuning is not really *improbable or surprising* at all under atheism, but simply follows from the fact that we exist. The response to this objection is to simply restate the argument in terms of our existence: our existence as embodied, intelligent beings is extremely unlikely under the atheistic single-universe hypothesis (since our existence requires fine-tuning), but not improbable under theism. Then, we simply apply the prime principle of confirmation to draw the conclusion that *our existence* strongly confirms theism over the atheistic single-universe hypothesis.

To further illustrate this response, consider the following "firing-squad" analogy. As John Leslie (1988, p. 304) points out, if fifty sharp shooters all miss me, the response "if they had not missed me I wouldn't be here to consider the fact" is not adequate. Instead, I would naturally conclude that there was some reason why they all missed, such as that they never really intended to kill me. Why would I conclude this? Because my continued existence would be very improbable under the hypothesis that they missed me by chance, but not improbable under the hypothesis that there was some reason why they missed me. Thus, by the prime principle of confirmation, my continued existence strongly confirms the latter hypothesis.

Objection 4: *The "Who Designed God?" Objection.* Perhaps the most common objection that atheists raise to the argument from design, of which the fine-tuning argument is one instance, is that postulating the existence of God does not solve the problem of design, but merely transfers it up one level. Atheist George Smith, for example, claims that:

> If the universe is wonderfully designed, surely God is even more wonderfully designed. He must, therefore, have had a designer even more wonderful than He is. If God did not require a designer, then there is no reason why such a relatively less wonderful thing as the universe needed one.[10]

Or, as philosopher J.J.C. Smart states the objection:

> If we postulate God in addition to the created universe we increase the complexity of our hypothesis. We have all the complexity of the universe itself, and we have in addition the at least equal complexity of God. (The designer of an artifact must be at least as complex as the designed artifact).... *If the theist can show the atheist that postulating God actually reduces the complexity of one's total world view, then the atheist should be a theist.*[11]

The first response to the above atheist objection is to point out that the atheist claim that the designer of an artifact must be as complex as the artifact designed is certainly not obvious. But I do believe that their claim has some intuitive plausibility: for example, in the world we experience, organized complexity seems only to be produced by systems that already possess it, such as the human brain/mind, a factory, or an organisms' biological parent.

The second, and better, response is to point out that, at most, the atheist objection only works against a version of the design argument that claims that all organized complexity needs an explanation, and that God is the best explanation of the organized complexity found in the world. The version of the argument I presented against the atheistic single-universe hypothesis, however, only required that the fine-tuning be more probable under theism than under the atheistic single-universe hypothesis. But this requirement is still met even if God exhibits tremendous internal complexity, far exceeding that of the universe. Thus, even if we were to grant the atheist assumption that the designer of an artifact must be as complex as the artifact, the fine-tuning would still give us strong reasons to prefer theism over the atheistic single-universe hypothesis.

To illustrate, consider the example of the "biosphere" on Mars presented at the beginning of this paper. As mentioned above, the existence of the biosphere would be much more probable under the hypothesis that intelligent life once visited Mars than under the chance hypothesis. Thus, by the prime principle of confirmation, the existence of such a "biosphere" would constitute strong evidence that intelligent, extraterrestrial life had once been on Mars, even though this alien life would most likely have to be much more complex than the "biosphere" itself.

The final response theists can give to this objection is to show that a super-mind such as God would not require a high degree of unexplained organized complexity to create the universe....

The many-universes hypothesis. In response to theistic explanation of fine-tuning of the cosmos, many atheists have offered an alternative explanation, what I will call the atheistic *many-universes hypothesis*. (In the literature it is more commonly referred to as the *Many Worlds hypothesis*, though I believe this name is somewhat misleading.) According to this hypothesis, there are a very large—perhaps infinite—number of universes, with the fundamental parameters of physics varying from universe to universe. Of course, in the vast majority of these universes the parameters of physics would not have life-permitting values. Nonetheless, in a small proportion of universes they would, and consequently it is no longer improbable that universes such as ours exist that are fine-tuned for life to occur.

Advocates of this hypothesis offer various types of models for where these universes came from. We will present what are probably the two most popular and plausible, the so-called *vacuum fluctuation* models and the *oscillating Big Bang* models. According to the vacuum fluctuation models, our universe, along with these other universes, were generated by quantum fluctuations in a pre-existing super-space.[12] Imaginatively, one can think of this pre-existing superspace as an infinitely extending ocean full of soap, and each universe generated out of this superspace as a soap-bubble which spontaneously forms on the ocean.

The other model, the oscillating Big Bang model, is a version of the *Big Bang* theory. According to the Big Bang theory, the universe came into existence in an "explosion" (that is, a "bang") somewhere between 10 and 15 billion years ago. According to the *oscillating* Big Bang theory, our universe will eventually collapse back in on itself (what is called the "Big Crunch") and then from that "Big Crunch" will arise another "Big Bang", forming a new universe, which will in turn itself collapse, and so on. According to those who use this model to attempt to explain the fine-tuning, during every cycle, the parameters of physics and the initial conditions of the universe are reset at random. Since this process of collapse, explosion, collapse, and explosion has been going on for all eternity, eventually a fine-tuned universe will occur, indeed infinitely many of them.

In the next section, we will list several reasons for rejecting atheistic many-universes hypothesis.

Reasons for rejecting the many-universes hypothesis. The first reason for rejecting the atheistic many-universes hypothesis, and preferring the theistic hypothesis, is the following general rule: *everything else being equal, we should prefer hypotheses for which we have independent evidence or that are natural extrapolations from what we already know.* Let's first illustrate and support this principle, and then apply it to the case of the fine-tuning.

Most of us take the existence of dinosaur bones to count as very strong evidence that dinosaurs existed in the past. But suppose a dinosaur skeptic claimed that she could explain the bones by postulating a "dinosaur-bone-producing-field" that simply materialized the bones out of thin air. Moreover, suppose further that, to avoid objections such as that there are no known physical laws that would allow for such a mechanism, the dinosaur skeptic simply postulated that we have not yet discovered these laws or detected these fields. Surely, none of us would let this skeptical hypothesis deter us from inferring to the existence of dinosaurs. Why? Because although no one has directly observed dinosaurs, we do have experience of other animals leaving behind fossilized remains, and thus the dinosaur explanation is a *natural extrapolation* from our common experience. In contrast, to explain the dinosaur bones, the dinosaur skeptic has invented a set of physical laws, and a set of mechanisms that are *not* a natural extrapolation from anything we know or experience.

In the case of the fine-tuning, we already know that minds often produce fine-tuned devices, such as Swiss watches. Postulating God—a supermind—as the explanation of the fine-tuning, therefore, is a natural extrapolation from what we already observe minds to do. In contrast, it is difficult to see how the atheistic many-universes hypothesis could be considered a natural extrapolation from what we observe. Moreover, unlike the atheistic many-universes hypothesis, we have some experiential evidence for the existence of God, namely religious experience. Thus, by the above principle, we should prefer the theistic explanation of the fine-tuning over the atheistic many-universes explanation, everything else being equal.

A second reason for rejecting the atheistic many-universe hypothesis is that the "many-universes generator" seems like it would need to be designed. For instance, in all current worked-out proposals for what this "universe generator" could be—such as the oscillating big bang and the vacuum fluctuation models explained above—the "generator" itself is governed by a complex set of physical laws that allow it to produce the universes. It stands to reason, therefore, that if these laws were slightly different the generator probably would not be able to produce any universes that could sustain life. After all, even my bread machine has to be made just right in order to work properly, and it only produces loaves of bread, not universes! Or consider a device as simple as a mouse trap: it requires that all the parts, such as the spring and hammer, be arranged just right in order to function. It is doubtful, therefore, whether the atheistic many-universe theory can entirely eliminate the problem of design the atheist faces; rather, at least to some extent, it seems simply to move the problem of design up one level....

A third reason for rejecting the atheistic many-universes hypothesis is that it cannot explain other features of the universe that seem to exhibit apparent design, whereas theism can. For example, many physicists, such as Albert Einstein, have observed that the basic laws of physics exhibit an extraordinary degree of beauty, elegance, harmony, and ingenuity. Nobel Prize winning physicist Steven Weinberg, for instance, devotes a whole chapter of his book *Dreams of a Final Theory*[13] to explaining how the criteria of beauty and elegance are commonly used to guide physicists in formulating the right laws....

Now such beauty, elegance, and ingenuity make sense if the universe was designed by God. Under the atheistic many-universes hypothesis, however, there is no reason to expect the fundamental laws to be elegant or beautiful. As theoretical physicist Paul Davies writes, "If nature is so 'clever' as to exploit mechanisms that amaze us with their ingenuity, is that not persuasive evidence for the existence of intelligent design behind the universe? If the world's finest minds can unravel only with difficulty the deeper workings of nature, how could it be supposed that those workings are merely a mindless accident, a product of blind chance?"[14]

This brings us to the final reason for rejecting the atheistic many-universes hypothesis, which may be the most difficult to grasp: namely, neither the atheistic many-universes hypothesis (nor the atheistic single-universe hypothesis) can at present adequately account for the improbable initial arrangement of matter in the universe required by the second law of thermodynamics. To see this, note that according to the second law of thermodynamics, the entropy of the universe is constantly increasing. The standard way of understanding this entropy increase is to say that the universe is going from a state of order to disorder. We observe this entropy increase all the time around us: things, such as a child's bedroom, that start out highly organized tend to "decay" and become disorganized unless something or someone intervenes to stop it.

Now, for purposes of illustration, we could think of the universe as a scrabble-board that initially starts out in a highly ordered state in which all the letters are arranged to form words, but which keeps getting randomly shaken. Slowly, the board, like the universe, moves from a state of order to disorder. The problem for the atheist is to explain how the universe could have started out in a highly ordered state, since it is extraordinarily improbable for such states to occur by chance. If, for example, one were to dump a bunch of letters at random on a scrabble-board, it would be very unlikely for most of them to form into words. At best, we would expect groups of letters to form into words in a few places on the board.

Now our question is, Could the atheistic many-universes hypothesis explain the high degree of initial order of our universe by claiming that given enough universes, eventually one will arise that is ordered and in which intelligent life occurs, and so it is no surprise that we find ourselves in an ordered universe? The problem with this explanation is that it is overwhelmingly more likely for local patches of order to form in one or two places than for the whole universe to be ordered, just as it is overwhelmingly more likely for a few words on the scrabble-board randomly to form words than for all the letters throughout the board randomly to form words. Thus, the overwhelming majority of universes in which intelligent life occurs will be ones in which the intelligent life will be surrounded by a small patch of order necessary for its existence, but in which the rest of the universe is disordered. Consequently, even under the atheistic many-universes hypothesis, it would still be enormously improbable for intelligent beings to find themselves in a universe such as ours which is highly ordered throughout.[15]

Conclusion. In the above sections we showed we have good, objective reasons for claiming that the fine-tuning provides strong evidence for theism. We first presented an argument for thinking that the fine-tuning provides strong evidence for preferring theism over the atheistic single-universe hypothesis, and then presented a variety of different reasons for rejecting the atheistic many-universes hypothesis as an explanation of the fine-tuning....

Notes

1. Freeman Dyson, *Disturbing the Universe* (New York: Harper & Row, 1979) 251.
2. Paul Davies, *The Cosmic Blueprint: New Discoveries in Nature's Creative Ability to Order the Universe* (New York: Simon and Schuster, 1988) 203.
3. Fred Hoyle, quoted in John Barrow and Frank Tipler, *The Anthropic Cosmological Principle* (Oxford: Oxford University Press, 1986) 22.
4. Paul Davies, *The Accidental Universe* (Cambridge: Cambridge University Press, 1982) 90-91.
5. John Leslie, "How to Draw Conclusions From a Fine-Tuned Cosmos," *Physics, Philosophy and Theology: A Common Quest for Understanding*, ed. Robert Russell, et.al. (Vatican City State: Vatican Observatory Press, 1988) 4, 35; Barrow and Tipler 322.
6. Davies, *Superforce* 242.
7. John Leslie, *Universes* (New York: Routledge, 1989) 39-40.
8. Leslie, "How to Draw Conclusions" 299.
9. Leslie, "How to Draw Conclusions" 300.
10. George Smith, "Atheism: The Case Against God," *An Anthology of Atheism and Rationalism*, ed. Gordon Stein (Prometheus Press, 1980) 56.
11. J.J.C. Smart, "Laws of Nature and Cosmic Coincidence," *The Philosophical Quarterly* Vol 35#140: 275-76; italics mine.

12. For example, see Quentin Smith, "World Ensemble Explanations," *Pacific Philosophical Quarterly* 67 (1986): 82.
13. Steven Weinberg, *Dreams of a Final Theory* (New York: Vintage Books, 1994) Chapter 6, "Beautiful Theories."
14. Davies, *Superforce* 235-36.
15. See Lawrence Sklar, *Physics and Chance: Philosophical Issues in the Foundation of Statistical Mechanics* (Cambridge: Cambridge University Press, 1993) Chapter 8, for a review of the non-theistic explanations for the ordered arrangement of the universe and the severe difficulties they face.

Discussion

1. You might not understand all of the science to which Collins appeals. Suppose we assume that what he says is roughly true. How unlikely is it that the universe would have just the right physical constants to permit the evolution of human life?
2. What are some reasons for rejecting some of the non-theistic explanations of the existence of human life? Do you think Collins has made a strong case for rational belief in God? Why or why not?
3. Does Collins' argument avoid Hume's criticisms?

Chapter 3

~~~

Moral Arguments

Euthyphro
*Plato**

Socrates. Come, then, and let us examine what we are saying. That thing or person which is dear to the gods is pious, and that thing or person which is hateful to the gods is impious, these two being the extreme opposites of one another. Was not that said?

Euthyphro. It was ...

Soc. And further, Euthyphro, the gods were admitted to have enmities and hatreds and differences?

Euth. Yes, that was also said.

Soc. And what sort of difference creates enmity and anger?... I will suggest that these enmities arise when the matters of difference are the just and unjust, good and evil, honourable and dishonourable. Are not these the points about which men differ, and about which when we are unable satisfactorily to decide our differences, you and I and all of us quarrel, when we do quarrel?

Euth. Yes, Socrates, the nature of the differences about which we quarrel is such as you describe.

Soc. And the quarrels of the gods, noble Euthyphro, when they occur, are of a like nature?

Euth. Certainly they are.

Soc. They have differences of opinion, as you say, about good and evil, just and unjust, honourable and dishonourable: there would have been no quarrels among them if there had been no such differences—would there now?

Euth. You are quite right.

Soc. Does not every man love that which he deems noble and just and good, and hate the opposite of them?

Euth. Very true.

Soc. But, as you say, people regard the same things, some as just and others as unjust,—about these they dispute; and so there arise wars and fightings among them.

---

*Plato founded the first school of philosophy (in the western world) in the fourth century B.C.

Euth. Very true.

Soc. Then the same things are hated by the gods and loved by the gods, and are both hateful and dear to them?

Euth. True.

Soc. And upon this view the same things, Euthyphro, will be pious and also impious?

Euth. So I should suppose.

Soc. Then, my friend, I remark with surprise that you have not answered the question which I asked. For I certainly did not ask you to tell me what action is both pious and impious: but now it would seem that what is loved by the gods is also hated by them. And therefore, Euthyphro, in thus chastising your father you may very likely be doing what is agreeable to Zeus but disagreeable to Cronos or Uranus, and what is acceptable to Hephaestus but unacceptable to Hera, and there may be other gods who have similar differences of opinion.

Euth. But I believe, Socrates, that all the gods would be agreed as to the propriety of punishing a murderer: there would be no difference of opinion about that....

Soc. ...There was a notion that came into my mind while you were speaking; I said to myself: "Well, and what if Euthyphro does prove to me that all the gods regarded the death of the serf as unjust, how do I know anything more of the nature of piety and impiety? For granting that this action may be hateful to the gods, still piety and impiety are not adequately defined by these distinctions, for that which is hateful to the gods has been shown to be also pleasing and dear to them." And therefore, Euthyphro, I do not ask you to prove this; I will suppose, if you like, that all the gods condemn and abominate such an action. But I will amend the definition so far as to say that what all the gods hate is impious, and what they love pious or holy; and what some of them love and others hate is both or neither. Shall this be our definition of piety and impiety?

Euth. Why not, Socrates?

Soc. Why not! certainly, as far as I am concerned, Euthyphro, there is no reason why not. But whether this admission will greatly assist you in the task of instructing me as you promised, is a matter for you to consider.

Euth. Yes, I should say that what all the gods love is pious and holy, and the opposite which they all hate, impious.

Soc. Ought we to enquire into the truth of this, Euthyphro, or simply to accept the mere statement on our own authority and that of others? What do you say?

Euth. We should enquire; and I believe that the statement will stand the test of enquiry.

Soc. We shall know better, my good friend, in a little while. The point which I should first wish to understand is whether the pious or holy is beloved by the gods because it is holy, or holy because it is beloved of the gods.

Euth. I do not understand your meaning, Socrates....

Soc. And what do you say of piety, Euthyphro: is not piety, according to your definition, loved by all the gods?

Euth. Yes.

Soc. Because it is pious or holy, or for some other reason?

Euth. No, that is the reason.

Soc. It is loved because it is holy, not holy because it is loved?

Euth. Yes.

Soc. And that which is dear to the gods is loved by them, and is in a state to be loved of them because it is loved of them?

Euth. Certainly.

Soc. Then that which is dear to the gods, Euthyphro, is not holy, nor is that which is holy loved of God, as you affirm; but they are two different things.

Euth. How do you mean, Socrates?

Soc. I mean to say that the holy has been acknowledge by us to be loved of God because it is holy, not to be holy because it is loved.

Euth. Yes.

Soc. But that which is dear to the gods is dear to them because it is loved by them, not loved by them because it is dear to them.

Euth. True.

Soc. But, friend Euthyphro, if that which is holy is the same with that which is dear to God, and is loved because it is holy, then that which is dear to God would have been loved as being dear to God; but if that which is dear to God is dear to him because it is loved by him, then that which is holy would have been holy because it is loved by him. But now you see that the reverse is the case, and that they are quite different from one another. For one is of a kind to be loved because it is loved, and the other is loved because it is of a kind to be loved. Thus you appear to me, Euthyphro, when I ask you what is the essence of holiness, to offer an attribute only, and not the essence—the attribute of being loved by all the gods. But you still refuse to explain to me the nature of holiness. And therefore, if you please, I will ask you not to hide your treasure, but to tell me once more what holiness or piety really is, whether dear to the gods or not (for that is a matter about which we will not quarrel) and what is impiety?

Euth. I really do not know, Socrates, how to express what I mean. For somehow or other our arguments, on whatever ground we rest them, seem to turn round and walk away from us.

Discussion

1. Suppose you believe that morality depends upon God. Which alternative would you find more palatable—arbitrariness or superfluousness? Why?

2. What are the religious motivations for maintaining that morality depends upon God?

3. If morality depends upon God, in what sense is God good? That is, if there is a criterion of goodness that stands over and judges people, in what sense is God good if the standard of goodness does not stand over him?

Moral Arguments for Theistic Belief

Robert Merrihew Adams *

Introduction. Moral arguments were the type of theistic argument most characteristic of the nineteenth and early twentieth centuries. More recently they have become one of philosophy's abandoned farms. The fields are still fertile, but they have not been cultivated systematically since the latest methods came in. The rambling Victorian farmhouse has not been kept up as well as similar structures, and people have not been stripping the sentimental gingerbread off the porches to reveal the clean lines of argument. This paper is intended to contribute to the remedy of this neglect. It will deal with quite a number of arguments, because I think we can understand them better if we place them in relation to each other. This will not leave time to be as subtle, historically or philosophically, as I would like to be, but I hope I will be able to prove something more than my own taste for Victoriana.

An argument from the nature of right and wrong. Let us begin with one of the most obvious, though perhaps never the most fashionable, arguments on the farm: an Argument from the Nature of Right and Wrong. We believe quite firmly that certain things are morally right and others are morally wrong (for example, that it is wrong to torture another person to death just for fun). Questions may be raised about the nature of that which is believed in these beliefs: what does the rightness or wrongness of an act consist in? I believe that the most adequate answer is provided by a theory that entails the existence of God—specifically, by the theory that moral rightness and wrongness consist in agreement and disagreement, respectively, with the will or commands of a loving God. One of the most generally accepted reasons for believing in the existence of anything is that its existence is implied by the theory that seems to account most adequately for some subject matter. I take it, therefore that my metaethical views provide me with a reason of some weight for believing in the existence of God.

Perhaps some will think it disreputably "tender-minded" to accept such a reason where the subject matter is moral. It may be suggested that the epistemological status of moral beliefs is so far inferior to that of physical beliefs, for example, that any moral belief found to entail the existence of an otherwise unknown object ought simply to be abandoned. But in spite of the general uneasiness about morality that pervades our culture, most of us do hold many moral beliefs with almost the highest degree of confidence. So long as we think it reasonable to argue at all from grounds that are not absolutely certain, there is no clear reason why such con-

---

*Robert Merrihew Adams is Chair of the Department of Philosophy at Yale University.

fident beliefs, in ethics as in other fields, should not be accepted as premises in arguing for the existence of anything that is required for the most satisfactory theory of their subject matter.[1]

Advantages. The divine command theory of the nature of right and wrong combines two advantages not jointly possessed by any of its nontheological competitors. These advantages are sufficiently obvious that their nature can be indicated quite briefly to persons familiar with the metaethical debate, though they are also so controversial that it would take a book-length review of the contending theories to defend my claims. The first advantage of divine command metaethics is that it presents facts of moral rightness and wrongness as objective, nonnatural facts—objective in the sense that whether they obtain or not does not depend on whether any human being thinks they do, and nonnatural in the sense that they cannot be stated entirely in the language of physics, chemistry, biology, and human or animal psychology. For it is an objective but not a natural fact that God commands, permits, or forbids something. Intuitively this is an advantage....

Alleged disadvantages. What we cannot avoid discussing, and at greater length than the advantages, are the alleged disadvantages of divine command metaethics. The advantages may be easily recognized, but the disadvantages are generally thought to be decisive. I have argued elsewhere, in some detail, that they are not decisive. Here let us concentrate on ... the gravest objection to the more extreme forms of divine command theory [which is] is that they imply that if God commanded us, for example, to make it our chief end in life to inflict suffering on other human beings, for no other reason than that he commanded it, it would be wrong not to obey. Finding this conclusion unacceptable, I prefer a less extreme, or modified, divine command theory, which identifies the ethical property of wrongness with the property of being contrary to the commands of a *loving* God. Since a God who commanded us to practice cruelty for its own sake would not be a loving God, this modified divine command theory does not imply that it would be wrong to disobey such a command....

Our discussion of the Argument from the Nature of Right and Wrong may be concluded with some reflections on the nature of the God in whose existence it gives us some reason to believe. (1) The appeal of the argument lies in the provision of an explanation of moral facts of whose truth we are already confident. It must therefore be taken as an argument for the existence of a God whose commands—and presumably, whose purposes and character as well—are in accord with our most confident judgments of right and wrong. I have suggested that he must be a loving God. (2) He must be an intelligent being, so that it makes sense to speak of his having a will and issuing commands. Maximum adequacy of a divine command theory surely requires that God be supposed to have enormous knowledge and understanding of ethically relevant facts, if not absolute omniscience. He should be a God "unto whom all hearts are open, all desires known, and from whom no secrets are hid." (3) The argument does not seem to imply very much about God's power, however—certainly not that he is omnipotent. (4) Nor is it obvious that the argument supports belief in the unity or uniqueness of God. Maybe the metaethical place of divine commands could be taken by the unanimous deliverances of a senate of deities, although that conception raises troublesome questions about the nature of the morality or quasi-morality that must govern the relations of the gods with each other.

Kantian arguments. The most influential moral arguments for theistic belief have been a family of arguments that may be called Kantian. They have a common center in the idea of a moral order of the universe and are arguments for belief in a God sufficiently powerful to establish and maintain such an order. The Kantian family has members on both sides of one of the most fundamental distinctions in this area: the distinction between theoretical and practical arguments. By "a theoretical moral argument for theistic belief" I mean an argument having an ethical premise and purporting to prove the *truth*, or enhance the *probability*, of theism. By "a practical argument for theistic belief" I mean an argument purporting only to give ethical or other practical reasons for *believing* that God exists. The practical argument may have no direct bearing at all on the truth or probability of the belief whose practical advantage it extols.

Arguments from the Nature of Right and Wrong are clearly theoretical moral arguments for theistic belief. Kant, without warning us of any such distinction, gives us sometimes a theoretical and sometimes a practical argument (in my sense of "theoretical" and "practical," not his). His theoretical argument goes roughly as follows:

(A) We ought (morally) to promote the realization of the highest good.
(B) What we ought to do must be possible for us to do.
(C) It is not possible for us to promote the realization of the highest good unless there exists a God who makes the realization possible.
(D) Therefore, there exists such a God.

Kant was not clear about the theoretical character of this argument, and stated as its conclusion that "it is morally necessary to assume the existence of God."[2] Its premises, however, plainly imply the more theoretical conclusion that God exists.

(C) needs explanation. Kant conceived of the highest good as composed of two elements. The first element, moral virtue, depends on the wills of moral agents and does not require divine intervention for its possibility. But the second element, the happiness of moral agents in strict proportion to their virtue, will not be realized unless there is a moral order of the universe. Such an order, Kant argues, cannot be expected of the laws of nature, without God.

Doubts may be raised whether Kant's conception of the highest good is ethically correct and whether there might not be some nontheistic basis for a perfect proportionment of happiness to virtue. But a more decisive objection has often been made to (A): In any reasonable morality we will be obligated to promote only the best attainable approximation of the highest good. For this reason Kant's theoretical moral argument for theism does not seem very promising to me.

Elsewhere Kant argues quite differently. He even denies that a command to promote the highest good is contained in, or analytically derivable from, the moral law. He claims rather that we will be "hindered" from doing what the moral law commands us to do unless we can regard our actions as contributing to the realization of "a final end of all things" which we can also make a "final end for all our actions and abstentions." He argues that only the highest good can serve morally as such a final end and that we therefore have a compelling moral need to believe in the possibility of its realization.[3] This yields only a practical argument for theistic belief. Stripped of some of its more distinctively Kantian dress, it can be stated in terms of "demoralization," by which I mean a weakening or deterioration of moral motivation.

(E) It would be demoralizing not to believe there is a moral order of the universe, for then we would have to regard it as very likely that the history of the universe will not be good on the whole, no matter what we do.

(F) Demoralization is morally undesirable.

(G) Therefore, there is moral advantage in believing that there is a moral order of the universe.

(H) Theism provides the most adequate theory of a moral order of the universe.

(J) Therefore, there is a moral advantage in accepting theism.

What is a moral order of the universe? I shall not formulate any necessary condition. But let us say that the following is *logically sufficient* for the universe's having a moral order: (1) A good world-history requires something besides human virtue (it might, as Kant thought, require the happiness of the virtuous); but (2) the universe is such that morally good actions will probably contribute to a good world-history. (I use 'world' as a convenient synonym for 'universe'.)

Avoiding demoralization. Theism has several secular competitors as a theory of a moral order of the universe in this sense. The idea of scientific and cultural progress has provided liberal thinkers, and Marxism has provided socialists, with hopes of a good world-history without God. It would be rash to attempt to adjudicate this competition here. I shall therefore not comment further on the truth of (H) but concentrate on the argument from (E) and (F) to (G). It is, after all, of great interest in itself, religiously and in other ways, if morality gives us a reason to believe in a moral order of the universe.

Is (E) true? Would it indeed be demoralizing not to believe there is a moral order of the universe? The issue is in large part empirical. It is for sociologists and psychologists to investigate scientifically what are the effects of various beliefs on human motivation.... But I have the impression there has not yet been very much hard, empirical research casting light directly on the question whether (E) is true.... Lacking scientifically established answers to the empirical aspects of our question, we may say, provisionally, what seems plausible to us. And (E) does seem quite plausible to me. Seeing our lives as contributing to a valued larger whole is one of the things that gives them a point in our own eyes. The morally good person cares about the goodness of what happens in the world and not just about the goodness of his own actions. If a right action can be seen as contributing to some great good, that increases the importance it has for him. Conversely, if he thinks that things will turn out badly no matter what he does, and especially if he thinks that (as often appears to be the case) the long-range effects of right action are about as likely to be bad as good, that will diminish the emotional attraction that duty exerts on him. Having to regard it as very likely that the history of the universe will not be good on the whole, no matter what one does, seems apt to induce a cynical sense of futility about the moral life, undermining one's moral resolve and one's interest in moral considerations. My judgment on this issue is subject to two qualifications, however.

(1) We cannot plausibly ascribe more than a demoralizing tendency to disbelief in a moral order of the universe. There are certainly people who do not believe in such an order, but show no signs of demoralization.

(2) It may be doubted how much most people are affected by beliefs or expectations about the history of the universe as a whole....

Some will object that those with the finest moral motivation can find all the inspiration they need in a tragic beauty of the moral life itself, even if they despair about the course of history. The most persuasive argument for this view is a presentation that succeeds in evoking moral emotion in connection with the thought of tragedy: Bertrand Russell's early essay "A Free Man's Worship"[4] is an eloquent example. But I remain somewhat skeptical. Regarded aesthetically, from the outside, tragedy may be sublimely beautiful; lived from the inside, over a long period of time, I fear it is only too likely to end in discouragement and bitterness, though no doubt there have been shining exceptions.

Defending practical arguments. But the main objection to the present argument is an objection to all practical arguments. It is claimed that none of them give justifying reasons for believing anything at all. If there are any practical advantages that are worthy to sway us in accepting or rejecting a belief, the advantage of not being demoralized is surely one of them. But can it be right, and intellectually honest, to believe something, or try to believe it, for the sake of any practical advantage, however noble?

I believe it can. This favorable verdict on practical arguments for theoretical conclusions is particularly plausible in "cases where faith creates its own verification," as William James puts it,[5] or where your wish is at least more likely to come true if you believe it will. Suppose you are running for Congress and an unexpected misfortune has made it doubtful whether you still have a good chance of winning. Probably it will at least be clear that you are more likely to win if you continue to believe that your chances are good. Believing will keep up your spirits and your alertness, boost the morale of your campaign workers, and make other people more likely to take you seriously. In this case it seems to me eminently reasonable for you to cling, for the sake of practical advantage, to the belief that you have a good chance of winning.

Another type of belief for which practical arguments can seem particularly compelling is trust in a person. Suppose a close friend of mine is accused of a serious crime. I know him well and can hardly believe he would do such a thing. He insists he is innocent. But the evidence against him, though not conclusive, is very strong. So far as I can judge the total evidence (including my knowledge of his character) in a cool, detached way, I would have to say it is quite evenly balanced. I want to believe in his innocence, and there is reason to think that I ought, morally, to believe in it if I can. For he may well be innocent. If he is, he will have a deep psychological need for someone to believe him. If no one believes him, he will suffer unjustly a loneliness perhaps greater than the loneliness of guilt. And who will believe him if his close friends do not? Who will believe him if I do not? Of course I could try to pretend to believe him. If I do that I will certainly be less honest with him, and I doubt that I will be more honest with myself, than if I really cling to the belief that he is innocent. Moreover, the pretense is unlikely to satisfy his need to be believed. If he knows me well and sees me often, my insincerity will probably betray itself to him in some spontaneous reaction.

The legitimacy of practical arguments must obviously be subject to some restrictions. Two important restrictions were suggested by William James. (1) Practical arguments should be employed only on questions that "cannot ... be decided on intellectual grounds."[6] There should be a plurality of alternatives that one finds intellectually plausible. (The option should be "living," as James would put it.) Faith ought not to be "believing what you know ain't so." It also ought not to short-circuit rational inquiry; we ought not to try to settle by practical argument an issue that we could settle by further investigation of evidence in the time available for settling it. (2) The question to be decided by practical argument should be urgent and of practical importance ("forced" and "momentous," James would say). If it can wait or is pragmatically inconsequential, we can afford to suspend judgment about it and it is healthier to do so....

Similarly I think that the rationality of trying for moral reasons to believe in a moral order of the universe depends in large measure on the antecedent strength of one's commitment to morality. If one is strongly committed, so that one wishes to be moral even if the world is not, and if one seeks, not reasons to be moral, but emotional undergirding for the moral life, then it may well be rational to be swayed by the practical argument for the belief....

Self-interest and morality. Both Kantian and Christian theism imply that true self-interest is in harmony with morality. Kant believed that in the long run one's happiness will be strictly proportioned to one's virtue. And if that would be denied by many Christian theologians for the sake of the doctrine of grace, they would at least maintain that no one can enjoy the greatest happiness without a deep moral commitment and that every good person will be very happy in the long run. They believe that the most important parts of a good person's self-interest are eternally *safe*, no matter how much his virtue or saintliness may lead him to sacrifice here below. The truth of these beliefs is surely another logically sufficient condition of the universe's having a moral order. (I assume that virtue is not so richly its own reward as to be sufficient in itself for happiness.)

There are both theoretical and practical arguments for theistic belief which are first of all arguments for faith in a moral world order that harmonizes self-interest with morality. As such, they belong to the Kantian type. For obvious reasons, let us call them "individualistic," by contrast with Kant's own, more "universalistic," arguments.

The practical arguments of this individualistic Kantian type depend on the claim that it would be demoralizing not to believe in a harmony of self-interest with virtue.... The conviction that every good person will be very happy in the long run has often contributed, in religious believers, to a cheerfulness and single-heartedness of moral devotion that they probably would not have had without it. This integration of motives may be regarded as morally advantageous even if its loss does not lead to criminality.

I anticipate the objection that self-interest has no place in the highest ethical motives, and that belief in the harmony of self-interest with morality therefore debases rather than elevates one's motivation. What could be nobler than the virtuous sacrifice of what one regards as one's only chance for great happiness? Yet such sacrifice is rendered impossible by faith in the sure reward of virtue.

I have two replies: (1) Self-interest remains a powerful motive in the best of us; a life of which that was not true would hardly be recognizable as human. It is not obvious that a hardwon victory over even the most enlightened self-interest is morally preferable to the integration of motives resulting from the belief that it will be well with the righteous in the long run. Those who hold that belief still have plenty of victories to win over shorter-sighted desires. And it is plausible to suppose—though I do not know that anyone has proved it—that we are more likely to attain to the goodness that is possible through an integration of motives, than to win a death struggle with our own deepest self-interest, since the latter is so hard.

(2) It is not only in our own case that we have to be concerned about the relation between self-interest and virtue. We influence the actions of other people and particularly of people we love. Morally, no doubt, we ought to influence them in the direction of always doing right (so far as it is appropriate to influence them deliberately at all). But as we care about their self-interest too, our encouragement

of virtue in them is apt to be more wholehearted and therefore more effective, if we believe that they will be happy in the long run if they do right. It is hard to see any ground for a charge of selfishness in this aspect of faith in the sure reward of virtue. It is not unambiguously noble (though it might be right) to encourage someone else—even someone you love—to make a great and permanent sacrifice of his true self-interest. We have no reason to regret the loss of opportunities to influence others so sadly....

I have focused, as most philosophical discussion of the moral arguments has, on the connections of theism with the nature of right and wrong and with the idea of a moral order of the universe. I am keenly aware that they form only part of the total moral case for theistic belief. Theistic conceptions of guilt and forgiveness,[7] for example, or of God as a friend who witnesses, judges, appreciates, and can remember all of our actions, choices, and emotions, may well have theoretical and practical moral advantages at least as compelling as any that we have discussed.

God's goodness. Perhaps moral arguments establish, at most, subsidiary advantages of belief in God's existence. They are more crucial to the case for his goodness. Causal arguments from the existence and qualities of the world may have some force to persuade us that there is a God, but they plainly have much less support to offer the proposition,

(K) If there is a God, he is morally very good.

(Here I define 'a God' as a creator and governor of the whole universe, supreme in understanding and knowledge as well as in power, so that (K) is not a tautology.)

There is a powerful moral argument for (K). Belief in the existence of an evil or amoral God would be morally intolerable. In view of his power, such belief would be apt to carry with it all the disadvantages, theoretical and practical, of disbelief in a moral order of the universe. But I am even more concerned about the consequences it would have in view of his knowledge and understanding. We are to think of a being who understands human life much better than we do—understands it well enough to create and control it. Among other things, he must surely understand our moral ideas and feelings. He understands everyone's point of view, and has a more objective, or at least a more complete and balanced view of human relationships than any of us can have. He has whatever self-control, stability, and integration of purpose are implied in his having produced a world as constant in its causal order as our own. And now we are to suppose that that being does not care to support with his will the moral principles that we believe are true. We are to suppose that he either opposes some of them, or does not care enough about some of them to act on them. I submit that if we really believed there is a God like that, who understands so much and yet disregards some or all of our moral principles, it would be extremely difficult for us to continue to regard those principles with the respect that we believe is due them. Since we believe that we ought to pay them that respect, this is a great moral disadvantage of the belief that there is an evil or amoral God....

Conclusion. In closing, I shall permit myself an argument *ad hominem*. The hypothesis that there is an amoral God is not open to the best known objection to theism, the argument from evil. Whatever may be said against the design argument for theism, it is at least far from obvious that the world was not designed. Yet hardly any philosopher takes seriously the hypothesis that it was designed by an amoral or evil being. Are there any good grounds for rejecting that hypothesis? Only moral grounds. One ought to reflect on that before asserting that moral arguments are out of place in these matters.

Notes

1. Cf. Henry Sidgwick, *The Methods of Ethics*, 7th ed. (New York: Dover, 1966), p. 509.
2. Immanuel Kant, *Critique of Practical Reason*, trans. L. W. Beck (New York: Liberal Arts Press, 1956), p. 130 (p. 125 of the Prussian Academy edition).
3. Immanuel Kant, *Religion within the Limits of Reason Alone*, trans. T. M. Greene and H. H. Hudson (New York: Harper, 1960), pp. 5-7. (The long footnote is particularly important.) In the *Critique of Practical Reason*, pp. 147-51 (142-6, Prussian Academy edition).
4. 1903, reprinted in Bertrand Russell, *Why I Am Not A Christian, and Other Essays on Religion and Related Subjects* (New York: Simon and Schuster, n.d.).
5. William James, "The Sentiment of Rationality," in his *The Will to Believe and Other Essays in Popular Philosophy* (New York: Dover Publications, 1956), p. 97.
6. William James, *The Will to Believe*, ibid., p. 11.
7. A theistic argument from the nature of guilt has been offered by A. E. Taylor, *The Faith of a Moralist*, vol. I (London: Macmillan, 1930), pp. 206-10. Cf. also H. P. Owen, *The Moral Argument for Christian Theism* (London: George Allen & Unwin, 1965), pp. 57-59.

Discussion

1. How does Adams attempt to solve the Euthyphro problem? Do you think he is successful?
2. Adams claims that the most adequate explanation of right and wrong is the agreement or disagreement with the commands of God. What are some other explanations of the nature of right and wrong? Is God's will more adequate?
3. Why does Adams think that the pursuit of morality, on some accounts of the nature of morality, would be demoralizing? How does theism improve on those competing accounts?

The Virtues of God and the Foundations of Ethics

*Linda Zagzebski**

"Nothing will be called good except in so far as it has a certain likeness of the divine goodness." *Summa Contra Gentiles* I. 40. 326.

Introduction. A moral theory is an abstract structure that aims to simplify, systematize, and justify our moral practices and beliefs. The human need to theorize is a powerful one. We want to understand the moral world as well as the natural world and, indeed, to understand the relation between the two. For Christians there is also the need to understand the relation between the moral world and the supernatural world. Christian philosophers have traditionally agreed that in some sense God is the foundation of moral value, and that makes the search for a foundationalist structure a natural one even though I would not claim that a belief in moral foundationalism is a requirement of Christianity.

In this paper I want to exhibit one way to structure a virtue ethics with a theological foundation; in fact, the theological foundation is an extension of virtue theory to God himself. It is, then, a divine virtue theory. I begin by describing a strong form of virtue ethics I call motivation-based.[1] This theory makes all moral concepts derivative from the concept of a good motive, the most basic component of a virtue, where what I mean by a motive is an emotion that initiates and directs action towards an end. I will then give motivation-based virtue theory a theological foundation by arguing that the motivations of one person in particular is the ultimate foundation of all moral value, and that person is God. I call the theory Divine Motivation Theory. This theory is structurally parallel to Divine Command Theory, but as I will show in the last section, it has many advantages over that theory while avoiding its well-known objections.

The theory without God: motivation-based virtue theory. In any foundationalist moral theory there is something that is good in the most basic way. If the goodness of something is really foundational, it cannot be justified or explained by the goodness of something else. Examples of foundational goods include Aristotle's idea of human flourishing—eudaimonia, or the Kantian good will. In the theory I will outline, it is good motivational states. Moral foundationalists almost always feel uneasy about the status of foundation itself, however, and so they look outside of ethics for something that is allegedly more basic than morality that is capable of grounding the entire structure. That something else could be human nature, reason, the will of God, or something else. I will propose that the ultimate ground of ethics is God's motivations. But before doing that I want to outline the theory without its deeper metaphysical basis.

---

*Linda Zagzebski is Kingfisher Chair of Philosophy at the University of Oklahoma.

In this theory the primary bearers of moral properties are emotions. Emotions are good or bad in themselves; they do not derive their goodness or badness from their relation to anything else that is good or bad. They are, therefore, intrinsically good or bad. Emotions are affective states with intentional objects. In an emotional state one feels a distinctive way *about* something, the intentional object, so emotion must have a cognitive component as well as an affective component since an emotional state involves taking or supposing or imagining the intentional object to be a certain way—e.g., threatening, exciting, boring, pitiful, contemptible, etc.[2] The feeling component accompanies seeing something as threatening, exciting, contemptible. So the agent feels threatened by something seen as threatening, feels excited by something seen as exciting, feels contemptuous of something seen as contemptible, and so on.

Emotions are individuated in part by their intentional object. So when I speak of an individual emotion, I do not mean fear or love, but love *of* something of a certain kind, or fear *that* something is the case. The goodness or badness of the emotion does not derive from the goodness or badness of the intentional object. For example, it is bad to take delight in the misfortune of others or to enjoy the sight of animals in pain, and the badness of these emotions is not derivative from the badness of the pain of animals or the misfortune of others. It is good to feel compassion for the suffering of another or to love another person, and the goodness of these emotions is not derivative from the badness of the suffering or the goodness of the other person.

Here it is important to make a distinction between two kinds of basic goodness and badness: the distinction between intrinsic and extrinsic goodness, and the distinction between goods as ends and goods as means.[3] Intrinsic goodness refers to the location or source of goodness rather than to the way we value things. Goodness as ends refers to the way we value things as objects of our desire or choice, not to the source of the goodness. When I say that an emotional state is intrinsically good, I mean that its goodness is ontologically basic; it does not derive its goodness from the goodness of anything else. But emotions are not typically good as ends. In contrast, good states of affairs are good as ends, as objects of choice, but they are not intrinsically good.[4]

A motive in the sense I mean is an emotion that initiates, sustains, and directs action towards an end. Not all motives are emotions since some motives are almost purely physiological, such as the motives of hunger, thirst, or fatigue, but the motives that have foundational ethical significance are emotions. It is also possible that not all emotions are motivating since some emotions may be purely passive, which is why emotions were formerly called "passions". Examples of passive emotions might include joy, sadness, tranquillity, and the enjoyment of beauty. But even these emotions probably can motivate in certain circumstances. It is usual to *call* an emotion a motive only when it actually operates to motivate on a particular occasion. But when an emotion that sometimes motivates does not operate to motivate at a particular time, it retains its motivational potential. So not all motives are emotions, but the morally significant ones are emotions, and most, if not all, emotions are or can be motives. That is, they have potential motivational force.[5]

Motives tend to be persistent and become dispositions, at which point they become components of enduring traits of character—virtues or vices. Each virtue has a motivational component which is the disposition to have an action-guiding emotion characteristic of the particular virtue. The virtuous person is disposed to perform acts motivated by such an emotion. So a person with the virtue of benevolence is disposed to act in ways motivated by the emotion of benevolence; a person with the virtue of courage is disposed to act in ways motivated by the distinctive emotion underlying the behavior of those who face danger when they judge it to be necessary to obtain a greater good; a person with the virtue of justice is disposed to act in ways expressing an attitude of equal respect for the humanity of others, and so on.[6]

A virtue also has a success component which is a component of reliability in reaching the end of the motivational component of the virtue. Some virtuous motives aim at *producing* a state of affairs of a certain kind. The state of affairs may either be internal to the agent or external to the agent. Other virtuous motives aim to *express* the emotion of the agent. Temperance is an example of a virtue whose motivational component aims at producing a state within the agent, whereas fairness is a virtue whose motivational component aims at producing a state of affairs external to the agent. Empathy and gratitude are examples of virtues whose motivational components aim at expressing the agent's emotional state. Successfully achieving the end of a virtuous motive, then, sometimes amounts to bringing about a state of affairs completely distinct from the motivating emotion, and sometimes success is achieved by merely expressing the emotion itself.

Some human motivations are good and others are bad. Good human motivations are components of virtues; bad human motivations are components of vices. If a human motive is a good one, reliable success in achieving its end is also a good thing. The goodness of the virtuous end is derivative from the goodness of the motive, not the other way around. The combination of a good human motivation with reliable success in reaching its end is a good human trait—a virtue. A vice is the combination of a bad human motivation with reliable success in reaching the end of the bad motivation.

The evaluative properties of acts are derivative from the evaluative properties of persons. Roughly, a right (permissible) act is an act a virtuous person might do. That is, it is not the case that she would not do it.[7] A wrong act is an act a virtuous person characteristically would not do. Vicious persons characteristically perform wrong acts, but so do persons who are neither vicious nor virtuous, and virtuous persons also may perform wrong acts, but uncharacteristically. A moral duty is an act a virtuous person characteristically *would* do. A virtuous act is one that expresses the motivational component of the virtue. For example, a compassionate act is one that expresses the motivation of compassion. It is an act in which the agent is motivated by compassion and acts with the intention of reaching the motivational end of compassion, the alleviation of the suffering of someone else. In the case of certain virtues, most especially justice, acts expressing the virtue are all moral duties. In the case of other virtues (e.g., compassion, kindness, mercy) many acts express the virtue but are not moral duties.[8]

The moral properties of states of affairs can also be defined in terms of good and bad motivations. Roughly, a good state of affairs is one that is the end of a good motive. A bad state of affairs is one that is the end of a bad motive.[9] What makes a certain outcome a just one, and hence, good, is that it is the aim of the motive distinctive of the virtue of justice. What makes a certain outcome a compassionate one, and hence, good, is that it is the aim of the motive of compassion, and so on. Goodness and badness of motives are therefore more fundamental than goodness and badness of states of affairs, at least states of affairs that are outcomes of human action. It follows that the value of outcomes cannot be identified independently of what virtuous persons do or are motivated to do.[10]

This is not to deny that certain states of affairs are final goods or ends of choice. The alleviation of suffering is such an end. It is worthy of choice in itself, not because it is a means to something else. But to return to the distinction between intrinsic value and value as an end, the position that just states of affairs are not intrinsically good but derive their goodness from the motivations of just persons is compatible with the position that just states of affairs are worthy of choice as final ends.

Therefore, the value of final ends is not the most basic kind of value. But these days it is not only common to think of the good of ends as the most basic sense of good, but "good" is sometimes defined as "worthy of choice." This, I believe, is a mistake, for to say that intrinsic goods are goods is not to say that they are worthy of choice. To be worthy of choice is to be a good in a certain way—as an end. To be intrinsically good is to have the source of goodness in itself. To say that God is good is not to say that God is worthy of choice. Even though there is a sense in which God *is* worthy of choice, saying God is good is not to say *that*. It is to say that the source of God's goodness is in himself. And what makes a good thing worthy of choice is that it is the object of intrinsically good motives.

In motivation-based virtue theory motives are good or bad in the most fundamental sense of good or bad. But what makes a motive good? My answer is that moral value is constituted by a harmony with the divine, not just a harmony within the soul. Human motives are good in so far as they are like God's motives. Since motives are emotions, this means that God must have emotions, a controversial position in Christian theology, although I will argue that the theory can stand without the claim that the states in God which are the counterparts of human emotions are also emotions. In any case, human virtues are modeled on the virtues of God. In humans virtues are finite representations of the traits of a perfect God. Since the gap between God and ourselves is infinite, it may seem to be hopelessly impractical, even if theologically and metaphysically desirable, to model our moral traits on God in this way. But we have Christ incarnate as our archetype. What I will propose in what follows is a way to give the traditional Christian idea of ethics as the imitation of Christ a theoretical structure.

The virtues of God. There are many accounts of virtue in the history of ethics, but all accounts agree that virtues are excellences; they are good personal traits. If we assume that the goodness of God is the metaphysical ground of all value, it is natural to ask whether God has virtues. It may seem that the answer is no, and in good Thomistic fashion I will start with the objections to the thesis before proceeding to argue that God does have virtues, and that the divine virtues include both a motivational component and a success component as described in the second section. More importantly, the divine virtues are not simply pale imitations of the more robust and richly nuanced traits of embodied and encultured beings. The relationship between divine and human virtues is, in fact, the reverse: Human virtues are pale imitations of the divine virtues. God is the only being who is virtuous in a pure and unqualified sense. As Aquinas says, all moral properties are attributed primarily to God and only analogously to humans. I believe that this includes the virtues and the primary component of virtue, a motivation.

The following objections arise from the high metaphysical view of God's nature that was developed in the medieval period and has its most subtle and penetrating expression in the thought of Aquinas. I will, however, propose a modification of that view since I submit that God has emotions.

Objection 1: God cannot have a virtue if a virtue includes a motivational component and a motive is an emotional state since God has no emotions. God cannot have emotions since (i) emotions involve the sense appetites and require a body, but God has no body or sensory appetites, and (ii) emotions are passions, ways of being acted upon, and that implies imperfection, but God is perfect and, hence, impassible.

Objection 2: Virtues are habits that involve overcoming contrary temptations and take time to develop, so they only make sense when attributed to imperfect beings who undergo change. But God does not *develop* his traits and has no contrary temptations; he is perfect and unchangeable.

Objection 3: Virtues are traditionally explained teleologically by reference to the natural end of a thing of a certain kind, an end that is not already actualized. This means that virtue presupposes potency. The virtues are goods *for* a thing as a member of a natural kind. But God is not lacking anything and has no potency, nor does God belong to a natural kind. Furthermore, it's hard to see how anything could be good for God.

Response: Virtues are the good traits of moral agents. The more perfect the moral agent, the more perfect the virtues. God is both a moral agent and a perfect being. Therefore, God has perfectly good moral traits—perfect virtues. Like all moral agents, God has motives, where motives are both explanations of and justifications for an agent's acts. In humans motives become dispositions, but if God has no dispositions, then God's motives are always *in act*, and God is always acting upon them. Since God is the perfect agent, God's motives are the perfect motives. God's love is the perfect motive of love; God's compassion is the perfect motive of compassion; God's mercy is the perfect motive of mercy, and so on. Since compassion, love, mercy, etc. are emotions, God's compassion, love, mercy, etc. are perfect emotions. I am not suggesting that it necessarily follows from the fact that God acts from compassion, and that the state of compassion in humans is an emotion, that God has emotions. I do think that having emotions is part of what makes a being a moral agent. But the minimum I want to insist upon in this paper is that God's virtues, like our virtues, include a component of motivation—a state that is act-directing, as well as reliably successful in bringing about the aim of the motive. God's motives are perfect, and his success is perfect as well. God is, therefore, not just reliable, he is perfectly reliable. A divine virtue, then, is the combination of a perfect motive with perfect success in bringing about the end of the motive.

Reply to objection 1: An emotion is a state of consciousness of a certain kind. I have suggested that that state includes a cognitive aspect whereby the emotion's intentional object is understood or construed to be a certain way. But an emotion is also an affective state; it has a certain "feel". Now the fact that God has no body precludes God from having emotions only if the possession of a body is a necessary condition for the states of consciousness in question, and that, of course, is denied by the Cartesian view of the relation between mind and body. Furthermore, even if Aquinas is right that sensory experience necessarily requires a body, it is not obvious that emotions necessarily have a sensory component if we mean by "sensory" a state that is of the same kind as states of consciousness that arise from the five senses or that are localized, such as the sensation of pain. But suppose we grant the objection. Suppose we agree with Aquinas that God has no passions (*passiones*) since these belong to the sensory appetites and the sensory appetites require a body. Aquinas agrees that God does have *affectiones* since the latter admits of two kinds, sensory and intellective. God has intellective appetites which belong to the will. In this category are included states that we call emotions—states such as love and joy. We see, then, that there are two words that refer to affective states in Aquinas, "*passiones*" and "*affectiones*." "*Passiones*" may be translated "passion" or "emotion," whereas Norman Kretzmann suggests "attitudes" as the translation for "*affectiones*."[11] As Kretzmann translates Aquinas, then, God has certain "attitudes" of love and joy, but these states are not emotions since Kretzmann maintains that Aquinas maintains that God has no emotions. But a case could be made for translating "*affectiones*" as "emotions" if it is true that even in us, states of emotion are not necessarily sensory. If some of our emotions are, or could be, intellective *affectiones* this would mean that the sensory aspect of an emotion is not essential to a state's being one of emotion. If so, a state could not be denied the categorization of an emotion on the grounds that it is not a sensory state. Thus, even if God has no sensory states it would not follow that he has no emotions.

Objection 1 gives a second reason for thinking that God cannot have emotions and that is that emotions are passions, ways of being acted upon, and thereby imply lack of perfection. I will not here address the issue of whether emotions are necessarily passive, but I do want to raise the question of whether emotion is an intrinsically defective state, a state that only makes sense when attributed to defective beings. I do not see that there is anything about emotion *per se* that implies imperfection, although there is no doubt that there are particular emotions that do have such an implication—e.g., fear, hope, jealousy, envy, hatred, bitterness. I hesitate to say that sadness implies a defect since sadness need not require any lack in the agent who has the emotion since it is a response to defects outside of the agent. The issue of whether the agent who has a certain emotion is defective does not correspond to the distinction that is sometimes made between positive and negative emotions. Some negative emotions such as sadness may imply no defect, whereas some positive emotions such as hope probably do imply a defect. In any case, we must admit that even if God does have emotions, he does not have the range of emotions that human beings have.

I have already said that it is not necessary to accept that God has emotions for the argument of this paper in spite of what I have said in this reply. Even if God does not have emotions, God nonetheless has states that are the counterparts of the states which in us are emotions. God has emotions in at least the same sense that God has beliefs. God's emotions may not be just like ours, but God's cognitive states are not just like ours either. What is of particular importance for Divine Motivation Theory is not so much that God's emotions are similar to ours in the way they feel, but that the divine states which are the counterparts of human emotions are motivations. That much should not be controversial. Since God is a moral agent, God acts from motives, and among those motives are compassion, forgiveness, and love.

Reply to objection 2: As Norman Kretzmann has pointed out to me, while Aquinas says that virtue is a habit, "*habitus*" to Aquinas means fundamentally the same thing as "having." The dispositional aspect of a *habitus* is important in his account of human virtues and vices because of our temporality and imperfection, but the idea of a disposition or habit is not essential to a *habitus* as Aquinas means it and does not prevent God from having qualities that in us would be habits or dispositions. For example, knowledge is a *habitus* and most human knowledge is dispositional. But the fact that God has no dispositions does not prevent God from having knowledge, nor does it prevent God's knowledge from being a *habitus* since God's knowledge is the eternal having of all truths. Similarly, even though a virtue such as compassion is a *habitus* which in us requires development over time culminating in a disposition distinctive of the virtue of compassion, that does not prevent God from having compassion, nor does it prevent compassion in God from being a *habitus*. God eternally has the emotion of compassion, not just as a disposition, but as an eternal motive-in-act.

Reply to objection 3: If a natural kind is a species, then God is not a natural kind, although God does have a nature and God *is* a certain kind of thing, namely, Absolutely Perfect Being, or Necessarily Existent Being. Each of the traditional arguments for the existence of God identifies a kind of thing that must be God, a kind of thing which, it must be argued, can have only one member. The divine virtues express the perfections of the kind God. There is no potency in God, but we can see that there is nothing inconsistent in the claim that a being with no potency has virtues since if, *per impossibile*, a human being reached full actualization of her potential with respect to some virtue, say, compassion, we certainly would not on that account deny that she is compassionate. The way in which a virtue is acquired is not essential to the virtue itself, although it may be essential to beings with a human nature to acquire virtue in a certain way. This means that there is nothing good *for* God if that means an extrinsic good that God needs for actualization, but there is still a sense in which God's virtues are good for him since even in the human case we do not cease claiming that what is good for us is good for us once it is attained. It is good for a human to have knowledge even when the knowledge is possessed; it is good for a knife to be sharp even when it *is* sharp. And it is good for God to be perfectly just, merciful, etc.[12]

Even though God has virtues and human virtues can be understood by their similarity to the divine virtues, this will have no practical usefulness to us in living a moral life unless we can see how to identify those human qualities that are like God's. We turn, then, to the doctrine of the Incarnation and its essential contribution to the ethics of *imitatio dei*.

Divine Motivation Theory. God has such virtues as justice, benevolence, mercy, forgiveness, kindness, love, compassion, loyalty, generosity, trustworthiness, integrity, and wisdom. God does not have courage, temperance, chastity, piety, nor does he have faith or hope. Each of the virtues in the latter group involve handling emotions that are distinctive of limited and embodied creatures like ourselves. Sexual feelings make no sense when applied to a disembodied being, and since God does not have to deal with fear, the awareness of inferiority to a superior being, the sense of powerlessness, nor the need for faith in God, which is to say, himself, it does not make sense to say that God has the virtues in this category. This means that God's virtues correspond to only some of the traits we consider human virtues. Of course, it does not follow that God's virtues are limited to these traits. It would be presumptuous of us to think that all divine virtues are perfections of human traits. If there are angels, God's virtues no doubt include perfections of angelic virtues, and if there are any other moral creatures in existence, God's virtues would include the perfections of the virtues of those beings as well. This position is expressed by Aquinas as follows:

> For just as God's being is universally perfect, in some way or other containing within itself the perfection of all beings, so also must his goodness in some way or other contain within itself the goodness of all things. Now a virtue is a goodness belonging to a virtuous person, for "it is in accordance with it that one is called good, and what one does is called good" [NE 1106a22-4]. Therefore, in its own way the divine goodness must contain all virtues (SCG I. 92.768).[13]

But this brings us to a practical problem. How can the idea of perfect justice, benevolence, generosity, mercy, etc. give us any practical guidance in the moral life? And how are we to get practical guidance in developing those virtues that I have conceded God does not have—virtues like chastity, faith, and courage? The answer, I suggest, is that we humans ought to think of Divine Motivation Theory in conjunction with the doctrine of the Incarnation in which the Father is revealed in the Son. To see Jesus is to see his Father (Jn 14:9). We learn to be moral, to develop the virtues, by the imitation of Christ.

The idea that humans should become as much like God as is humanly possible is the basis of the primary ethical doctrine of the Hebrew Bible, that of *imitatio Dei*.[14] "You shall be holy, for I the Lord your God am holy" (Lev. 19:2). In the Hebrew Scriptures, to become like God is to follow God's commands: "The Lord will establish you as a people holy to himself, as he has sworn to you, if you keep the commandments of the Lord your God, and walk in his ways" (Deut 28: 9). The doctrine of the Incarnation, however, shifts the ethical direction since through Christ, the Word made flesh, we have access to the Father and come to share in the divine nature. (See. Eph 1:9.) Christ says "Be perfect even as your heavenly father is perfect" (Matt 5:48), but we become perfect through Christ. Christian ethics, then, focuses less on following divine commands than on imitating the virtues of Christ, and the focus of the New Testament is primarily on the motivational component of these virtues. We see Jesus in a variety of human circumstances that produce recognizable human emotions, including temptation, weariness, anxiety, sadness, and anger. Jesus makes very few commands, but when he does, his injunctions generally call us to have motivations (emotion-dispositions) which I claim are the basic components of virtues, as in the Beatitudes and the two great commandments of love. The New Testament does not typically call us to will, but to be motivated in a virtuous way, so St. Paul says, "Owe no one anything but to love one another" (Romans 13:8). The Golden Rule appeals to a motive, not to a volition. We imagine how we would want to be treated and imaginatively project our own wants onto others. This leads us to have an emotional response to other persons that motivates our treatment of them. Our motive for loving and forgiving is not that we are to follow God's commands, but that God himself loves and forgives. And we see that there is no limit on the forgiveness of injuries because it corresponds to God's forgiveness of us, not because it will win over the offender or because God wills it (Matthew 18:21ff). The Incarnation is also a beautiful expression of the humility of God. A king rides a donkey and a Rabbi washes his disciples' feet. We are called to do the same (John 13: 13-14). In the words of Irenaeus, the first great Christian theologian: "In His immeasurable love He became what we are in order to make us what He is."[15]

Divine Motivation Theory gives an abstract structure for a long tradition of Christian ethics based on the imitation of Christ. Much of that work uses the narrative approach to ethics, and it is important to see that narrative ethics need not be in competition with theoretical ethics, but that DM theory can give it a theoretical grounding. Likewise, it gives a theoretical structure to a practical ethics that examines the individual virtues based on Scripture and the Christian tradition of veneration of the saints.

Advantages of DM theory over DC theory. Divine Motivation Theory is structurally parallel to Divine Command Theory in that DM theory makes moral properties derivative from God's motives, whereas DC theory makes moral properties derivative from God's will. In this section I will briefly compare the two theories to show how DM theory avoids the well-known problems of DC theory and has some decided advantages.

Divine Command Theory makes the divine will the source of moral value. Roughly, good states of affairs are what God wills to exist; bad states of affairs are what God wills not to exist. The focus of the theory, however, is generally on the rightness and wrongness of human acts. An act is morally required (a duty) just in case God commands us to do it; an act is morally wrong just in case God forbids us to do it. Since a divine command is the expression of God's will with respect to human and other creaturely acts, the divine will is the fundamental source of the moral properties of acts as well as of states of affairs.

The nature of the relation between God's commands and moral requirements is an important issue for DC theorists. To say that "x is morally required" just *means* "x is commanded by God" is too strong since that has the consequence that to say "x is right because God commands it" is a mere tautology; it is just to say "x is commanded by God because x is commanded by God." On the other hand, to say that God's commands and moral requirements are extensionally equivalent is too weak. That would be compatible with the lack of any metaphysical connection whatever between the existence of moral properties and God's will. Divine Command Theory, then, aims at something in between identity of meaning and mere extensional equivalence. It should turn out that God's will *makes* what's good to be good and what's right to be right. States of affairs are good/bad and acts are right/wrong *because* of the will of God. God's will is the metaphysical ground of all moral properties. This is also the sense in which God's motives ground moral value in Divine Motivation Theory.

An important objection to Divine Command Theory goes back to Plato's *Euthyphro* where Socrates asks, "Is what is holy holy because the gods approve it, or do they approve it because it is holy?" As applied to DC theory this question produces a famous dilemma: If God wills the good because it is good, then goodness is independent of God's will and the latter does not explain the former. On the other hand, if something is good because God wills it, then it looks as if the divine will is arbitrary. God is not constrained by any moral reason from willing anything whatever, and it is hard to see how any non-moral reason could be the right sort of reason to determine God's choice of what to make good or bad. The apparent consequence is that good/bad and right/wrong are determined by an arbitrary divine will; God could have commanded cruelty or hatred, and if he had done so, cruel and hateful acts would have been right, even duties. This is not only an unacceptable consequence for our sense of the essentiality of the moral properties of acts of certain kinds, but it also makes it hard to see how it can be true that God himself is good in any important, substantive sense of good.

Robert Adams has attempted to address this problem by modifying DC theory to say that the property of rightness is the property of being commanded by a *loving* God. This permits Adams to allow that God could command cruelty for its own sake, but if God did so he would not love us, and if that were the case, Adams argues, morality would break down. Morality is dependent upon divine commands, but they are dependent upon the commands of a deity with a certain nature. If God's nature were not loving, morality would fall apart.[16]

But even if Adams's proposal succeeds at answering the objection it is designed to address, it seems to me that it is unsatisfactory because it is *ad hoc*. There is no intrinsic connection between a command and the property of being loving, so to tie morality to the commands of a loving God is to tie it to two distinct properties of God. In Divine Motivation Theory, however, there is no need to solve the problem of whether God could make it right that we brutalize the innocent by making any such modification to the theory since being loving is one of God's essential motives. The right thing for humans to do is to act on motives that imitate the divine motives. Brutalizing the innocent is not an act that expresses a motive that imitates the divine motives. Hence, it is impossible for brutalizing the innocent to be right as long as (i) it is impossible for such an act to be an expression of a motive that is like the motives of God, and (ii) it is impossible for God to have different motives. (ii) follows from the highly plausible assumption that God's motives are part of his nature.[17]

DC theory also can argue that God's will is part of his nature, and Stump and Kretzmann have used the Thomistic doctrine of divine simplicity, which has the consequence that God's will is identical with his nature, to solve both the arbitrariness problem and the problem that God could command something like cruelty.[18] This solution is not *ad hoc*, but it requires argument to make the needed connection between the divine will and the divine nature. That is because a will is logically separable from its possessor in a way that motives are not. In fact, the feature of a will that led to the theory of the existence of a will in the first place, namely, its freedom, is the very feature that seems to have that consequence. In contrast, God's love, mercy, justice, compassion, etc., make God what he is. There is no need to overcome by argument a prior expectation that God's motives are dissociated from his nature as in the case of God's commands.

The arbitrariness problem may or may not be answerable in a DC theory, but the problem does not even arise in DM theory. That is because a will needs a reason, but a motive *is* a reason. The will, according to Aquinas, always chooses "under the aspect of good," which means that reasons are not inherent in the will itself. In contrast, motives provide not only the impetus to action, but the reason *for* the action. If we know that God acts from a motive of love, there is no need to look for a further reason for the act. On the other hand, a divine command requires a reason, and if the reason is or includes fundamental divine motivational states such as love, it follows that even DC theory needs to refer to God's motives to avoid the consequence that moral properties are arbitrary and God himself is not good. This move makes divine motives more basic than the divine will even in DC theory.

In addition to avoiding these difficulties inherent in Divine Command Theory, Divine Motivation Theory has two important theoretical advantages. First, DM theory gives us a unitary theory of all evaluative properties, divine as well as human, whereas DC theory does not. DC theory is most naturally interpreted as an ethics of law, a divine deontological theory, wherein the content of the law is promulgated by divine commands. But God's own goodness and the rightness of God's own acts are not connected to divine commands, and must be given an independent analysis. In contrast, DM theory makes the features of the divine nature in virtue of which God is morally good the foundation for the moral goodness of those same features in creatures. Second, as we have already seen, DM theory shows the importance of Christology for ethics, whereas DC theory does not. DC theory ignores the doctrines of the Trinity and the Incarnation, focusing on the will of the Creator-God as the source of moral value. It is, in effect, an Old Testament theory. The features of Christian ethics that derive from the life of Christ do not appear in the theory, at least not in any straightforward way. The fact that DM theory integrates these features into the theory makes it theologically preferable as well as easier to apply.

Notes

1. *Virtues of the Mind: An Inquiry into the Nature of Virtue and the Ethical Foundations of Knowledge* (Cambridge University Press, 1996), Part II. Earlier, I described this theory in the first of my Jellema Lectures, "Making Motivation Ethically Primary," delivered at Calvin College in March 1995.
2. Compare Robert Roberts' definition of an emotion as a "concern-based construal" in "What an Emotion Is: A Sketch," *Philosophical Review* 97, 2 (April 1988), 183-209. I agree with Roberts that some aspect of the world is construed to be such-and-such in an emotional state. I add the suggestion that the such-and-such is a concept of the type listed above. These concepts are or include what Bernard Williams calls thick ethical concepts, but I will not discuss this part of my theory of emotion here. I pursue that question in "Emotion and Moral Judgment."
3. Christine Korsgaard called attention to this distinction in "Two Distinctions in Goodness," *Philosophical Review* XCII, 2 (April 1983), 169-195.
4. Of course, the occurrence of an emotional state is a state of affairs, so this claim has to be qualified.
5. Kant's so-called pure motive of duty might be an exception to my thesis that all morally significant motives are emotions. I doubt that it is an exception, but will not discuss it here.

6. One of the problems in discussing motives is that our vocabulary about emotions and virtues is rather limited. Often we have no word for an emotion that is a component of a particular virtue or vice when we have a word for the virtue or vice itself. This is probably the case with courage and cowardice, fairness and unfairness. On the other hand, sometimes the word for the virtue or vice is borrowed from the word for the component emotion. This is probably the case with benevolence, compassion, cruelty, kindness, and many others.

7. I am using a modification of the Lewis definition of "might" in terms of "would" that appears in *Counterfactuals* (Cambridge: Harvard University Press, 1973). Lewis's definition applies to "would" and "might" as they appear in counterfactual conditionals; mine does not.

8. This distinction roughly corresponds to the distinction between perfect and imperfect duties.

9. A bad state of affairs can also be defined as one that a good motive would attempt to prevent or to eliminate, and a good state of affairs can be defined as one that a bad motive would attempt to prevent or to eliminate.

10. This theory therefore avoids the impasse between consequentialists and deontologists on the issue of the morality of performing an act that otherwise would be bad for the sake of a good outcome. Consequentialists and deontologists, of course, give different answers to that question, but they agree that the question makes sense. On the view I am proposing, the question does not make sense since an outcome is not something whose value is determined independently of attitudes virtuous persons have towards it.

11. See Norman Kretzmann, *The Metaphysics of Theism: Aquinas's Natural Theology in Summa Contra Gentiles I* (Oxford: Clarendon Press, 1997) for the most detailed commentary on Aquinas's natural theology in recent decades. The translation to which I refer appears in Chapter Eight.

12. I am grateful to the late Norman Kretzmann for suggesting this line of reply to the objection that nothing is good for God.

13. Translation by Norman Kretzmann, quoted in Kretzmann, p. 251.

14. See Menachem Kellner, "Jewish Ethics," *A Companion to Ethics*, ed. by Peter Singer (Blackwell, 1991), p. 84.

15. *The Scandal of the Incarnation*, selected and introduced by Hans Urs von Balthasar, trans. by John Saward, San Francisco: Ignatius Press, 1990, p. 54.

16. Adams, "Divine Command Metaethics Modified Again," *Journal of Religious Ethics* 7 (1979), 66-79.

17. This is assuming, of course, that the motives of which we are speaking are suitably general. Love is essential to God, but love of Adam and Eve is not.

18. Eleonore Stump and Norman Kretzmann, "Absolute Simplicity," *Faith and Philosophy* 2 (1985), 353-382. Stump and Kretzmann present the same view in "Being and Goodness," *Divine and Human Action*, ed. Thomas V. Morris (Ithaca: Cornell University Press, 1988).

Discussion

1. How does Zagzebski's Divine Motivation Theory overcome the Euthyphro problem? Do you think she is successful?
2. What are the moral and theological advantages of morality being rooted in emotions as opposed to actions?
3. In what ways is Zagzebski's Divine Motivation Theory compatible with the New Testament? In what ways is it incompatible? Is her view compatible, as far as you know, with the Holy Writ of other religious traditions?

Chapter 4

◈

Religious Experience

Perceiving God
*William Alston**

The position. I want to explore and defend the idea that the experience, or, as I shall say, the perception, of God plays an epistemic role with respect to beliefs about God importantly analogous to that played by sense *perception* with respect to beliefs about the physical world. The nature of that latter role is, of course, a matter of controversy, and I have no time here to go into those controversies. It is admitted, however, on (almost) all hands that sense perception provides us with knowledge (justified belief) about current states of affairs in the immediate environment of the perceiver and that knowledge of this sort is somehow required for any further knowledge of the physical world. The possibility I wish to explore is that what a person takes to be an experience of God can provide him/her with knowledge (justified beliefs) about what God is doing, or how God is "situated," vis-à-vis that subject at that moment. Thus, by experiencing the presence and activity of God, S can come to know (justifiably believe) that God is sustaining her in being, filling her with His love, strengthening her, or communicating a certain message to her.

Let's call beliefs as to how God is currently related to the subject *M-beliefs* ('M' for manifestation); these are the "perceptual beliefs" of the theological sphere. I shall suppose that here too the "perceptual" knowledge one acquires from experience is crucial for whatever else we can learn about God, though I won't have time to explore and defend that part of the position; I will have my hands full defending the claim that M-beliefs are justified. I will just make two quick points about the role of M-beliefs in the larger scheme. First, just as with our knowledge of the physical world, the recognition of a crucial role for perceptual knowledge is compatible with a wide variety of views as to just how it figures in the total system and as to what else is involved. Second, an important difference between the two spheres is that in the theological sphere perceptual beliefs as to what God has "said" (communicated, revealed) to one or another person play a major role.

---

*William Alson is Professor Emeritus of Philosophy at Syracuse University.

I have been speaking alternatively of perceptual *knowledge* and of the *justification* of perceptual beliefs. In this paper I shall concentrate on justification, leaving to one side whatever else is involved in knowledge. It will be my contention that (putative) experience of God is a source of justification for M-beliefs, somewhat in the way that sense experience is a source of justification for perceptual beliefs.

Again, it is quite controversial what this latter way is. I shall be thinking of it in terms of a direct-realist construal of sense perception, according to which I can be justified in supposing that my dog is wagging his tail just because something is visually presenting itself to me as (looks like) my dog wagging his tail; that is, it looks to me in such a way that I am thereby justified in thereby supposing it to be my dog wagging his tail. Analogously I think of the "experience of God" as a matter of something's presenting itself to one's experience as God (doing so and so); so that here too the subject is justified in believing that God is present to her, or is doing so and so vis-à-vis her, just because that is the way in which the object is presented to her experience. (For the purposes of this paper let's focus on those cases in which this presentation is not via any *sensory* qualities or sensorily perceivable objects. The experience involved will be nonsensory in character.) It is because I think of the experience of God as having basically the same structure as the sense perception of physical objects that I feel entitled to speak of "perceiving God." But though I construe the matter in direct-realist terms, most of what I have to say here will be relevant to a defense of the more general claim that the experiential justification of M-beliefs is importantly parallel to the experiential justification of perceptual beliefs about the physical environment, on any halfway plausible construal of the latter, at least on any halfway plausible realist construal.

Response to objections. I shall develop the position by way of responding to a number of objections. This procedure reflects my conviction that the very considerable incidence of putative perceptions of God creates a certain initial presumption that these experiences are what they seem to be and that something can thereby be learned about God.

Objection I. What reason do we have for supposing that anyone ever does really perceive God? In order for S to perceive God it would have to be the case that (1) God exists, and (2) God is related to S or to his experience in such a way as to be perceivable by him. Only after we have seen reason to accept all that will we take seriously any claim to perceive God.

Answer. It all depends on what you will take as a reason. What you have in mind, presumably, are reasons drawn from some source other than perceptions of God, e.g., metaphysical arguments for the existence and nature of God. But why do you think you are justified in that restriction? We don't proceed in this way with respect to sense perception. Although in determining whether a particular alleged perception was genuine we don't make use of the results of *that* perception, we do utilize what has been observed in many other cases. And what alternative is there? The conditions of veridical sense perception have to do with states of affairs and causal interactions in the physical world, matters to which we have no cognitive access that is not based on sense perception. In like fashion, if there is a divine reality why suppose that the conditions of veridically perceiving it could be ascertained without relying on perceptions of *it*? In requiring external validation in this case but not the other you are arbitrarily imposing a double standard.

Objection II. There are many contradictions in the body of M-beliefs. In particular, persons report communications from God that contradict other reported communications. How, then, can one claim that all M-beliefs are justified?

Answer. What is (should be) claimed is only *prima facie* justification. When a person believes that God is experientially present to him, that belief is justified *unless* the subject has sufficient reasons to suppose it to be false or to suppose that the experience is not, in these circumstances, sufficiently indicative of the truth of the belief. This is, of course, precisely the status of individual perceptual beliefs about the physical environment. When, seeming to see a lake, I believe there to be a lake in front of me, my belief is thereby justified unless I have sufficient reason to suppose it false or to suppose that, in these circumstances, the experience is not sufficiently indicative of the truth of the belief.

Objection III. It is rational to form beliefs about the physical environment on the basis of the way that environment appears to us in sense experience (call this practice of belief formation *SP*) because that is a generally reliable mode of belief formation. And it is reliable just because, in normal conditions, sense experience varies concomitantly with variations in what we take ourselves to be perceiving. But we have no reason to suppose any such regular covariation for putative perception of God. And hence we lack reason for regarding as rational the parallel practice of forming M-beliefs on the basis of what is taken to be a perception of God (call that practice *RE*).

Answer. This is another use of a double standard. How do we know that normal sense experience varies concomitantly with perceived objects? We don't know this *a priori*. Rather, we have strong empirical evidence for it. That is, by relying on sense perception for our data we have piled up evidence for the reliability of SP. Let's call the kind of circularity exhibited here *epistemic circularity*. It is involved whenever the premises in an argument for the reliability or rationality of a belief-forming practice have themselves been acquired by that practice.[1] If we allow epistemically circular arguments, the reliability of RE can be supported in the same way. Among the things people have claimed to learn from RE is that God will enable people to experience His presence and activity from time to time in a veridical way. By relying on what one learns from the practice of RE, one can show that RE is a reliable belief-forming practice. On the other hand, if epistemically circular arguments are not countenanced, there can be no significant basis for a reliability claim in either case.

Objection IV. A claim to perceive *X*, and so to form reliable perceptual beliefs about *X* on the basis of this, presupposes that the experience involved is best explained by the activity of *X*, *inter alia*. But it seems that we can give adequate explanations of putative experiences of God in purely naturalistic terms, without bringing God into the explanation at all. Whereas we can't give adequate explanations of normal sense experience without bringing the experienced external objects into the explanation. Hence RE, but not SP, is discredited by these considerations.

Answer. I do not believe that much of a case can be made for the adequacy of any naturalistic explanation of experiences of God. But for present purposes I want to concentrate on the way in which this objection once more depends on a double standard. You will have no case at all for your claim unless you, question-beggingly, restrict yourself to sources of evidence that exclude RE. For from RE and systems built up on its output we learn that God is involved in the explanation of every fact whatever. But you would not proceed in that way with SP. If it is a question of determining the best explanation of sense experience you will, of course, make use of what you think you have learned from SP. Again, you have arbitrarily applied different standards to the two practices.

Here is another point. Suppose that one could give a purely psychological or physiological explanation of the experiences in question. That is quite compatible with God's figuring among their causes and, hence, coming into an ideally complete explanation. After all, it is presumably possible to give an adequate causal explanation of sense experience in terms of what goes on within the skull, but that is quite compatible with the external perceived objects' figuring further back along the causal chain.

Objection V. You have been accusing me of *arbitrarily* employing a double standard. But I maintain that RE differs from SP in ways that make different standards appropriate. SP is a pervasive and inescapable feature of our lives. Sense experience is insistent, omnipresent, vivid, and richly detailed. We use it as a source of information during all our waking hours. RE, by contrast, is not universally shared; and even for its devotees its practice is relatively infrequent. Moreover, its deliverances are, by comparison, meager, obscure, and uncertain. Thus when an output of RE does pop up, it is naturally greeted with more skepticism, and one properly demands more for its validation than in the case of so regular and central part of our lives as SP.

Answer. I don't want to deny either the existence or the importance of these differences. I want to deny only that they have the alleged bearing on the epistemic situation. Why should we suppose that a cognitive access enjoyed only by a part of the population is less likely to be reliable than one that is universally distributed? Why should we suppose that a source that yields less detailed and less fully understood beliefs is more suspect than a richer source? *A priori* it would seem just as likely that some aspects of reality are accessible only to persons that satisfy certain conditions not satisfied by all human beings as that some aspects are equally accessible to all. *A priori* it would seem just as likely that some aspects of reality are humanly graspable only in a fragmentary and opaque manner as that some aspects are graspable in a more nearly complete and pellucid fashion. Why view the one sort of cognitive claim with more suspicion than the other? I will agree that the spotty distribution of RE calls for explanation, as does the various cognitively unsatisfactory features of its output. But, for that matter, so does the universal distribution and cognitive richness of SP. And in both cases explanations are forthcoming, though in both cases the outputs of the practices are utilized in order to achieve those explanations. As for RE, the limited distribution may be explained by the fact that many persons are not prepared to meet the moral and other "way of life" conditions that God has set for awareness of Himself. And the cognitively unsatisfactory features of the doxastic output are explained by the fact that God infinitely exceeds our cognitive powers.

Objection VI. When someone claims to see a spruce tree in a certain spot, the claim is checkable. Other people can take a look, photographs can be taken, the subject's condition can be diagnosed, and so on. But there are no comparable checks and tests available in RE. And how can we take seriously a claim to have perceived an objective state of affairs if there is, in principle, no intersubjective way of determining whether that claim is correct?

Answer. The answer to this objection is implicit in a point made earlier, viz., that putative experience of God yields only *prima facie* justification, justification (unqualifiedly) provided there are no sufficient overriding considerations. This notion has a significant application only where there is what we may call an *overrider system*, i.e., ways of determining whether the facts are such as to indicate a belief from the range in question to be false and ways of determining whether conditions are such that the basis of the belief is sufficiently indicative of its truth. SP does contain such a system. What about RE? Here we must confront a salient difference between the two spheres. If we consider the way in which a body of beliefs has been developed on the basis of SP we find pretty much the same system across all cultures. But our encounters with God have spawned a number of different religious communities with beliefs and practices of worship which are quite different, though with some considerable overlap. These differences carry with them differences in overrider systems. But it remains true that if we consider any particular religious community which exhibits a significant commonality in doctrine and worship it will feature a more or less definite overrider system. For concreteness let's think of what I will call the *mainline Christian community.* (From this point onward I will use the term 'RE' for the practice of forming M-beliefs as it goes on in this community.) In that community a body of doctrine has developed concerning the nature of God, His purposes, and His interactions with mankind, including His appearances to us. If an M-belief contradicts this system that is a reason for deeming it false. Moreover there is a long and varied history of experiential encounters with God, embodied in written accounts as well as oral transmission. This provides bases for regarding particular experiences as more or less likely to be veridical, given the conditions, psychological or otherwise, in which they occurred, the character of the subject, and the effects in the life of the subject. Thus a socially established religious doxastic practice like RE will contain a rich system of overriders that provides resources for checking the acceptability of any particular M-beliefs.

Overriders for RE beliefs
are within the religious community

But perhaps your point is rather that there are no *external* checks on a particular report, none that do not rely on other claims of the same sort. Let's agree that this is the case. But why suppose that to be any black mark against RE? Here is the double standard again. After all, particular claims within SP cannot be checked without relying on what we have learned from SP. Suppose I claim to see a fir tree in a certain spot. To check on this one would have to rely on other persons' perceptual reports as to what is at that spot, our general empirical knowledge of the likelihood of a fir tree in that locality, and so on. Apart from what we take ourselves to have learned from SP, we would have nothing to go on. One can hardly determine whether my report was accurate by intuiting self-evident truths or by consulting divine revelation. But if SP counts as having a system of checks even though this system involves relying on some outputs of the practice in order to put others to the test, why should RE be deemed to have no such system when its procedures exhibit the same structure? Once more you are, arbitrarily, setting quite different requirements for different practices.

Perhaps your point was that RE's system of checks is unlike SP's. In particular, the following difference can be discerned. Suppose I report seeing a morel at a certain spot in the forest. Now suppose that a number of qualified observers take a good look at that spot at that time and report that no morel is to be seen. In that case my report would have been decisively disconfirmed. But nothing like that is possible in RE. We can't lay down any conditions (of a sort the satisfaction of which we can determine) under which a properly qualified person will experience the presence of God if God is "there" to be experienced. Hence a particular report cannot be decisively disconfirmed by the experience of others.

But what epistemic relevance does this difference have? Why should we suppose that RE is rendered dubious for lacking checkability of this sort? Let's consider what makes this kind of intersubjective test possible for SP. Clearly it is that we have discovered fairly firm regularities in the behavior of physical things, including human sense perception. Since there are stable regularities in the ways in which physical objects disclose themselves to our perception, we can be assured that if X exists at a certain time and place and if S satisfies appropriate conditions then S is sure to perceive X. But no such tight regularities are discoverable in God's appearances to our experience. We can say something about the way in which such matters as the distribution of attention and the moral and spiritual state of the subject are conducive to such appearances; but these most emphatically do not add up to the sort of lawlike connections we get with SP. Now what about this difference? Is it to the epistemic discredit of RE that it does not enable us to discover such regularities? Well, that all depends on what it would be reasonable to expect if RE does put us into effective cognitive contact with God. Given what we have learned about God and our relations to Him (from RE, supplemented by whatever other sources there be), should we expect to be able to discover such realities if God really exists? Clearly not. There are several important points here, but the most important is that it is contrary to God's plans for us to give us that much control, cognitive and practical. Hence it is quite understandable, if God exists and is as RE leads us to suppose, that we should not be able to ascertain the kinds of regularities that would make possible the kinds of intersubjective tests exhibited by SP. Hence, the epistemic status of RE is in no way diminished by its lack of such tests. Once more RE is subjected to an inappropriate standard. This time, however, it is not a double standard, but rather an inappropriate single standard. RE is being graded down for lacking positive features of other practices, where these features cannot reasonably be supposed to be generally necessary conditions of epistemic excellence, even for experiential practices. Thus my critic is exhibiting what we might term *epistemic chauvinism*, judging alien forms of life according to whether they conform to the home situation, a procedure as much to be deplored in the epistemic as in the political sphere.

Objection VII. How can it be rational to take RE as a source of justification when there are incompatible rivals that can lay claim to that status on exactly the same grounds? M-beliefs of different religious communities conflict to a considerable extent, particularly those concerning alleged divine messages, and the bodies of doctrine they support conflict even more. We get incompatible accounts of God's plans for us and requirements on us, of the conditions of salvation, and so on. This being the case, how can we pick out just one of these communal practices as yielding justified belief?

Answer. I take this to be by far the most serious difficulty with my position. I have chosen to concentrate on what I take to be less serious problems, partly because their consideration brings out better the main lineaments of the position, and partly because any serious treatment of this last problem would spill beyond the confines of this paper. Here I shall have to content myself with making one basic point. We are not faced with the necessity of choosing only one such practice as yielding *prima facie* justified M-beliefs. The fact that there are incompatibilities between systems of religious beliefs, in M-beliefs and elsewhere, shows that not all M-beliefs can be true, but not that they cannot all be *prima facie* justified. After all, incompatible beliefs *within* a system can all be *prima facie* justified; that's the point of the *prima facie* qualification. When we are faced with a situation like that, the hope is that the overrider system and other winnowing devices will weed out the inconsistencies. To be sure, intersystem winnowing devices are hazier and more meager than those which are available within a system; but consistency, consonance with other well-entrenched beliefs and doxastic practices, and general reasonability and plausibility give us something to go on. Moreover, it may be that some religious ways of life fulfill their own promises more fully than others. Of course, there is never any guarantee that a unique way of resolving incompatibilities will present itself, even with a system. But where there are established practices of forming beliefs on the basis of experience, I believe the rational course is to regard each such belief as thereby *prima facie* justified, hoping that future developments, perhaps unforeseeable at present, will resolve fundamental incompatibilities.

Conclusion. In conclusion I will make explicit the general epistemological orientation I have been presupposing in my defense of RE. I take our human situation to be such that we engage in a plurality of basic doxastic practices, each of which involves a distinctive sort of input to belief-forming "mechanisms," a distinctive range of belief contents (a "subject matter" and ways of conceiving it), and a set of like functions that determine belief contents as a function of input features. Each practice is socially established: socially shared, inculcated, reinforced, and propagated. In addition to experiential practices, with which we have been concerned in this paper, there are, e.g., inferential practices, the input of which consists of beliefs, and the practice of forming memory beliefs. A doxastic practice is not restricted to the formation of first-level beliefs; it will also typically involve criteria and procedures of criticism of the beliefs thus formed; here we will find the "overrider systems" of which we were speaking earlier. In general, we learn these practices and engage in them long before we arrive at the stage of explicitly formulating their principles and subjecting them to critical reflection. Theory is deeply rooted in practice.

Nor, having arrived at the age of reason, can we turn our back on all that and take a fresh start, in the Cartesian spirit, choosing our epistemic procedures and criteria anew, on a purely "rational" basis. Apart from reliance on doxastic tendencies with which we find ourselves, we literally have nothing to go on. Indeed, what Descartes did, as Thomas Reid trenchantly pointed out, was arbitrarily to pick one doxastic practice he found himself engaged in—accepting propositions that seem self-evident—and set that as a judge over all the others, with what results we are all too familiar. This is not to say that we must acquiesce in our prereflective doxastic tendencies in every respect. We can tidy things up, modify our established practices so as to make each more internally consistent and more consistent with the others. But, on the whole and for the most part, we have no choice but to continue to form beliefs in accordance with these practices and to take these ways of forming beliefs as paradigmatically conferring epistemic justification. And this is the way that epistemology has in fact gone, except for some arbitrary partiality. Of course it would be satisfying to economize our basic commitments by taking one or a few of these practices as basic and using them to validate the others; but we have made little progress in this enterprise over the centuries. It is not self-evident that sense perception is reliable, nor can we establish its reliability if we restrict ourselves to premises drawn from introspection; we cannot show that deductive reasoning is valid without using deductive reasoning to do so; and so on. We are endowed with strong tendencies to engage in a number of distinct doxastic practices, none of which can be warranted on the basis of others. It is clearly the better part of wisdom to recognize beliefs that SP emerge from these practices to be rational and justified, at least once they are properly sifted and refined.

In this paper I have undertaken to extend this account to doxastic practices that are not universally practiced. Except for that matter of distribution and the other peripheral matters mentioned in Objection V and except for being faced with actually existing rivals, a religious experiential doxastic practice like RE seems to me to be on all fours with SP and other universal practices. It too involves a distinctive range of inputs, a range of belief contents, and functions that map features of the former onto contents of the latter. It is socially established within a certain community. It involves higher-level procedures of correction and modification of its first-level beliefs. Though it *may* be acquired in a deliberate and self-conscious lay fashion, it is more typically acquired in a practical, prereflective form. Though it is obviously avoidable in a way SP, e.g., is not, for many of its practitioners it is just about as firmly entrenched.

These similarities lead me to the conclusion that if, as it seems we must concede, a belief is *prima facie* justified by virtue of emerging from one of the universal basic practices, we should also concede the same status to the products of RE. I have sought to show that various plausible-sounding objections to this position depend on the use of a double standard or reflect arbitrary epistemic chauvinism. They involve subjecting RE to inappropriate standards. Once we appreciate these points, we can see the strength of the case for RE as one more epistemically autonomous practice of belief formation and source of justification.

Notes

1. See my "Epistemic Circularity," *Philosophy and Phenomenological Research*, XLVII, 1 (September 1986): 1-30.

Discussion

1. In what ways is religious experience like sensory experience?
2. In what ways is religious unlike sensory experience?
3. How does Alston respond to the alleged dissimilarities between sensory and religious experience? Do you think his responses are adequate?
4. What do you consider to be the most powerful objection to the veridicality of religious experience? Can ordinary sensory experience overcome this sort of objection?

Chapter 5

꘡

Naturalism Refuted?

The Self-Refutation of Naturalism

Alvin Plantinga *

Proper function.... Most of us think (or would think on reflection) that at least *a* function or purpose of our cognitive faculties is to provide us with true beliefs. Moreover, we go on to think that when they function properly, in accord with our design plan, then for the most part they do precisely that....

... Over a vast area of cognitive terrain we take it both that the purpose (function) of our cognitive faculties is to provide us with true or verisimilitudinous beliefs and that, for the most part, that is just what they do. We suppose, for example, that most of the deliverances of memory are at least approximately correct. True, if you ask five witnesses how the accident happened, you may get five different stories. Still, they will agree that there was indeed an *accident* and that it was an *automobile* accident (as opposed, say, to a naval disaster or a volcanic eruption); there will usually be agreement as to the number of vehicles involved (particularly if it is a small number), as well as the rough location of the accident (Aberdeen, Scotland, as opposed to Aberdeen, South Dakota), and so on. And all this is against the background of massive and much deeper agreement: that there are automobiles; that they do not disappear when no one is looking; that if released from a helicopter they fall down rather than up, that they are driven by people who use them to go places, that they are seldom driven by three-year-olds, that their drivers have purposes, hold beliefs, and often act on those purposes and beliefs, that few of them (or their drivers) have been more than a few miles from the surface of the earth, that the world has existed for a good long time—much longer than ten minutes, say—and a million more such Moorean truisms. (Of course, there is the occasional dissenter—in the grip, perhaps, of cognitive malfunction or a cognitively crippling philosophical theory.)

We think our faculties much better adapted to reach the truth in some areas than others; we are good at elementary arithmetic and logic, and the perception of

---

*Alvin Plantinga is John A. O'Brien Professor of Philosophy at University of Notre Dame. Prior to his Notre Dame appointment, he taught for twenty years at Calvin College.

middle-sized objects under ordinary conditions. We are also good at remembering certain sorts of things: I can easily remember what I had for breakfast this morning, where my office was located yesterday, and whether there was a large explosion in my house last night. Things get more difficult, however, when it comes to an accurate reconstruction of what it was like to be, say, a fifth century B.C. Greek (not to mention a bat), or whether the axiom of choice or the continuum (hypothesis) is true; things are even more difficult, perhaps, when it comes to figuring out how quantum mechanics is to be understood, and what the subnuclear realm of quark and gluon is really like, if indeed there really is a subnuclear realm of quark and gluon. Still, there remains a vast portion of our cognitive terrain where we think that our cognitive faculties do furnish us with truth.

The problem. But isn't there a problem, here, for the naturalist? At any rate for the naturalist who thinks that we and our cognitive capacities arrived upon the scene after some billions of years of evolution (by way of natural selection, genetic drift, and other blind processes working on such sources of genetic variation as random genetic mutation)? Richard Dawkins (according to Peter Medawar, "one of the most brilliant of the rising generation of biologists") once leaned over and remarked to A. J. Ayer at one of those elegant, candle-lit, bibulous Oxford college dinners, that he couldn't imagine being an atheist before 1859 (the year Darwin's *Origin of Species* was published); "although atheism might have been logically tenable before Darwin," said he, "Darwin made it possible to be an intellectually fulfilled atheist."[1]

Now Dawkins thinks Darwin made it possible to be an intellectually fulfilled atheist. But perhaps Dawkins is dead wrong here. Perhaps the truth lies in the opposite direction. If our cognitive faculties have originated as Dawkins thinks, then their ultimate purpose or function (if they *have* a purpose or function) will be something like *survival* (of individual, species, gene, or genotype); but then it seems initially doubtful that among their functions—ultimate, proximate, or otherwise—would be the production of true beliefs. Taking up this theme, Patricia Churchland declares that the most important thing about the human brain is that it has evolved; hence, she says, its principal function is to enable the organism to *move* appropriately:

> Boiled down to essentials, a nervous system enables the organism to succeed in the four F's: feeding, fleeing, fighting and reproducing. The principle chore of nervous systems is to get the body parts where they should be in order that the organism may survive.... Improvements in sensorimotor control confer an evolutionary advantage: a fancier style of representing is advantageous *so long as it is geared to the organism's way of life and enhances the organism's chances of survival* [Churchland's emphasis]. Truth, whatever that is, definitely takes the hindmost.[2]

Her point, I think, is that (from a naturalistic perspective) what evolution guarantees is (at most) that we *behave* in certain ways—in such ways as to promote survival, or survival through childbearing age. The principal function or purpose, then, (the 'chore' says Churchland) of our cognitive faculties is not that of producing true or verisimilitudinous beliefs, but instead that of contributing to survival by getting the body parts in the right place. What evolution underwrites is only (at most) that our *behavior* be reasonably adaptive to the circumstances in which our ancestors found themselves; hence (so far forth) it does not guarantee mostly true or verisimilitudinous beliefs. Of course our beliefs *might* be mostly true or verisimilitudinous (hereafter I'll omit the 'verisimilitudinous'); but there is no particular reason to think they *would* be: natural selection is interested not in truth, but in appropriate behavior. What Churchland says suggests, therefore, that naturalistic evolution—that is, the conjunction of metaphysical naturalism with the view that we and our cognitive faculties have arisen by way of the mechanisms and processes proposed by contemporary evolutionary theory—gives us reason to doubt two things: (a) that a *purpose* of our cognitive systems is that of serving us with true beliefs, and (b) that they *do*, in fact, furnish us with mostly true beliefs.

W.V.O. Quine and Karl Popper, however, apparently demur. Popper argues that since we have evolved and survived, we may be pretty sure that our hypotheses and guesses as to what the world is like are mostly correct.[3] And Quine says he finds encouragement in Darwin:

> What does make clear sense is this other part of the problem of induction: why does our innate subjective spacing of qualities accord so well with the functionally relevant groupings in nature as to make our inductions tend to come out right? Why should our subjective spacing of qualities have a special purchase on nature and a lien on the future?
>
> There is some encouragement in Darwin. If people's innate spacing of qualities is a gene-linked trait, then the spacing that has made for the most successful inductions will have tended to predominate through natural selection. Creatures inveterately wrong in their inductions have a pathetic but praiseworthy tendency to die before reproducing their kind.[4]

Indeed, Quine finds a great deal more encouragement in Darwin than Darwin did: "With me," says Darwin,

> the horrid doubt always arises whether the convictions of man's mind, which has been developed from the mind of the lower animals, are of any value or at all trustworthy. Would any one trust in the convictions of a monkey's mind, if there are any convictions in such a mind?[5]

So here we appear to have Quine and Popper on one side and Darwin and Churchland on the other. Who is right? But a prior question: what, precisely, is the issue? Darwin and Churchland seem to believe that (naturalistic) evolution gives one a reason to doubt that human cognitive faculties produce for the most part true or beliefs: call this 'Darwin's Doubt'. Quine and Popper, on the other hand, apparently hold that evolution gives us reason to believe the opposite: that human cognitive faculties *do* produce for the most part true beliefs. How shall we understand this opposition?

Darwin's doubt. One possibility: perhaps Darwin and Churchland mean to propose that a certain objective conditional probability is relatively low: the probability of human cognitive faculties' being reliable (producing mostly true beliefs), given that human beings *have* cognitive faculties (of the sort we have) and given that these faculties have been produced by evolution (Dawkin's blind evolution, unguided by the hand of God or any other person). If metaphysical naturalism and this evolutionary account are both true, then our cognitive faculties will have resulted from blind mechanisms like natural selection, working on such sources of genetic variation as random genetic mutation. Evolution is interested, not in true belief, but in survival or fitness. It is therefore unlikely that our cognitive faculties have the production of true belief as a proximate or any other function, and the probability of our faculties' being reliable (given naturalistic evolution) would be fairly low. Popper and Quine on the other side, judge that probability fairly high.

The issue, then, is the value of a certain conditional probability: P(R/(N&E&C)).[6] Here N is metaphysical naturalism. It isn't easy to say precisely what naturalism *is*, but perhaps that isn't necessary in this context; prominent examples would be the views of (say) David Armstrong, the later Darwin, Quine and Bertrand Russell. (Crucial to metaphysical naturalism, of course, is the view that there is no such person as the God of traditional theism.) E is the proposition that human cognitive faculties arose by way of the mechanisms to which contemporary evolutionary thought directs our attention; and C is a complex proposition whose precise formulation is both difficult and unnecessary, but which states what cognitive faculties we have—memory, perception, reason, Reid's sympathy—and what sorts of beliefs they produce. R, on the other hand, is the claim that our cognitive faculties are reliable (on the whole, and with the qualifications mentioned), in the sense that they produce mostly true beliefs in the sorts of environments that are normal for them. And the question is: what is the probability of R on N&E&C? (Alternatively, perhaps the interest of *that* question lies in its bearing on *this* question: what is the probability that a belief produced by human cognitive faculties is *true*, given N&E&C?) And if we construe the dispute in this way, then what Darwin and Churchland propose is that this probability is relatively low, whereas Quine and Popper think it fairly high....

The doubt developed.... In order to avoid irrelevant distractions, suppose we think, first, not about ourselves and our ancestors, but about a hypothetical population of creatures a lot like ourselves on a planet similar to Earth. (Darwin proposed that we think about another species, such as monkeys.) Suppose these creatures have cognitive faculties, hold beliefs, change beliefs, make inferences, and so on; and suppose these creatures have arisen by way of the selection processes endorsed by contemporary evolutionary thought. What is the probability that their faculties are reliable? What is P(R/(N&E&C)), specified not to us, but to them? According to Quine and Popper, the probability in question would be rather high: belief is connected with action in such a way that extensive false belief would lead to maladaptive behavior, in which case it is likely that the ancestors of those creatures would have displayed that pathetic but praiseworthy tendency Quine mentions.

But now for the contrary argument. First, perhaps it is likely that their *behavior* is adaptive; but nothing follows about their *beliefs*. We aren't given, after all, that their beliefs are so much as causally connected with their behavior; for we aren't given that their beliefs are more than mere epiphenomena, not causally involved with behavior at all. Perhaps their beliefs neither figure into the causes of their behavior, nor are caused by that behavior. (No doubt beliefs would be caused by *something* in or about these creatures, but it need not be by their behavior.)....

A second possibility is that the beliefs of these creatures are not among the *causes* of their behavior, but are *effects* of that behavior, or effects of proximate causes that also cause behavior. Their beliefs might be like a sort of decoration that isn't involved in the causal chain leading to action. Their waking beliefs might be no more causally efficacious, with respect to their behavior, than our dream beliefs are with respect to ours.... Under these conditions, of course, their beliefs could be wildly false. It *could* be that one of these creatures believes that he is at that elegant, bibulous Oxford dinner, when in fact he is slogging his way through some primeval swamp, desperately fighting off hungry crocodiles. Under this possibility, as under the first, beliefs would not have (or need not have) any purpose or function; they would be more like unintended by-products. Under this possibility as under the first, the probability that their cognitive faculties are reliable, is low.

A third possibility is that beliefs do indeed have causal efficacy with respect to behavior, but not by virtue of their *content*; to put it in currently fashionable jargon, this would be the suggestion that while beliefs are causally efficacious, it is only by virtue of their *syntax*, not by virtue of their *semantics*.... I read a poem very loudly, so loudly as to break a glass; the sounds I utter have meaning, but their meaning is causally irrelevant to the breaking of the glass. In the same way it might be that these creatures' beliefs have causal efficacy, but not by way of the content of those beliefs. A substantial share of probability must be reserved for this option; and under this option, as under the preceding two, the likelihood that the beliefs of these creatures would be for the most part true would be low....

A [fourth] (and final) possibility is that the beliefs of our hypothetical creatures are indeed both causally connected with their behavior and also adaptive. Assume, then, that our creatures have belief systems and that these systems are adaptive: they produce adaptive behavior, and at not too great a cost in terms of resources. What is the probability (on this assumption together with N&E&C) that their cognitive faculties are reliable; and what is the probability that a belief produced by those faculties will be true?

Not as high as you might think. For, of course, beliefs don't causally produce behavior *by themselves*; it is beliefs, desires, and other things that do so together. Suppose we oversimplify a bit and say that my behavior is a causal product just of my beliefs and desires. Then the problem is that clearly there will be any number of *different* patterns of belief and desire that would issue in the same action; and among those there will be many in which the beliefs are wildly false. Paul is a prehistoric hominid; the exigencies of survival call for him to display tiger-avoidance behavior. There will be many behaviors that are appropriate: fleeing, for example, or climbing a steep rock face, or crawling into a hole too small to admit the tiger, or leaping into a handy lake. Pick any such appropriately specific behavior *B*. Paul engages in *B*, we think, because, sensible fellow that he is, he has an aversion to being eaten and believes that *B* is a good means of thwarting the tiger's intentions.

But clearly this avoidance behavior could be a result of a thousand other belief-desire combinations: indefinitely many other belief-desire systems fit *B* equally well.... Perhaps Paul very much *likes* the idea of being eaten, but whenever he sees a tiger, always runs off looking for a better prospect, because he thinks it unlikely that the tiger he sees will eat him. This will get his body parts in the right place so far as survival is concerned, without involving much by way of true belief. (Of course we must postulate other changes in Paul's ways of reasoning, including how he changes belief in response to experience, to maintain coherence.) Or perhaps he thinks the tiger is a large, friendly, cuddly pussycat and wants to pet it; but he also believes that the best way to pet it is to run away from it. Or perhaps he confuses running *toward* it with running *away* from it, believing of the action that is really running away from it, that it is running toward it; or perhaps he thinks the tiger is a regularly recurring illusion, and, hoping to keep his weight down, has formed the resolution to run a mile at top speed whenever presented with such an illusion; or perhaps he thinks he is about to take part in a sixteen-hundred-meter race, wants to win, and believes the appearance of the tiger is the starting signal; or perhaps.... Clearly there are any number of belief-cum-desire systems that equally fit a given bit of behavior where the beliefs are mostly false. Indeed, even if we fix desire, there will still be any number of systems of belief that will produce a given bit of behavior: perhaps Paul does not want to be eaten, but (a) thinks the best way to avoid being eaten is to run toward the tiger, and (b) mistakenly believes that he is running toward it when in fact he is running away.

But these possibilities are wholly preposterous, you say. Following Richard Grandy, you point out that when we ascribe systems of belief and desire to persons, we make use of "principles of humanity," whereby we see others as resembling what we take ourselves to be.[7] You go on to endorse David Lewis's suggestion that a theory of content requires these "principles of humanity" in order to rule out as "deeply irrational" those nonstandard belief-desire systems; the contents involved are "unthinkable," and are hence disqualified as candidates for someone's belief-desire structure.[8] Surely you (and Grandy and Lewis) are right: in ascribing beliefs to others, we *do* think of them as like what we think we are. (This involves, among other things, thinking that the (a) purpose or function of their cognitive systems, like that of ours, is the production of true beliefs.) And a theory of content ascription does indeed require more than just the claim that the content of my beliefs must fit my behavior and desires: that leaves entirely too much latitude as to what that content, on a given occasion, might in fact be. These principles of humanity will exclude vast hordes of logically possible belief-desire systems as systems (given human limitations) no human being *could* have.... These principles will also exclude some systems as systems we think no properly functioning human being *would* have: accordingly, I will not attribute to Paul the view that emeralds are grue, or the belief that it would be good to have a nice saucer of mud for lunch.[9]

These points are quite correct; but they do not bear on the present question. It is true that a decent theory of content ascription must require more than that the belief fit the behavior; for a decent theory of content ascription must also respect or take for granted what we ordinarily think about our desires, beliefs, and circumstances and the relations between these items. But in the case of our hypothetical population, these "principles of humanity" are not relevant. For we are not given that its members are human; more important, we are not given that those principles of humanity, those commonsense beliefs about how their behavior, belief, and desire are related, are true of them. We can't assume that their beliefs, for given circumstances, would be similar to what *we* take it we would believe in those circumstances. We must ask what sorts of belief-desire systems are *possible* for these creatures, given only that they have evolved according to the principles of contemporary evolutionary theory; clearly these gerrymanders are perfectly possible. So perhaps their behavior has been adaptive, and their systems of belief and desire such as to fit that adaptive behavior; those beliefs could nonetheless be wildly wrong. There are indefinitely many belief-desire systems that fit adaptive behavior, but where the beliefs involved are not for the most part true. A share of probability has to be reserved for these possibilities as well.

Our question was this: given our hypothetical population along with N&E&C, what is the probability that the cognitive systems of beliefs these creatures display is reliable? Suppose we briefly review. First, on the condition in question, there is some probability that their beliefs are not causally connected with behavior at all. It would be reasonable to suppose, on that condition, that the probability of a given belief's being true would not be far from 1/2, and hence reasonable to suppose that the probability that their cognitive faculties are reliable (produce a substantial preponderance of verisimilitudinous beliefs) is very low. Second, there is some probability that their beliefs are causally connected with behavior, but only as epiphenomenal effect of causes that also cause behavior; in that case too it would be reasonable to suppose that the probability of their cognitive systems' being reliable is very low. Third, there is the possibility that belief is only 'syntactically', not 'semantically', connected with behavior; on this possibility too, there would be a low probability that their cognitive faculties are reliable.... [Fourth], there is also some probability that their beliefs are causally connected with their behavior, and are adaptive; as we saw, however, there are indefinitely many belief-desire systems that would yield adaptive behavior, but are unreliable. Here one does not quite know what to say about the probability that their cognitive systems would produce mainly true beliefs, but perhaps it would be reasonable to estimate it as somewhat more than 1/2. These possibilities are mutually exclusive and jointly exhaustive; if we had definite probabilities for each of the five cases and definite probabilities for R on each of them, then the probability of R would be the weighted average of the probabilities for R on each of those possibilities—weighted by the probabilities of those possibilities. (Of course we don't have definite probabilities here, but only vague estimates; it imparts a spurious appearance of precision to so much as mention the relevant formula.)

Trying to combine these probabilities in an appropriate way, then, it would be reasonable to suppose that the probability of R, of these creatures' cognitive systems being reliable, is relatively low, somewhat less than 1/2. More exactly, a reasonable posture would be to think it very unlikely that the statistical probability of their belief-producing mechanisms' being reliable, given that they have been produced in the suggested way, is very high; and rather likely that (on N&E&C) R is less probable than its denial.

Now return to Darwin's Doubt. The reasoning that applies to these hypothetical creatures, of course, also applies to *us*; so if we think the probability of R with respect to *them* is relatively low on N&E&C, we should think the same thing about the probability of R with respect to *us*. Something like this reasoning, perhaps, is what underlay Darwin's doubt.... So taken, his claim is that P(R/N&E&C) (specified to us) is rather low, perhaps somewhat less than 1/2. Arguments of this sort are less than coercive; but it would be perfectly sensible to estimate these probabilities in this way.

An argument against naturalism. Suppose you do estimate these probabilities in roughly this way: suppose you concur in Darwin's Doubt, taking P(R/(N&E&C)) to be fairly low. But suppose you also think, as most of us do, that in fact our cognitive faculties *are* reliable (with the qualifications and nuances introduced previously). Then you have a straightforward probabilistic argument against naturalism—and for traditional theism, if you think these two the significant alternatives. According to Bayes' Theorem,

$$P((N\&E\&C)/R) = \frac{P(N\&E\&C) \times P(R/(N\&E\&C))}{P(R)}$$

where P(N&E&C) is your estimate of the probability for N&E&C independent of the consideration of R. You believe R, so you assign it a probability near 1 and you take P(R/(N&E&C)) to be no more than 1/2. Then P((N&E&C)/R) will be no greater than 1/2 times P(N&E&C), and will thus be fairly low. You believe C (the proposition specifying the sorts of cognitive faculties we have); so you assign it a very high probability; accordingly P((N&E)/R) will also be low. No doubt you will also assign a very high probability to the conditional *if naturalism is true, then our faculties have arisen by way of evolution*; then you will judge that P(N/R) is also low. But you do think R is true; you therefore have evidence against N. So your belief that our cognitive faculties are reliable gives you a reason for rejecting naturalism and accepting its denial.

The same argument will not hold, of course, for traditional theism; on that view the probability that our cognitive faculties are reliable will be much higher than 1/2; for, according to traditional (Jewish, Christian, Moslem) theism, God created us in his image, a part of which involves our having knowledge over a wide range of topics and areas.[10] So (provided that for you the prior probabilities of traditional theism and naturalism are comparable) P(traditional theism/R) will be considerably greater than P(N/R)....

The argument developed. By way of brief review: Darwin's Doubt can be taken as the claim that the probability of R on N&E&C is fairly low; as I argued, that is plausible. But Darwin's Doubt can also be taken as the claim that the rational attitude to take, here, is agnosticism about that probability; that is more plausible. Still more plausible is the disjunction of these two claims: either the rational attitude to take toward this probability is the judgment that it is low, or the rational attitude is agnosticism with respect to it. But then the devotee of N&E has a defeater for any belief *B* he holds. Now the next thing to note is that *B might be N&E itself*; our devotee of N&E has an undercutting defeater for N&E, a reason to doubt it, a reason to be agnostic with respect to it. (This also holds if he isn't agnostic about P(R/(N&E&C)) but thinks it low, as in the preliminary argument; he has a defeater either way.) If he has no defeater for this defeater and no independent evidence—if his reason for doubting N&E, remains undefeated—then the rational course would be to reject belief in N&E....

What we have seen so far, therefore, is that the devotee of N&E has a defeater for any belief he holds, and a stronger defeater for N&E itself. If he has no defeater for this defeater, and no independent evidence, then the rational attitude toward N&E would be one of agnosticism.

... [T]he friend of N&E is ... likely to suggest that we consult the scientific results on the matter—what does science tell us about the likelihood that our cognitive faculties are reliable? But this can't work either. For consider any argument from science (or anywhere else) he might produce. This argument will have premises; and these premises, he claims, give him good reason to believe R (or N&E). But note that he has the very same defeater for each of those premises that he has for R and for N&E; and he has the same defeater for his belief that those premises constitute a good reason for R (or N&E). For that belief, and for each of the premises, he has a reason for doubting it, a reason for being agnostic with respect to it. This reason, obviously, cannot be defeated by an ultimately undefeated defeater. For every defeater of this reason he might have, he knows that he has a defeater-defeater: the very undercutting defeater that attached itself to R and to N&E in the first place.

We could also put it like this: any argument he offers, for R, is in this context delicately circular or question-begging. It is not *formally* circular; its conclusion does not appear among its premises. It is instead (we might say) *pragmatically* circular in that it purports to give a reason for trusting our cognitive faculties, but is itself trustworthy only if those faculties (at least the ones involved in its production) are indeed trustworthy. In following this procedure and giving this argument, therefore, he subtly assumes the very proposition he proposes to argue for. Once I come to doubt the reliability of my cognitive faculties, I can't properly try to allay that doubt by producing an *argument*; for in so doing I rely on the very faculties I am doubting. The conjunction of evolution with naturalism gives its adherents a reason for doubting that our beliefs are mostly true; perhaps they are mostly wildly mistaken. But then it won't help to *argue* that they can't be wildly mistaken; for the very reason for mistrusting our cognitive faculties generally will be a reason for mistrusting the faculties generating the beliefs involved in the argument....

What we really have here is one of those nasty dialectical loops to which Hume calls our attention.[11]... When the devotee of N&E notes that he has a defeater for R, then at that stage he also notes (if apprised of the present argument) that he has a defeater for N&E; indeed, he notes that he has a defeater for anything he believes. Since, however, his having a defeater for N&E depends upon some of his beliefs, what he now notes is that he has a defeater for his defeater of R and N&E; so now he no longer *has* that defeater for R and N&E. So then his original condition of believing R and assuming N&E reasserts itself: at which point he again has a defeater for R and N&E. But then he notes that *that* defeater is also a defeater of the defeater of R and N&E; hence.... So goes the paralyzing dialectic. After a few trips around this loop, we may be excused for throwing up our hands in despair, or disgust, and joining Hume in a game of backgammon. The point remains, therefore: one who accepts N&E (and is apprised of the present argument) has a defeater for N&E, a defeater that cannot be defeated by an ultimately undefeated defeater. And isn't it irrational to accept a belief for which you know you have an ultimately undefeated defeater?

Hence the devotee of N&E has a defeater D for N&E—a defeater, furthermore, that can't be ultimately defeated; for obviously D attaches to any consideration one might bring forward by way of attempting to defeat it. If you accept N&E, you have an ultimately undefeated reason for rejecting N&E: but then the rational thing to do is to reject N&E. If, furthermore, one also accepts the conditional *if N is true, then so is E*, one has an ultimately undefeated defeater for N. One who contemplates accepting N, and is torn, let's say, between N and theism, should reason as follows: if I were to accept N, I would have good and ultimately undefeated reason to be agnostic about N; so I should not accept it. Unlike the preliminary argument, this is not an argument for the *falsehood* of naturalism and thus (given that naturalism and theism are the live options) for the truth of theism; for all this argument shows, naturalism might still be true. It is instead an argument for the conclusion that (for one who is aware of the present argument) accepting naturalism is irrational. It is like the self-referential argument against classical foundationalism: classical foundationalism is either false or such that I would be unjustified in accepting it; so (given that I am aware of this fact) I can't justifiably accept it.[12] But of course it does not follow that classical foundationalism is not *true*; for all this argument shows, it could be true, though not rationally acceptable. Similarly here; the argument is not for the falsehood of naturalism, but for the irrationality of accepting it. The conclusion to be drawn, therefore, is that the conjunction of naturalism with evolutionary theory is self-defeating: it provides for itself an undefeated defeater. Evolution, therefore, presents naturalism with an undefeated defeater. But if naturalism is true, then, surely, so is evolution. Naturalism, therefore, is unacceptable.

Proper function and belief in God. The traditional theist, on the other hand, isn't forced into that appalling loop. On this point his set of beliefs is stable. He has no corresponding reason for doubting that it is a purpose of our cognitive systems to produce true beliefs, nor any reason for thinking that $P(R/(N\&E\&C))$ is low, nor any reason for thinking the probability of a belief's being true, given that it is a product of his cognitive faculties, is no better than in the neighborhood of 1/2. He may indeed endorse some form of evolution; but if he does, it will be a form of evolution guided and orchestrated by God. And *qua* traditional theist—*qua* Jewish, Moslem, or Christian theist—he believes that God is the premier knower and has created us human beings in his image, an important part of which involves his endowing them with a reflection of his powers as a knower....

Once again, therefore, we see that naturalistic epistemology flourishes best in the garden of supernaturalistic metaphysics. Naturalistic epistemology conjoined with naturalistic metaphysics leads *via* evolution to skepticism or to violation of canons of rationality; conjoined with theism it does not. The naturalistic epistemologist should therefore prefer theism to metaphysical naturalism.[13]

Notes

1.   Richard Dawkins, *The Blind Watchmaker* (New York: Norton, 1986), pp. 6, 7.
2.   Patricia Churchland, *Journal of Philosophy*, 84 (October 1987), p. 548.
3.   Karl Popper, *Objective Knowledge: An Evolutionary Approach* (Oxford: Clarendon Press, 1972), p. 261.
4.   W.V.O. Quine, "Natural Kinds," in *Ontological Relativity and Other Essays* (New York: Columbia University Press, 1969), p. 126.
5.   Letter to William Graham Down, July 3, 1881, in *The Life and Letters of Charles Darwin Including an Autobiographical Chapter*, ed. Francis Darwin (London: John Murray, Albermarle Street, 1887), 1:315-16.
6.   We could think of this probability in two ways: as a conditional *epistemic* probability, or as a conditional *objective* probability. Either will serve for my argument, but I should think the better way to think of it would be as objective

probability; for in this sort of context epistemic probability, presumably, should follow known (or conjectured) objective probability.

7. Richard Grandy, "Reference, Meaning and Belief," *Journal of Philosophy* 70 (1973), pp. 443ff.

8. David Lewis, *On the Plurality of Worlds* (Oxford: Basil Blackwell, 1986), pp. 38ff., 107-8.

9. See Elizabeth Anscombe's *Intention* (Oxford: Basil Blackwell, 1957), sec. 38.

10. Thus, for example, Thomas Aquinas:

    Since human beings are said to be in the image of God in virtue of their having a nature that includes an intellect, such a nature is most in the image of God in virtue of being most able to imitate God. (*Summa Theologiae*, la, q. 93, a. 4)

    Only in rational creatures is there found a likeness of God which counts as an image .... As far as a likeness of the divine nature is concerned, rational creatures seem somehow to attain a representation of [that] type in virtue of imitating God not only in this, that he is and lives, but especially in this, that he understands. (*Summa Theologiae*, Ia, q. 93 a. 6)

11. David Hume, *A Treatise of Human Nature*, with an analytical index, ed. L. A. Selby-Bigge (Oxford: Clarendon Press, 1888), I, IV, i, p. 187.

12. See my "Reason and Belief in God," in *Faith and Rationality: Reason and Belief in God* (Notre Dame, Indiana: University of Notre Dame Press, 1983).

13. Victor Reppert reminds me that the argument of this chapter bears a good bit of similarity to arguments to be found in chapters III and XIII of C. S. Lewis' *Miracles* (New York: Macmillan 1947); the argument also resembles Richard Taylor's argument in Chapter X of his *Metaphysics*.

Discussion

1. Try to state the point of Plantinga's argument against naturalism in a clear paragraph. Is Plantinga's argument an argument against evolution? Why or why not?

2. What is the alleged advantage of theism when it comes to explaining the proper functioning of our cognitive faculties?

3. Does Plantinga's argument provide adequate grounds for rational belief in God? Why or why not?

Chapter 6

≈

The Balance of Probabilities

A Cumulative Case for the Existence of God
Richard Swinburne*

The justification of religious belief.... [O]nce I had seen what makes scientific theories meaningful and justified, I saw that any metaphysical theory, such as the Christian theological system, is just a superscientific theory. Scientific theories each seek to explain a certain limited class of data: Kepler's laws sought to explain the motions of the planets; natural selection seeks to explain the fossil record and various present features of animals and plants. But some scientific theories are on a higher level than others and seek to explain the operation of the lower-level theories and the existence in the first place of the objects with which they deal. Newton's laws explained why Kepler's laws operated; chemistry has sought to explain why primitive animals and plants existed in the first place. A metaphysical theory is a highest-level-of-all theory. It seeks to explain why there is a universe at all, why it has the most general laws of nature that it does (especially such laws as lead to the evolution of animals and humans), as well as any particular phenomena that lower-level laws are unable to explain. Such a theory is meaningful if it can be stated in ordinary words, stretched a bit in meaning perhaps. And it is justified if it is a simple theory and leads you to expect the observable phenomena when you would not otherwise expect them. Once I had seen this, my program was there—to use the criteria of modern natural science, analyzed with the careful rigor of modern philosophy, to show the meaningfulness and justification of Christian theology.

At this time I discovered that someone else had attempted to use the best science and philosophy of his day rigorously to establish Christian theology. I read part one of the *Summa Theologiae* of Thomas Aquinas. He too started from where the secular world was in his day—the thirteenth century—and used the best secular philosophy available, that of Aristotle, instead of the initially more Christian-looking philosophy of Plato; and he sought to show that reflection on the observable world, as described by Aristotelian science, led inescapably to its creator God. The *Summa* doesn't start from faith or religious experience or the Bible; it starts from the observ-

---

*Richard Swinburne is Nolloth Professor of the Philosophy of the Christian Religion, Oxford University.

able world. After an introductory question, its first main question is *Utrum Deus Sit*, whether there is a God; and it provides five "ways" or arguments from the most evident general phenomena of experience: that things change, that things cause other things, and so on—to show that there is. I do not think that those five ways work too well in detail; and it is interesting that often where the argument goes wrong it is not because Aquinas had relied unjustifiably on Christian theology but because he had relied too much on Aristotelian science. While I realized that the details were not always satisfactory, it seemed to me that the approach of the *Summa* was 100 percent right. I came to see that the irrationalist spirit of modern theology was a modern phenomenon, a head-in-the-sand defensive mechanism. In general, I believe, it is the spirit of St. Thomas rather than the spirit of Kierkegaard that has been the more prevalent over two millennia of Christian theology. But each generation must justify the Christian system by using the best secular knowledge of its own day; and that is why true disciples of St. Thomas cannot rely on the *Summa*—they have to carry out Thomas's program, using the knowledge of their own day....

Scientific versus personal explanation. The basic idea of *The Existence of God*[1] is that the various traditional arguments for theism—from the existence of the world (the cosmological argument), from its conformity to scientific laws (a version of the teleological argument), and so on—are best construed not as deductive arguments but as inductive arguments to the existence of. God. A valid deductive argument is one in which the premises (the starting points) infallibly guarantee the truth of the conclusion; a correct inductive argument is one in which the premises confirm the conclusion (that is, make it more probable than it would otherwise be). Science argues from various limited observable phenomena to their unobservable physical causes, and in so doing it argues inductively. My claim was that theism is the best justified of metaphysical theories. The existence of God is a very simple hypothesis that leads us to expect various very general and more specific phenomena that otherwise we would not expect; and for that reason it is rendered probable by the phenomena. Or rather, as with any big scientific theory, each group of phenomena adds to the probability of the theory—together they make it significantly more probable than not.

When explaining phenomena we have available two different kinds of explanation. One is *scientific explanation*, whereby we explain a phenomenon E in terms of some prior state of affairs F (the cause) in accordance with some regularity or natural law L that describes the behavior of objects involved in F and E. We explain why a stone took two seconds to fall from a tower to the ground (E) by its having been liberated from rest at the top of the tower 64 feet from the ground (F) and by the regularity derivable from Galileo's law of fall that all bodies fall toward the surface of the earth with an acceleration of 32 ft/sec^2 (L); E follows from F and L. And, as I noted earlier, science can also explain the operation of a regularity or law in some narrow area in terms of the operation of a wider law. Thus it can explain why Galileo's law of fall holds for small objects near the surface of the earth. Galileo's law follows from Newton's laws, given that the earth is a body of a certain mass far from other massive bodies and the objects on its surface are close to it and small in mass in comparison.

The other way that we use all the time and see as a proper way of explaining phenomena is what I call *personal explanation*. We often explain some phenomenon *E* as brought about by a person *P* in order to achieve some purpose or goal *G*. The present motion of my hand is explained as brought about by me for the purpose of picking up a glass. The motion of my legs earlier toward a room is explained by my purpose of going there to give a lecture. In these cases I bring about a state of my body that then itself causes some state of affairs outside my body. But it is I (*P*) who bring about the bodily state (*E*) conducive to producing that further state (*G*) rather than some other.

The kind of explanation involved here is a different way of explaining things from the scientific. Scientific explanation involves laws of nature and previous states of affairs. Personal explanation involves persons and purposes. In each case the grounds for believing the explanation to be correct are, as stated earlier, the fact that to explain the cited phenomenon and many other similar phenomena we need few entities (for example, one person rather than many), few kinds of entities with few, easily describable properties, behaving in mathematically simple kinds of ways (such as a person having certain capacities and purposes that do not change erratically) that give rise to many phenomena. In seeking the best explanation of phenomena we may seek explanations of either kind, and if we cannot find a scientific one that satisfies the criteria, we should look for a personal one.

We should seek explanations of all things; but we have seen that we have reason for supposing that we have found one only if the purported explanation is simple and leads us to expect what we find when that is otherwise not to be expected. The history of science shows that we judge that the complex, miscellaneous, coincidental and diverse needs explaining, and that it is to be explained in terms of something simpler. The motions of the planets (subject to Kepler's laws), the mechanical interactions of bodies on earth, the behavior of pendula, the motions of tides, the behavior of comets and so forth formed a pretty miscellaneous set of phenomena. Newton's law of motion constituted a simple theory that led us to expect these phenomena, and so was judged a true explanation of them. The existence of thousands of different chemical substances combining in different ratios to make other substances was complex. The hypothesis that there were only a hundred or so chemical elements of which the thousands of substances were made was a simple hypothesis that led us to expect the complex phenomena. When we reach the simplest possible starting point for explanation that leads us to expect the phenomena that we find, there alone we should stop and believe that we have found the ultimate brute fact on which all other things depend.

The cosmological argument. The cosmological argument argues from the existence of a complex physical universe (or something as general as that) to God who keeps it in being. The premise is the existence of our universe for so long as it has existed (whether a finite time or, if it has no beginning, an infinite time). The universe is a complex thing with lots and lots of separate chunks. Each of these chunks has a different finite and not very natural volume, shape, mass and so forth—consider the vast diversity of galaxies, stars and planets, and pebbles on the seashore. Matter is inert and has no powers that it can choose to exert; it does what it has to do. There is a limited amount of it in any region, and it has a limited amount of energy and velocity. There is a complexity, particularity and finitude about the universe that looks for explanation in terms of something simpler.

The existence of the universe is something evidently inexplicable by science. For, as we saw, a scientific explanation as such explains the occurrence of one state of affairs in terms of a previous state of affairs and some law of nature that makes states like the former bring about states like the latter. It may explain the planets being in their present positions by a previous state of the system (the sun and planets being where they were last year) and the operation of Kepler's laws, which postulate that states like the latter are followed a year later by states like the former. And so it may explain the existence of the universe this year in terms of the existence of the universe last year and the laws of cosmology. But either there was a first state of the universe or there has always been a universe. In the former case, science cannot explain why there was the first state; and in the latter case it still cannot explain why any matter exists (or, more correctly, matter-energy) for the laws of nature to get a grip on, as it were. By its very nature science cannot explain why there are any states of affairs at all.

But a God can provide an explanation. The hypothesis of theism is that the universe exists because there is a God who keeps it in being and that laws of nature operate because there is a God who brings it about that they do. He brings it about that the laws of nature operate by sustaining in every object in the universe its liability to behave in accord with those laws (including the law of the conservation of matter, that at each moment what was there before continues to exist). The universe exists because at each moment of finite or infinite time, he keeps in being objects with this liability. The hypothesis of theism is like a hypothesis that a person brings about certain things for some purpose. God acts directly on the universe, as we act directly on our brains, guiding them to move our limbs (but the universe of course is not his body).

As we have seen, personal explanation and scientific explanation are the two ways we have of explaining the occurrence of phenomena. Since there cannot be a scientific explanation of the existence of the universe, either there is a personal explanation or there is no explanation at all. The hypothesis that there is a God is the hypothesis of the existence of the simplest kind of person that there could be. A person is a being with *power* to bring about effects, *knowledge* of how to do so and *freedom* to choose which effects to bring about. God is by definition an omnipotent (that is, infinitely powerful), omniscient (that is, all-knowing) and perfectly free person: he is a person of infinite power, knowledge and freedom; a person to whose power, knowledge and freedom there are no limits except those of logic. The hypothesis that there exists a being with infinite degrees of the qualities essential to a being of that kind is the postulation of a very simple being. The hypothesis that there is one such God is a much simpler hypothesis than the hypothesis that there is a god who has such and such limited power, or the hypothesis that there are several gods with limited powers. It is simpler in just the same way that the hypothesis that some particle has zero mass or infinite velocity is simpler than the hypothesis that it has 0.32147 of some unit of mass or a velocity of 221,000 km/sec. A finite limitation cries out for an explanation of why there is just that particular limit, in a way the limitlessness does not. God provides the simplest stopping-point for explanation.

That there should exist anything at all, let alone a universe as complex and as orderly as ours, is exceedingly strange. But if there is a God, it is not vastly unlikely that he should create such a universe. A universe such as ours is a thing of beauty, a theater in which humans and other creatures can grow and work out their destiny, a point that I shall develop further below. So the argument from the universe to God is an argument from a complex phenomenon to a simple entity, which leads us to expect (thought does not guarantee) the existence of the former far more than it would be expected otherwise. Therefore, I suggest, it provides some evidence for its conclusion.

The argument from design. The teleological argument, or argument from design, has various forms. One form is the argument from temporal order. This has as its premises the operation of the most general laws of nature, that is, the orderliness of nature in conforming to very general laws. What exactly these laws are, science may not yet have discovered-perhaps they are the field equations of Einstein's general theory of relativity, or perhaps there are some yet more fundamental laws. Now, as we have seen, science can explain the operation of some narrow regularity or law in terms of a wider or more general law. But what science by its very nature cannot explain is why there are the most general laws of nature that there are; for *ex hypothesi*, no wider law can explain their operation.

The conformity of objects throughout endless time and space to simple laws cries out for explanation. For let us consider to what this amounts. Laws are not things, independent of material objects. To say that all objects conform to laws is simply to say that they all behave in exactly the same way. To say, for example, that the planets obey Kepler's laws is just to say that each planet at each moment of time has the property of moving in the ways that Kepler's laws state. There is, therefore, this vast coincidence in the behavioral properties of objects at all times and in all places. If all the coins of some region have the same markings, or all the papers in a room are written in the same handwriting, we seek an explanation in terms of a common source of these coincidences. We should seek a similar explanation for that vast coincidence which we describe as the conformity of objects to laws of nature—such as the fact that all electrons are produced, attract and repel other particles, and combine with them in exactly the same way at each point of endless time and space.

That there is a universe and that there are laws of nature are phenomena so general and pervasive that we tend to ignore them. But there might so easily not have been a universe at all, ever. Or the universe might so easily have been a chaotic mess. That there is an *orderly* universe is something very striking, yet beyond the capacity of science ever to explain. Science's inability to explain these things is not a temporary phenomenon, caused by the backwardness of twentieth-century science. Rather, because of what a scientific explanation is, these things will ever be beyond its capacity to explain. For scientific explanations by their very nature terminate with some ultimate natural law and ultimate physical arrangement of physical things, and the question with which I am concerned is why there are natural laws and physical things at all.

There is available again the simple explanation of the temporal orderliness of the universe, that God makes protons and electrons move in an orderly way, just as we might make our bodies move in the regular patterns of a dance. He has *ex hypothesi* the power to do this. But why should he choose to do so? The orderliness of the universe makes it a beautiful universe, but, even more importantly, it makes it a universe that humans can learn to control and change. For only if there are simple laws of nature can humans predict what will follow from what—and unless they can do that, they can never change anything. Only if they know that by sowing certain seeds, weeding and watering them, they will get corn, can they develop an agriculture. And humans can acquire that knowledge only if there are easily graspable regularities of behavior in nature. It is good that there are human beings, embodied minicreators who share in God's activity of forming and developing the universe through their free choice. But if there are to be such, there must be laws of nature. There is, therefore, some reasonable expectation that God will bring them about; but otherwise that the universe should exhibit such very striking order is hardly to be expected.

The form of "argument from design" that has been most common in the history of thought and was very widely prevalent in the eighteenth and early nineteenth centuries is the argument from spatial order. The intricate organization of animals and plants that enabled them to catch the food for which their digestive apparatus was suited and to escape from predators suggested that they were like very complicated machines and hence that they must have been put together by a master machine-maker, who built into them at the same time the power to reproduce. The frequent use of this argument in religious apologetic came to an abrupt halt in 1859, when Darwin produced his explanation of why there were complexly organized animals and plants, in terms of the laws of evolution operating on much simpler organisms. There seemed no need to bring God into the picture.

That reaction was, however, premature. For the demand for explanation can be taken back a further stage. Why are there laws of evolution that have the consequence that over many millennia simple organisms gradually give rise to complex organisms? No doubt because these laws follow from the basic laws of physics. But then why do the basic laws of physics have such a form as to give rise to laws of evolution? And why were there primitive organisms in the first place? A plausible story can be told of how the primeval "soup" of matter-energy at the time of the "big bang" (a moment some 15,000 million years ago at which, scientists now tell us, the universe, or at least the present stage of the universe, began) gave rise over many millennia, in accordance with physical laws, to those primitive organisms. But then why was there matter suitable for such evolutionary development in the first place?

With respect to the laws and with respect to the primeval matter, we have again the same choice: saying that these things cannot be further explained or postulating a further explanation. Note that the issue here is not why there are laws at all (the premise of the argument from temporal order) or why there is matter-energy at all (the premise of the cosmological argument), but why the laws and the matter-energy have this peculiar character of being already wound up to produce plants, animals and humans. Since the most general laws of nature have this special character, there can be no scientific explanation of why they are as they are. And although there might be a scientific explanation of why the matter at the time of the big bang had the special character it did, in terms of its character at some earlier time, clearly if there was a first state of the universe, it must have been of a certain kind; or if the universe has lasted forever, its matter must have had certain general features if at any time there was to be a state of the universe suited to produce plants, animals and humans. Scientific explanation comes to a stop. The question remains whether we should accept these particular features of the laws and matter of the universe as ultimate brute facts or whether we should move beyond them to a personal explanation in terms of the agency of God.

What the choice turns on is how likely it is that the laws and initial conditions should by chance have just this character. Recent scientific work has drawn attention to the fact that the universe is fine tuned. The matter-energy at the time of the big bang has to have a certain density and a certain velocity of recession; increase or decrease in these respects by one part in a million would have had the effect that the universe was not life-evolving. For example, if the big bang had caused the quanta of matter-energy to recede from each other a little more quickly, no galaxies, stars or planets, and no environment suitable for life would have been formed. If the recession had been marginally slower, the universe would have collapsed in on itself before life could be formed. Similarly, the constants in the laws of nature needed to lie within very narrow limits if life was to be formed. It is, therefore, most unlikely that laws and initial conditions should have by chance a life-producing character. God is able to give matter and laws this character. If we can show that he would have reason to do so, then that gives support to the hypothesis that he has done so. There is available again the reason (in addition to the reason of its beauty) that was a reason why God would choose to bring about an orderly universe at all—the worthwhileness of the sentient embodied beings that the evolutionary process would bring about, and above all of humans who can themselves make informed choices as to what sort of a world there should be.

The cumulative case. A similar pattern of argument from various other phenomena such as the existence of conscious beings, the providential ordering of things in certain respects, the occurrence of certain apparently miraculous events in history and the religious experiences of many millions is ... available to establish theism (when all the arguments are taken together) as overall significantly more probable than not.

Notes

1. Richard Swinburne, *The Existence of God* (Oxford: The Clarendon Press, 1979).

Discussion

1. The simplicity of hypotheses plays a major role in Swinburne's arguments. Do you think the simple, all things considered, is a sign of the true? Why or why not?
2. Consider your favorite scientific hypothesis. — Does Swinburne's account of the justification of scientific hypotheses make sense?
3. Is the case for theism strengthened when one considers the cosmological argument together with, for example, the argument from design, religious experience, apparently miraculous events, etc.? Why or why not?
4. Has Swinburne ignored any relevant counter-evidence?

The Balance of Probabilities

*J. L. Mackie**

Bad arguments. We can now bring together the many different arguments for theism which we have discussed, and consider their combined effect.... [T]here is at
least one interesting and important possibility of consilience, namely that which
would bring together (1) reported miracles, (2) inductive versions of the design and
consciousness arguments, picking out as "marks of design" both the fact that there
are causal regularities at all and the fact that the fundamental natural laws and
physical constants are such as to make possible the development of life and consciousness, (3) an inductive version of the cosmological argument, seeking an
answer to the question "Why is there any world at all?" (4) the suggestion that there
are objective moral values whose occurrence likewise calls for further explanation,
and (5) the suggestion that some kinds of religious experience can be best understood as direct awareness of something supernatural. These various considerations
might be held jointly to support the hypothesis that there is a personal or quasi-
personal god.

The cumulative argument. In evaluating this possibility, we must note how in
principle a hypothesis can be supported by the consilience of different considerations, each of which, on its own, leaves the balance of probabilities against that
hypothesis. Suppose that there are several pieces of evidence, e_1, e_2, and e_3, each of
which would fit in with a hypothesis h, but each of which, on its own, is explained
with less initial improbability on some other grounds, say by g_1, g_2, and g_3 respectively. Yet if the improbability involved in postulating h is less than the *sum* of the
improbabilities involved in the rival explanations g_1, g_2, and g_3, though it is greater
than each of these improbabilities separately, the balance of probabilities when we
take e_1, e_2, and e_3 together will favour the hypothesis h. It is important that it is just
the one initial improbability of h that is weighed in turn against the improbabilities
of g_1, g_2, and g_3 and then against the sum of these.

But the supposed consilience of theistic arguments does not satisfy the
requirements of this formal pattern. As we have seen, the first and fifth of these
considerations are extremely weak: all the evidence that they can muster is easily
explained in natural terms, without any improbabilities worth taking into account.
Consciousness and the actual phenomena of morality and valuing as a human
activity are explained without further improbabilities, given that the natural world
is such as to allow life to evolve, so the only improbabilities to be scored against the
naturalistic kind of explanation are whatever may be involved in there being causal
regularities, the fundamental laws and physical constants being as they are, and
there being any world at all. Against the rival theistic hypothesis we should have to

---

*J. L. Mackie (1917-1981) taught at Oxford University.

score the (significant) improbability that if there were a god he (or it) would create a world with causal laws, and one with our specific causal laws and constants, but also the great improbability of there being a process of the unmediated fulfilment of will, and, besides, the basic improbability of there being a god at all. For while the naturalist had admittedly no reply to Leibniz's question "Why is there a world at all?," the theist, once deprived of the illusory support of the ontological argument, is equally embarrassed by the question "Why is there a god at all?" Whatever initial improbability there may be in the unexplained brute fact that there is a world, there is a far greater initial improbability in what the theist has to assert as the unexplained brute fact that there is a god capable of creating a world.

In the end, therefore, we can agree with what Laplace said about God: we have no need of that hypothesis. This conclusion can be reached by an examination precisely of the arguments advanced in favour of theism, without even bringing into play what have been regarded as the strongest considerations on the other side, the problem of evil and the various natural histories of religion. When these are thrown into the scales, the balance tilts still further against theism. Although we could not ... rule out the possibility that some acceptable modification of traditional theism might enable it to accommodate the occurrence of evils, we saw that no sound solution of this sort has yet been offered; the extreme difficulty that theism has in reconciling *its own* doctrines with one another in this respect must tell heavily against it. Also, although the clear possibility of developing an adequate natural explanation of the origin, evolution, and persistence of religious belief is not a primary argument against theism, and could be brushed aside if there were any cogent positive case for the existence of a god, yet, since there is no such case, it helps to make the negative case still more conclusive. It removes the vague but obstinate feeling that where so many people have believed so firmly—and sometimes fervently—and where religious thought and organization have been so tenacious and so resilient "there must be something in it." We do not need to invoke the "higher causes" by which Machiavelli (with his tongue in his cheek) said that ecclesiastical principalities are upheld.[1] The occurrence, even the continuing occurrence, of theism is not, in Hume's phrase, a continued miracle which subverts all the principles of our understanding.

Conclusion. The balance of probabilities, therefore, comes out strongly against the existence of a god.... There is ... no easy way of defending religion once it is admitted that the literal, factual, claim that there is a god cannot be rationally sustained.

Notes

1. N. Machiavelli, *The Prince* (many editions), Chapter 11.

Discussion

1. Is all of the evidence *easily* explainable, as Mackie alleges, in naturalistic terms? Why or why not?

2. Compare Mackie's with Swinburne's cumulative argument. Give several reasons for preferring one argument over the other.
3. What sorts of evidence does Mackie think counts against God's existence? Do you find his claims compelling?

Arguing for God

Alvin Plantinga *

Introduction. Some two-thirds of the world's population of approximately five billion people profess belief in God—the God of Abraham, Isaac, and Jacob, God as he is conceived of by Jews, Moslems, Christians, and others. So thought of, God is an immaterial person who is all-knowing, all-powerful, perfectly good, and the creator and sustainer of the world.... This characterization of God is what we might call *standard theism*....

[I]n contemporary philosophy (contemporary western philosophy anyway), perhaps the most widely discussed philosophical problem about belief in God is ... something like this: is it rational, or reasonable, or sensible, or intellectually acceptable, or in accord with one's intellectual obligations to believe in God? (This question has been very much with us for at least the last couple of hundred years, ever since the Enlightenment.) Many apparently think not; they think contemporary science, or modern historical methods, or perhaps just what those who are enlightened and in the know now think—they think these things make it unreasonable to believe in God or at any rate unreasonable for those who are sufficiently aware of contemporary science and culture. This question—the reasonableness or rationality of belief in God—is the topic of this [essay].

Traditional arguments for the existence of God. The most widely accepted method of approaching this question is to consider the arguments for and against belief in God. What more natural than to look at the evidence? If the arguments *for* the existence of God (theistic arguments, as they are called) are stronger than the arguments *against* his existence, then it is rational or reasonable to believe in God; on the other hand, if the arguments against theism outweigh the arguments for it, then the rational procedure is to reject belief in God in favor of atheism or agnosticism.... As I say, this procedure seems initially, sensible; and ... I shall briefly consider some of these arguments....

There are many arguments for the existence of God; they have been discussed for a long time by many acute philosophers and theologians; here it won't be possible to do more than barely indicate some of the most important arguments and some of the most important lines of discussion. Theistic arguments go back at least to the time of Aristotle (and perhaps considerably further back than that). Such arguments were extensively studied and discussed in the Middle Ages; one thinks particularly of Anselm's Ontological Argument and of Thomas Aquinas's celebrated five ways (five theistic proofs) at the beginning of his massive and monumental *Summa Theologiae*. In the Middle Ages, the principal reason for constructing theis-

---

*Alvin Plantinga is John A. O'Brien Professor of Philosophy at University of Notre Dame. Prior to his Notre Dame appointment, he taught for twenty years at Calvin College.

tic proofs was not to convince people that there really is such a person as God (then, as now, most people already believed that) but to show that we human beings can *know* that there is such a person, can have *scientific* or *demonstrative* knowledge of the existence of God. Early modern philosophy and the Enlightenment saw a great flurry of theistic proofs; Descartes, Locke, Leibniz, Malebranche, Berkeley, Paley, and many others all offered proofs or arguments for the existence of God (prompting the remark that nobody doubted the existence of God until the philosophers tried to prove it). Here the aim wasn't so much to show that we can have demonstrative knowledge of the existence of God as to show that it is reasonable or rational to accept theistic belief. This attempt to provide good theistic arguments continues to the present day.

Immanuel Kant, one of the greatest commentators on the theistic arguments, divided them into three large categories: *Ontological Arguments, Cosmological Arguments*, and *Teleological Arguments*.

In some ways the most interesting of these is the utterly fascinating *Ontological Argument*, first offered in the eleventh century by Anselm of Canterbury (1033-1109).... Anselm's argument has been the subject of enormous controversy ever since he had the temerity to spring it on an unsuspecting world. It has fascinated nearly every great philosopher from Anselm's day to the present. Many utterly reject it; Kant claimed to have finally and definitively refuted it; Schopenhauer thought it was a charming joke; many philosophers since have thought it was a joke alright, but more like a *dumb* joke. And indeed the argument does have about it a suggestion of trumpery and deceit. Nonetheless there have been and are many who think some version of this argument a perfectly valid argument for the existence of God; it does not lack for contemporary defenders.[1]

Turn now to *Cosmological Arguments*. These arguments typically proceed from some very general fact about the world—that there is *motion* for example, or *causation*; they then move to the conclusion that there must be a first unmoved mover or first uncaused cause—a being that is not itself caused to exist by anything else, but causes everything else to exist. An interesting variant is presented by the argument from *contingency*. This argument begins from the fact that there are many, contingent beings—beings that (like you and me) *do* exist, but could have *failed* to exist; it moves to the conclusion that there is a *necessary* being, a being such that it is not possible that it fail to exist. (It would remain to be shown that such a being would be God.) Perhaps the strongest version of the Cosmological Arguments would combine the argument from contingency with first cause and first mover arguments.[2]

The third kind of argument, says Kant, is the *Teleological Argument* or argument from design—more exactly, the teleological arguments, since there are several different arguments of this type. A fine formulation of such an argument is given by David Hume (who, however, does not himself accept it).... Many facets of the universe strongly suggest that it has been created or designed: the delicate articulated beauty of a tiny flower, the night sky viewed from the side of a mountain, the fact that the cosmological constants (including in particular the rate of expansion of the universe) must be extremely accurately adjusted if there is to be intelligent life in the universe, and so on.

The nature of proof. Now these classical arguments as classically presented typically take the form of *conclusive* or *coercive* arguments, or rather would-be conclusive or coercive arguments. They take the form of attempted *demonstrations*; the idea is that any rational person who is intellectually honest will believe the premises and will see that the premises do indeed entail the intended conclusions. Taken as coercive demonstrations, it is fair to say, I think, that they fail. None of these arguments seems to be a real demonstration. None seems to be the sort of argument which (like, say, the Pythagorean Theorem ...) really leaves no room for doubt or disagreement. Taken as *demonstrations*, the theistic arguments fail. But why should they be taken like that? After all, scarcely any arguments for any serious philosophical conclusion qualify as real demonstrations—are really such that anyone who understands them is obliged to accept them on pain of irrationality or intellectual dishonesty. Take your favorite argument for any serious philosophical conclusion; there will be plenty of people who don't accept that argument, and are not thereby shown to be either unusually dense or intellectually dishonest. So why should it be different with theistic arguments? Even if there aren't any knockdown drag-out *demonstrations* for the existence of God, there might still be plenty of good arguments. A good argument would be one that started from premises many people rationally accept (or are inclined to accept) and proceeds via steps many people reasonably endorse to the conclusion that there is such a person as God. Perhaps there aren't any demonstrations; it doesn't follow that there aren't any good arguments. As a matter of fact, I think we can see that there are a host of good theistic arguments....

So suppose we take these theistic proofs in a different spirit (in the spirit appropriate to philosophical arguments generally): not as knockdown drag-out arguments which no sane person can honestly reject, but instead as arguments whose premises and inferential moves will be found attractive by many who reflect on the matter. Then I think we must conclude that the ontological argument, even in the forms in which it commits no fallacies, doesn't have a great deal of force (despite the fact that, as I think, it is a perfectly valid argument). Perhaps it has *some* force; but probably not many who reflect on the argument and understand it will find the premise—that it is possible that there be a greatest possible being—plausible unless they already accept the conclusion. The cosmological argument, however, is much stronger, and the teleological arguments, stronger yet.

Non-traditional arguments. So far the traditional arguments. In addition to these, however, there are also a large number of other theistic arguments, some of which resist easy statement and don't fall easily under the traditional rubrics. There is ... a wide variety of *epistemological* arguments, arguments that take their premises or starting points in some fact about human knowledge. Consider, for example, *The Argument from the Confluence of Proper Function and Reliability*, which goes as follows. Most of us assume that when our intellectual or cognitive faculties are functioning properly (in the right sort of environment, the sort of environment for which they seem to be designed), they are for the most part reliable; for the most part the beliefs they produce are true. According to theism, God has created us in his image; he has created us in such a way as to resemble him in being able to know the truth over a wide range of topics and subjects. This provides an easy, natural explanation of the fact (as we see it) that when our cognitive faculties are not subject to dysfunction, the beliefs they produce are for the most part true.

And this explanation has no real competitors (at least among beliefs that are live options for us). It is sometimes suggested that nontheistic evolutionism is such a competitor; but this is a mistake. First, there is the problem I noted above: we don't have an evolutionary explanation of human cognitive capacities, and we don't even know that it is possible that there be one. But second, nontheistic evolution would at best explain our faculties' being reliable with respect to beliefs that have survival value. (That would exclude [among others] beliefs involving reasonably recondite mathematical truths, relativity theory, and quantum mechanics, and, more poignantly, scientific beliefs of the sort involved in thinking evolution is a plausible explanation of the flora and fauna we see around us.) "At best," I say; but it wouldn't really explain even that. True beliefs *as such* don't have survival value; they have to be linked with the right kind of dispositions to behavior. What evolution really requires is that our *behavior* have survival value, not necessarily that our beliefs be true; it is sufficient for the demand of evolution that we be programmed to act in adaptive ways. But there are many ways in which our behavior could be adaptive, even if our beliefs were for the most part false. (For example, our whole belief structure might be a sort of by-product or epiphenomenon, having no real connection with truth, and no real connection with our action.) So there is no explanation in evolution for the confluence of proper function and reliability. As Patricia Churchland (not noted as a defender of theism) puts it, from an evolutionary point of view, "The principal chore of nervous systems is to get the body parts where they should be in order that the organism may survive.... Truth, whatever that is, definitely takes the hindmost."[3]

The argument from the confluence of reliability and proper function is one epistemological theistic argument; but there are many more. For example, there are arguments from the nature of warrant or positive epistemic status, from induction, from the rejection of global skepticism, from reference, from modal intuition, and from intuition generally. But there are also a variety of *moral* arguments, arguments from the phenomena of morality. Among the best are Robert Adams' favored version[4] which, stated in simple fashion, goes as follows. A person might find herself utterly convinced (as I do) that (1) morality is objective, not dependent upon what human beings know or think, that (2) the rightness or wrongness of an action (for example, the wrongness of the action of killing someone just for the thrill of it) cannot be explained in terms of any "natural" facts about human beings or other things—that is, it can't ultimately be explained in terms of physical, chemical, or biological facts, and that (3) there couldn't *be* such objective non-natural moral facts unless there were such a person as God who, in one way or another, brings them into being, or legislates them. This is the obverse side of the thought that in a naturalistic universe, objective moral facts somehow wouldn't make sense, wouldn't fit in.[5]

In addition to moral, epistemological, and metaphysical arguments, there are several others that don't fit well into those categories. For example, there are arguments from love, from beauty and the appreciation of beauty, from play, enjoyment, humor, and adventure. (At bottom, these arguments claim that love in its many manifestations, or a Mozart piano concerto, or a great adventure have a kind of value that can't be explained in naturalistic terms.) There are also arguments from colors and flavors, and from the meaning of life.

The most important thing to see here, I think, is this. Once we recognize that a good theistic argument doesn't have to be a proof that will coerce any reasonable intellect (once we apply the same standards to theistic arguments that we apply to other arguments), we see that there are a large number of good theistic arguments—in fact it is extremely difficult to think of any other important philosophical thesis for which there are so many importantly different arguments. Indeed, the fact that there *are* so many different arguments (the fact that theism is of explanatory value in so many, and so many different areas of thought) is itself still another argument in its favor.

Anti-theistic arguments.... [B]y far the most important atheological argument [is] the celebrated argument from evil. This argument goes all the way back to Epicurus.[6] The objector begins by reminding us of the sheer *extent* of suffering and evil in the world, and indeed there is an enormous amount of it. There is also the cruelly ironic character of some evil; a man who drives a cement mixer truck comes home for lunch, lingers a bit too long in the warmth and love of his family, hurriedly jumps into his truck, backs out—and kills his three-year-old daughter who had been playing behind the wheels. Why didn't God prevent something so savagely ironic? A woman in a Nazi concentration camp is compelled to choose which of her two children shall go to the gas chamber and which shall be saved; here we have evil naked and unalloyed; and if God is what theists claim he is—omnipotent and wholly good—then why does he permit such abominations in his world?...

So the objector begins with this question: if God is omnipotent and wholly good, then why is there all this evil? The theist must concede, I think, that she doesn't know—that is, she doesn't know in any detail. On a quite general level, she may know or think she knows that God permits evil because he can achieve a world he sees as better by permitting evil than by preventing it; and what God sees as better is, of course, better. But we cannot see why *our* world, with all its ills, would be better than others we think we can imagine, nor what, in any detail, is God's reason for permitting a given specific evil. Not only can we not see this, we can't, I think, envision any very good possibilities. And here I must remark that most of the attempts to explain why God permits evil—*theodicies*, as we might call them—seem to me tepid and shallow.

Of course the fact that the theist can't answer Epicurus' question—the fact that for many or most specific evils, she has no real idea what God's reason for permitting that specific evil might be—that fact does not in itself prove much of anything. Our grasp of the fundamental way of things is at best limited; there is no reason to think that if God *did* have a reason for permitting the evil in question, we would be the first to know. Something further must be added, if the objector is to make a worthwhile point. Granted: we don't know why God permits evil; but where, so far, is the problem?

Here the objector is quick to oblige. And (at least until recently) his most popular response has been to offer some version of the *deductive anti-theistic argument from evil* ... [J. L. Mackie, for example,] claims that the existence of evil—and of course the theist will himself agree that there is evil—entails that there is no God, or at any rate no God as conceived by standard theism. Mackie puts the claim as follows: "... [I]t can be shown, not merely that religious beliefs lack rational support, but that they are positively irrational, that the several parts of the essential theological doctrine are inconsistent with one another."[7] He goes on to argue that the existence of God is incompatible with the existence of evil; he concludes that since the theist is committed to both God and evil, theistic belief is irrational. It ought to be discouraged; and those who accept it, presumably, ought to give it up.

At present, I think, it is fairly widely conceded (contrary to Mackie's claim) that there is nothing like straightforward contradiction or inconsistency or necessary falsehood in the joint affirmation of God and evil. It is logically possible that God should have a reason for permitting all the evil there is; but if so, then the existence of God is not incompatible with the existence of the evil the world displays. This suggestion is developed, for example, in the Free Will Defense, according to which God must put up with at least some evil if he is to create genuinely free creatures. The Free Will Defense goes all the way back to Augustine in the fifth century and is widely accepted at present.[8]

Accordingly, atheologians have turned from deductive to *probabilistic* arguments from evil. The typical atheological claim at present is not that the existence of God is logically *incompatible* with that of evil. The claim is instead that

(1) there is an omnipotent, omniscient and perfectly good God

is *improbable* or *unlikely* with respect to

(2) There are 10^{13} turps of evil (where the *turp*, is the basic unit of evil).

According to William Rowe, for example, it is probable that

(3) "There exist instances of intense suffering which an omnipotent, omniscient being could have prevented without thereby losing some greater good or permitting some evil equally bad or worse."[9]

This is probable, he says, because

> It seems quite unlikely that *all* the instances of intense suffering occurring daily in our world are intimately related to the occurrence of greater goods or the prevention of evils at least as bad; and even more unlikely, should they somehow all be so related, that an omnipotent omniscient being could not have achieved at least some of these goods (or prevented some of those evils) without permitting the instances of intense suffering that are supposedly related to them.

The atheologian, therefore, claims that (1) is improbable with respect to (2). But he doesn't make this point for the sheer academic charm of it all; something further is supposed to follow. The fact, if it is a fact, that (1) is thus improbable is supposed to show that there is something wrong or misguided about belief in God, that it is irrational, or intellectually irresponsible, or noetically second class, or not such as to measure up to the appropriate standards for proper belief.

But *is* (1) improbable on (2) (or some other reasonably plausible proposition about evil)? Why should we think so? Rowe's claim is that there is much *apparently pointless* evil; there is much which is such that we have no idea what reason God (if there is such a person) could have for permitting it. He considers a hypothetical state of affairs in which a fawn is burned in a forest fire and refers to the fawn's "apparently pointless" suffering; this suffering he says, "was preventable, and so far as we can see, pointless." He seems to be arguing that (1) is improbable with respect to (2) because

> (3) Many cases of evil are apparently pointless,

that is, many cases of evil are apparently not such that an omniscient and omnipotent God would be obliged to put up with them in order to achieve a world as good as ours.

But how shall we understand Rowe here? In particular, how shall we understand this "apparently pointless"? Here there are two possibilities. First, he may be holding that

> (4) In fact there *are* many cases of evil such that *it is apparent that* an omnipotent and omniscient God, if he existed, would not have a reason for permitting them.

But this is much too strong. There aren't cases of evil such that it is just *obvious* or *apparent* that God could have no reason for permitting them. The most we can sensibly say is that there are many cases of evil such that we can't think of any good reason why he would permit them; but of course that doesn't mean that it is apparent to us that he doesn't *have* a reason. As Stephen Wykstra quite properly points out,[10] we could sensibly claim this latter only if we had reason to think that if such a God *did* have a reason for permitting such evils, we would be likely to have some insight into what it is. But why think *that*? There is no reason to think that if there is such a person as God, and if he had a reason for permitting a particular evil state of affairs, *we* would have a pretty good idea of what that reason might be. On the theistic conception our cognitive powers, as opposed to God's, are a bit slim for that. God might have reasons we cannot so much as understand; he might have reasons involving other creatures—angels, devils, the principalities and powers of whom St. Paul speaks—creatures of whose nature and activities we have no knowledge.

Shall we take (3) as pointing out, then, that there are many evils such that we have no idea what God's reason, if any, is for permitting them? That seems right; but why suppose it shows that (1) is improbable with respect to (2)? We could sensibly claim *that* only if we had good reason to think that we would be privy to God's reasons for permitting evil, if he had some; but of course we don't have good reason to think that. We know very little of God's alternatives; perhaps, for example, we and our suffering figure into transactions involving beings we know nothing at all about....

Say that an evil is *inscrutable* if it is such that we can't think of any reason God (if there is such a person) could have for permitting it. Clearly, the crucial problem for this probabilistic argument from evil is just the fact that nothing much follows from the fact that some evils are inscrutable; if theism is true, we would expect that there would be inscrutable evil. Indeed, it is only *hubris* which would tempt us to think that we could so much as grasp God's plans here, even if he proposed to divulge them to us. But then the fact that there is inscrutable evil does not make it improbable that God exists. The argument from evil, therefore, may have some degree of strength, but its weaknesses are evident.

Is argument required for belief in God? As I said at the beginning, perhaps the most widely discussed philosophical question having to do with belief in God is the question whether such belief is rational, or reasonable, or intellectually up to snuff, or such that a person who was reasonable and well informed could accept it. And the typical way of approaching this question has been to examine the arguments for and against the existence of God. But is it really clear that discussing those arguments is the only or best way to approach this question of the rational justification of theistic belief? The assumption seems to be that if the arguments for theism are stronger than those for atheism, then belief in God is rational; but if the arguments for atheism are stronger, then atheism, or at any rate agnosticism, is the more reasonable attitude. But why suppose that the rational status of theistic beliefs—its reasonability or intellectual acceptability—depends upon whether there are good theistic arguments available? Consider an analogy. We all believe that there has been a past and that we know something about it. As Bertrand Russell pointed out, however, it is possible (possible in the broadly logical sense) that the world is only five minutes old, having been created just five minutes ago complete with all its apparent traces of the past, all the apparent memories, dusty books, faded pictures, crumbling mountains, massive oak trees, and the like. So what about the belief that there has been a substantial past, that the world has been here for more than five minutes? Surely that belief is rational, justified, and reasonable. But is there a good non-circular, non-question begging *argument* for it? (Of course if we are content with *circular* arguments, the theist can produce plenty of such arguments for theism.) It is certainly hard to see what they might be; no one, so far as I know, has ever come up with much of a candidate. So our belief in the past is rational or justified even though we don't have a good non-circular argument for it; so a belief can be justified in the absence of such reason; so why suppose we need arguments or evidence (evidence in the sense of other supporting beliefs) for the existence of God? Why can't belief in God be properly basic?

We can approach this same question from a slightly different direction. Many philosophers (and others as well) object that theistic belief is irrational or intellectually sub par because, as they say, there is *insufficient evidence* for it. Bertrand Russell was once asked what he would say if, after dying, he were brought into the presence of God and asked why he hadn't been a believer. Russell's reply: "I'd say 'Not enough evidence God! Not enough evidence!'"[11] We needn't speculate as to how such a reply would be received; what is clear is that Russell held theistic belief to be unreasonable because there is insufficient evidence for it. W. K. Clifford, that "delicious *enfant terrible*" as William James called him, insisted that it is wrong, immoral, wicked, and monstrous to accept a belief for which you don't have sufficient evidence. As he puts it in his characteristically restrained fashion, "Whoso would deserve well of his fellows in this matter will guard the purity of his belief with a very fanaticism of jealous care, lest at anytime it should rest on an unworthy object, and catch a stain which can never be wiped away"; and he concludes by saying, "To sum up: it is wrong always, everywhere, and for anyone to believe anything upon insufficient evidence."[12] So it is wrong to accept belief in God without sufficient evidence; numberless hordes of philosophers have joined Clifford in this opinion, and in the further opinion that indeed there is not sufficient evidence for belief in God.[13]

So the evidentialist objection has two premises:

(a) It is irrational to believe in God unless there is sufficient evidence (good arguments) for theistic belief

and

(b) there is no evidence, or at least no sufficient evidence, for theistic belief.

Now I have already argued that (b) is at best dubious. There are many good theistic arguments, and putting them all together results in an impressive case indeed. But our present concern is the *other* premise of the objector's argument: the claim that in the absence of evidence, belief in God is irrational or unjustifiable or intellectually unacceptable. Why should we believe a thing like that? Why do those who offer the evidentialist objection believe it? We don't think the same thing about belief in other minds, the past, material objects. So why here? One answer, I think, is that those who think thus, think of theism as a *scientific hypothesis*, or a quasi-scientific hypothesis, or relevantly *like* a scientific hypothesis—something like Special Relativity, for example, or Quantum Mechanics, or the Theory of Evolution. According to J. L. Mackie, for example, "Against the rival theistic hypothesis we should have to score the (significant) improbability that if there were a god he (or it) would create a world with causal laws, and one with our specific causal laws and constants, but also the great improbability of there being a process of the unmediated fulfillment of will." And speaking of religious experience, he makes the following characteristic remark: "Here, as elsewhere, the supernaturalist hypothesis fails because there is an adequate and much more economical naturalistic alternative."[14] Clearly these remarks are relevant only if we think of belief in God as or as like a sort of scientific hypothesis, a theory designed to explain some body of evidence, and acceptable to the degree that it explains that evidence. On this way of looking at the matter, there is a relevant body of evidence shared by believer and unbeliever alike; theism is a hypothesis designed to explain that body of evidence; and theism is rationally defensible only to the extent that it is a good explanation thereof.

But why should we think of theism like this? Clearly there are perfectly sensible alternatives. Consider our beliefs about the past: one could take a Mackie-like view here as well. One could hold that our beliefs about the past are best thought of as like a scientific hypothesis, designed to explain such present phenomena as (among other things) apparent memories; and if there were a more "economical" explanation of these phenomena that did not postulate past facts, then our usual beliefs in the past "could not be rationally defended." But here this seems clearly mistaken (not to say silly); the availability of such an "explanation" wouldn't in any way tell against our ordinary belief that there has really been a past. Why couldn't the same hold for theism?

In responding to Hume, Thomas Reid brilliantly discusses a similar network of questions. Here the topic under discussion is not God, but material objects or an external world. Suppose it is proposed that my belief in material objects is "rationally defensible" only if it is more probable than not with respect to a body of knowledge that includes no physical object propositions but only, say, self-evident truths together with experiential propositions specifying how I am appeared to. Add (as the history of modern philosophy strongly suggests) that it is impossible to show that physical object statements *are* more probable than not with respect to such a body of evidence; or add, more strongly, that in fact physical object propositions are *not* more probable than not with respect to such propositions. What would follow from that? One of Reid's most important and enduring contributions was to point out that nothing of much interest would follow from that. In particular it would not follow that belief in physical objects ought to be discouraged as somehow improper, or irrational, or intellectually out of order.

But why, then, should we think it follows in the case of theism? Suppose theistic belief is not more probable than not with respect to the body of beliefs shared by theists and nontheists: why should we conclude that it is not rationally defensible? Perhaps it is perfectly rational to take belief in God in the way we ordinarily take belief in other minds, material objects, the past, and the like. Why isn't it perfectly sensible to *start with* belief in God? Why does belief in God have to be probable with respect to some *other* body of evidence in order to be rationally defensible?...

Conclusion. So the question about the rationality of theistic belief can't anywhere nearly be settled just by paying attention to the arguments for and against belief in God. At least as important is the question whether belief in God is properly basic—whether, that is, proper and rational belief in God can resemble (say) memory beliefs in not ordinarily being accepted by way of reliance upon arguments or evidential support from other beliefs. The most promising way to investigate that question, I think, is to consider what rationality, or warrant, or positive epistemic status *is*; once we are clear about that, then we can ask whether basic belief in God can have it. I myself believe such investigation reveals that belief in God taken in the basic way is perfectly proper, and rational, and acceptable; indeed, I think we can *know* that God exists without believing on the basis of arguments. But that is a topic for another time.

Notes

1. See, for example, Charles Hartshorne's *Man's Vision of God* (New York: Harper and Row, 1941); and Norman Malcolm's "Anselm's Ontological Arguments," (*Philosophical Review*, 1960). There is a development and defense of a version of this argument in my *God, Freedom and Evil* (Grand Rapids: Eerdman's, 1978) and *The Nature of Necessity* (Oxford University Press, 1974).
2. As in David Braine's *The Reality of Time and the Existence of God* (Oxford: Oxford University Press, 1988).
3. Patricia Churchland, "Epistemology in the Age of Neuroscience," *Journal of Philosophy* 84 (October, 1987), pp. 548.
4. See Robert Merrihew Adams, "Moral Arguments for Theistic Belief" [see Chapter 3, #11 of this collection].
5. See George Mavrodes, "Religion and the Queerness of Morality," in *Rationality, Religious Belief and Moral Commitment*, ed. by Robert Audi and William Wainwright (Ithaca, NY: Cornell University Press, 1986).
6. Diogenes Laertius, *Lives of Eminent Philosophers*, trans. by R. D. Hicks (Cambridge: Harvard, 1979), 8K. X, 80-82.
7. "Evil and Omnipotence," *Mind*, 64 (1955). In Mackie's posthumous *The Miracle of Theism* (Oxford: Oxford University Press, 1982), Mackie wavers between his earlier claim that the existence of God is straightforwardly inconsistent with that of evil, and the claim that the existence of evil is powerful but not conclusive evidence against the existence of God. (See pp. 150-175, and see my "Is Theism Really a Miracle?" in *Faith and Philosophy*, 3, April 1986, pp. 298-313.

8. And (as I see it) rightly so; see my *The Nature of Necessity* (Oxford: Clarendon Press, 1974), Chap. IX, and *God Freedom and Evil* (New York: Harper and Row, 1974; and Grand Rapids: W. B. Eerdmans, 1980), pp. 7-64.

9. William Rowe, "The Problem of Evil and Some Varieties of Atheism" [see chapter 13 #30 of this collection].

10. Stephen Wykstra, "The Humean Obstacle to Evidential Arguments from Suffering: on Avoiding the Evils of Appearance," *International Journal for the Philosophy of Religion* 16 (1984), pp. 85.

11. Bertrand Russell, quoted in W. Salmon's "Religion and Science: a New Look at Hume's Dialogues," *Philosophical Studies* 33 (1978), pp. 176.

12. W.K. Clifford, "The Ethics of Belief "[see chapter 7 #19 of this collection].

13. For example, Brand Blanshard, *Reason and Belief* (London: Allen and Unwin, 1974), pg. 400 ff.; Antony Flew, *The Presumption of Atheism* (London: Pemberton, 1976), pp. 87 ff. —essay 20 of this collection; Bertrand Russell, "Why I am not a Christian," in *Why I am not a Christian* (New York: Simon and Schuster, 1957), pg. 3 ff.; J. L. Mackie, *The Miracle of Theism* (Oxford: The Clarendon Press, 1982); Michael Scriven, *Primary Philosophy* (New York: McGraw Hill, 1966) pp. 87 ff.; and many others. This objection is even more popular in the oral tradition than in published work; and it ordinarily has the character of an unspoken assumption more than that of an explicit objection.

14. Mackie, *The Miracle of Theism*, pp. 252-53. Ibid., pp. 198.

Discussion

1. Plantinga distinguishes between coercive demonstrations and arguments which some reasonable people find attractive. Defend the view that the latter is adequate for theistic arguments. Or defend the view that non-coercive, non-demonstrative arguments are not intellectualy adequate.

2. How might one develop an argument for the existence of God based on, as Plantinga suggests, love, beauty and the appreciation of beauty, play, enjoyment, humor and adventure?

3. Plantinga's loosening of the criteria for arguments and widening of the phenomena that might best be explained by God makes theism more intellectually respectable. Explain your agreement or disagreement with this statement.

The Nature of Reason

*William J. Wainwright**

The Lockean background. In *An Essay Concerning Human Understanding,* John Locke defines reason as "the discovery of the certainty or probability of such propositions or truths, which the mind arrives at by deduction made from such ideas, which it has got by the use of its natural faculties; viz. by sensation or reflection" (iv. 1& 2).[1] Rational belief is proportionate to the strength of the evidence at one's disposal. "The mind, if it *will proceed rationally,* ought to examine all the grounds of probability, and see how they make more or less for or against any proposition, before it assents to or dissents from it; and upon a due balancing of the whole, reject or receive it, with more or less firm assent, proportionably to the preponderancy of the greater grounds of probability on one side or the other" (iv. 15. 5). What is true of beliefs in general is true of religious beliefs in particular. They are rational only if (I) they are properly basic (immediately grounded in the mind's intuitive awareness of its own ideas), or (2) inferred from those ideas by sound deductive or inductive standards, or (3) are the content of a revelation whose credentials are certified by beliefs meeting the first or second condition. While modern intellectuals may doubt whether religious beliefs meet these standards, Locke did not. God's existence can be demonstrated, and the evidence at our disposal makes it probable that the Bible is God's revelation.

Richard Swinburne would agree with the substance of Locke's remarks. His books *The Existence of God* and *Faith and Reason* persuasively argue that the evidence at our disposal makes God's existence probable and the Christian revelation credible.[2] Swinburne's work as a whole is informed by a conception of reason which is similar to Locke's in spirit if not always in letter. "To believe that *p* is to believe that *p* is more probable than any alternative.... The kind of probability at stake here is ... epistemic probability," and "epistemic probability is relative to evidence" *(FR* 18)....

Swinburne recognizes, of course, that apparently rational people differ over such things as the prior probability of hypotheses.... Swinburne also notes that people's beliefs in reports of experience, deliverances of reason, and other basic propositions differ "in the degrees of confidence with which they hold" them.... People's inferential standards also differ.... Finally, people's assessments of the *overall* probability of theories and hypotheses differ....

Swinburne admits that these disagreements are very much the product of our "upbringing," but insists that if progress is to be made in rational enquiry, "we must make the judgments which seem to us to be intuitively right." The relativity of our understanding "does not mean that our understanding is in error" *(EG* 56).

*William Wainwright is Professor of Philosophy at University of Wisconsin, Milwaukee.

I believe that this is correct. But I also think that differences over prior probability, the overall probability of a hypothesis, and so on, are differences in judgment, and that differences in judgment are typically affected by what William James called our "willing" or "passional" nature—our temperament, needs, concerns, fears, hopes, passions, and "divinations." Simplicity, for example, is partly a matter of intelligibility or naturalness. But the conviction that a hypothesis is intelligible or natural is partly a product of familiarity, and is affected by our attachments and attitudes. A hypothesis that seems intelligible or natural to a traditional Christian theist like Swinburne may not seem intelligible or natural to a [confirmed and critical atheist like] J. L. Mackie.

Our assessments of the overall probability of a hypothesis like theism are also affected by our passional nature; for when it comes to "the question, what is to come of the evidence, being what it is," each of us must finally decide "according to (what is called) the state of his heart."[3] In the last analysis, I can only view the evidence "in the medium of *my* primary mental experiences, under the aspects which they spontaneously present to *me*, and with the aid of *my* best illative [inferential] sense."[4] Our assessments of the evidence depend on our view of prior probabilities, of the evidence's overall weight, and so on. But because these "have no definite ascertained value and are reducible to no scientific standard, what are such to each individual, depends on his moral temperament" and personal history, as well as investigation and argument.[5]

Swinburne would not deny that our willing nature affects our judgment, but would, I think, insist that its influence is epistemically harmful.... This attitude towards the effect of "passion" on reason is hardly unusual. But is it correct? [I] will offer a partial defense of the claim that the influence of the heart can be epistemically benign.

Cognitive faculties rightly disposed. The position I will defend was once a Christian commonplace: that reason is capable of knowing God—but only when one's cognitive faculties are rightly disposed. It should be distinguished from two others which have dominated modern thought. The first claims that God can be known by "objective reason"—that is, by an understanding that systematically excludes "passional factors" from the process of reasoning. The other insists that God can be known only "subjectively," or by the heart. Both views identify reason with ratiocination. They also assume that reasoning is objective only when unaffected by wants, interests, and desires. The tradition I will discuss steers between these two extremes. It places a high value on proofs, arguments, and inferences, yet also believes that a properly disposed heart is needed to see their force. The most articulate spokesman for this position is Jonathan Edwards.

Edwards was strongly influenced by Continental rationalists like Malebranche, by some of the Cambridge Platonists (Henry More, for example), and by the empiricists (especially Locke). He was also excited by Newton and the new science. Although these traditions were diverse, they had an important common feature—an almost uncritical confidence in reason's power and scope. Edwards's practice reflects this confidence. Philosophical arguments are deployed to demolish critics, justify the principal Christian doctrines, and erect a speculative metaphysics (a subjective idealism like Berkeley's). But Edwards was also a Calvinist who shared the Reformed tradition's distrust of humanity's natural capacities and its skepticism about natural theology.

These diverse strands are reflected in the apparent ambiguity of Edwards's remarks on reason. Thus, he can say, on the one hand, that "arguing for the being of a God according to the natural powers from everything we are conversant with is short, easy, and what we naturally fall into" (Misc. 268, T 78), and yet, on the other hand, insist that, in thinking about God, reason is baffled by "mystery," "paradox," and "seeming inconsistence.".... [6]

... [A]lthough reason *can* prove God's existence, determine the nature of many of his attributes, discern our obligations to him, and establish the credibility of Scripture, grace is needed to help "the natural principles against those things that tend to stupify it and to hinder its free exercise" (Misc. 626, T 111). It is also needed to "sanctify the reasoning faculty and assist it to see the clear evidence there is of the truth of religion in rational arguments" (Misc. 628, T 251)....

Edwards on "reason." Edwards uses "reason" in two closely related senses. Sometimes the term refers to "ratiocination, or a power of inferring by arguments" (DSL 18). At others it refers to "the power ... an intelligent being has to judge of the truth of propositions ... immediately by only looking on the propositions" as well as to ratiocination (Misc. 1340, T 219). The difference between these characterizations isn't important; in both cases, "reason's work is to perceive truth and not excellency" (DSL 18). Excellency and what pertains to it are perceived by the heart. While Edwards concedes that there is a more extended sense in which "reason" refers to "the faculty of mental perception in general" (DSL 18), he clearly prefers the stricter usage. His official view is that of other modern philosophers who deny that reason has an affective dimension (a love of the good, for example, or a delight in excellence).

Grace affects reason as well as the heart. "Common grace" helps the faculties "to do that more fully which they do by nature," strengthening "the natural principles [for example, conscience] against those things that tend to stupify it and to hinder its free exercise." "Special grace," on the other hand, "causes those things to be in the soul that are above nature; and causes them to be in the soul habitually" (Misc. 626, T 111). Special grace sanctifies by infusing benevolence or true virtue—namely, the love of being in general. Infused benevolence is the basis of a new epistemic principle; a sense of the heart which tastes, relishes, and perceives the beauty of holiness (that is, benevolence). By its means, the sanctified acquire a new simple idea (the idea of "true beauty") which the unredeemed lack. Because this idea is needed to properly understand divine matters, the "saints" are in a superior epistemic position. One can't rightly understand God's moral attributes, for example, if one doesn't perceive their beauty. Nor can one adequately grasp truths which logically or epistemically depend on God's holiness and its splendor such as the infinite heinousness of sin or the appropriateness of God's aiming at his own glory. The saints also behold old data with new eyes. They perceive the stamp of divine splendor on the world's order and design and upon the events recorded in sacred history. They thereby acquire a more accurate sense of this evidence's force and impressiveness.

[Let us consider an] epistemic effect of special grace. The new principle that God infuses

> sanctifies the reasoning faculty and assists it to see the clear evidence there is of the truth of religion in rational arguments, and that in two ways, viz., as it removes prejudices and so lays the mind more open to the force of arguments, and also secondly, as it positively enlightens and assists it to see the force *of* rational arguments ... by adding greater light, clearness and strength to the judgment (Misc. 628, T 251).

There is nothing intrinsically supernatural about many of these benefits. The *cause* of the mind's reasoning soundly is supernatural, but the effect (sound reasoning) often is not; the spirit simply helps us use our natural epistemic faculties rightly.

What sorts of "prejudices" interfere with reason's "free exercise"? "Opinions arising from imagination" are one example. They

> take us as soon as we are born, are beat into us by every act of sensation, and so grow *up* with us from our very births; and by that means grow into us so fast that it is almost impossible to root them out, being as it were so incorporated with our very minds that whatsoever is objected to them, contrary thereunto, is as if it were dissonant to the very constitution of them. Hence, men come to make what they can actually perceive by their senses, or immediate and outside reflection into their own souls, the standard of possibility and impossibility ("Prejudices," 196).

Biases arising from temperament, education custom and fashion furnish other examples....

Sin's essence is a failure to obey the love commandment. Those who don't love being in general love "private systems." Their loves are partial, extending to only some beings. They are also inordinate; lives are centered on the self or more extensive private systems rather than on God (who is "in effect" being in general) and the creatures who are absolutely dependent on him and reflect his glory.

Sin has noetic consequences. Edwards refers, for example, to "the great subjection of the soul in its fallen state to the external senses" (Misc. 782, T 122). (This subjection is presumably a consequence of the soul's inordinate love of temporal goods.) Again, self-love blinds us to everything that doesn't bear on immediate self-interest (OS 145-57)....

Our corrupt inclinations even affect our sense of what is and isn't reasonable. "Common inclination or the common dictates of inclination, are often called common sense." A person who says that the doctrine of eternal damnation offends common sense is using the expression in this way. But the inclinations behind this judgment have been shaped by an insensibility to "the great evil of sin." They are therefore corrupt (Misc. Obs. 253)....

Grace frees the mind from these "prejudices." An unprejudiced reason, however, isn't dispassionate. For it is affected by *epistemically benign* feelings and inclinations. A love of wider systems alone checks self-interest. Nor is it sufficient to replace hostility towards religion with indifference or neutrality; the heart must be receptive to it. An unprejudiced reason is also affected by natural motions of the heart—gratitude for one's being, for example, or a sense that it would be unfitting for the injustice that evades human tribunals to escape punishment. And since our love of temporal goods is inordinate because it isn't subordinate to a love of eternity, the latter is needed to correct it.

Another point is relevant as well. Natural reason reveals many truths about God and our relation to him. Yet even at the level of nature these truths aren't properly understood if the heart lacks a due sense of the natural good and evil in them (a proper sense of the natural unfittingness of disobeying the world's sovereign, for example, and a horror of the natural evils consequent upon offenses against him, or a proper sense of the natural benefits he has bestowed upon us and of the obligations these gifts create).

I conclude, then, that *common* grace not only inhibits the action of passional factors corrupting reason; it (at least temporarily) causes better affections to influence it. *Sanctifying* grace replaces the effects of corrupt affections by the influences of true benevolence. A reason that is exercising itself "freely" and without "prejudice," therefore, is affected by passional factors.

But grace does more than remove the impediments ("prejudices") hindering reason's free exercise by restructuring our affections....

It should by now be clear how sin affects reasoning. Our immersion in temporal concerns distracts us so that we don't attend to our ideas. Our subjection to the senses aggravates the tendency to substitute words and other sensible signs for ideas, and our disordered lives make it difficult for us to appreciate even the natural goods and evils associated with religion. (For example, our blunted conscience blinds us to the natural fittingness of obeying God's commands, and our inordinate attachment to the present life leads us to neglect more important natural goods that extend beyond it.) A lack of true benevolence (which is sin's essence) makes it impossible to understand God's holiness (which consists in it) or to appreciate its beauty.

We are now also in a position to understand why rational arguments for religious truths aren't always convincing. Miscellanies 201 (T 246 ff.) and 408 (T 249 ff.) imply that a conviction of reality is created (1) by an idea's clarity and liveliness, (2) by its internal coherence and its coherence with our other ideas, and (3) by its agreement with "the nature and constitution of our minds themselves." Why, then, do religious ideas so often fail to carry conviction? Partly because the clarity and intensity of spiritual ideas is a function of "the practice of virtue and holiness" (Misc. 123, T 246) and our own practice falls woefully short, and partly because the "tempers" or "frames" of the ungodly aren't suited to them.... It is possible that those without spiritual frames can't even discern their coherence....

Special, or sanctifying, grace remedies these defects by enabling us to attend more easily to the actual ideas that the words of religion stand for and by disposing the heart to be suitably affected by the natural and supernatural good and evil associated with them. Common grace has similar effects, but (because it doesn't replace the love of private systems with true benevolence) doesn't furnish the mind with actual ideas of true virtue and true beauty, affecting it only with a sense of the relevant *natural* goods and evils.

The sense of divine beauty alone is intrinsically supernatural. A reason which has been freed from the bonds of imagination, prejudice, and narrow self-interest, attends to ideas of God's being, power, knowledge, justice, munificence, and other "natural" attributes, and is suitably affected by the natural good and evil associated with them isn't functioning above its nature. A reason which has been strengthened in these ways is capable, however, of seeing the force of rational arguments for the truths of "natural religion"—that is, truths about God which neither logically nor epistemically depend on the ideas of holiness and true beauty. A suitably disposed natural reason is thus capable of establishing God's existence and general nature. Truths which depend on the ideas of holiness and true beauty can also be established by rational arguments, but the force of these can be appreciated only by people with spiritual frames.

Desires and beliefs. Edwards was the philosophical heir to rationalists, and empiricists whose confidence in reason was relatively unqualified. He was the theological heir to a Reformed tradition which distrusted humanity's natural capacities. Did he succeed in coherently weaving these apparently inconsistent strands together? The answer, I believe, is a qualified "Yes."

The key is a distinction between good rational arguments and the conditions necessary for their acceptance. I may have a good argument against smoking, for example, but my desire to smoke may prevent me from appreciating its force. What is needed isn't a better argument, but a reorientation of my desires.

Edwards's position is roughly this. While reason is capable of generating good rational arguments for God's existence, his providential government of human affairs, predestination, and many other theological and metaphysical doctrines, self-deception, prejudice, self-interest, and other passional factors make it difficult for us to see their force. These faults can't be corrected by applying Descartes's rules for correct thinking, Locke's "measures ... to regulate our assent and moderate our persuasion,"[7] or other methods of this sort. What is needed is a set of epistemic excellences which are themselves expressions of morally desirable character traits and rightly ordered affections. The defects distorting human reasoning are deeply rooted in human nature, and can only be eliminated by the appropriate virtues.

Two features of Edwards's position are especially significant. First, the epistemic virtues aren't merely negative; they involve more than the exclusion of the passions and selfish partialities which subvert reason. Nor are the epistemic virtues confined to noncontroversial excellences like the love of truth. They include properly ordered natural affections such as gratitude and a love of being in general which God infuses into the hearts of his elect. These affections not only cast out others which adversely affect reasoning; they affect it themselves. Under their influence, we reason differently and more accurately.

The other significant feature is this. Two views should be distinguished. One is that there are circumstances in which it is legitimate for people's passions and affections to make up deficiencies in the evidence. Although the (objective) evidence isn't sufficient to warrant belief, one is entitled to let one's passional nature tip the balance. The other is that a person's passional nature is sometimes needed to evaluate the evidence properly (to accurately assess its force). The first view is often attributed to James. Edwards holds the second.

Edwards's position differs significantly from the more familiar positions of James, Kierkegaard, and others who appeal to passional factors. Edwards is an evidentialist. A proper, and therefore rational, religious belief must be self-evident or based on adequate evidence. But, unlike most evidentialists, Edwards believes that passional factors are needed to appreciate the evidence's *force*. Only those with properly disposed hearts can read the evidence rightly.

Edwards's view thus also differs from Locke's and Swinburne's. Fully rational judgments are determined not only by one's evidence and inductive standards; they are also determined by feelings and attitudes that express theological virtues....

True benevolence's assessment of the evidence isn't a nonrational ground for belief in this sense. It doesn't lead the saints to construct new inductive standards, to forget about some of the evidence, or to engage in selective investigation. Nor does it provide them with a *reason* for doing so. True benevolence isn't a nonrational ground for belief in Swinburne's sense, because it isn't a *ground* for belief at all, although its presence *does* partially explain why the saints hold the beliefs they do. In the same way, a good scientist's impartiality, intellectual honesty, and desire for truth help explain why she holds the beliefs she does and not the views of some less scrupulous or more credulous colleague. But they aren't *grounds* for her belief.

The position Edwards represents must be distinguished, then, from other more familiar views. Is it true or plausible? I am not sure. But I am convinced that the two strongest objections to it are inconclusive. I will discuss the more serious of the two in the following section.

Defending the passions. That passional factors *should* affect reasoning strikes most philosophers as epistemically, or even morally, objectionable. [This objection] rest[s] on a common assumption that our passional nature isn't a reliable guide to objective truth. Since Edwards (and also, I think, Pascal, Kierkegaard, and James) denies this, th[is] objections beg the question.

Let me begin with two preliminary comments. First, people like Edwards aren't recommending that we cultivate certain beliefs by viewing the evidence selectively. Edwards isn't advising us to *ignore* evidence, but to view *all* the evidence (assess its force) in a certain way. Second, the sort of partiality exhibited by those with holy dispositions doesn't exclude other intellectual virtues closely associated with impartiality.... The truly benevolent *are* partial in the sense that they allow their judgments to be influenced by their new wants and interests. Whether this sort of selectivity or partiality is undesirable is another matter....

The best argument against cognitive voliting [knowingly allowing one's beliefs to be influenced by passional factors] is inductive. Extensive experience has shown that need, desire, and other passional factors can adversely affect judgment. It has also shown that methodical efforts to reduce their influence can serve the cause of truth. Science is the most impressive example.

This argument, however, is also inconclusive. Edwards would agree with James. "Almost always" in science, "and even in human affairs in general," we should "save ourselves from any chance of believing falsehood, by not making up our minds at all till objective evidence has come." They would agree, in other words, that passional considerations are out of order in most cases *like those in the sample.* Both would deny that we can legitimately extrapolate from these cases to others with different subject-matters (the metaphysical and moral structure of reality, for example, or things of the spirit). As we have just seen, they have arguments purporting to show that, with respect to these subject-matters, some passional factors *are* reliable guides to truth. To simply assume that the generalization concerning the adverse effects of passional factors can be extended to areas like these begs the question. It may not, for example, apply to ethics. Aristotle argued that moral reasoning goes astray when it isn't informed by a correct understanding of the good life. The latter, however, depends on properly cultivated dispositions as well as sound reasoning. If one's emotional temper is defective or has been perverted by corrupt education, one can't appreciate the good. As a result, one misconstrues the nature of the good life, and one's practical deliberations miscarry. Now according to classical theism, God is the good. One would therefore expect a properly cultivated heart to be a necessary condition for grasping truths about him.

If theism is true, and if it is also true that subjective qualifications would be needed to know God if God existed, then there is reason to think that cognitive voliting is sometimes reliable. In refusing to allow our passional nature to affect our judgment on religious matters, we may, therefore, be prejudging the case against people like Edwards....

The relevance of Edwards. Why should Edwards's account of the proper use of our epistemic faculties still interest us? For two reasons. First, his account is the most carefully articulated version known to me of an epistemic theory deeply embedded in important strands of the Christian tradition. Calvin, for example, thought that rational arguments for the authority of Scripture "will not obtain full credit in the hearts of men until they are sealed by the inward testimony of the Spirit."[8] And while Aquinas believed that there is good evidence for the divine origin of Christian teaching, he didn't think that it was sufficient to compel assent without the inward movement of a will grounded in a "supernatural principle."[9]... The notion that a proper disposition is needed to appreciate the force of rational arguments for the authority of the Gospel can be easily extended to rational arguments for the truths of "natural religion" when these, too, come under attack....

The other reason for taking Edwards seriously is this. I suggest that theists who think that there are rational arguments for the truths of religion and who, in the light of their beliefs, think through the implications of their disagreements with intelligent, well-informed, honest, and philosophically astute critics will be forced to draw similar conclusions. They believe that these critics' assessment of the overall force of the evidence is in error. This error can't plausibly be attributed to such things as lack of intelligence, unfamiliarity with relevant evidence, obvious prejudice, or an unwillingness to consider counterclaims. Edwards would ascribe it to a failure of the heart. Modern theists may be reluctant to agree. (Partly because of their respect for these critics.) Yet if theism *is* true, and there *is* good evidence for it, what other explanation could there be of the failure of so many to appreciate its force?

Notes

1. John Locke, *An Essay Concerning Human Understanding* (2 vols., New York: Dover Publications, Inc., 1959).
2. *The Existence of God* (Oxford: Clarendon Press, 1979); *Faith and Reason* (Oxford: Clarendon Press, 1981); hereafter *EG* and *FR* respectively.
3. John Henry Newman, "Love the Safeguard of Faith against Superstition," in *University Sermons* (Westminster, Md.: Christian Classics, 1966), 227.
4. Newman, *Grammar of Assent* (Garden City, NY. Image Books, 1955), 318.
5. Newman, "Faith and Reason Contrasted as Habits of Mind," in *University Sermons*, 191.
6. Edwards's principal discussions of reason are located in the "Miscellanies" (a number of which can be found in *The Philosophy of Jonathan Edwards from his Private Notebooks*, ed. Harvey G. Townsend (Eugene, Oreg.: University of Oregon monographs, 1955), hereafter Misc., T; "A Divine and Supernatural Light" and "Miscellaneous Observations," in *The Works of President Edwards* (1968 repr. of Leeds edn. reissued with a 2-VOL. supplement in Edinburgh, 1847), viii, hereafter DSL and Misc. Obs., respectively; "The Mind," "Subjects to be Handled in the Treatise on the Mind," and "Of the Prejudices of Imagination," in *Scientific and Philosophical Writings*, ed. Wallace E. Anderson (New

Haven, Conn.: Yale University Press, 1980), hereafter "Mind," "Subjects" and "Prejudices," respectively, and *Original Sin* (New Haven, Conn.: Yale University Press, 1970), hereafter *OS*. Other relevant material can be found in *Religious Affections* (New Haven, Conn.: Yale University Press, 1959), hereafter *RA*; *The Nature of True Virtue*, in *Ethical Writings*, ed. Paul Ramsey (New Haven, Conn.: Yale University Press, 1989), hereafter *TV*; *History of the Work of Redemption* (New Haven, Conn.: Yale University Press, 1989); and *Freedom of the Will*, hereafter *FW*.

7. Locke, *Essay*, introd., 3.
8. John Calvin, *Institutes of the Christian Religion* (Grand Rapids, Mich.: Eerdmans, 1957), I.I, 7.4.
9. St Thomas Aquinas, *The Summa Theologica* (New York: Benziger Bros.,), VOL 2, part II-II, q. 6, a. I.

Discussion

1. What is Wainwright's explanation of disagreement concerning the power of theistic arguments?
2. If you disagree with Wainwright, what is your alternative explanation?
3. Suppose we concede that desires and aversions play a role in the assessment of arguments. How can we tell who is being misled by their improper desires and aversions?

Arguments for the Existence of God

Suggestions for Further Study

Alston, William. *Perceiving God.* Ithaca, NY: Cornell University Press, 1991.

Craig, William Lane and Smith, Quentin. *Theism, Atheism and Big Bang Cosmology.* Oxford: Clarendon Press, 1993.

Davis, Stephen. *God, Reason and Theistic Proofs.* Grand Rapids, MI: Eerdmans Publishing Company, 1997.

Helm, Paul, ed. *Divine Commands and Morality.* Oxford: Oxford University Press, 1981.

Le Poidevin, Robin. *Arguing for Atheism.* New York: Routledge, 1996.

Leslie, John. *Universes.* New York: Routledge, 1989.

Martin, Michael. *Atheism: A Philosophical Justification.* New York: Temple University Press, 1990.

Mitchell, Basil. *The Justification of Religious Belief.* New York: Seabury Press, 1973.

Michael Murray, ed. *Reason for the Hope Within.* Grand Rapids, MI: Eerdmans Publishing Company, 1999.

Newman, John Henry. *A Grammar of Assent.* Notre Dame: University of Notre Dame Press, 1979.

Rowe, William. *The Cosmological Argument.* Princeton: Princeton University Press, 1975.

Rowe, William. *Philosophy of Religion: An Introduction.* Belmont: Wadsworth Publishing Company, 1978.

Swinburne, Richard. *The Existence of God.* Oxford: Clarendon Press, 1979.

Part Two

Reason and Belief in God

Introduction

~~~~~

Reason
and Belief in God

Introduction. There is a tremendous variety of positions concerning the relationship of faith to reason. One extreme contends that rational faith demands proof of a rather stringent sort and the other extreme claims that faith should be maintained contrary to or in defiance of reason. While there is certainly a philosopher or two who have held such extreme positions, most philosophers locate themselves somewhere in the middle.

The most hotly contested recent debate on faith and reason centers around *evidentialism* which maintains that one must have evidence or arguments for one's beliefs (in God) to be rational. Since the time of the Enlightenment, many people have felt the demand to hold all beliefs, including belief in God, up to the searching light of reason. A belief is rational, according to this view, only if it can be supported by evidence or argument. Atheistic or agnostic evidentialists have generated a popular objection to the rationality of religious belief; *the evidentialist objection to belief in God* holds that it is irrational to believe in God without sufficient evidence or argument; and there is not sufficient evidence or argument for the existence of God. Hence, although God might actually exist, in the absence of evidence it is irrational to believe in God. The evidentialist objection is not an attempt to *disprove* belief in God, but it does attempt to *discredit* belief in God.

There have been several responses to the evidentialist objection to belief in God. Some theists have endorsed *theistic evidentialism* which contends that belief in God is rational only if there is sufficient evidence for the existence of God, and there *is* sufficient evidence for the existence of God (either in the form of the traditional theistic arguments or based on religious experience). This view comes in extreme forms and in more moderate forms. The more moderate view has been fetchingly called (by its creator, Stephen Wykstra) "sensible evidentialism" (opposing "stupid" evidentialism?!). *Sensible evidentialism* is the view that belief in God is rational because someone in the theistic community has evidence for the truth of their beliefs; sensible evidentialism concedes that there is a need for evidence for belief to be rational, but resists the awkward implication that each and every person is under some sort of obligation to become a quasi-philosopher—required to carefully study all of the alleged proofs and disproofs of God's existence. Both theistic and sensible evidentialism accept the basic contention of evidentialism—that rational belief in God requires the support of evidence or argument.

One might likewise accept this basic contention yet believe in defiance of the evidence. *Fideism* holds that belief in God ought to be accepted and maintained in the absence of or contrary to reason. If reason were to oppose faith, so much the worse for reason. It is difficult to find many recent defenses of fideism, it being a term as unpopular in Western philosophy as "communist" or "fundamentalist."

The most intriguing recent development in matters of faith and reason is the so-called "Reformed epistemology." This view has been developed by, among others, Alvin Plantinga and Nicholas Wolterstorff, who have been deeply influenced by John Calvin, one of the Protestant Reformers (hence the name). *Reformed epistemology* holds that one can perfectly rationally believe in God without the support of propositional evidence. One need not have carefully considered a theistic argument and refuted the counter-arguments to maintain rational belief in God. Belief in God is *properly basic*: a rational, foundational belief that one reasons *from* and not *to*. Reformed epistemology, as you might imagine, has been subject to tremendous criticism from the philosophical community which prizes argument, perhaps inordinately (if Reformed epistemology is correct).

The need for evidence. No textbook in philosophy of religion could be complete without the contribution of W.K. Clifford. It is difficult to resist his impassioned demand for evidence. His potent illustration of the corrupt ship-owner suggests that just as there is an ethics of action, there is also an ethics of belief. All beliefs, in every circumstance, for every person, require (morally) the support of evidence. It is wrong, so Clifford's famous maxim goes, always and everywhere for anyone to believe anything on insufficient evidence.

Antony Flew, a contemporary Cliffordian, defends the rational requirement of evidence by analogy to a debate. When debating the existence of God, the burden of proof is on the one who affirms the existence of God. Flew imperceptibly shifts from talk of proper debate protocol to belief policies. The lesson that he seems to draw from his discussion of debates is that there is a presumption of atheism which, in each individual's case, can be overcome only by adducing adequate grounds.

Wittgensteinian fideism. I stated earlier that few contemporary philosophers defend fideism. Nonetheless, contemporary philosophers have been accused of endorsing fideism. One such position has been called "Wittgensteinian fideism." Ludwig Wittgenstein's later writings both noticed and affirmed the tremendous variety of our beliefs that are not held because of reasons—such beliefs are, according to Wittgenstein, groundless. A curious number of Wittgenstein's most prominent students are religious believers, many of whom applied his general insights into the structure of human belief to religious belief. Norman Malcolm favorably compares belief in God to the belief that things don't vanish into thin air. Both are part of the untested and untestable framework of human belief. These framework beliefs are ones that we are inculcated into from the earliest ages. They form the system of beliefs *within which* testing of other beliefs can take place. While we can justify beliefs within the framework, we cannot justify the framework itself. The giving of reasons must come to an end. And then we believe, groundlessly.

Not surprisingly, many philosophers have criticized Wittgensteinian fideism. Kai Nielsen contends that religious belief consists in more than belief that God exists; religious belief is an interrelated system of beliefs about the after-life, morality and human happiness (to name a few). Each of these issues raises philosophical questions which nag us for answers. The entire kit and kaboodle of religious beliefs cannot be isolated from philosophical criticism and justification. Nielsen attributes the unwillingness of Wittgensteinians to justify religious belief to their anti-realist commitments: they do not really believe that there is an object (or subject), over and above the heavens and the earth, which satisfies the definition of "God." For Wittgensteinians, "God" does not function grammatically as ordinary terms do. Nielsen, no believer himself, is a friend of the orthodox believer on this count—belief in God is about something independent of believers themselves.

Pragmatic justification of religious belief. Suppose it simply cannot be decided on the basis of the evidence whether or not God exists. Since it is nonetheless possible that God exists, there may yet be consequences for belief or unbelief; indeed, such consequences may be eternal. Pascal's famous wager relies on the undecidability of belief in God on the basis of the evidence as well as the potential consequences of belief and unbelief. At the time of his death, Pascal left a series of notes that he had intended to complete in a full and final defense of Christian belief. These intriguing notes were published in 1600 as Pascal's *Pensées*. The best that these suggestive notes can provide are hints and guesses about Pascal's final project. *Pascal's wager,* the most famous portion of the *Pensées*, is intended to show that even though there is not sufficient evidence for or against the existence of God, it is better to gain the potential benefits of eternal bliss and to avoid the potential costs of eternal damnation by committing oneself to belief in God. I have included other sections to demonstrate that this is not all that Pascal had to say about rational religious belief. He seemed concerned to shock disinterested and easily distracted people into caring about the most important matter—their eternal destiny. He also seemed to believe that there is adequate evidence for the truth of Christianity but that one must care about the evidence in order to see it; that is, one's passions need to be properly ordered to comprehend the truth.

Calling Clifford a "delicious *enfant terrible*," William James defends the right to believe in God in the absence of sufficient evidence. His attack on Clifford, and the incessant Enlightenment demand for evidence, is two-pronged. He first argues that the person who accepts Clifford's rules of truth-seeking has made a passional (i.e. non-rational) decision. Each person, he argues, has the right to choose their own risks concerning their approach to belief-acquisition. One can be a Cliffordian who avoids false beliefs at all costs but misses out on many true beliefs. Or one can be more, shall we say, Jamesian—generously accepting many true beliefs (without adequate evidence) and so running the risk of admitting many false beliefs. James concludes his essay by demonstrating the deficiencies of Clifford's belief policies in matters of fundamental human concern: personal relationships, morality and God. The belief policy that is most likely to secure what we want in these areas is to commit ourselves ahead of or in the absence of sufficient evidence.

Reformed epistemology. We have already mentioned the major tenet of reformed epistemology: belief in God is perfectly proper without the support of a theistic argument. Clark defends reformed epistemology by illustrating how actual people actually acquire beliefs. A great many of our beliefs are acquired without evidential support. Belief properly begins with trust rather than suspicion; beliefs are innocent until proven guilty. So, too, belief in God may be accepted without adequate propositional evidence (unless or until one has adequate reason to give up belief in God).

Phil Quinn has offered some of the most important criticisms of reformed epistemology. Quinn's intuition is that most intellectually sophisticated adult theists in our culture cannot properly believe in God in a basic manner. That is, if such people are to reasonably believe in God they must have understood and embraced the evidence for God's existence. Quinn contends that belief in God cannot be properly basic because of the evidence against the existence of God (such evidence is a defeater of belief in God). The initial believing state seems to be one in which evil and naturalistic explanations of God are so detrimental to rational belief in God that they need to be overcome by substantial evidence.

Chapter 7

~

The Need for Evidence

The Ethics of Belief
*W.K. Clifford**

The shipowner. A Shipowner was about to send to sea an emigrant-ship. He knew that she was old, and not over-well built at the first; that she had seen many seas and climes, and often had needed repairs. Doubts had been suggested to him that possibly she was not seaworthy. These doubts preyed upon his mind and made him unhappy; he thought that perhaps he ought have her thoroughly overhauled and refitted, even though this should put him to great expense. Before the ship sailed, however he succeeded in overcoming these melancholy reflections. He said to himself that she had gone safely through many voyages and weathered so many storms that it was idle to suppose she would not come safely home from this trip also. He would put his trust in Providence, which could hardly fail to protect all these unhappy families that were leaving their fatherland to seek for better times elsewhere. He would dismiss from his mind all ungenerous suspicions about the honesty of builders and contractors. In such ways he acquired a sincere and comfortable conviction that his vessel was thoroughly safe and seaworthy; he watched her departure with a light heart, and benevolent wishes for the success of the exiles in their strange new home that was to be; and he got his insurance money when she went down in mid-ocean and told no tales.

What shall we say of him? Surely this, that he was verily guilty of the death of those men. It is admitted that he did sincerely believe in the soundness of his ship; but the sincerity of his conviction can in no wise help him, because *he had no right to believe on such evidence as was before him*. He had acquired his belief not by honestly earning it in patient investigation, but by stifling his doubts. And although in the end he may have felt so sure about it that he could not think otherwise, yet inasmuch as he had knowingly and willingly worked himself into that frame of mind, he must be held responsible for it.

Let us alter the case a little, and suppose that the ship was not unsound after all; that she made her voyage safely, and many others after it. Will that diminish the

---

*W. K. Clifford (1845-1879) was a British physicist and mathematician.

guilt of her owner? Not one jot. When an action is once done, it is right or wrong for ever; no accidental failure of its good or evil fruits can possibly alter that. The man would not have been innocent, he would only have been not found out. The question of right or wrong has to do with the origin of his belief, not the matter of it; not what it was, but how he got it; not whether it turned out to be true or false, but whether he had a right to believe on such evidence as was before him....

It may be said, however, that ... it is not the belief which is judged to be wrong, but the action following upon it. The shipowner might say, "I am perfectly certain that my ship is sound, but still I feel it my duty to have her examined, before trusting the lives of so many people to her."...

Belief and actions.... [I]t is not possible so to sever the belief from the action it suggests as to condemn the one without condemning the other.... Nor is that truly a belief at all which has not some influence upon the actions of him who holds it. He who truly believes that which prompts him to an action has looked upon the action to lust after it, he has committed it already in his heart. If a belief is not realized immediately in open deeds, it is stored up for the guidance of the future. It goes to make a part of that aggregate of beliefs which is the link between sensation and action at every moment of all our lives, and which is so organized and compacted together that no part of it can be isolated from the rest, but every new addition modifies the structure of the whole. No real belief, however trifling and fragmentary it may seem, is ever truly insignificant; it prepares us to receive more of its like, confirms those which resembled it before, and weakens others; and so gradually it lays a stealthy train in our inmost thoughts, which may some day explode into overt action, and leave its stamp upon our character for ever.

And no one man's belief is in any case a private matter which concerns himself alone. Our lives are guided by general conception of the course of things which has been created by society for social purposes. Our words, our phrases, our forms and processes and modes of thought, are common property, fashioned and perfected from age to age; an heirloom which every succeeding generation inherits as a precious deposit and a sacred trust to be handed on to the next one, not unchanged but enlarged and purified, with some clear marks of its proper handiwork. Into this, for good or ill, is woven every belief of every man who has speech of his fellows. An awful privilege, and an awful responsibility, that we should help to create the world in which posterity will live.

All beliefs and believers. In the ... case which [has] been considered, it has been judged wrong to believe on insufficient evidence, or to nourish belief by suppressing doubts and avoiding investigation. The reason of this judgment is not far to seek: it is that ... the belief held by one man was of great importance to other men. But forasmuch as no belief held by one man, however seemingly trivial the belief, and however obscure the believer, is ever actually insignificant or without its effect on the fate of mankind, we have no choice but to extend our judgment to all cases of belief whatever. Belief, that sacred faculty which prompts the decisions of our will, and knits into harmonious working all the compacted energies of our being, is ours not for ourselves, but for humanity. It is rightly used on truths which have been established by long experience and waiting toil, and which have stood in the fierce light of free and fearless questioning. Then it helps to bind men together, and to strengthen and direct their common action. It is desecrated when given to unproved and unquestioned statements, for the solace and private pleasure of the believer; to add a tinsel splendour to the plain straight road of our life and display a bright mirage beyond it; or even to drown the common sorrows of our kind by a self-deception which allows them not only to cast down, but also to degrade us. Whoso would deserve well of his fellows in this matter will guard the purity of his belief with a very fanaticism of jealous care, lest at any time it should rest on an unworthy object, and catch a stain which can never be wiped away.

It is not only the leader of men, statesman, philosopher, or poet, that owes this bounden duty to mankind. Every rustic who delivers in the village alehouse his slow, infrequent sentences, may help to kill or keep alive the fatal superstitions which clog his race. Every hard-worked wife of an artisan may transmit to her children beliefs which shall knit society together, or rend it in pieces. No simplicity of mind, no obscurity of station, can escape the universal duty of questioning all that we believe.

It is true that this duty is a hard one, and the doubt which comes out of it is often a very bitter thing. It leaves us bare and powerless where we thought that we were safe and strong. To know all about anything is to know how to deal with it under all circumstances. We feel much happier and more secure when we think we know precisely what to do, no matter what happens, than when we have lost our way and do not know where to turn. And if we have supposed ourselves to know all about anything, and to be capable of doing what is fit in regard to it, we naturally do not like to find that we are really ignorant and powerless, that we have to begin again at the beginning, and try to learn what the thing is and how it is to be dealt with—if indeed anything can be learnt about it. It is the sense of power attached to a sense of knowledge that makes men desirous of believing, and afraid of doubting.

Duty to mankind. This sense of power is the highest and best of pleasures when the belief on which it is founded is a true belief, and has been fairly earned by investigation. For then we may justly feel that it is common property, and holds good for others as well as for ourselves. Then we may be glad, not that I have learned secrets by which I am safer and stronger, but that *we men* have got mastery over more of the world; and we shall be strong, not for ourselves, but in the name of Man and in his strength. But if the belief has been accepted on insufficient evidence, the pleasure is a stolen one. Not only does it deceive ourselves by giving us a sense of power which we do not really possess, but it is sinful, because it is stolen in defiance of our duty to mankind. That duty is to guard ourselves from such beliefs as from a pestilence, which may shortly master our own body and then spread to the rest of the town. What would be thought of one who, for the sake of a sweet fruit, should deliberately run the risk of bringing a plague upon his family and his neighbours?

And, as in other such cases, it is not the risk only which has to be considered; for a bad action is always bad at the time when it is done, no matter what happens afterwards. Every time we let ourselves believe for unworthy reasons, we weaken our powers of self-control, of doubting, of judicially and fairly weighing evidence. We all suffer severely enough from the maintenance and support of false beliefs and the fatally wrong actions which they lead to, and the evil born when one such belief is entertained is great and wide. But a greater and wider evil arises when the credulous character is maintained and supported, when a habit of believing for unworthy reasons is fostered and made permanent. If I steal money from any person, there may be no harm done by the mere transfer of possession; he may not feel the loss, or it may prevent him from using the money badly. But I cannot help doing this great wrong towards Man, that I make myself dishonest. What hurts society is not that it should lose its property, but that it should become a den of thieves; for then it must cease to be society. This is why we ought not to do evil that good may come; for at any rate this great evil has come, that we have done evil and are made wicked thereby. In like manner, if I let myself believe anything on insufficient evidence, there may be no great harm done by the mere belief; it may be true after all, or I may never have occasion to exhibit it in outward acts. But I cannot help doing this great wrong towards Man, that I make myself credulous. The danger to society is not merely that it should believe wrong things, though that is great enough; but that it should become credulous, and lose the habit of testing things and inquiring into them; for then it must sink back into savagery.

The harm which is done by credulity in a man is not confined to the fostering of a credulous character in others, and consequent support of false beliefs. Habitual want of care about what I believe leads to habitual want of care in others about the truth of what is told to me. Men speak the truth to one another when each reveres the truth in his own mind and in the other's mind; but how shall my friend revere the truth in my mind when I myself am careless about it, when I believe things because I want to believe them, and because they are comforting and pleasant? Will he not learn to cry, "Peace," to me, when there is no peace? By such a course I shall surround myself with a thick atmosphere of falsehood and fraud, and in that I must live. It may matter little to me, in my cloud-castle of sweet illusions and darling lies; but it matters much to Man that I have made my neighbours ready to deceive. The credulous man is father to the liar and the cheat; he lives in the bosom of this his family, and it is no marvel if he should become even as they are. So closely are our duties knit together, that whoso shall keep the whole law, and yet offend in one point, he is guilty of all.

The ethics of belief. To sum up: it is wrong always, everywhere, and for any one, to believe anything upon insufficient evidence.

If a man, holding a belief which he was taught in childhood or persuaded of afterwards, keeps down and pushes away any doubts which arise about it in his mind, purposely avoids the reading of books and the company of men that call in question or discuss it, and regards as impious those questions which cannot easily be asked without disturbing it—the life of that man is one long sin against mankind....

Inquiry into the evidence of a doctrine is not to be made once for all, and then taken as finally settled. It is never lawful to stifle a doubt; for either it can be honestly answered by means of the inquiry already made, or else it proves that the inquiry was not complete.

"But," says one, "I am a busy man; I have no time for the long course of study which would be necessary to make me in any degree a competent judge of certain questions, or even able to understand the nature of the arguments." Then he should have no time to believe.

Discussion

1. Give three reasons for thinking that beliefs ought to be supported by evidence.
2. If you were to adhere to Clifford's ethics of belief, how would your beliefs be different?
3. Criticize Clifford's views on reason.

The Presumption of Atheism
Antony Flew *

Burden of proof.... What I want to examine is the contention that the debate about the existence of God should properly begin from the presumption of atheism, that the onus of proof must lie upon the theist.

The word "atheism," however, has in this contention to be construed unusually. Whereas nowadays the usual meaning of "atheist" in English is "someone who asserts that there is no such being as God," I want the word to be understood not positively but negatively. I want the originally Greek prefix "a" to be read in the same way in "atheist" as it customarily is read in such other Greco-English words as "amoral," "atypical," and "asymmetrical." In this interpretation an atheist becomes: not someone who positively asserts the non-existence of God; but someone who is simply not a theist. Let us, for future ready reference, introduce the labels "positive atheist" for the former and "negative atheist" for the latter.

The introduction of this new interpretation of the word "atheism" may appear to be a piece of perverse Humpty-Dumptyism, going arbitrarily against established common usage. "Whyever," it could be asked, "don't you make it not the presumption of atheism but the presumption of agnosticism?" ...[F]ollowing the present degenerate usage, an agnostic is one who, having entertained the proposition that God exists, now claims not to know either that it is or that it is not true. To be in this ordinary sense an agnostic you have already to have conceded that there is, and that you have, a legitimate concept of God; such that, whether or not this concept does in fact have application, it theoretically could. But the atheist in my peculiar interpretation, unlike the atheist in the usual sense, has not as yet and as such conceded even this.

This point is important, though the question whether the word "agnosticism" could bear the meaning which I want now to give to the word "atheism" is not. What the protagonist of my presumption of atheism wants to show is that the debate about the existence of God ought to be conducted in a particular way, and that the issue should be seen in a certain perspective. His thesis about the onus of proof involves that it is up to the theist: first, to introduce and to defend his proposed concept of God; and, second, to provide sufficient reason for believing that this concept of his does in fact have an application....

The case for the presumption of atheism. What does show the presumption of atheism to be the right one is what we have now to investigate.

(i) An obvious first move is to appeal to the old legal axiom: *"Ei incumbit probatio qui dicit, non qui negat."* Literally and unsympathetically translated this

---

*Antony Flew is Emeritus Professor of Philosophy at Reading University.

becomes: "The onus of proof lies on the man who affirms, not on the man who denies." To this the objection is almost equally obvious. Given just a very little verbal ingenuity, the content of any motion can be rendered alternatively in either a negative or a positive form: either, "That this house denies the existence of God"; or, "That this house takes its stand for positive atheism." So interpreted, therefore, our axiom provides no determinate guidance.

Suppose, however, that we take the hint already offered in the previous paragraph. A less literal but more sympathetic translation would be: "The onus of proof lies on the proposition, not on the opposition." The point of the change is to bring out that this maxim was offered in a legal context, and that our courts are institutions of debate. An axiom providing no determinate guidance outside that framework may nevertheless be fundamental for the effective conduct of orderly and decisive debate. Here the outcome is supposed to be decided on the merits of what is said within the debate itself, and of that alone. So no opposition can set about demolishing the proposition's case until and unless that proposition has first provided them with a case for demolition: "You've got to get something on your plate before you can start messing it around."[1]

Of course our maxim even when thus sympathetically interpreted still offers no direction on which contending parties ought to be made to undertake which roles. Granting that courts are to operate as debating institutions, and granting that this maxim is fundamental to debate, we have to appeal to some further premise principle before we become licensed to infer that the prosecution must propose and the defence oppose. This further principle is, once again, the familiar presumption of innocence. Were we, while retaining the conception of a court as an institution for reaching decisions by way of formalised debate, to embrace the opposite presumption, the presumption of guilt, we should need to adopt the opposite arrangements. In these the defence would first propose that the accused is after all innocent, and the prosecution would then respond by struggling to disintegrate the case proposed.

(ii) The first move examined cannot, therefore, be by itself sufficient. To have considered it does nevertheless help to show that to accept such a presumption is to adopt a policy. And policies have to be assessed by reference to the aims of those for whom they are suggested. If for you it is more important that no guilty person should ever be acquitted than that no innocent person should ever be convicted, then for you a presumption of guilt must be the rational policy. For you, with your preference structure, a presumption of innocence becomes simply irrational. To adopt this policy would be to adopt means calculated to frustrate your own chosen ends; which is, surely, paradigmatically irrational. Take, as an actual illustration, the controlling elite of a ruling Leninist party, which must as such refuse to recognise any individual rights if these conflict with the claims of the party, and which in fact treats all those suspected of actual or potential opposition much as if they were already known "counter-revolutionaries," "enemies of socialism," "friends of the United States," "advocates of free elections," and all other like things bad. I can, and do, fault this policy and its agents on many counts. Yet I cannot say that for them, once granted their scale of values, it is irrational.

What then are the aims by reference to which an atheist presumption might be justified? One key word in the answer, if not the key word, must be "knowledge." The context for which such a policy is proposed is that of inquiry about the existence of God; and the object of the exercise is, presumably, to discover whether it is possible to establish that the word "God" does in fact have application. Now to establish must here be either to show that you know or to come to know. But knowledge is crucially different from mere true belief. All knowledge involves true belief, not all true belief constitutes knowledge. To have a true belief is simply and solely to believe that something is so, and to be in fact right. But someone may believe that this or that is so, and his belief may in fact be true, without its thereby and necessarily constituting knowledge. If a true belief is to achieve this more elevated status, then the believer has to be properly warranted so to believe. He must, that is, be in a position to know.

Obviously there is enormous scope for disagreement in particular cases: both about what is required in order to be in a position to know; and about whether these requirements have actually been satisfied. But the crucial distinction between believing truly and knowing is recognised as universally as the prior and equally vital distinction between believing and believing what is in fact true. If, for instance, there is a question whether a colleague performed some discreditable action, then all of us, though we have perhaps to admit that we cannot help believing that he did, are rightly scrupulous not to assert that this is known unless we have grounds sufficient to warrant the bolder claim. It is, therefore, not only incongruous but also scandalous in matters of life and death, and even of eternal life and death, to maintain that you know either on no grounds at all, or on grounds of a kind which on other and comparatively minor issues you yourself would insist to be inadequate.

Conclusion. It is by reference to this inescapable demand for grounds that the presumption of atheism is justified. If it is to be established that there is a God, then we have to have good grounds for believing that this is indeed so. Until and unless some such grounds are produced we have literally no reason at all for believing; and in that situation the only reasonable posture must be that of either the negative atheist or the agnostic. So the onus of proof has to rest on the proposition. It must be up to them: first, to give whatever sense they choose to the word "God," meeting any objection that so defined it would relate only to an incoherent pseudo-concept; and, second, to bring forward sufficient reasons to warrant their claim that, in their present sense of the word "God," there is a God. The same applies, with appropriate alterations, if what is to be made out is, not that theism is known to be true, but only—more modestly—that it can be seen to be at least more or less probable.

Notes

1. J.L. Austin, *Sense and Sensibilia* (Oxford: Clarendon Press, 1962), 142.

Discussion

1. Defend the debate policy that the burden of proof falls on the person who affirms.
2. Think of several instances where the burden of proof (in a debate) falls on the person who denies.
3. Suppose that we concede that in debates about the existence of God, the burden of proof is on those who affirm God's existence. What is the relevance of this practice to our belief policies?

Chapter 8

~~~~~

Wittgensteinian Fideism

The Groundlessness of Belief
Norman Malcolm[*]

Groundless believing. In his final notebooks Wittgenstein wrote that it is difficult "to realize the groundlessness of our believing."[1] He was thinking of how much mere acceptance, on the basis of no evidence, forms our lives. This is obvious in the case of small children. They are told the names of things. They accept what they are told. They do not ask for grounds. A child does not demand a proof that the person who feeds him is called "Mama." Or are we to suppose that the child reasons to himself as follows: "The others present seem to know this person who is feeding me, and since they call her 'Mama' that probably is her name"? It is obvious on reflection that a child cannot consider evidence or even doubt anything until he has already learned much. As Wittgenstein puts it: "The child learns by believing the adult. Doubt comes *after* belief" (*OC*, 160).

What is more difficult to perceive is that the lives of educated, sophisticated adults are also formed by groundless beliefs. I do not mean eccentric beliefs that are out on the fringes of their lives, but fundamental beliefs. Take the belief that familiar material things (watches, shoes, chairs) do not cease to exist without some physical explanation. They don't "vanish in thin air." It is interesting that we do use that very expression: "I *know* I put the keys right here on this table. They must have vanished in thin air!" But this exclamation is hyperbole; we are not speaking in literal seriousness. I do not know of any adult who would consider, in all gravity, that the keys might have inexplicably ceased to exist....

The framework of thinking. Our attitude in this matter is striking. We would not be willing to consider it as even improbable that a missing lawn chair had "just ceased to exist." We would not entertain such a suggestion. If anyone proposed it we would be sure he was joking. It is no exaggeration to say that this attitude is part of the foundations of our thinking. I do not want to say that this attitude is *un*reasonable; but rather that it is something that we do not *try* to support with

---

[*]Norman Malcolm (1911-1990), student and friend of Ludwig Wittgenstein, taught at Cornell University.

grounds. It could be said to belong to "the framework" of our thinking about material things.

Wittgenstein asks: "Does anyone ever test whether this table remains in existence when no one is paying attention to it?" (*OC* 163). The answer is: Of course not. Is this because we would not call it "a table" if that were to happen? But we do call it "a table" and none of us makes the test. Doesn't this show that we do not regard that occurrence as a possibility? People who did so regard it would seem ludicrous to us. One could imagine that they made ingenious experiments to decide the question; but this research would make us smile. Is this because experiments were conducted by our ancestors that settled the matter once and for all? I don't believe it. The principle that material things do not cease to exist without physical cause is an unreflective part of the framework within which physical investigations are made and physical explanations arrived at....

A "system" provides the boundaries within which we ask questions, carry out investigations, and make judgments. Hypotheses are put forth and challenged, *within* a system. Verification, justification, the search for evidence, occur *within* a system. The framework propositions of the system are not put to the test, not backed up by evidence. This is what Wittgenstein means when he says, "Of course there is justification; but justification comes to an end" (*OC*, 192); and when he asks "Doesn't testing come to an end?" (*OC*, 164); and when he remarks that "whenever we test anything we are already presupposing something that is not tested" (*OC*, 163).

Beginning with trust. That this is so is not to be attributed to human weakness. It is a conceptual requirement that our inquiries and proofs stay within boundaries.... We are taught, or we absorb, the systems within which we raise doubts, make inquiries, draw conclusions. We grow into a framework. We don't question it. We accept it trustingly. But this acceptance is not a consequence of reflection. We do not decide to accept framework propositions. We do not decide that we live on the earth, any more that we decide to learn our native tongue. We do come to adhere to a framework proposition, in the sense that it forms the way we think. The framework propositions that we accept, grow into, are not idiosyncrasies but common ways of speaking and thinking that are pressed on us by our human community. For our acceptances to have been withheld would have meant that we had not learned how to count, to measure, to use names, to play games, or even *to talk*. Wittgenstein remarks that "a language-game is only possible if one trusts something." Not *can* but *does* trust something (*OC*, 509). I think he means by this trust or acceptance what he calls belief "in the sense religious belief" (*OC*, 459). What does he mean by belief "in the sense of religious belief"? He explicitly distinguishes it from *conjecture*. I think this means that there is nothing tentative about it, it is not adopted as a hypothesis that might later be withdrawn in the light of new evidence. This also makes explicit an important feature of Wittgenstein's understanding of belief, in the sense of "religious belief," namely, that it does not rise or fall on the basis of evidence or grounds: it is "groundless."

Evidentialism. In our Western academic philosophy, religious belief is commonly regarded as unreasonable and is viewed with condescension or even contempt. It is said that religion is a refuge for those who, because of weakness of intellect or character, are unable to confront the stern realities of the world. The objective, mature, *strong* attitude is to hold beliefs solely on the basis of *evidence*.

It appears to me that philosophical thinking is greatly influenced by this veneration of evidence. We have an aversion to statements, reports, declarations, beliefs, that are not based on grounds....

"WHY? Why? why?" Suppose that a pupil has been given thorough training in some procedure, whether it is drawing patterns, building fences, or proving theorems. But then he has to carry on by himself in new situations. How does he know what to do? Wittgenstein presents the following dialogue: "'However you instruct him in the continuation of a pattern—how can he *know* how he is to continue by himself?'—Well, how do *I* know?—If that means 'Have I grounds?', the answer is: the grounds will soon give out. And then I shall act, without grounds" (*PI*, 211). Grounds come to an end. Answers to How-do-we-know? questions come to an end. Evidence comes to an end. We must speak, act, live, without evidence. This is so, not just on the fringes of life and language, but at the center of our most regularized activities. We do learn rules and learn to follow them. But our training was in the past! We had to leave it behind and proceed on our own.

It is an immensely important fact of nature that as people carry on an activity in which they have received a common training, they do largely *agree* with one another, accepting the same examples and analogies, taking the same steps. We agree in what to say, in how to apply language. We agree in our responses to particular cases.

As Wittgenstein says: "That is not agreement in opinions but in form of life" (*PI*, 241). We cannot explain this agreement by saying that we are just doing what the rules tell us—for our agreement in applying rules, formulae, and signposts is what gives them their *meaning*.

One of the primary pathologies of philosophy is the feeling that we must *justify* our language-games. We want to establish them as well-grounded. But we should consider here Wittgenstein's remark that a language-game "is not based on grounds. It is there—like our life" (*OC*, 559).

Within a language-game there is justification and lack of justification, evidence and proof, mistakes and groundless opinions, good and bad reasoning and correct measurements and incorrect ones. One cannot properly apply these terms to a language-game itself. It may, however, be said to be "groundless," not in the sense of a groundless opinion, but in the sense that we accept it, we live it. We can say, "This is what we do. This is how we are."

In this sense religion is groundless and so is chemistry. Within each of these two systems of thought and action there is controversy and argument. Within each there are advances and recessions of insight into the secrets of nature or the spiritual condition of humankind and the demands of the Creator, Savior, Judge, Source. Within the framework of each system there is criticism, explanation, justification. But we should not expect that there might be some sort of rational justification of the framework itself....

It is intellectually troubling for us to conceive that a whole system of thought might be groundless, might have no rational justification. We realize easily enough, however, that grounds soon give out—that we cannot go on giving reasons for our reasons. There arises from this realization the conception of a reason that is *self-justifying*—something whose credentials as a reason cannot be questioned....

There is nothing wrong with this. How else could we have disciplines, systems, games? But our fear of groundlessness makes us conceive that we are under some logical compulsion to terminate at *those particular* stopping points. We imagine that we have confronted the self-evident reason, the self-justifying explanation, the picture or symbol whose meaning cannot be questioned. This obscures from us the *human* aspect of our concepts—the fact that what we call "a reason," "evidence," "explanation," "justification" is what appeals to and satisfies *us*.

God and the proofs. The desire to provide a rational foundation for a form of life is especially prominent in the philosophy of religion, where there is an intense preoccupation with purported proofs of the existence of God. In American universities there must be hundreds of courses in which these proofs are the main topic. We can be sure that nearly always the critical verdict is that the proofs are invalid and consequently that, up to the present time at least, religious belief has received no rational justification.

Well, of course not! The obsessive concern with the proofs reveals the assumption that in order for religious belief to be intellectually respectable it *ought* to have a rational justification. *That* is the misunderstanding. It is like the idea that we are not justified in relying on memory until memory has been proved reliable....

The groundlessness of religious belief. Religion is a form of life; it is language embedded in action—what Wittgenstein calls a "language-game." Science is another. Neither stands in need of justification, the one no more than the other....

Notes

1. Ludwig Wittgenstein, *On Certainty*, ed. G.E.M. Anscombe and G.H. von Wright; English translation by D. Paul and G.E.M. Anscombe (Oxford, 1969), paragraph 166. Henceforth I include references to his work in the text, employing the abbreviation "OC" followed by paragraph number.... References to his *Philosophical Investigations*, ed. G.E.M. Anscombe and R. Rhees;

English translation by Anscombe (Oxford, 1967) are indicated by "PI" followed by paragraph number. In OC and PI, I have mainly used the translations of Paul and Anscombe but with some departures.

Discussion

1. Are the foundations of our beliefs self-justifying or simply convenient stopping points? Defend your view.
2. If belief in God is groundless, could unbelief be groundless? If so, how?
3. Suppose our beliefs are ultimately groundless. What would follow about our grasp of reality?

Religion and Groundless Believing
Kai Nielsen *

Religious language-games. It is a fundamental religious belief of Jews and Christians that a human being's chief end is to glorify God and to enjoy Him forever. Human beings are not simply creatures who will rot and die, but they will survive the death of their present bodies. They will, after the Last Judgment, if they are saved, come into a blissful union with God, free finally of all sin, and they will be united in Heaven in human brotherhood and love. But for now, that is, in our "earthly" condition of life, we stand in division both inwardly as self-divided creatures and against each other as well; a kingdom of heaven on earth is far from being realized. We humans—or so Jews and Christians believe—are sinful creatures standing before the God of mercy and of love whose forgiveness we need and to whom everything is owed.

The thing to see here is that being a Jew or a Christian is not just the having of one framework-belief, namely a belief that there is a God. And it is not just, as some philosophers seem to assume, the having of that belief and the having of another, namely that we will survive the death of our bodies. Rather, as Wittgenstein and Malcolm stress, what we have with a religion is a system, or as I would prefer to call it, a cluster of interlocking beliefs, qualifying and giving each other sense and mutual support.[1] We have here a world-picture which not only tells us, or purports to tell us, what is the case but orients and guides our lives and can touch profoundly—if we can accept such a world-picture—our hopes and expectations as well. To be a Jew or a Christian is to be a person whose sense of self and sense of the meaningfulness of life is tied up with that world-picture.

No place to stand. It has seemed to many philosophers, believers and nonbelievers alike, that key concepts in this world-picture—God, heaven, hell, sin, the Last Judgement, a human being's chief end, being resurrected and coming to be a new man with a new body—are all in one degree or another problematic concepts whose very intelligibility or rational acceptability are not beyond reasonable doubt. Yet it is just this skeptical thrust—or so at least it would appear—that Wittgenstein and certain Wittgensteinians oppose as itself a product of *philosophical* confusion.[2] In the systemic home of various ongoing and deeply entrenched language-games, these concepts have a place, and in that context they are, and must be, perfectly in order as they are. Within those language-games no genuine questions of their intelligibility or rational acceptability can arise and criticisms from the outside—from the vantage point of some other language-game—are always irrelevant, for the criteria of intelligibility or rational acceptability are

---

*Kai Nielsen is Professor of Philosophy at University of Calgary.

always in part dependent on a particular language-game. It might be thought that the phrase "genuine question" in the above is a tip-off marking what in effect is a *persuasive* definition and showing, as clearly as can be, that such questions can and do arise over such general criteria within the parameters of such language-games. But the response would be that no one who commanded a clear view of what she or he was saying and doing would try to make such a challenge or search for such general criteria of intelligibility or rationality, for she would be perfectly aware that she had no place to stand in trying to gain such a critical vantage point. There just are no criteria of intelligibility or rationality *überhaupt* [overall or in general]. Such a person has and can have no Archimedean point in accordance with which she could carry out such a critique.

Genuine criticism, such Wittgensteinians argue, will have to proceed piecemeal and within the parameters of these different but often interlocking language-games. Critique, if it is to cut deep and be to the point, must be concrete (specific) and involve an extended examination of the forms of life from *within*. For such a criticism to be a genuine possibility the critics must have a sensitive participant's or participant-like understanding of these forms of life as they are exhibited in the language-games with which they are matched....

In such a context criticism is in order and is an indispensable tool in the *development* of a tradition, but there is—so the claim goes—no genuinely relevant criticism possible of language-games as a whole or of forms of life. There is no coherent sense, such Wittgensteinians argue, in which we can speak of a confused language-game or an irrational form of life or of a full-fledged, conceptually distinct practice which is irrational or incoherent. Our language-games are rooted in these practices and are not in need of justification or of a foundation. In fact the whole idea of foundations or grounds or justification here is without sense. Foundationalism is a philosophical mythology. There is no logic which can give us the *a priori* order of the world. Rather our logical distinctions are found in or become a codification of distinctions found in our various language-games. But the sense—the intelligibility—of our language-games cannot be coherently questioned. There is, they claim, no coherent sense to the phrase "a confused language-game" or "a confused but conceptually distinct practice" or "an irrational form of life." We indeed have a deep philosophical penchant to go on to question, to ask for foundations for, to try to justify such practices, language-games, or forms of life. But it is just here that we fall into transcendental illusion. We do not recognize the import of Wittgenstein's full stop and we dream of justification where none exists or even could exist.

Both understanding and genuine criticism must, initially at least, proceed by seeing how the various concepts interlock and how in the form of a whole system—a cluster of concepts—they make sense. There is no understanding them in isolation. We come to understand their use by coming to see their place—their various roles—in the system. There is no understanding "the chief end of man" outside of something like a religious context and there is no understanding the distinctive end of man envisioned by Christianity without understanding its concept of God. And there is no, so the claim goes, even tolerable understanding of Christianity's concept of God without understanding the Christian concept of the end of man and man's highest good.... These concepts and many others like them cluster together, and we cannot understand them in isolation. Moreover, they stand and fall together.

Genuine criticism. Yet, these crucial Wittgensteinian points notwithstanding, there is a certain probing of those concepts which is quite natural and which can—or so it at least appears—be carried out in relative isolation from the examination of the other concepts of the cluster, provided we have something like a participant's grasp of the whole cluster. We, in wondering about the resurrection body in the resurrection world, naturally wonder how identity is preserved in the switch or in the resurrection or reconstitution of the body. Who is it that is me in the interim between the decay of the "old body" and the emergence of the "new" one, and in what space and in what world in relation to our present familiar world of everyday life and physics is this resurrection world? Is it even logically or conceptually possible for a rocket to be shot up to it? Somehow this all seems fatuous—a plain getting of it wrong—but what then is a getting of it right, what is it that we are talking about, and does it make sense? Does it help our understanding at all to say that we must just understand it in its own terms? Does it help particularly the perplexities we feel at this juncture to relate such conceptions to the other conceptions in our religious language-game? It is not at all clear to me that, about these particular worries, it does help much, if at all, to relate these philosophically perplexing conceptions to other religious conceptions.

Even more important is the role of the concept of God here. While gaining its meaning in a certain determinate context in a cluster of concepts, the concept of God can still have, in relative isolation, certain questions addressed to it. We glorify God and find our chief joy in Him, but *who* or *what* is this God we enjoy and how appropriate is the use of personal pronouns in such talk? We have the word 'God' but is it a proper name, an abbreviated definite description, a special kind of descriptive predicable or what? It surely appears to be some kind of referring expression, but what does it refer to? How could we be acquainted with, or could we be acquainted with or otherwise come to know, what it stands for or characterizes? How do we—or do we—identify God, how do we individuate God, what are we talking about when we talk of God, do we succeed in making any successful reference when we speak of God? What or who is this God we pray to, love, find our security in, make sense of our lives in terms of, and the like? Our cluster of religious concepts will help us somewhat here. We know He is the God of love who transcends in His might and mystery our paltry understanding.... This helps to some extent to locate God in *conceptual* space but only to some extent, for still the nagging question persists: *what* is it or *who* is it that is this being of infinite love, mercy, power, and understanding of whom we stand in need? What literally are we talking about when we speak of this being or what kind of reality or putative reality do we speak of when we speak of or even talk to God? (If we have no conception of what it is to speak literally here, then we can have no understanding of the possibility of speaking metaphorically or analogically either, for the possibility of the latter is parasitic on the possibility of the former.) Suppose someone says there is no reality here and 'God' answers to nothing at all—stands for, makes reference to, nothing at all. How are we to answer him and show he is mistaken? And how are we to answer the other chap who looks on the scene and says he does not know how to decide such an issue? He does not understand what it would be like to succeed in making reference with 'God', but not knowing that, he also does not know—indeed cannot know—that 'God' does *not* stand for anything either. If we don't understand what could count as success, how could we understand what could count as failure? All these people can play Jewish or Christian language-games with such a cluster of concepts, but they remain thoroughly perplexed about what, if anything, they are talking about in speaking of God. If that is so, how can we possibly be justified in saying that the concepts in question are unproblematic and are in order as they are? We know what it is religious people do with such words.... But though we can speak and act and at least seem to share a common understanding, we cannot decide whether 'God' does, or even could (given its meaning), secure reference—stand for something, refer to something actually real, and we do not agree about or understand how to go about settling or resolving or even dissolving that issue. But how then can these key concepts or conceptions be unproblematic?

Wittgensteinian anti-realism. Some, whom I have called—perhaps tendentiously—Wittgensteinian Fideists, would respond that the core mistake in what I have been arguing is that I continue to construe God as an object or a thing or entity of some sort. That this is a governing assumption for me, as it is for Flew as well, is revealed in my and his repeated request for a specification of the referent (denotation) of 'God', in our asking repeatedly *who* or *what* is God.[3] We both are, it could be argued, looking for the substance answering to the substantive and sometimes at least that is a mistake of such an order as to show a fundamental confusion about the logic of God. It confuses the surface grammar of the concept with its depth grammar.

There is no more question, they claim, of finding out whether God exists than there is of finding out whether physical objects exist. The putative question "Is God real?" makes no more sense than does the question-form "Do material objects exist?" It is true that a man who rejects religious belief and does not believe in God is not cut off from reason—is not thereby shown to be irrational—as is the man who does not believe there are any physical objects. Indeed we would not know what to make of a child's doubting the reality of physical objects, but we would understand very well a child's not believing in God or an adult's coming not to believe in God. The kind of unquestionable propositions that Moore and Wittgenstein take to be bedrock unquestionable propositions may, in their normal employments in normal contexts, very well be propositions it really makes no sense to question. They are framework beliefs. Whatever other differences they may exhibit, they are propositions which are not, or at least so these Wittgensteinians claim, *testable empirically* and thus are, in that way, not grounded in experience. There is no finding out whether they are true or false. The fact that the basic teachings of religion cannot properly be called knowledge should cease to be paradoxical, shocking, or perplexing when we reflect on this and on the fact that these various framework beliefs—certain of them as we are—are still not bits of knowledge. Moreover, that is not distinctive of religion and ideology but is a feature, as Wittgenstein shows, of many quite unproblematic domains as well.[4] All language-games have their framework propositions and, as they are something we cannot be mistaken about or in any way test or establish, they are not bits of knowledge. Doubting, establishing, believing, finding out, and knowing are activities which only make sense within the confines of language-games, and they require each other for any such single activity to be possible. But such contrastive conceptions cannot be applied to the framework propositions themselves. And while it is perfectly true that cultural changes can and do bring about changes in what we do and do not regard as reasonable, what realism requires, Wittgenstein argues, is a recognition that we do not have and cannot come to have a historical vantage point which will tell us what, such historical contexts apart, is "really reasonable."[5] (Indeed such talk may very well have no coherent sense.) What we have in various areas are different and often incommensurable beliefs which are, for many at least, unshakable beliefs which regulate their lives. But there is no finding out which, if any of them, are really true. There is, such Wittgensteinians argue, no establishing "philosophical foundations" which show that some or all of them have a rational underpinning. Such rationalist hopes are utterly misguided.[6]

To understand what we mean by 'God', to grasp its role in the stream of life, is to come to understand its role in such religious activities as worship, prayer, and the praise of God. That is where we come to understand what it is that we believe in when we believe in God. That is where the experience of God will have some reality, and it is in those surroundings that "Thou art God" has a clear sense. There God becomes a reality in our lives, and it is there where it becomes clear to us that the existence of God is neither a theoretical nor a quasi-theoretical nor even a metaphysical question.... Some Wittgensteinians have even claimed that "God exists" in its actual logical form (its depth grammar) is not something which actually is, as it appears to be, in the indicative mood. Most definitely, such Wittgensteinians claim, it is not a statement of fact or even a putative statement of fact. 'God', they also claim, is not a term concerning which it makes any sense at all to look for its referent. In Christian and Jewish language-games "God is real" is a grammatical truth.

Religious realism. These claims deserve a critical reception. "God is unreal. God is but a figment of our imaginations borne of our deepest needs" are not deviant English sentences. There are a number of language-games in which such talk is quite at home. But as believers don't speak that way, it will be claimed that the above skeptical utterances are not at home in religious language-games. (But again, believers could act in a play and speak that way or write novels, as Dostoevski did, in which characters say such things.) At least some believers understand such talk and there are many ex-believers and doubting Thomases and people struggling in various ways with religious belief. In their struggles and in their expectable and understandable wrestlings with faith, such talk has a home. Questions about whether God is really a figment of our imagination quite naturally arise. Moreover, their typical contexts are not the bizarre and metaphysical contexts in which we can ask whether physical objects are real or whether memory beliefs are even reliable. In our lives, that is, they are, for believer and nonbeliever alike, not idling questions like "Is time real?"

... That some people—even that many people—do not question these propositions does not show they are "unquestionable propositions."...

Granted 'God' does not stand for an object among objects, but still what does 'God' stand for? None of the above has shown that to be a pseudoquestion.

Critique. Wittgensteinians—as is most evident in the work of Winch, Dilman, and Phillips—try very hard to avoid facing that issue. Indeed they struggle to show that in reality there is no such issue at all.[7] I have tried to expose the nerve of some of the issues here and to maintain against them that there appears at least to be a real issue here.

Wittgensteinians will contend that language-games and forms of life are neither well-founded nor ill-founded. They are just there like our lives. Our understanding of them and assurance concerning them is shown by the way we go on—by how we employ them—whether we claim, in our philosophical moments, to understand them or not. There is no showing that the evaluative conceptions and norms, including the norms of reasonability embedded in them, require a justification, a foundation, or even an explanation.... The urge to attempt such justifications and explanations is very deep—as deep as the very subject that has traditionally been called "philosophy." But Wittgenstein schools us to resist this urge. If he is near to the mark, reason—the use by human beings of the various canons of rationality—requires that we resist it. Such general inquiries about religion and reality are senseless. There neither is nor can be a *philosophical* underpinning of religion or anything else. But such philosophical foundationalism is not needed. It is not something the loss of which undermines our capacity to make sense of our lives. Bad philosophy gives us the illusion that religion requires such a foundation and sometimes succeeds in so infiltrating religious conceptions that they do come to have incoherent elements which should not be accepted. Good philosophy will help us spot and excise those nonsensical, metaphysical elements. But when purified of such extraneous metaphysical elements, religious belief is both foundationless and not in the slightest need of foundations or of some philosophical justification.

... I don't want to speak of that grand issue here but only to face some of its implications for religion, if one takes to heart Wittgenstein's critique of the pretensions of philosophy. I agree, of course, that religion can have no such philosophical or metaphysical foundations. I do not even have a tolerably clear sense of what it means to say that there is some *distinctive philosophical* knowledge that would give us "the true grounds" of religious belief. I am no more concerned than are the Wittgensteinians to defend such a metaphysical religiosity and I am not concerned to replace it with some distinctive atheological *"philosophical* knowledge."

However, our perplexities and difficulties about God and religion are not just in a second-order context where the engine is idling. Most of them are not like perplexities about how we can know whether there is an external world or whether induction is justified or whether our memory beliefs are ever reliable. It is not just the talk about God-talk that perplexes us but certain central bits of the first-order talk itself. People with a common culture and a common set of language-games are very much at odds over whether we can know or justifiably believe that there is a God and this can be, and often is, linked for some with an intense desire to believe in God or, for that matter (though much less frequently), not to believe in God....

Using their own procedures, procedures I take within a certain scope to be perfectly proper, I started by looking at religious language-games we all can play and concerning which we at least have a knowledge by *wont.* When we look at certain religious language-games and—indeed from inside them—put questions which are perfectly natural, questions that plain people ask, and ask without suffering from metaphysical hunger, we will see that perplexities *arise* about to whom or to what we could be praying, supplicating, or even denying when we talk in this manner. Where 'God' is construed non-anthropomorphically, as we must construe 'God' if our conception is not to betray our belief as a superstition, it appears at least to be the case that we do not understand who or what it is we believe in when we speak of believing in God. It is not just that we do not understand these matters very well—that is certainly to be expected and is quite tolerable—but that we are utterly at sea here.

Religious skepticism. Such considerations make skepticism about the reality of such a conception very real indeed. And that very skepticism—as Dostoevski teaches us—can even come from someone who has a genuine need or at least a desire to believe. That skepticism is common enough and, if I am near to my mark, could be well-founded, even in complete innocence of or in utter irony about philosophical foundations for or against religious belief.

Notes

1. Ludwig Wittgenstein, *On Certainty*, trans. Denis Paul and G. E. M. Anscombe (Oxford: Basil Blackwell, 1969) and Norman Malcolm, [the previous essay in this collection].

2. Wittgenstein in *On Certainty* and again in a somewhat different way in his *Philosophical Investigations*. See Rush Rhees, *Without Answers* (London: Routledge and Kegan Paul, 1969); the article cited in the previous note from Malcolm; D.Z. Phillips, *The Concept of Prayer* (London: Routledge and Kegan Paul, 1965), *Death and Immortality* (New York: St. Martin's Press, 1970), *Faith and Philosophical Enquiry* (London: Routledge and Kegan Paul, 1970) and *Religion Without Explanation* (Oxford: Basil Blackwell, 1976).

3. See my *Contemporary Critiques of Religion* (New York: Herder and Herder, 1971) and my *Scepticism* (New York: St. Martin's, 1973), and see A.G.N. Flew's *God and Philosophy* (London: Hutchinson, 1966) and A.G.N. Flew's *The Presumption of Atheism* (New York: Barnes and Noble, 1976).

4. Ludwig Wittgenstein, *On Certainty* and G.H. von Wright, "Wittgenstein On Certainty," in G.H. von Wright, ed., *Problems in the Theory of Knowledge* (The Hague: Martinus Nijhoff, 1972), pp. 47-60.

5. Wittgenstein, *On Certainty*, pp. 43 and 80.

6. Again, *On Certainty* seems to me a crucial reference here. See also Stanley Cavell, *Must We Mean What We Say?* (New York: Charles Scribner's Sons, 1969).

7. Such accounts have been powerfully criticized by Robert C. Coburn, "Animadversions on a Wittgensteinian Apologe." *Perkins Journal*, Spring 1971, pp. 25-36, and by Michael Durrant, "Is the Justification of Religious Belief a Possible Enterprise?" *Religious Studies*, vol. 9 (1971), pp. 440-54 and in his "Some Comments on 'Meaning and Religious Language,'" in Stuart Brown, ed., *Reason and Religion*, pp. 222-32.

Discussion

1. What sorts of beliefs are criticizable and what sorts of beliefs are beyond criticism (i.e., bedrock unquestionable propositions)?
2. Where would you place religious beliefs? Why?
3. What are some legitimate questions that religious belief must answer?

Chapter 9

〜

Pragmatic Justification of Religious Belief

The Wager
*Blaise Pascal**

184. A letter to incite to the search after God.

And then to make people seek Him among the philosophers, sceptics, and dogmatists, who disquiet him who inquires of them.

187. ... Men despise religion; they hate it and fear it is true. To remedy this, we must begin by showing that religion is not contrary to reason; that it is venerable, to inspire respect for it; then we must make it lovable, to make good men hope it is true; finally, we must prove it is true....

194. ... The immortality of the soul is a matter which is of so great consequence to us and which touches us so profoundly that we must have lost all feeling to be indifferent as to knowing what it is. All our actions and thoughts must take such different courses, according as there are or are not eternal joys to hope for, that it is impossible to take one step with sense and judgment unless we regulate our course by our view of this point which ought to be our ultimate end.

Thus our first interest and our first duty is to enlighten ourselves on this subject, whereon depends all our conduct. Therefore among those who do not believe, I make a vast difference between those who strive with all their power to inform themselves and those who live without troubling or thinking about it.

I can have only compassion for those who sincerely bewail their doubt, who regard it as the greatest of misfortunes, and who, sparing no effort to escape it, make of this inquiry their principal and most serious occupation.

But as for those who pass their life without thinking of this ultimate end of life, and who, for this sole reason that they do not find within themselves the lights which convince them of it, neglect to seek them elsewhere, and to examine thoroughly whether this opinion is one of those which people receive with credulous simplicity, or one of those which, although obscure in themselves, have nevertheless a solid and immovable foundation, I look upon them in a manner quite different.

---

*Blaise Pascal (1623-1662) was a French mathematician and philosopher.

This carelessness in a matter which concerns themselves, their eternity, their all, moves me more to anger than pity; it astonishes and shocks me; it is to me monstrous. I do not say this out of the pious zeal of a spiritual devotion. I expect, on the contrary, that we ought to have this feeling from principles of human interest and self-love; for this we need only see what the least enlightened persons see. We do not require great education of the mind to understand that here is no real and lasting satisfaction; that our pleasures are only vanity; that our evils are infinite; and, lastly, that death, which threatens us every moment, must infallibly place us within a few years under the dreadful necessity of being for ever either annihilated or unhappy....

Nothing is so important to man as his own state, nothing is so formidable to him as eternity; and thus it is not natural that there should be men indifferent to the loss of their existence, and to the perils of everlasting suffering. They are quite different with regard to all other things. They are afraid of mere trifles; they foresee them; they feel them. And this same man who spends so many days and nights in rage and despair for the loss of office, or for some imaginary insult to his honour, is the very one who knows without anxiety and without emotion that he will lose all by death. It is a monstrous thing to see in the same heart and at the same time this sensibility to trifles and this strange insensibility to the greatest objects. It is an incomprehensible enchantment, and a supernatural slumber....

198. The sensibility of man to trifles, and his insensibility to great things, indicates a strange inversion.

205. When I consider the short duration of my life, swallowed up in the eternity before and after, the little space which I fill and even can see, engulfed in the infinite immensity of spaces of which I am ignorant and which know me not, I am frightened and am astonished at being here rather than there; for there is no reason why here rather than there, why now rather than then. Who has put me here? By whose order and direction have this place and time been allotted to me?...

228. Objection of atheists: "But we have no light."

229. This is what I see and what troubles me. I look on all sides, and I see only darkness everywhere. Nature presents to me nothing which is not matter of doubt and concern. If I saw nothing there which revealed a Divinity, I would come to a negative conclusion; if I saw everywhere the signs of a Creator, I would remain peacefully in faith. But, seeing too much to deny and too little to be sure, I am in a state to be pitied....

233. ... "God is, or He is not." But to which side shall we incline? Reason can decide nothing here.... A game is being played at the extremity of this infinite distance where heads or tails will turn up. What will you wager? According to reason, you can do neither the one thing nor the other; according to reason, you can defend neither of the propositions....

Yes; but you must wager. It is not optional. You are embarked. Which will you choose then? Let us see. Since you must choose, let us see which interests you least. You have two things to lose, the true and the good; and two things to stake, your reason and your will, your knowledge and your happiness; and your nature has two things to shun, error and misery. Your reason is no more shocked in choosing one rather than the other, since you must of necessity choose. This is one point settled. But your happiness? Let us weigh the gain and the loss in wagering that God is. Let us estimate these two chances. If you gain, you gain all; if you lose, you lose nothing. Wager, then, without hesitation that He is. "That is very fine. Yes, I must wager; but I may perhaps wager too much." Let us see. Since there is an equal risk of gain and of loss, if you had only to gain two lives, instead of one, you might still wager. But if there were three lives to gain, you would have to play (since you are under the necessity of playing), and you would be imprudent, when you are forced to play, not to chance your life to gain three at a game where there is an equal risk of loss and gain. But there is an eternity of life and happiness. And this being so, ... you would still be right in wagering one to win two, and you would act stupidly, being obliged to play, by refusing to stake one life against three at a game.... But there is here an infinity of an infinitely happy life to gain, a chance of gain against a finite number of chances of loss, and what you stake is finite. It is all divided; wherever the infinite is and there is not an infinity of chances of loss against that of gain, there is no time to hesitate, you must give all.... For it is no use to say it is uncertain if we will gain, and it is certain that we risk, and that the infinite distance between the certainly of what is staked and the uncertainty of what will be gained, equals the finite good which is certainly staked against the uncertain infinite. It is not so, as every player stakes a certainty to gain an uncertainty....

"I confess it, I admit it. But, still, is there no means of seeing the faces of the cards?" Yes, Scripture and the rest, etc. "Yes, but I have my hands tied and my mouth closed; I am forced to wager, and am not free. I am not released, and am so made that I cannot believe. What, then, would you have me do?"

True. But at least learn your inability to believe, since reason brings you to this, and yet you cannot believe. Endeavour, then, to convince yourself, not by increase of proofs of God, but by the abatement of your passions. You would like to attain faith and do not know the way; you would like to cure yourself of unbelief and ask the remedy for it. Learn of those who have been bound like you, and who now stake all their possessions. These are people who know the way which you would follow, and who are cured of an ill of which you would be cured. Follow the way by which they began; by acting as if they believed, taking the holy water, having masses said, etc. Even this will naturally make you believe, and deaden your acuteness. "But this is what I am afraid of." And why? What have you to lose? But to show you that this leads you there, it is this which will lessen the passions, which are your stumbling-blocks.

The end of this discourse. —Now, what harm will befall you in taking this side? You will be faithful, humble, grateful, generous, a sincere friend, truthful. Certainly you will not have those poisonous pleasures, glory and luxury; but will you not have others? I will tell you that you will thereby gain in this life, and that, at each step you take on this road, you will see so great certainty of gain, so much nothingness in what you risk, that you will at last recognise that you have wagered for something certain and infinite, for which you have given nothing....

253. Two extremes: to exclude reason, to admit reason only....

564. The prophecies, the very miracles and proofs of our religion, are not of such a nature that they can be said to be absolutely convincing. But they are also of such a kind that it cannot be said that it is unreasonable to believe them. Thus there is both evidence and obscurity to enlighten some and confuse others. But the evidence is such that it surpasses, or at least equals, the evidence to the contrary; so that it is not reason which can determine men not to follow it, and thus it can only be lust or malice of heart. And by this means there is sufficient evidence to condemn, and insufficient to convince; so that it appears in those who follow it that it is grace, and not reason, which makes them follow it; and in those who shun it, that it is lust, not reason, which makes them shun it.

Discussion

1. How much of your life is focussed on trivialities? On considering your eternal destinies? What would it take to make you care about eternity?
2. What would motivate one to believe on the basis of the wager? Are such motivations adequate grounds for genuine faith?
3. Pascal seems to think that our passions, emotions and pride can hinder the perception of the truth. Can you think of other beliefs that are affected by our passions, emotions and pride?

The Will To Believe

William James *

Introduction. I have long defended to my own students the lawfulness of voluntarily adopted faith; but as soon as they have got well imbued with the logical spirit, they have as a rule refused to admit my contention to be lawful philosophically, even though in point of fact they were personally all the time chock-full of some faith or other themselves. I am all the while, however, so profoundly convinced that my own position is correct, that your invitation has seemed to me a good occasion to make my statements more clear....

Hypotheses and options. Let us give the name of *hypothesis* to anything that may be proposed to our belief; and just as the electricians speak of live and dead wires, let us speak of any hypothesis as either *live* or *dead*. A live hypothesis is one which appeals as a real possibility to him to whom it is proposed. If I asked you to believe in the Mahdi, the notion makes no electric connection with your nature,—it refuses to scintillate with any credibility at all. As an hypothesis it is completely dead. To an Arab, however (even if he be not one of the Mahdi's followers), the hypothesis is among the mind's possibilities: it is alive. This shows that deadness and liveness in an hypothesis are not intrinsic properties, but relations to the individual thinker. They are measured by his willingness to act. The maximum of liveness in an hypothesis, means willingness to act irrevocably. Practically, that means belief; but there is some believing tendency wherever there is willingness to act at all.

Next, let us call the decision between two hypotheses an *option*. Options may be of several kinds. They may be—1. *living* or *dead*; 2. *forced* or *avoidable*; 3. *momentous* or *trivial*; and for our purposes we may call an option a *genuine* option when it is of the forced, living, and momentous kind.

1. A living option is one in which both hypotheses are live ones. If I say to you: "Be a theosophist or be a Mohammedan," it is probably a dead option, because for you neither hypothesis is likely to be alive. But if I say: "Be an agnostic or be a Christian," it is otherwise: trained as you are, each hypothesis makes some appeal, however small, to your belief.

2. Next, if I say to you: "Choose between going out with your umbrella or without it," I do not offer you a genuine option, for it is not forced. You can easily avoid it by not going out at all. Similarly, if I say, "Either love me or hate me," "Either call my theory true or call it false," your option is avoidable. You may remain indifferent to me, neither loving nor hating, and you may decline to offer any judgment as to my theory. But if I say, "Either accept this truth or go without it," I put on you a forced option, for there is no standing place outside of the alter-

---

*William James (1842-1910) was a Harvard psychologist and philosopher.

native. Every dilemma based on a complete logical disjunction, with no possibility of not choosing, is an option of this forced kind.

3. Finally, if I were Dr. Nansen and proposed to you to join my North Pole expedition, your option would be momentous; for this would probably be your only similar opportunity, and your choice now would either exclude you from the North Pole sort of immortality altogether or put at least the chance of it into your hands. He who refuses to embrace a unique opportunity loses the prize as surely as if he tried and failed. *Per contra*, the option is trivial when the opportunity is not unique, when the stake is insignificant, or when the decision is reversible if it later prove unwise. Such trivial options abound in the scientific life. A chemist finds an hypothesis live enough to spend a year in its verification: he believes in it to that extent. But if his experiments prove inconclusive either way, he is quit for his loss of time, no vital harm being done.

It will facilitate our discussion if we keep all these distinctions well in mind....

Clifford's Maxim.... [T]hat delicious *enfant terrible* Clifford writes: "Belief is desecrated when given to unproved and unquestioned statements for the solace and private pleasure of the believer.... Whoso would deserve well of his fellows in this matter will guard the purity of his belief with a very fanaticism of jealous care, lest at any time it should rest on an unworthy object, and catch a stain which can never be wiped away.... If [a] belief has been accepted on insufficient evidence," [even though the belief be true, as Clifford on the same page explains] "the pleasure is a stolen one.... It is sinful because it is stolen in defiance of our duty to mankind. That duty is to guard ourselves from such beliefs as from a pestilence which may shortly master our own body and then spread to the rest of the town.... It is wrong always, everywhere, and for every one, to believe anything upon insufficient evidence."

James's thesis.... The thesis I defend is, briefly stated, this: *Our passional nature not only lawfully may, but must, decide an option between propositions, whenever it is a genuine option that cannot by its nature be decided on intellectual grounds; for to say, under such circumstances, "Do not decide, but leave the question open," is itself a passional decision,—just like deciding yes or no,—and is attended with the same risk of losing the truth....*

Two different sorts of risk.... There are two ways of looking at our duty in the matter of opinion,—ways entirely different, and yet ways about whose difference the theory of knowledge seems hitherto to have shown very little concern. *We must know the truth;* and *we must avoid error,*—these are our first and great commandments as would-be knowers; but they are not two ways of stating an identical commandment, they are two separable laws....

Believe truth! Shun error—these, we see, are two materially different laws; and by choosing between them we may end by coloring differently our whole intellectual life. We may regard the chase for truth as paramount, and the avoidance of error as secondary; or we may, on the other hand, treat the avoidance of error as more imperative, and let truth take its chance. Clifford, in the instructive passage which I have quoted, exhorts us to the latter course. Believe nothing, he tells us, keep your mind in suspense forever, rather than by closing it on insufficient evidence incur the awful risk of believing lies. You, on the other hand, may think that the risk of being in error is a very small matter when compared with the blessings of real knowledge, and be ready to be duped many times in your investigation rather than postpone indefinitely the chance of guessing true. I myself find it impossible to go with Clifford....

For my own part, I have also a horror of being duped; but I can believe that worse things than being duped may happen to a man in this world: so Clifford's exhortation has to my ears a thoroughly fantastic sound. It is like a general informing his soldiers that it is better to keep out of battle forever than to risk a single wound. Not so are victories either over enemies or over nature gained. Our errors are surely not such awfully solemn things. In a world where we are so certain to incur them in spite of all our caution, a certain lightness of heart seems healthier than this excessive nervousness on their behalf....

The risks of belief.... Wherever the option between losing truth and gaining it is not momentous, we can throw the chance of *gaining truth* away, and at any rate save ourselves from any chance of *believing falsehood*, by not making up our minds at all till objective evidence has come. In scientific questions, this is almost always the case; and even in human affairs in general, the need of acting is seldom so urgent that a false belief to act on is better than no belief at all. Law courts, indeed, have to decide on the best evidence attainable for the moment.... But in our dealings with objective nature we obviously are recorders, not makers, of the truth; and decisions for the mere sake of deciding promptly and getting on to the next business would be wholly out of place. Throughout the breadth of physical nature facts are what they are quite independently of us, and seldom is there any such hurry about them that the risks of being duped by believing a premature theory need be faced. The questions here are always trivial options, the hypotheses are hardly living (at any rate not living for us spectators), the choice between believing truth or falsehood is seldom forced. The attitude of skeptical balance is therefore the absolutely wise one if we would escape mistakes. What difference, indeed, does it make to most of us whether we have or have not a theory of the Rontgen rays, whether we believe or not in mind-stuff, or have a conviction about the causality of conscious states? It makes no difference. Such options are not forced on us. On every account it is better not to make them, but still keep weighing reasons *pro et contra* with an indifferent hand.

I speak, of course, here of the purely judging mind. For purposes of discovery such indifference is to be less highly recommended, and science would be far less advanced than she is if the passionate desires of individuals to get their own faiths confirmed had been kept out of the game.... The most useful investigator, because the most sensitive observer, is always he whose eager interest in one side of the question is balanced by an equally keen nervousness lest he become deceived.[1]

Science has organized this nervousness into a regular *technique*, her so-called method of verification; and she has fallen so deeply in love with the method that one may even say she has ceased to care for truth by itself at all. It is only truth as technically verified that interests her. The truth of truths might come in merely affirmative form, and she would decline to touch it. Such truth as that, she might repeat with Clifford, would be stolen in defiance of her duty to mankind. Human passions, however, are stronger than technical rules. "Le coeur a ses raisons," as Pascal says, "que la raison ne connait pas"; and however indifferent to all but the bare rules of the game the umpire, the abstract intellect, may be, the concrete players who furnish him the materials to judge of are usually, each one of them, in love with some pet 'live hypothesis' of his own. Let us agree, however, that wherever there is no forced option, the dispassionately judicial intellect with no pet hypothesis, saving us, as it does, from dupery at any rate, ought to be our ideal.

The question next arises: Are there not somewhere forced options in our speculative questions, and can we (as men who may be interested at least as much in positively gaining truth as in merely escaping dupery) always wait with impunity till the coercive evidence shall have arrived? It seems *a priori* improbable that the truth should be so nicely adjusted to our needs and powers as that. In the great boarding-house of nature, the cakes and the butter and the syrup seldom come out so even and leave the plates so clean....

Faith may bring forth its own verification. *Moral questions* immediately present themselves as questions whose solution cannot wait for sensible proof. A moral question is a question not of what sensibly exists, but of what is good, or would be good if it did exist. Science can tell us what exists; but to compare the *worths*, both of what exists and of what does not exist, we must consult not science, but what Pascal calls our heart. Science herself consults her heart when she lays it down that the infinite ascertainment of fact and correction of false belief are the supreme goods for man....

Turn now from these wide questions of good to a certain class of questions of fact, questions concerning personal relations, states of mind between one man and another. *Do you like me or not?*—for example. Whether you do or not depends, in countless instances, on whether I meet you half-way, am willing to assume that you must like me, and show you trust and expectation. The previous faith on my part in your liking's existence is in such cases what makes your liking come. But if I stand aloof, and refuse to budge an inch until I have objective evidence, until you shall have done something apt, ... ten to one your liking never comes.... The desire for a certain kind of truth here brings about that special truth's existence; and so it is in innumerable cases of other sorts. Who gains promotions, boons, appointments, but the man in whose life they are seen to play the part of live hypotheses, who discounts them, sacrifices other things for their sake before they have come, and takes risks for them in advance? His faith acts on the powers above him as a claim, and creates its own verification.

A social organism of any sort whatever, large or small, is what it is because each member proceeds to his own duty with a trust that the other members will simultaneously do theirs. Wherever a desired result is achieved by the co-operation of many independent persons, its existence as a fact is a pure consequence of the precursive faith in one another of those immediately concerned. A government, an army, a commercial system, a ship, a college, an athletic team, all exist on this condition, without which not only is nothing achieved, but nothing is even attempted.... There are, then, cases where a fact cannot come at all unless a preliminary faith exists in its coming. *And where faith in a fact can help create the fact*, that would be an insane logic which should say that faith running ahead of scientific evidence is the 'lowest kind of immorality' into which a thinking being can fall. Yet such is the logic by which our scientific absolutists pretend to regulate our lives!

Logical conditions of religious belief. In truths dependent on our personal action, then, faith based on desire is certainly a lawful and possibly an indispensable thing.

But now, it will be said, these are all childish human cases, and have nothing to do with great cosmical matters, like the question of religious faith. Let us then pass on to that. Religions differ so much in their accidents that in discussing the religious question we must make it very generic and broad. What then do we now mean by the religious hypothesis? Science says things are; morality says some things are better than other things; and religion says essentially two things.

First, she says that the best things are the more eternal things.... The second affirmation of religion is that we are better off even now if we believe her first affirmation to be true.

Now, let us consider what the logical elements of this situation are *in case the religious hypothesis in both its branches be really true....* So proceeding, we see, first, that religion offers itself as a *momentous* option. We are supposed to gain, even now, by our belief, and to lose by our nonbelief, a certain vital good. Secondly, religion is a *forced* option, so far as that good goes. We cannot escape the issue by remaining skeptical and waiting for more light, because, although we do avoid error in that way *if religion be untrue*, we lose the good, *if it be true*, just as certainly as if we positively chose to disbelieve. It is as if a man should hesitate indefinitely to ask a certain woman to marry him because he was not perfectly sure that she would prove an angel after he brought her home. Would he not cut himself off from that particular angel-possibility as decisively as if he went and married some one else? Skepticism, then, is not avoidance of option; it is option of a certain particular kind of risk. *Better risk loss of truth than chance of error,*—that is your faith-vetoer's exact position. He is actively playing his stake as much as the believer is; he is backing the field against the religious hypothesis, just as the believer is backing the religious hypothesis against the field.

To preach skepticism to us as a duty until 'sufficient evidence' for religion be found, is tantamount therefore to telling us, when in presence of the religious hypothesis, that to yield to our fear of its being error is wiser and better than to yield to our hope that it may be true. It is not intellect against all passions, then; it is only intellect with one passion laying down its law. And by what, forsooth, is the supreme wisdom of this passion warranted? Dupery for dupery, what proof is there that dupery through hope is so much worse than dupery through fear? I, for one, can see no proof; and I simply refuse obedience to the scientist's command to imitate his kind of option, in a case where my own stake is important enough to give me the right to choose my own form of risk. If religion be true and the evidence for it be still insufficient, I do not wish, by putting your extinguisher upon my nature (which feels to me as if it had after all some business in this matter), to forfeit my sole chance in life of getting upon the winning side,—that chance depending, of course, on my willingness to run the risk of acting as if my passional need of taking the world religiously might be prophetic and right.

... Now to most of us religion comes in a still further way that makes a veto on our active faith even more illogical. The more perfect and more eternal aspect of the universe is represented in our religions as having personal form. The universe is no longer a mere *It* to us, but a *Thou*, if we are religious; and any relation that may be possible from person to person might be possible here.... To take a trivial illustration: just as a man who in a company of gentlemen made no advances, asked a warrant for every concession, and believed no one's word without proof, would cut himself off by such churlishness from all the social rewards that a more trusting spirit would earn,—so here, one who should shut himself up in snarling logicality and try to make the gods extort his recognition willy-nilly, or not get it at all, might cut himself off forever from his only opportunity of making the gods' acquaintance.... I, therefore, for one, cannot see my way to accepting the agnostic rules for truth-seeking, or willfully agree to keep my willing nature out of the game. I cannot do so for this plain reason, that *a rule of thinking which would absolutely prevent me from acknowledging certain kinds of truth if those kinds of truth were really there, would be an irrational rule.* That for me is the long and short of the formal logic of the situation, no matter what the kinds of truth might materially be.

Conclusion. I confess I do not see how this logic can be escaped. But sad experience makes me fear that some of you may still shrink from radically saying with me, *in abstracto*, that we have the right to believe at our own risk any hypothesis that is live enough to tempt our will.... When I look at the religious question as it really puts itself to concrete men, and when I think of all the possibilities which both practically and theoretically it involves, then this command that we shall put a stopper on our heart, instincts, and courage, and *wait*—acting of course meanwhile more or less as if religion were *not* true—till doomsday, or till such time as our intellect and senses working together may have raked in evidence enough,—this command, I say, seems to me the queerest idol ever manufactured in the philosophic cave.

Notes

1. Compare Wilfrid Ward's Essay, "The Wish to Believe," in his *Witness to the Unseen*, Macmillan & Co., 1893.

Discussion

1. Clifford says that it is wrong to believe without sufficient evidence. James says that we are within our rights to believe (certain propositions) without sufficient evidence. Defend one or the other view.
2. What prevents someone who follows James's beliefs policies from believing anything they want?
3. How have your judgments about how to approach beliefs changed now that you are fully apprised of the risks?

Chapter 10

~~~

Reformed Epistemology

Without Evidence or Argument
Kelly James Clark *

Introduction. Suppose a stranger, let's call him David, sends you a note that declares that your wife is cheating on you. No pictures are included, no dates or times, no names. Just the assertion of your wife's unfaithfulness. You have had already fifteen good, and so far as you know, faithful years with your wife. Her behavior hasn't changed dramatically in the past few years. Except for David's allegation, you have no reason to believe there has been a breach in the relationship. What should you do? Confront her with what you take to be the truth, straight from David's letter? Hire a detective to follow her for a week and hope against hope the letter is a hoax? Or do you simply remain secure in the trust that you have built up all those years?

Suppose, even worse, that your son Clifford comes home after taking his first philosophy course in college. He persuades you of the truth of the so-called "problem of other minds." How do you know that other minds and, therefore, other people exist? How do you know that people are not simply cleverly constructed robots with excellent makeup jobs? How do you know that behind the person facade lies a person—someone with thoughts, desires and feelings? You can't experience another person's feelings; you can't see another person's thoughts (even if you were to cut off the top of their head and peer into their brain); and even Bill Clinton can't really feel another person's pain. Yet thoughts, desires, and feelings are all essential to being a person. So you can't tell from the outside or just by looking, so to speak, if someone is a person. I can know that *I* am a person because I experience my own thoughts, feelings and desires. But I can't know, because I don't have any access to your inner-experience, if you, or anyone else, is a person.

Since you can't know if anyone else is a person, you rightly infer that you can't know if your wife is a person. Unsure that your wife is a person, how do you treat her? Do you hire a philosophical detective to search the philosophical literature for a proof that people-like things really are people? Do you avoid cuddling in the

---

*Kelly James Clark is Professor of Philosophy at Calvin College.

meantime, given your aversion to snuggling with machines? Or do you simply trust your deep-seated conviction that, in spite of the lack of evidence, your wife is a person and deserves to be treated as such?

Two final "Supposes." Suppose that you come to believe that there is a God because your parents taught you from the cradle up that God exists. Or suppose that you are on a retreat or on the top of a mountain and have a sense of being loved by God or that God created the universe. You begin to believe in God, not because you are persuaded by the argument from design—you are simply taken with belief in God. You just find yourself believing, what you had heretofore denied, that God exists. Now you have come across the writings of David Hume and W.K. Clifford who insist that you base all of your beliefs on evidence. Hume raises a further point: your belief in an all-loving, omnipotent God is inconsistent with the evil that there is in the world. Given the fact of evil, God cannot exist. To meet this demand for evidence, do you become a temporary agnostic and begin perusing the texts of Aquinas, Augustine and Paley for a good proof of God's existence? Do you give up belief in God because you see Hume's point and can't see how God and evil could be reconciled? Or do you remain steady in your trust in God in spite of the lack of evidence and even in the face of counter-evidence?

My Suppose-This and Suppose-That Stories are intended to raise the problem of the relationship of our important beliefs to evidence (and counter-evidence). Since the Enlightenment, there has been a demand to expose all of our beliefs to the searching criticism of reason. If a belief is unsupported by the evidence, it is irrational to believe it. It is the position of Reformed epistemology (likely the position that Calvin held) that belief in God, like belief in other persons, does not require the support of evidence or argument in order for it to be rational. This view has been defended by some of the world's most prominent philosophers including Alvin Plantinga, Nicholas Wolterstorff, and William Alston.[1]

The claim that belief in God is rational without the support of evidence or argument is startling for many an atheist or theist. Most atheist intellectuals feel comfort in their disbelief in God because they judge that there is little or no evidence for God's existence. Many theistic thinkers, however, insist that belief in God requires evidence and that such a demand should and can be met. So the claim that a person does not need evidence in order to rationally believe in God runs against the grain for atheist thinkers and has raised the ire of many theists. In spite of the vitriolic response to Reformed epistemology, I believe it is eminently defensible. In order to defend it, let us examine its critique of the Enlightenment demand for evidence.

The demand for evidence. W.K. Clifford, in an oft-cited article, claims that it is wrong, always and everywhere, for anyone to believe anything on insufficient evidence. Such a strong claim makes one speculate on Clifford's childhood: one imagines young W.K. constantly pestering his parents with "Why? Why? Why?..." It is this childish attitude toward inquiry and the risks that belief requires that leads

William James to chastise Clifford as an *enfant terrible*. But, rather than disparage his character, let's examine the deficiencies of his claim that everything must be believed only on the basis of sufficient evidence (Relevance: If everything must be based on sufficient evidence, so must belief in God).

The first problem with Clifford's universal demand for evidence is that it cannot meet its own demand. Clifford offers two fetching examples (a shipowner who knowingly sends an unseaworthy ship to sea and, in the first example, it sinks and, in the second example, it makes the trip) in support of his claim. The examples powerfully demonstrate that in cases like the example, rational belief requires evidence. No one would disagree: some beliefs require evidence for their rational acceptability. But *all* beliefs in *every* circumstance? That's an exceedingly strong claim to make and, it turns out, one that cannot be based on evidence.

Consider what someone like Clifford might allow us to take for evidence: beliefs that we acquire through sensory experience and beliefs that are self-evident like logic and mathematics. Next rainy day, make a list of all of your experiential beliefs: The sky is blue, grass is green, most trees are taller than most grasshoppers, slugs leave a slimy trail.... Now add to this list all of your logical and mathematical beliefs: $2 + 2 = 4$, every proposition is either true or false, all of the even numbers that I know of are the sum of two prime numbers, in Euclidean geometry the interior angles of triangles equal 180. From these propositions, try to deduce the conclusion that it is wrong, always and everywhere, for anyone to believe anything on insufficient evidence. None of the propositions that are allowed as evidence have anything at all to do with the conclusion. So Clifford's universal demand for evidence cannot satisfy its own standard! Therefore, by Clifford's own criterion, it must be irrational. More likely, however, the demand is simply false and it is easy to see why.

We, finite beings that we are, simply cannot meet such a demand. Consider all of the beliefs that you currently hold. How many of those have met Clifford's strict demand for evidence? Clifford intends for all of us, like a scientist in a laboratory, to test all of our beliefs all of the time. Could your beliefs survive Clifford's test? Think of how many of your beliefs, even scientific ones, are acquired *just because someone told you*. Not having been to Paraguay, I only have testimonial evidence that Paraguay is a country in South America. For all I know, all of the mapmakers have conspired to delude us about the existence of Paraguay (and even South America!). And, since I have been to relatively few countries around the world, I must believe in the existence of most countries (and that other people inhabit them and speak in that language) without support of evidence. I believe that $e=mc^2$ and that matter is made up of tiny little particles not because of experiments in a chemistry or physics lab (for all of my experiments failed) but because my science teachers told me so. Most of the beliefs that I have acquired are based on my trust in my teachers and not on careful consideration of what Clifford would consider adequate evidence. And in this busy day and age, I don't really have the time to live up to Clifford's demand for evidence! If we had the leisure to test all of our beliefs, perhaps we could meet the demand. But since we cannot meet that demand, we cannot be obligated to do so.

Even if we had the time, however, we could not meet this universal demand for evidence. The demand for evidence simply cannot be met in a large number of cases with the cognitive equipment that we have. No one, as mentioned above, has ever been able to prove the existence of other persons. No one has ever been able to prove that we were not created five minutes ago with our memories intact. No one has been able to prove the reality of the past or that, in the future, the sun will rise. This list could go on and on. There is a limit to the things that human beings can prove. A great deal of what we believe is based on faith, not on evidence or arguments.

I use the term "faith" here but that it is misleading. I don't mean to oppose faith to knowledge in these instances. For surely we know that the earth is more than five minutes old and that the sun will rise tomorrow (although, maybe not in cloudy Grand Rapids!) and that Paul converted to Christianity (and lots of other truths about the past), etc., etc., etc. In these cases, we know lots of things but we cannot prove them. We have to trust or rely on the cognitive faculties which produce these beliefs. We rely on our memory to produce memory beliefs (I remember having coffee with my breakfast this morning). We rely on an inductive faculty to produce beliefs about the veracity of natural laws (If I let go of this book, it will fall to the ground). We rely on our cognitive faculties when we believe that there are other persons, there is a past, there is a world independent of our mind, or what other people tell us. We can't help but trust our cognitive faculties.

It is easy to see why. Reasoning must start somewhere. Suppose we were required to offer evidence or arguments for all of our beliefs. If we offer statements 1-4 as evidence for 5, we would have to offer arguments to support 1-4. And then we would have to offer arguments in support of the arguments that are used to support 1-4. And then we would need arguments.... You get the point. Reasoning must start somewhere. There have to be some truths that we can just accept and reason from. Why not start with belief in God?

Without evidence or argument. We have been outfitted with cognitive faculties that produce beliefs that we can reason from. The number of beliefs we do and must reason to is quite small compared to the number of beliefs that we do and must accept without the aid of a proof. That's the long and short of the human believing condition. We, in most cases, must rely on our God-given intellectual equipment to produce beliefs, without evidence or argument, in the appropriate circumstances. Is it reasonable to believe that God has created us with a cognitive faculty which produces belief in God without evidence or argument?

There are at least three reasons to believe that it is proper or rational for a person to accept belief in God without the need for an argument. First, there are very few people who have access to or the ability to assess most theistic arguments. It is hard to imagine, therefore, that the demand for evidence would be a requirement of reason. My grandmother, a paradigm of the non-philosophical believer, would cackle if I informed her that her belief in God was irrational because she was unable to understand Aquinas's second Way or to refute Hume's version of the argument from evil. The demand for evidence is an imperialistic attempt to make philosophers out of people who have no need to become philosophers. It is curious that very few philosophers (like most ordinary folk) have come to belief in God on the basis of theistic arguments. I commissioned and published a collection of spiritual autobiographies from prominent Christian philosophers just to see if philosophers were any different from my Grandmother on this count. They weren't.[2]

Second, it seems that God has given us an awareness of himself that is not dependent on theistic arguments. It is hard to imagine that God would make rational belief as difficult as those that demand evidence contend. I encourage anyone who thinks that evidence is required for rational belief in God, to study very carefully the theistic arguments, their refutations and counter-refutations, and their increasing subtlety yet decreasing charm. Adequate assessment of these arguments would require a lengthy and torturous tour through the history of philosophy and may require the honing of one's logical and metaphysical skills beyond the capacity of most of us. Why put that sort of barrier between us and God? John Calvin believed that God had provided us with a sense of the divine. He writes:

> There is within the human mind, and indeed by natural instinct, an awareness of divinity. This we take to be beyond controversy. To prevent anyone from taking refuge in the pretense of ignorance, God himself has implanted in all men a certain understanding of his divine majesty. Ever renewing its memory, he repeatedly sheds fresh drops.... Indeed, the perversity of the impious, who though they struggle furiously are unable to extricate themselves from the fear of God, is abundant testimony that this conviction, namely that there is some God, is naturally inborn in all, and is fixed deep within, as it were in the very marrow. From this we conclude that it is not a doctrine that must first be learned in school, but one of which each of us is master from his mother's womb and which nature itself permits no one to forget.[3]

Calvin contends that people are accountable to God for their unbelief not because they have failed to submit to a convincing theistic proof, but because they have suppressed the truth that God has implanted within their minds. It is natural to suppose that if God created us with cognitive faculties which by and large reliably produce beliefs without the need for evidence, he would likewise provide us with a cognitive faculty which produces belief in him without the need for evidence.

Third, belief in God is more like belief in a person than belief in a scientific theory. Consider the examples that started this essay. Somehow the scientific approach—doubt first, consider all of the available evidence, and believe later—seems woefully inadequate or inappropriate to personal relations. What seems manifestly reasonable for physicists in their laboratory is desperately deficient in human relations. Human relations demand trust, commitment and faith. If belief in God is more like belief in other persons than belief in atoms, then the trust that is appropriate to persons will be appropriate to God. We cannot and should not arbitrarily insist that the scientific method is appropriate to every kind of human practice. The fastidious scientist, who cannot leave the demand for evidence in her laboratory, will find herself cut off from relationships that she could otherwise reasonably maintain—with friends, family and, perhaps even, God.

With or without evidence. I haven't said that belief in God could not or, in some cases, should not be based on evidence or argument. Indeed, I am inclined to think that the theistic arguments do provide some, non-coercive, evidence of God's existence. By non-coercive, I mean that the theistic arguments aren't of such power and illumination that they should be expected to persuade all rational creatures. Rational people could rationally reject the theistic proofs. Rational people, and this is a fact that we must live with, rationally disagree. Nonetheless, I believe that someone could rationally believe in God on the basis of theistic arguments, but no one needs to.[4]

Reformed epistemologists also believe, like Calvin, that the natural knowledge of himself that God has implanted within us has been overlaid by sin. Part of the knowledge process may require the removal of the effects of sin on our minds. Attention to theistic arguments might do that. Also, some of the barriers to religious belief—such as the problem of evil or the alleged threat of science to religion—may need to be removed before one can see the light that has been shining within all along.

But the scales can fall from the "mind's eye" in a wide variety of means: on a mountaintop or at the ocean, looking at a flower, through a humbling experience, or by reading *The Chronicles of Narnia*. The list goes on yet a certain common feature should be noticed (and not the fact that few people have ever acquired belief in God as a result of the study of theistic proofs). The primary obstacle to belief in God seems to be more moral than intellectual. On the mountains one may feel one's smallness in relation to the grandness of it all. The flower may arouse one's sense of beauty. The loss of a job or a divorce may reveal one's unjustified pride. And *The Chronicles of Narnia* may awaken the dormant faith of a child. In all of these cases, the scales slide off the mind's eye when the overweening self is dethroned (not to mix too many metaphors!). Humility, not proofs, may be necessary to the realization of belief in God.

Conclusion. This approach to belief in God has been rather descriptive. We need to pay a lot more attention to how actual people actually acquire beliefs. The psychology of believing may tell us a lot about our cognitive equipment. The lessons learned from observing people and their beliefs support the position that I have defended: rational people may rationally believe in God without evidence or argument.

Notes

1. Alvin Plantinga, "Reason and Belief in God," Nicholas Wolterstorff, "Can Belief in God Be Rational If It Has No Foundations?" and William Alston, "Christian Experience and Christian Belief" in *Faith and Rationality*, Plantinga and Wolterstorff eds., (Notre Dame, Indiana: University of Notre Dame Press, 1983); William Alston, *Perceiving God* (Ithaca, New York: Cornell University Press, 1991); Alvin Plantinga, *Warranted Christian Belief* (New York and Oxford: Oxford University Press, 1999).
2. See Kelly James Clark, *Philosophers Who Believe* (Downers Grove, IL: InterVarsity Press, 1993).
3. *Institutes of the Christian Religion*, Bk. 1, Ch. 3.
4. I argue this in some detail in my *Return to Reason* (Grand Rapids, Michigan: Eerdmans Publishing Company, 1990).

Discussion

1. How much of what you believe was acquired because someone told you?
2. What beliefs (other than belief in God) might be held without evidence or argument?
3. Could Reformed epistemology be used to defend any wacky belief?
4. Defend or criticize Clark's descriptive (as opposed to evidentialism's more normative) approach to a theory of knowledge.

On Finding the Foundations of Theism

*Philip L. Quinn**

Varieties of foundationalism. Foundationalism comes in two varieties. Descriptive foundationalism is a thesis about the structure of a body of beliefs, and normative foundationalism is a thesis about the structure of epistemic justification for a body of beliefs. Both varieties partition a body of beliefs into two subclasses, a foundational class and a founded class. For descriptive foundationalism, the foundational class is the class of basic beliefs. A belief is basic for a person at a time provided it is accepted by that person at that time but is not accepted by that person at that time on the basis of any of his or her other beliefs at that time. For normative foundationalism, the foundational class is the class of properly basic beliefs. A belief is properly basic for a person at a time just in case it is basic for the person at the time and its being basic for the person at the time is contrary to no correct canon of epistemic propriety and results from no epistemic deficiency on his or her part at that time. For descriptive foundationalism, the founded class is the class of beliefs based on basic beliefs, and, for normative foundationalism, the founded class is the class of beliefs properly based on properly basic beliefs.

It surely is possible that, for some human persons at some times, certain propositions which self-evidently entail that God exists are basic. But is it also possible that, for some human persons at some times, certain propositions which self-evidently entail that God exists are *properly* basic? In other words, could such propositions *be*, or at least *be among*, the normative foundations of theism, at least for some people at some times? The answers to these question depend, of course, on what the correct criteria for proper basicality turn out to be.

Recently Alvin Plantinga has been arguing that it is in order for a religious epistemologist to return affirmative answers to these questions.[1] There are two prongs to Plantinga's argument. The first is destructive: it is an attempt to show that certain criteria for proper basicality, according to which propositions which self-evidently entail the existence of God could not be properly basic, are seriously defective and must be rejected. The second is constructive: it is an attempt to elaborate a procedure for justifying criteria for proper basicality which will allow that some propositions self-evidently entailing that God exists could turn out to be properly basic.

[In this paper I will argue] that such propositions would seldom, if ever, be properly basic for intellectually sophisticated adult theists in our culture....

What if belief in God could be properly basic? [I contend that Plantinga] fails to prove that belief in propositions which self-evidently entail God's existence could

---

*Philip L. Quinn is John A. O'Brien Professor of Philosophy at University of Notre Dame.

ever be properly basic for anyone. But it might be true that belief in such propositions could be properly basic, even if Plantinga has not proved it. And if it were, what would be the consequences for religious epistemology? I now turn to an exploration of this issue.

Plantinga's examples of beliefs which could be properly basic in the right conditions include the following items:

(5) God is speaking to me.
(6) God disapproves of what I have done.

and

(7) God forgives me for what I have done.

And according to Plantinga the right conditions include a component which is, broadly speaking, experiential. He says:

> Upon reading the Bible, one may be impressed with a deep sense that God is speaking to him. Upon having done what I know is cheap, or wrong, or wicked I may feel guilty in God's sight and form the belief *God disapproves of what I've done*. Upon confession and repentance, I may feel forgiven, forming the belief *God forgives me for what I've done*.[2]

It strikes me that part of what makes the suggestion that beliefs like those expressed by (5)-(7) could be properly basic in conditions like those partially described in the quoted passage seem attractive is an analogy with an extremely plausible view about how certain Moorean commonsense beliefs are often justified. When I have the experience of seeming to see a hand in front of me in the right conditions, I may be justified in believing

(8) I see a hand in front of me....

... Hence the proposition expressed by (8) may be basic, and quite properly so, in the right conditions. And if this is, as I believe it to be, an attractive view about how believing the proposition expressed by (8) can be, and sometimes is, justified, then there is an argument from analogy for supposing that propositions like those expressed by (5)-(7) may also be properly basic in conditions which include an experiential component of the right sort for grounding such beliefs. To be sure, there are significant disanalogies. The direct justification of the belief expressed by (8) is grounded in a mode of sensory experience which is now generally believed by non-skeptical epistemologists to be reliable in the right conditions. By contrast, the direct justification of the beliefs expressed by (5)-(7) is grounded in a mode of experience which, though it may be reliable in the right conditions, is not now generally believed by non-skeptical epistemologists to be so. But, although such considerations might be taken to show that the analogical argument is not very strong, it does not deprive the positive analogy of heuristic and explanatory capabilities. I am going to make use of these capabilities in the remainder of the discussion....

There is another salient feature of directly justified Moorean beliefs like the one expressed by (8) which would have an analogue in the case of religious beliefs like those expressed by (5)-(7) if they could be properly basic in the right conditions. This is that the kind of justification conferred on such Moorean beliefs by direct grounding in experience of the right sort is defeasible. So, for example, a potential defeater for the proposition expressed by (8) is this:

(11) I am now hallucinating a hand.

If propositions such as (8) are taken to be properly basic in the right conditions, then a full specification of those conditions must include reference to the status of potential defeaters such as (11). What would it be reasonable to say about potential defeaters when specifying in fuller detail the right conditions for proper basicality of the proposition expressed by (8)? Several possibilities come to mind.

It might be suggested that conditions are right for the proposition expressed by (8) to be properly basic for me only if none of its potential defeaters is true. This suggestion clearly misses the mark. When I have the experience of seeming to see a hand in front of me, it may be that the proposition expressed by (8) is true and the proposition expressed by (11) is false, and yet I am justified in rejecting the former and accepting the latter because, for instance, I remember taking a large dose of some hallucinogen only an hour ago and hallucinating wildly in the interval. Merely to insist that potential defeaters be false in order for conditions to be right for proper basicality is to require much too little.

Alternatively, it might be suggested that conditions are right for the proposition expressed by (8) to be properly basic for me only if each of its potential defeaters is such that I have some reason to think it is false. Clearly this suggestion errs in the direction of demanding too much. I have never exhaustively enumerated the potential defeaters of the proposition expressed by (8), and I am inclined to doubt that I would ever complete such a task if I began it. I have certainly never mobilized or acquired a reason against each of them. No one I know has ever tried to do such a thing in defense of all of his or her Moorean commonsense beliefs. So if such beliefs frequently are properly basic in virtue of being directly grounded in sensory experience, as I think they are, conditions are often right for proper basicality without such an elaborate structure of reasons for the falsity of potential defeaters having been mobilized.

It does, however, seem initially plausible to suppose that conditions are right for the proposition expressed by (8) to be properly basic for me only if I have no sufficiently substantial reasons to think that any of its potential defeaters is true and this is not due to epistemic negligence on my part. Two features of this claim require a bit of explanation. First, if the only reason I have to think that some potential defeater of the proposition expressed by (8) is true is, for instance, that I remember once, long ago, having mistaken a tree's branches for a hand, then that will not usually suffice to undermine the *prima facie* justification the proposition expressed by (8) has in the right experiential conditions to such an extent that that proposition is not properly basic.... It takes a sufficiently substantial reason for thinking one of its potential defeaters is true to rob a proposition of proper basicality in conditions in which it would otherwise be properly basic.[3] Second, if I happen to lack sufficiently substantial reasons to think that any potential defeater of the proposition expressed by (8) is true merely because, for example, I have negligently failed to recall that I ingested some hallucinogenic substance only an hour ago and have been hallucinating wildly in the interval, then clearly conditions are not right for the proposition expressed by (8) to be properly basic for me, even though it may in fact be basic for me. More generally, a proposition is not *prima facie* justified if one negligently ignores good reasons for thinking one of its potential defeaters is true which would be sufficiently substantial to undermine the proposition's *prima facie* justification to such an extent that it would not be *prima facie* justified. Such epistemic negligence would constitute an epistemic deficiency.

Rational defeaters and belief in God. By analogy, it also seems initially plausible to say that conditions are right for the propositions expressed by (5)-(7) to be properly basic for me only if I have no sufficiently substantial reasons to think that any of their potential defeaters is true and this is not due to epistemic negligence on my part. But there is the rub. A potential defeater of the propositions expressed by (5)-(7) is this:

(12) God does not exist.

And, unfortunately, I do have very substantial reasons for thinking that the proposition expressed by (12) is true. My reasons derive mainly from one of the traditional problems of evil. What I know, partly from experience and partly from testimony, about the amount and variety of non-moral evil in the universe confirms highly for me the proposition expressed by (12). Of course, this is not indefeasible confirmation of the proposition expressed by (12). It could be defeated by other things I do not know. Perhaps it is not even undefeated confirmation. Maybe it even is defeated by other things I do know. Nevertheless, it does furnish me with a very substantial reason for thinking that the proposition expressed by (12) is true. Moreover, I dare say that many, perhaps most, intellectually sophisticated adults in our culture are in an epistemic predicament similar to mine. As I see it, an intellectually sophisticated adult in our culture would have to be epistemically negligent not to have very substantial reasons for thinking that what (12) expresses is true. After all, non-trivial atheological reasons, ranging from various problems of evil to naturalistic theories according to which theistic belief is illusory or merely projective, are a pervasive, if not obtrusive, component of the rational portion of our cultural heritage.

But, even if such reasons are very substantial, are they sufficiently substantial to make it the case that the propositions expressed by (5)-(7) would no longer be properly basic in conditions of the sort described by Plantinga in which, we are supposing, they could have been properly basic but for the presence of such substantial reasons? On reflection, I am convinced that such reasons are, taken collectively, sufficiently substantial, though I confess with regret that I cannot at present back up my intuitive conviction with solid arguments. But I conjecture that many, perhaps most, intellectually sophisticated adults in our culture will share my intuitive conviction on this point. And so I conclude that many, perhaps most, intellectually sophisticated adult theists in our culture are seldom, if ever, in conditions which are right for propositions like those expressed by (5)-(7) to be properly basic for them.

Intellectually sophisticated adults. It does not follow from this conclusion that intellectually sophisticated adult theists in our culture cannot be justified in believing propositions like those expressed by (5)-(7). For all that I have said, some such propositions are such that, for every single one of their potential defeaters which is such that there is some very substantial reason to think it is true, there is an even better reason to think it is false. And so, for all I know, some intellectually sophisticated adult theists in our culture could be, or perhaps even are, in the fortunate position, with respect to some such propositions and their potential defeaters, of having, for each potential defeater which some epistemically non-negligent, intellectually sophisticated adult in our culture has a very substantial reason to think is true, an even better reason to think it is false. But if there are such fortunate theists in our culture, they are people who have already accomplished at least one of the main tasks traditionally assigned to natural theology. Although they may know of no proof of the existence of God, they possess reasons good enough to defend some proposition which self-evidently entails the existence of God against all of its potential defeaters which epistemically non-negligent, intellectually sophisticated adults in our culture have very substantial reasons to believe. I tend to doubt that many intellectually sophisticated adult theists in our culture are in this fortunate position for any appreciable portion of their lives....

... Consider again our hypothetical fortunate person who has reasons good enough to defend theistic belief against all of its potential defeaters which epistemically non-negligent, intellectually sophisticated adults in our culture have very substantial reasons to believe. I would say that, for such a person, theistic belief would be based, in a broad sense, on all the reasons which are parts of the person's total case for the rationality of theistic belief. In employing this broad conception of the basing relation, I am aiming to draw attention to the fact that, if the person did not have all those reasons and were like many, perhaps most, intellectually sophisticated adults in our culture, theistic belief would not be rational for the person, or at least its rationality would be diminished to an appreciable extent if some of those reasons were absent. On this broad conception of the basing relation, I would not need to revise the principle concerning the right conditions for certain propositions to be, in the broad sense, properly basic for me, to which I had ascribed initial plausibility, in order to accommodate the hypothetical fortunate person, for the fortunate person's theistic belief would be, in the broad sense, properly based on all the reasons which comprise his or her total case for the rationality of theistic belief. Reasons which are, in the broad sense, part of a basis for theistic belief need not be related to a proposition which self-evidently entails the existence of God in the same way that the premises of an inference are related to its conclusion.... [T]hey may provide part of a basis for theistic belief in much the same way Richard Swinburne's argument in *The Coherence of Theism* that the claim that God exists is not demonstrably incoherent provides part of the basis for Swinburne's claim in *The Existence of God* that God's existence is more probable than not. And if I am right about the epistemic predicament of many, perhaps most, intellectually sophisticated adult theists in our culture, for them theistic belief stands in need of at least some basis of this kind if it is to be rational. This may, in the end, be a point on which Plantinga and I have a disagreement which is not merely verbal. I would insist, and Plantinga, for all I know, might not, that many, perhaps most, intellectually sophisticated adult theists in our culture must, if their belief in God is to be rational, have a total case for the rationality of theistic belief which includes defenses against defeaters which have very substantial support.

Notes

1. Alvin Plantinga, "Is Belief in God Properly Basic?", *Nous* 15 (1981). Additional discussion related to the charge that modern foundationalism is self-referentially incoherent may be found in Alvin Plantinga, "Is Belief in God Rational?", *Rationality and Religious Belief*, ed. C.F. Delaney (Notre Dame: University of Notre Dame Press, 1979).... [S]ome of the same themes are further amplified in Alvin Plantinga, "Reason and Belief in God," *Faith and Rationality*, ed. Alvin Plantinga and Nicholas Wolterstorff (Notre Dame: University of Notre Dame Press, 1983).
2. *Ibid.*, p. 46.
3. I came to appreciate this point as a result of reflecting on comments by Jonathan Malino and William P. Alston.

Discussion

1. Do you agree with Quinn about the epistemic predicament of most intellectually sophisticated adult theists in our culture? Why or why not?
2. If intellectually sophisticated adult theists are in the predicament that Quinn describes, does it follow that belief in God cannot be properly basic for such persons? Why or why not?
3. What would a religious believer need to do, according to Quinn, to get out of their predicament? Do you think this is possible?

Reason and Belief in God

Suggestions for Further Study

Clark, Kelly James. *Philosophers Who Believe*. Downers Grove, IL: InterVarsity Press, 1993.

Clark, Kelly James. *Return to Reason*. Grand Rapids, MI: Eerdmans Publishing Company, 1991.

Evans, C. Stephen. *Faith Beyond Reason*. Grand Rapids, MI: Eerdmans Publishing Company, 1998.

Helm, Paul. *Faith and Understanding*. Grand Rapids, MI: Eerdmans Publishing Company, 1997.

Kenny, Anthony. *What is Faith?* Oxford: Oxford University Press, 1992.

Mavrodes, George. *Belief in God*. New York: Random House, 1970.

Morris, Thomas. *Making Sense of It All: Pascal and the Meaning of Life*. Grand Rapids, MI: Eerdmans Publishing Company, 1992.

Penelhum, Terence, ed. *Faith*. New York: Macmillan, 1989.

Penelhum, Terence. *Reason and Religious Faith*. Boulder, CO: Westview Press, 1995.

Phillips, D. Z. *Faith After Foundationalism*. London: Routledge, 1988.

Plantinga, Alvin and Nicholas Wolterstorff. *Faith and Rationality*. Notre Dame: University of Notre Dame Press, 1983.

Sessions, William Lad. *The Concept of Faith: A Philosophical Investigation*. Ithaca: Cornell University Press, 1994.

Swinburne, Richard. *Faith and Reason*. Oxford: Oxford University Press, 1981.

Wainwright, William. *Reasons and the Heart: A Prolegomenon to a Critique of Passional Reasons*. Ithaca: Cornell University Press, 1995.

Part Three

God and Human Suffering

≈≈≥

The Problem of Evil

Introduction. The mournful cry "Why God?" is as ancient as belief in God itself. Human suffering, without the consolation of divine clarification, is its own source of spiritual suffering. God, when most needed, seems angry, vindictive, hidden, wicked or even non-existent. And these accusations have come from believers! (See, for example, the book of Job.) Little wonder that evil has been taken by agnostics and atheists as evidence against the existence of God.

The problem of evil is often raised against the backdrop of two classes of evil: natural and moral. Natural evils arise solely from nature: earthquakes, pestilence, famine, drought, flooding, mudslides and hurricanes (to mention just a few). Moral evils are due to the free choices of human beings and include, for example, war, poverty and racism.

The basic argument from evil draws consequences from attributes of God and conjoins them with the simple fact of evil (either moral or natural):

1. God is omnipotent and wholly good.
2. If God is omnipotent, he can eliminate evil.
3. If God is wholly good, he would want to eliminate evil.
4. There is evil.
5. Therefore, God does not exist.

As stated, the argument leaves a little to be desired. First, it should include reference to omniscience—God might be willing and able to eliminate evil but not know how to eliminate evil. Second, even if it is a good argument it does not disprove the existence of God; at best it demonstrates that God is either not omnipotent, wholly good or omniscient. By rejecting any one of these divine attributes, God's existence might be maintained. But who would wish to worship a perverse bully or a well-intentioned wimp? Denying any of the three attributes—omniscience, omnipotence, perfect goodness—seems to denigrate divinity.

In his *Dialogues Concerning Natural Religion*, Hume's interlocutors discuss the evidence for and against God's existence. In this selection the problem of evil is raised: "Is he willing to prevent evil, but not able? then is he impotent. Is he able, but not willing? then is he malevolent. Is he both able and willing? whence then is evil?" The import of Hume's challenge is not clear. Perhaps he intends to show that given the fact of evil, God cannot exist. However, this discussion occurs within a book that discusses the argument from design which seeks the limits of what can be known about God from nature. Hume might be arguing that God is not good in any sense analogous to human goodness. Given God's sure and certain power and wisdom but also all of the immense human infelicity, God's goodness cannot be at all like human goodness. Some find refuge in this sort of mystery; however, God's moral attributes (more than God's power, surely) are central to his divinity. To call God good, if Hume is right, is tantamount to calling God "fobbertival" or any other nonsense term.

Theodicy. Are there ways of justifying belief in God's existence in the face of evil? A theodicy is just such an attempt to justify God given the facts of evil. God, after all, may very well be omnipotent, omniscient and wholly good yet have a perfectly good reason (or two) for allowing evil. The most important suggestion of God's reason for allowing evil dates to Augustine—the free will theodicy. The free will defense has been recently rejuvenated by Alvin Plantinga with all of the resources of recent developments in logic.[1] The free will defense assumes that human beings are *free* in the sense that their actions are *uncaused*—no antecedent state of affairs can cause or coerce free actions. A "caused free action" is a contradiction in terms, no more possible than a square circle. If it is not possible for there to be caused free actions, then it is not possible for God to cause free actions.[2] If God cannot cause free actions, that is if significantly free human actions are up to us, then God cannot prevent free human choices even if those choices are for evil. God may be able to prevent us from making evil choices, but not without violating our free will. If God values free will, then the evil that free will unleashes might be justified.

John Hick's soul-making theodicy unites the free-will explanation of moral evil with a view of human nature as less than perfect. On the traditional, Augustinian view of human nature, humans were created perfect (but with free will) and placed in paradise. How, given these circumstances, humans could possibly fail is surely a mystery (or a contradiction). If human beings are less than perfect, however, and are not placed in paradise then human failure seems almost inevitable. What could justify God's putting people a lot like us in harm's way? According to Hick, facing real dangers and challenges is the only way that God could accomplish the goal that he set for human beings—to (freely) become children of God. Hick's "soul-making theodicy" explains how natural evils assist in the development of such virtues as courage, patience and generosity. Evil is justified because it is necessary for immature, incomplete people to become heirs of eternal life.

Appealing to distinctly religious (even Christian) goods, Marilyn McCord Adams focuses on the troubling "horrendous evils"—evils such that, if one suffered them, one would have good reason to doubt that one's life was a great good on the whole. Adams outlines the deficiencies of classical theodicies for explaining horrendous evils. Her own solution appeals to a more adequate conception of divine goodness—God is good to created persons. Adams believes we are incapable of understanding—because of the vast intellectual distance between humans and God—God's reasons why people suffer horrendously. Nonetheless, she believes that God has shown us three ways that he can defeat horrendous evil within the context of the sufferer's life: by identifying with Christ, divine gratitude, or vision into the inner life of God. By appealing to distinctively Christian beliefs, Adams contends that she can show that God and evil—even horrendous evil—are not incompatible.

The evidential problem of evil. The focus of discussion of the problem of evil has shifted in the past twenty years. Virtually everyone, atheist and theist alike, concedes that Plantinga has demonstrated that God and evil are not logically incompatible. Nonetheless some philosophers contend that there is simply too much evil, or that some evil is too horrific, for God to exist or for a person to reasonably believe that God exists.

William Rowe contends that the fact that there is some evil, apparently pointless evil, gives us reason to believe that God does not exist. Rowe does not believe that he has disproved God's existence but he does believe that he has given good reasons for believing that God does not exist. His argument may be stated, roughly, as follows:

1. If there is a God, there would be no pointless evil.
2. We have reason to believe that there is pointless evil.
3. Therefore, we have reason to believe that God does not exist.

Suppose we grant the truth of the first premise, how could Rowe demonstrate the truth of the second premise? He does so by offering the example of a fawn who suffers serious burns and dies days later. Because we can see no point to the fawn's suffering, Rowe contends that we have reason to believe that there is no point to the fawn's suffering. And if the fawn's suffering is indeed pointless then he has established the second premise of his argument. And from (1) and (2) it surely follows that it is unreasonable to believe that God exists.

Rowe's famous essay elicited a flurry of responses; Daniel Howard-Snyder brings together some of the most important of them. Howard-Snyder carefully outlines Rowe's argument, showing Rowe's explicit inferences as well as his hidden assumptions. The crucial assumption involves what have been called "Noseeum Inferences." One makes a Noseeum Inference when one assumes that because one can't see something, it isn't there. Rowe makes such inferences when he argues that because we can't see the point to some suffering, it is reasonable to believe that there is no point to that suffering. Howard-Snyder takes Rowe to task, contending that, at least with respect to certain areas of human inquiry, Noseeum Inference are not valid. This is certainly true, Howard-Snyder contends, with respect to God. With our puny cognitive abilities we simply should not expect to see certain kinds of reasons even if they exist.

No doubt Rowe and other non-theists are at this very moment dreaming up powerful responses to the likes of Plantinga, Hick, Adams and Howard-Snyder. The lively debate over God and evil is not likely to end soon.

Notes

1. Alvin Plantinga, *God, Freedom and Evil* (Grand Rapids, MI: Eerdmans Publishing Company, 1977). Plantinga distinguishes between a "defense" and a "theodicy." A theodicy must offer plausible, indeed true reasons that God might have for allowing evil. A defense is simply an attempt to demonstrate the logical consistency of God and evil and, as such, need not restrict itself to consideration of plausible or true explanations.
2. I am assuming that God cannot do the logically impossible.

Chapter 11

~~~~~

The Problem Stated

God and Evil
*David Hume**

Philo: On the contrary, it is here chiefly, cried Philo, that the uniform and equal maxims of Nature are most apparent. Man, it is true, can, by combination, surmount all his real enemies, and become master of the whole animal creation.... This very society, by which we surmount those wild beasts, our natural enemies; what new enemies does it not raise to us? What woe and misery does it not occasion? Man is the greatest enemy of man. Oppression, injustice, contempt, contumely, violence, sedition, war, calumny, treachery, fraud; by these they mutually torment each other; and they would soon dissolve that society which they had formed, were it not for the dread of still greater ills, which must attend their separation.

Demea: But though these external insults, said Demea, from animals, from men, from all the elements, which assault us, form a frightful catalogue of woes, they are nothing in comparison of those which arise within ourselves, from the distempered condition of our mind and body. How many lie under the lingering torment of diseases? Hear the pathetic enumeration of the great poet.

Intestine stone and ulcer, colic-pangs,
Demoniac frenzy, moping melancholy,
And moon-struck madness, pining atrophy,
Marasmus, and wide-wasting pestilence.
Dire was the tossing, deep the groans: *despair*
Tended the sick, busiest from couch to couch.
And over them triumphant *death* his dart
Shook: but delay'd to strike, though oft invok'd
With vows, as their chief good and final hope. [Milton, *Paradise Lost*]

---

*David Hume (1711-1776) was a Scottish philosopher best known for his skeptical views.

The disorders of the mind, continued Demea, though more secret, are not perhaps less dismal and vexatious. Remorse, shame, anguish, rage, disappointment, anxiety, fear, dejection, despair; who has ever passed through life without cruel inroads from these tormentors? How many have scarcely ever felt any better sensations? Labour and poverty, so abhorred by every one, are the certain lot of the far greater number; and those few privileged persons, who enjoy ease and opulence, never reach contentment or true felicity. All the goods of life united would not make a very happy man; but all the ills united would make a wretch indeed; and any one of them almost (and who can be free from every one?) nay often the absence of one good (and who can possess all?) is sufficient to render life ineligible....

Philo: And is it possible ... said Philo, that after all these reflections, and infinitely more, which might be suggested, you can still persevere in your Anthropomorphism, and assert the moral attributes of the Deity, his justice, benevolence, mercy, and rectitude, to be of the same nature with these virtues in human creatures? His power we allow is infinite: whatever he wills is executed: but neither man nor any other animal is happy: therefore he does not will their happiness. His wisdom is infinite: He is never mistaken in choosing the means to any end: But the course of Nature tends not to human or animal felicity: therefore it is not established for that purpose. Through the whole compass of human knowledge, there are no inferences more certain and infallible than these. In what respect, then, do his benevolence and mercy resemble the benevolence and mercy of men?

Epicurus's old questions are yet unanswered.

Is he willing to prevent evil, but not able? then is he impotent. Is he able, but not willing? then is he malevolent. Is he both able and willing? whence then is evil?

Discussion

1. What are the different kinds of evils that Philo and Demea speak of? Are any of these easier to reconcile with God's goodness and power than any others?
2. If you don't know what anthropomorphism means, look it up in a dictionary. Is anthropomorphism, when applied to God, good or bad? Defend your answer.
3. What conclusion do you think Hume is drawing here? Support your position.

Chapter 12

Theodicy

The Soul-Making Theodicy
John Hick *

The Augustinian legacy. Within the Augustinian tradition, which has dominated the thought of Western Christendom since the fifth century, the doctrine of a fearful and calamitous fall of man long ago in the "dark backward and abysm of time," and of a subsequent participation by all men in the deadly entail of sin, is, as we have seen, deeply entrenched. According to this conception in its developed form, man was created finitely perfect, but in his freedom he rebelled against God and has existed ever since under the righteous wrath and just condemnation of his Maker. For the descendants of Adam and Eve stand in a corporate unity and continuity of life with the primal pair and have inherited both their guilt and a corrupted and sin-prone nature. We are accordingly born as sinners, and endowed with a nature that is bound to lead us daily into further sin; and it is only by God's free, and to us incomprehensible, grace that some (but not all) are eventually to be saved.

It is helpful to distinguish two separable elements within this tradition: namely, the assertion of an inherited *sinfulness* or tendency to sin, and the assertion of a universal human *guilt* in respect of Adam's crime, falling upon us on account of a physical or mystical presence of the whole race in its first forefather. As we shall see, the former idea is common to all Christian traditions—whether in the form of a physiologically or of a socially transmitted moral distortion—whilst the latter idea is peculiar to Augustinian and Calvinist theology.

The Augustinian picture is so familiar that it is commonly thought of as *the* Christian view of man and his sinful plight. Nevertheless it is only *a* Christian view....

The Irenaean tradition. Fortunately there is another and better way. As well as the "majority report" of the Augustinian tradition, which has dominated Western

---

*John Hick is Emeritus Professor of Philosophy at Claremont Graduate School and University of Birmingham.

Christendom, both Catholic and Protestant, since the time of Augustine himself, there is the "minority report" of the Irenaean tradition. This latter is both older and newer than the other, for it goes back to St. Irenaeus and others of the early Hellenistic Fathers of the Church in the two centuries prior to St. Augustine, and it has flourished again in more developed forms during the last hundred years.

Instead of regarding man as having been created by God in a finished state, as a finitely perfect being fulfilling the divine intention for our human level of existence, and then falling disastrously away from this, the minority report sees man as still in process of creation. Irenaeus himself expressed the point in terms of the (exegetically dubious) distinction between the "image" and the "likeness" of God referred to in Genesis i. 26: "Then God said, Let us make man in our image, after our likeness." His view was that man as a personal and moral being already exists in the image, but has not yet been formed into the finite likeness of God. By this "likeness" Irenaeus means something more than personal existence as such; he means a certain valuable quality of personal life which reflects finitely the divine life. This represents the perfecting of man, the fulfillment of God's purpose for humanity, the "bringing of many sons to glory" the creating of "children of God" who are "fellow heirs with Christ" of his glory.

And so man, created as a personal being in the image of God, is only the raw material for a further and more difficult stage of God's creative work. This is the leading of men as relatively free and autonomous persons, through their own dealings with life in the world in which He has placed them, towards that quality of personal existence that is the finite likeness of God. The features of this likeness are revealed in the person of Christ, and the process of man's creation into it is the work of the Holy Spirit. In St. Paul's words, "And we all, with unveiled faces, beholding the glory of the Lord, are being changed into his likeness ... from one degree of glory to another; for this comes from the Lord who is the Spirit"; or again, "For God knew his own before ever they were, and also ordained that they should be shaped to the likeness ... of his Son." In Johannine terms, the movement from the image to the likeness is a transition from one level of existence, that of animal life (*Bios*), to another and higher level, that of eternal life (*Zoe*), which includes but transcends the first. And the fall of man was seen by Irenaeus as a failure within the second phase of this creative process, a failure that has multiplied the perils and complicated the route of the journey in which God is seeking to lead mankind.

In the light of modern anthropological knowledge some form of two-stage conception of the creation of man has become an almost unavoidable Christian tenet. At the very least we must acknowledge as two distinguishable stages the fashioning of *homo sapiens* as a product of the long evolutionary process, and his sudden or gradual spiritualization as a child of God. But we may well extend the first stage to include the development of man as a rational and responsible person capable of personal relationship with the personal Infinite who has created him. This first stage of the creative process was, to our anthropomorphic imaginations, easy for divine omnipotence. By an exercise of creative power God caused the physical universe to exist, and in the course of countless ages to bring forth within it organic life, and finally to produce out of organic life personal life; and when man had thus emerged out of the evolution of the forms of organic life, a creature had been made who has the possibility of existing in conscious fellowship with God. But the second stage of the creative process is of a different kind altogether. It cannot be performed by omnipotent power as such. For personal life is essentially free and self-directing. It cannot be perfected by divine fiat, but only through the uncompelled responses and willing cooperation of human individuals in their actions and reactions in the world in which God has placed them. Men may eventually become the perfected persons whom the New Testament calls "children of God," but they cannot be created ready-made as this.

The value-judgement that is implicitly being invoked here is that one who has attained to goodness by meeting and eventually mastering temptations, and thus by rightly making responsible choices in concrete situations, is good in a richer and more valuable sense than would be one created *ab initio* in a state either of innocence or of virtue. In the former case, which is that of the actual moral achievements of mankind, the individual's goodness has within it the strength of temptations overcome, a stability based upon an accumulation of right choices, and a positive and responsible character that comes from the investment of costly personal effort. I suggest, then, that it is an ethically reasonable judgement, even though in the nature of the case not one that is capable of demonstrative proof, that human goodness slowly built up through personal histories of moral effort has a value in the eyes of the Creator which justifies even the long travail of the soul-making process.

The picture with which we are working is thus developmental and teleological. Man is in process of becoming the perfected being whom God is seeking to create. However, this is not taking place—it is important to add—by a natural and inevitable evolution, but through a hazardous adventure in individual freedom. Because this is a pilgrimage within the life of each individual, rather than a racial evolution, the progressive fulfillment of God's purpose does not entail any corresponding progressive improvement in the moral state of the world. There is no doubt a development in man's ethical situation from generation to generation through the building of individual choices into public institutions, but this involves an accumulation of evil as well as of good. It is thus probable that human life was lived on much the same moral plane two thousand years ago or four thousand years ago as it is today. But nevertheless during this period uncounted millions of souls have been through the experience of earthly life, and God's purpose has gradually moved towards its fulfillment within each one of them, rather than within a human aggregate composed of different units in different generations.

The soul-making theodicy. If, then, God's aim in making the world is "the bringing of many sons to glory," that aim will naturally determine the kind of world that He has created. Antitheistic writers almost invariably assume a conception of the divine purpose which is contrary to the Christian conception. They assume that the purpose of a loving God must be to create a hedonistic paradise; and therefore to the extent that the world is other than this, it proves to them that God is either not loving enough or not powerful enough to create such a world. They think of God's relation to the earth on the model of a human being building a cage for a pet animal to dwell in. If he is humane he will naturally make his pet's quarters as pleasant and healthful as he can. Any respect in which the cage falls short of the veterinarian's ideal, and contains possibilities of accident or disease, is evidence of either limited benevolence or limited means, or both. Those who use the problem of evil as an argument against belief in God almost invariably think of the world in this kind of way. David Hume, for example, speaks of an architect who is trying to plan a house that is to be as comfortable and convenient as possible. If we find that "the windows, doors, fires, passages, stairs, and the whole economy of the building were the source of noise, confusion, fatigue, darkness, and the extremes of heat and cold" we should have no hesitation in blaming the architect. It would be in vain for him to prove that if this or that defect were corrected greater ills would result: "still you would assert in general, that, if the architect had had skill and good intentions, he might have formed such a plan of the whole, and might have adjusted the parts in such a manner, as would have remedied all or most of these inconveniences."

But if we are right in supposing that God's purpose for man is to lead him from human *Bios*, or the biological life of man, to that quality of *Zoe*, or the personal life of eternal worth, which we see in Christ, then the question that we have to ask is not, Is this the kind of world that an all-powerful and infinitely loving being would create as an environment for his human pets? or, Is the architecture of the world the most pleasant and convenient possible? The question that we have to ask is rather, Is this the kind of world that God might make as an environment in which moral beings may be fashioned, through their own free insights and responses, into "children of God"?

Such critics as Hume are confusing what heaven ought to be, as an environment for perfected finite beings, with what this world ought to be, as an environment for beings who are in process of becoming perfected. For if our general conception of God's purpose is correct the world is not intended to be a paradise, but rather the scene of a history in which human personality may be formed towards the pattern of Christ. Men are not to be thought of on the analogy of animal pets, whose life is to be made as agreeable as possible, but rather on the analogy of human children, who are to grow to adulthood in an environment whose primary and overriding purpose is not immediate pleasure but the realizing of the most valuable potentialities of human personality.

Needless to say, this characterization of God as the heavenly Father is not a merely random illustration but an analogy that lies at the heart of the Christian faith. Jesus treated the likeness between the attitude of God to man, and the attitude of human parents at their best towards their children, as providing the most adequate way for us to think about God. And so it is altogether relevant to a Christian understanding of this world to ask, How does the best parental love express itself in its influence upon the environment in which children are to grow up? I think it is clear that a parent who loves his children, and wants them to become the best human beings that they are capable of becoming, does not treat pleasure as the sole and supreme value. Certainly we seek pleasure for our children, and take great delight in obtaining it for them; but we do not desire for them unalloyed pleasure at the expense of their growth in such even greater values as moral integrity, unselfishness, compassion, courage, humour, reverence for the truth, and perhaps above all the capacity for love. We do not act on the premise that pleasure is the supreme end of life; and if the development of these other values sometimes clashes with the provision of pleasure, then we are willing to have our children miss a certain amount of this, rather than fail to come to possess and to be possessed by the finer and more precious qualities that are possible to the human personality. A child brought up on the principle that the only or the supreme value is pleasure would not be likely to become an ethically mature adult or an attractive or happy personality. And to most parents it seems more important to try to foster quality and strength of character in their children than to fill their lives at all times with the utmost possible degree of pleasure. If, then, there is any true analogy between God's purpose for his human creatures, and the purpose of loving and wise parents for their children, we have to recognize that the presence of pleasure and the absence of pain cannot be the supreme and overriding end for which the world exists. Rather, this world must be a place of soul-making. And its value is to be judged, not primarily by the quantity of pleasure and pain occurring in it at any particular moment, but by its fitness for its primary purpose, the purpose of soul-making.[1]...

Conclusion. This, then, is the starting-point from which we propose to try to relate the realities of sin and suffering to the perfect love of an omnipotent Creator. And as will become increasingly apparent, a theodicy that starts in this way must be eschatological in its ultimate bearings. That *is* to say, instead of looking to the past for its clue to the mystery of evil, it looks to the future, and indeed to that ultimate future to which only faith can look. Given the conception of a divine intention working in and through human time towards a fulfillment that lies in its completeness beyond human time, our theodicy must find the meaning of evil in the part that it is made to play in the eventual outworking of that purpose; and must find the justification of the whole process in the magnitude of the good to which it leads. The good that outshines all ill is not a paradise long since lost but a kingdom which is yet to come in its full glory and permanence.

Notes

1. The phrase "the vale of Soul-making" was coined by the poet John Keats in a letter written to his brother and sister in April 1819. He says, "The common

cognomen of this world among the misguided and superstitious is "a vale of tears" from which we are to be redeemed by a certain arbitrary interposition of God and taken to Heaven—What a little circumscribed straightened notion! Call the world if you Please 'The vale of Soul-making.'" In this letter he sketches a teleological theodicy. "Do you not see," he asks "how necessary a World of Pains and troubles is to school an Intelligence and make it a Soul?" (*The Letters of John Keats*, ed. by M. B. Forman. London: Oxford University Press, 4th ed., 1952, pp. 334-5.)

Discussion

1. Is the end of soul-making a great enough good to explain all of human suffering?
2. Can you think of evils which are so horrific that they couldn't possibly contribute to soul-making? How do you think Hick might explain these?
3. Could we become virtuous without facing real dangers? Show why this is or is not the case.

Horrendous Evils and the Goodness of God
Marilyn McCord Adams*

Introduction. Over the past thirty years, analytic philosophers of religion have defined "the problem of evil" in terms of the *prima facie* difficulty in consistently maintaining

(1) God exists, and is omnipotent, omniscient, and perfectly good.

And

(2) Evil exists.

In a crisp and classic article, "Evil and Omnipotence,"[1] J. L. Mackie emphasized that the problem is not that (1) and (2) are logically inconsistent by themselves, but that they together with quasi-logical rules formulating attribute-analyses—such as

(P1) A perfectly good being would always eliminate evil so far as it could,

and

(P2) There are no limits to what an omnipotent being can do—

constitute an inconsistent premiss-set....

In debates about whether the argument from evil can establish the irrationality of religious belief, care must be taken, both by the atheologians who deploy it and the believers who defend against it, to insure that the operative attribute-analyses accurately reflect that religion's understanding of Divine power and goodness. It does the atheologian no good to argue for the falsity of Christianity on the ground that the existence of an omnipotent, omniscient, pleasure-maximizer is incompossible with a world such as ours, because Christians never believed God was a pleasure-maximizer anyway....

The moral ... might be summarized thus: where the internal coherence of a system of religious beliefs is at stake, successful arguments for its inconsistency must draw on premises (explicitly or implicitly) internal to that system or obviously acceptable to its adherents; likewise for successful rebuttals or explanations of consistency. The thrust of my argument is to push both sides of the debate towards more detailed attention to and subtle understanding of the religious system in question.

---

*Marilyn McCord Adams is Professor of Medieval Theology at Yale University.

As a Christian philosopher, I want to focus in this paper on the problem for the truth of Christianity raised by what I shall call "horrendous" evils. Although our world is riddled with them, the Biblical record punctuated by them, and one of them—viz., the passion of Christ, according to Christian belief, the judicial murder of God by the people of God—is memorialized by the Church on its most solemn holiday (Good Friday) and in its central sacrament (the Eucharist), the problem of horrendous evils is largely skirted by standard treatments for the good reason that they are intractable by them. After showing why, I will draw on other Christian materials to sketch ways of meeting this, the deepest of religious problems.

Defining the category. For present purposes, I define "horrendous evils" as "evils the participation in (the doing or suffering of) which gives one reason *prima facie* to doubt whether one's life could (given their inclusion in it) be a great good to one on the whole." Such reasonable doubt arises because it is so difficult humanly to conceive how such evils could be overcome.... [H]orrendous evils seem *prima facie*, not only to balance off but to engulf the positive value of a participant's life. Nevertheless, that very horrendous proportion, by which they threaten to rob a person's life of positive meaning, cries out not only to be engulfed, but to be made meaningful through positive and decisive defeat.

I understand this criterion to be objective, but relative to individuals. The example of habitual complainers, who know how to make the worst of a good situation, shows individuals not to be incorrigible experts on what ills would defeat the positive value of their lives. Nevertheless, nature and experience endow people with different strengths; one bears easily what crushes another. And a major consideration in determining whether an individual's life is/has been a great good to him/her on the whole, is invariably and appropriately how it has seemed to him/her.

I offer the following list of paradigmatic horrors: the rape of a woman and axing off of her arms, psychophysical torture whose ultimate goal is the disintegration of personality, betrayal of one's deepest loyalties, cannibalizing one's own offspring, child abuse of the sort described by Ivan Karamazov, child pornography, parental incest, slow death by starvation, participation in the Nazi death camps, the explosion of nuclear bombs over populated areas, having to choose which of one's children shall live and which be executed by terrorists, being the accidental and/or unwitting agent of the disfigurement or death of those one loves best. I regard these as *paradigmatic* because I believe most people would find in the doing or suffering of them *prima facie* reason to doubt the positive meaning of their lives.[2]...

For better or worse, the by-now-standard strategies for "solving" the problem of evil are powerless in the face of horrendous evils.

Seeking the reason-why. In his model article "Hume on Evil,"[3] Pike takes up Mackie's challenge, arguing that (Pl) fails to reflect ordinary moral intuitions (more to the point, I would add, Christian beliefs), and traces the abiding sense of trouble to the hunch that an omnipotent, omniscient being could have no reason compatible with perfect goodness for permitting (bringing about) evils, because all legitimate excuses arise from ignorance or weakness. Solutions to the problem of evil have thus been sought in the form of counter-examples to this latter claim, i.e., logically possible reasons why that would excuse even an omnipotent, omniscient God! The putative logically possible reasons offered have tended to be *generic* and *global*: generic insofar as some *general* reason is sought to cover all sorts of evils; global insofar as they seize upon some feature of the world as a whole. For example, philosophers have alleged that the desire to make a world with one of the following properties—"the best of all possible worlds," "a world a more perfect than which is impossible," "a world exhibiting a perfect balance of retributive justice,"[4] "a world with as favorable a balance of (created) moral good over moral evil as God can weakly actualize"—would constitute a reason compatible with perfect goodness for God's creating a world with evils in the amounts and of the kinds found in the actual world. Moreover, such general reasons are presented as so powerful as to do away with any need to catalogue types of evils one by one, and examine God's reason for permitting each in particular. Plantinga explicitly hopes that the problem of horrendous evils can thus be solved without being squarely confronted.[5]

The insufficiency of global defeat. A pair of distinctions is in order here: (i) between two dimensions of divine goodness in relation to creation—viz., "producer of global goods" and "goodness to" or "love of individual created persons"; and (ii) between the overbalance/defeat of evil by good on the global scale, and the overbalance/defeat of evil by good within the context of an individual person's life. Correspondingly, we may separate two problems of evil parallel to the two sorts of goodness mentioned in (i).

In effect, generic and global approaches are directed to the first problem: they defend divine goodness along the first (global) dimension by suggesting logically possible strategies for the global defeat of evils. But establishing God's excellence as a producer of global goods does not automatically solve the second problem, especially in a world containing horrendous evils. For God cannot be said to be good or loving to any created persons the positive meaning of whose lives He allows to be engulfed in and/or defeated by evils—that is, individuals within whose lives horrendous evils remain undefeated. Yet, the only way unsupplemented global and generic approaches could have to explain the latter, would be by applying their general reasons-why to particular cases of horrendous suffering.

Unfortunately, such an exercise fails to give satisfaction. Suppose for the sake of argument that horrendous evil could be included in maximally perfect world orders; its being partially constitutive of such an order would assign it that generic and global positive meaning. But would knowledge of such a fact, defeat for a mother the *prima facie* reason provided by her cannibalism of her own infant to wish that she had never been born? Again, the aim of perfect retributive balance confers meaning on evils imposed. But would knowledge that the torturer was being tortured give the victim who broke down and turned traitor under pressure any more reason to think his/her life worthwhile? Would it not merely multiply reasons for the torturer to doubt that his/her life could turn out to be a good to him/her on the whole? Could the truck-driver who accidentally runs over his beloved child find consolation in the idea that this middle-known[6] but unintended side-effect was part of the price God accepted for a world with the best balance of moral good over moral evil He could get?

Not only does the application to horrors of such generic and global reasons for divine permission of evils fail to solve the second problem of evil; it makes it worse by adding generic *prima facie* reasons to doubt whether human life would be a great good to individual human beings in possible worlds where such divine motives were operative. For, taken in isolation and made to bear the weight of the whole explanation, such reasons-why draw a picture of divine indifference or even hostility to the human plight. Would the fact that God permitted horrors because they were constitutive means to His end of global perfection, or that He tolerated them because He could obtain that global end anyway, make the participant's life more tolerable, more worth living for him/her? Given radical human vulnerability to horrendous evils, the ease with which humans participate in them, whether as victim or perpetrator, would not the thought that God visits horrors on anyone who caused them, simply because he/she deserves it, provide one more reason to expect human life to be a nightmare?

Those willing to split the two problems of evil apart might adopt a divide-and-conquer strategy, by simply denying divine goodness along the second dimension. For example, many Christians do not believe that God will insure an overwhelmingly good life to each and every person He creates. Some say the decisive defeat of evil with good is promised only within the lives of the obedient, who enter by the narrow gate. Some speculate that the elect may be few. Many recognize that the sufferings of this present life are as nothing compared to the hell of eternal torment, designed to defeat goodness with horrors within the lives of the damned.

Such a road can be consistently travelled only at the heavy toll of admitting that human life in worlds such as ours is a bad bet. Imagine (adapting Rawls' device) persons in a pre-original position, considering possible worlds containing managers of differing power, wisdom, and character, and subjects of varying fates. The question they are to answer about each world is whether they would willingly enter it as a human being, from behind a veil of ignorance as to which position they would occupy. Reason would, I submit, dictate a negative verdict for worlds whose omniscient and omnipotent manager permits *ante-mortem* horrors that remain undefeated within the context of the human participant's life; *a fortiori*, for worlds in which some or most humans suffer eternal torment....

The how of God's victory. Up to now, my discussion has given the reader cause to wonder whose side I am on anyway? For I have insisted, with rebels like Ivan

Karamazov and John Stuart Mill, on spot-lighting the problem horrendous evils pose. Yet, I have signalled my preference for a vision of Christianity that insists on both dimensions of Divine goodness, and maintains not only (a) that God will be good enough to created persons to make human life a good bet, but also (b) that each created person will have a life that is a great good to him/her on the whole. My critique of standard approaches to the problem of evil thus seems to reinforce atheologian Mackie's verdict of "positive irrationality" for such a religious position.

Whys versus hows. The inaccessibility of reasons-why seems especially decisive.[7] For surely an all-wise and all-powerful God, who loved each created person enough (a) to defeat any experienced horrors within the context of the participant's life, and (b) to give each created person a life that is a great good to him/her on the whole, would not permit such persons to suffer horrors for no reason. Does not our inability even to conceive of plausible candidate reasons suffice to make belief in such a God positively irrational in a world containing horrors? In my judgment, it does not.

To be sure, motivating reasons come in several varieties relative to our conceptual grasp: There are (i) reasons of the sort we can readily understand when we are informed of them (e.g., the mother who permits her child to undergo painful heart surgery because it is the only humanly possible way to save its life). Moreover, there are (ii) reasons we would be cognitively, emotionally, and spiritually equipped to grasp if only we had a larger memory or wider attention span (analogy: I may be able to memorize small town street plans; memorizing the road networks of the entire country is a task requiring more of the same, in the way that proving Gödel's theorem is not). Some generic and global approaches insinuate that Divine permission of evils has motivating reasons of this sort. Finally, (iii) there are reasons that we are cognitively, emotionally, and/or spiritually too immature to fathom (the way a two-year old child is incapable of understanding its mother's reasons for permitting the surgery). I agree with Plantinga that our ignorance of Divine reasons for permitting horrendous evils is not of types (i) or (ii), but of type (iii).

Nevertheless, if there are varieties of ignorance, there are also varieties of reassurance. The two-year old heart patient is convinced of its mother's love, not by her cognitively inaccessible reasons, but by her intimate care and presence through its painful experience. The story of Job suggests something similar is true with human participation in horrendous suffering. God does not give Job His reasons-why, and implies that Job isn't smart enough to grasp them; rather Job is lectured on the extent of divine power, and sees God's goodness face to face! Likewise, I suggest, to exhibit the logical compossibility of both dimensions of divine goodness with horrendous suffering, it is not necessary to find logically possible reasons *why* God might permit them. It is enough to show *how* God can be good enough to created persons despite their participation in horrors—by defeating them within the context of the individual's life and by giving that individual a life that is a great good to him/her on the whole.

What sort of valuables? In my opinion, the reasonableness of Christianity can be maintained in the face of horrendous evils only by drawing on resources of religious value theory. For one way for God to be *good to* created persons is by relating them appropriately to relevant and great goods. But philosophical and religious theories differ importantly on what valuables they admit into their ontology. Some maintain that "what you see is what you get," but nevertheless admit a wide range of valuables, from sensory pleasures, the beauty of nature and cultural artifacts, the joys of creativity, to loving personal intimacy. Others posit a transcendent good (e.g., the Form of the Good in Platonism, or God, the Supremely Valuable Object, in Christianity). In the spirit of Ivan Karamazov, I am convinced that the depth of horrific evil cannot be accurately estimated without recognizing it to be incommensurate with any package of merely non-transcendent goods and so unable to be balanced off, much less defeated thereby.

Where the *internal* coherence of Christianity is the issue, however, it is fair to appeal to its own store of valuables. From a Christian point of view, God is a being a greater than which cannot be conceived, a good incommensurate with both created goods and temporal evils. Likewise, the good of beatific, face-to-face intimacy with God is simply incommensurate with any merely non-transcendent goods or ills a person might experience. Thus, the good of beatific face-to-face intimacy with God would *engulf* ... even the horrendous evils humans experience in this present life here below, and overcome any *prima facie* reasons the individual had to doubt whether his/her life would or could be worth living

Personal meaning, horrors defeated. *Engulfing* personal horrors within the context of the participant's life would vouchsafe to that individual a life that was a great good to him/her on the whole. I am still inclined to think it would guarantee that immeasurable divine goodness to any person thus benefitted. But there is good theological reason for Christians to believe that God would go further, beyond engulfment to defeat. For it is the nature of persons to look for meaning, both in their lives and in the world. Divine respect for and commitment to created personhood would drive God to make all those sufferings which threaten to destroy the positive meaning of a person's life meaningful through positive defeat.

How could God do it? So far as I can see, only by integrating participation in horrendous evils into a person's relationship with God. Possible dimensions of integration are charted by Christian soteriology. I pause here to sketch three:

(i) First, because God in Christ participated in horrendous evil through His passion and death, human experience of horrors can be a means of *identifying* with Christ, either through *sympathetic* identification (in which each person suffers his/her own pains, but their similarity enables each to know what it is like for the other) or through *mystical* identification (in which the created person is supposed literally to experience a share of Christ's pain[8]).

(ii) Julian of Norwich's description of heavenly welcome suggests the possible defeat of horrendous evil through divine gratitude. According to Julian, before the elect have a chance to thank God for all He has done for them, God will say, "Thank you for all your suffering, the suffering of your youth." She says that the creature's experience of divine gratitude will bring such full and unending joy as could not be merited by the whole sea of human pain and suffering throughout the ages.[9]

(iii) A third idea identifies temporal suffering itself with a vision into the inner life of God, and can be developed several ways. Perhaps, contrary to medieval theology, God is not impassible, but rather has matched capacities for joy and for suffering. Perhaps, as the Heidelberg catechism suggests, God responds to human sin and the sufferings of Christ with an agony beyond human conception. Alternatively, the inner life of God may be, strictly speaking and in and of itself, beyond both joy and sorrow.... And if a face-to-face vision of God is a good for humans incommensurate with any non-transcendent goods or ills, so any vision of God (including horrendous suffering) would have a good aspect insofar as it is a vision of God (even if it has an evil aspect insofar as it is horrendous suffering). For the most part, horrors are not recognized as experiences of God (any more than the city slicker recognizes his visual image of a brown patch as a vision of Beulah the cow in the distance). But, Christian mysticism might claim, at least from the *post-mortem* perspective of the beatific vision, such sufferings will be seen for what they were, and retrospectively no one will wish away any intimate encounters with God from his/her life-history of this world. The created person's experience of the beatific vision together with his/her knowledge that intimate divine presence stretched back over his/her *ante-mortem* life and reached down into the depths of his/her worst suffering, would provide retrospective comfort independent of comprehension of the reasons-why akin to the two-year-old's assurance of its mother's love. Taking this third approach, Christians would not need to commit themselves about what in any event we do not know: viz., whether we will (like the two-year-old) ever grow up enough to understand the reasons why God permits our participation in horrendous evils. For by contrast with the best of earthly mothers, such divine intimacy is an incommensurate good and would cancel out for the creature any need to know why.

Conclusion. The worst evils demand to be defeated by the best goods. Horrendous evils can be overcome only by the goodness of God. Relative to human nature, participation in horrendous evils and loving intimacy with God are alike disproportionate: for the former threatens to engulf the good in an individual human life with evil, while the latter guarantees the reverse engulfment of evil by good. Relative to one another, there is also disproportion, because the good that God *is*, and intimate relationship with Him, is incommensurate with created goods and evils alike. Because intimacy with God so outscales relations (good or bad) with any creatures, integration into the human person's relationship with God confers significant meaning and positive value even on horrendous suffering. This result coheres with basic Christian intuition: that the powers of darkness are stronger than humans, but they are no match for God!

Standard generic and global solutions have for the most part tried to operate within the territory common to believer and unbeliever, within the confines of religion-neutral value theory. Many discussions reflect the hope that substitute attribute-analyses, candidate reasons-why and/or defeaters could issue out of values shared by believers and unbelievers alike. And some virtually make this a requirement on an adequate solution.... But agreement on truth-value is not necessary to consensus on internal consistency. My contention has been that it is not only legitimate, but, given horrendous evils, necessary for Christians to dip into their richer store of valuables to exhibit the consistency of (1) and (2). I would go one step further: assuming the pragmatic and/or moral (I would prefer to say, broadly speaking, religious) importance of believing that (one's own) human life is worth living, the ability of Christianity to exhibit how this could be so despite human vulnerability to horrendous evil, constitutes a pragmatic/moral/religious consideration in its favor, relative to value schemes that do not....

Notes

1. J.L. Mackie, "Evil and Omnipotence," *Mind*, 64 (1955).
2. Most people would agree that a person *p*'s doing or suffering of them constitutes *prima facie* reason to doubt whether *p*'s life can be, given such participation, a great good to *p* on the whole.
3. "Hume on Evil," *Philosophical Review*, 72 (1963), 180-97.
4. Augustine, *On Free Choice of Will* iii, 93-102.
5. Alvin Plantinga, "Self-Profile," in James E. Tomberlin and Peter Van Inwagen (eds.), *Profiles: Alvin Plantinga* (Dordrecht, Boston: Reidel, 1985), 38.
6. Middle knowledge, or knowledge of what is "in between" the actual and the possible, is the sort of knowledge of what a free creature *would do* in every situation in which that creature could possibly find himself....
7. Following Plantinga, where horrendous evils are concerned, not only do we not know God's *actual* reason for permitting them; we cannot even *conceive* of any plausible candidate sort of reason consistent with worthwhile lives for human participants in them.
8. For example, Julian of Norwich tells us that she prayed for and received the latter (*Revelations of Divine Love*, chapter 17). Mother Theresa of Calcutta seems to construe Matthew 25: 31-46 to mean that the poorest and the least *are* Christ, and that their sufferings *are* Christ's (Malcolm Muggeridge, *Something Beautiful for God*, Harper & Row Publishers, New York 1960), 72-75.
9. *Revelations of Divine Love*, ch. 14.

Discussion

1. Do you think "producer of global goods" is an adequate understanding of divine goodness? If not, what ramifications would adding "good to created persons" to divine goodness have for one's theodicy?
2. Why are non-transcendent goods inadequate to make up for horrific suffering?
3. Are the goods that Adams offers—identifying with Christ, divine gratitude, vision into the inner life of God—adequate consolations for victims of horrendous suffering? Do you think any of these reason likely to be true?

Chapter 13

≈

The Evidential Problem of Evil

The Problem of Evil and Some Varieties of Atheism
*William Rowe**

Introduction. This paper is concerned with three interrelated questions. The first is: Is there an argument for atheism based on the existence of evil that may rationally justify someone in being an atheist? To this first question I give an affirmative answer and try to support that answer by setting forth a strong argument for atheism based on the existence of evil.[1] The second question is: How can the theist best defend his position against the argument for atheism based on the existence of evil? In response to this question I try to describe what may be an adequate rational defense for theism against any argument for atheism based on the existence of evil. The final question is: What position should the informed atheist take concerning the rationality of theistic belief? Three different answers an atheist may give to this question serve to distinguish three varieties of atheism: unfriendly atheism, indifferent atheism, and friendly atheism. In the final part of the paper I discuss and defend the position of friendly atheism....

The argument stated. In developing the argument for atheism based on the existence of evil, it will be useful to focus on some particular evil that our world contains in considerable abundance. Intense human and animal suffering, for example, occurs daily and in a great plenitude in our world. Such intense suffering is a clear case of evil. Of course, if the intense suffering leads to some greater good, a good we could not have obtained without undergoing the suffering in question, we might conclude that the suffering is justified, but it remains an evil nevertheless. For we must not confuse the intense suffering in and of itself with the good things to which it sometimes leads or of which it may be a necessary part. Intense human or animal suffering is in itself bad, an evil, even though it may sometimes be justified by virtue of being a part of, or leading to, some good which is unobtainable without it. What is evil in itself may sometimes be good as a means because it leads to something that is good in itself. In such a case, while remaining an evil in itself, the

---

*William Rowe is Professor of Philosophy at Purdue University.

intense human or animal suffering is, nevertheless, an evil which someone might be morally justified in permitting.

Taking human and animal suffering as a clear instance of evil which occurs with great frequency in our world, the argument for atheism based on evil can be stated as follows:

1. There exist instances of intense suffering which an omnipotent, omniscient being could have prevented without thereby losing some greater good or permitting some evil equally bad or worse.
2. An omniscient, wholly good being would prevent the occurrence of any intense suffering it could, unless it could not do so without thereby losing some greater good or permitting some evil equally bad or worse.
3. There does not exist an omnipotent, omniscient, wholly good being.

What are we to say about this argument for atheism, an argument based on the profusion of one sort of evil in our world? The argument is valid; therefore, if we have rational grounds for accepting its premises, to that extent we have rational grounds for accepting atheism. Do we, however, have rational grounds for accepting the premises of this argument?

Let's begin with the second premise.... Premise (2) says that an omniscient, wholly good being would prevent the occurrence of any intense suffering it could, unless it could not do so without thereby losing some greater good or permitting some evil equally bad or worse. This premise (or something not too distant from it) is, I think, held in common by many atheists and nontheists. Of course, there may be disagreement about whether something is good, and whether, if it is good, one would be morally justified in permitting some intense suffering to occur in order to obtain it. Someone might hold, for example, that no good is great enough to justify permitting an innocent child to suffer terribly. Again, someone might hold that the mere fact that a given good outweighs some suffering and would be lost if the suffering were prevented, is not a morally sufficient reason for permitting the suffering. But to hold either of these views is not to deny (2). For (2) claims only that *if* an omniscient, wholly good being permits intense suffering *then* either there is some greater good that would have been lost, or some equally bad or worse evil that would have occurred, had the intense suffering been prevented. (2) does not purport to describe what might be a *sufficient* condition for an omniscient, wholly good being to permit intense suffering, only what is a *necessary* condition. So stated, (2) seems to express a belief that accords with our basic moral principles, principles shared by both theists and nontheists. If we are to fault the argument for atheism, therefore, it seems we must find some fault with its first premise.

Suppose in some distant forest lightning strikes a dead tree, resulting in a forest fire. In the fire a fawn is trapped, horribly burned, and lies in terrible agony for several days before death relieves its suffering. So far as we can see, the fawn's intense suffering is pointless. For there does not appear to be any greater good such that the prevention of the fawn's suffering would require either the loss of that good or the occurrence of an evil equally bad or worse. Nor does there seem to be any equally bad or worse evil so connected to the fawn's suffering that it would have had to occur had the fawn's suffering been prevented. Could an omnipotent, omniscient being have prevented the fawn's apparently pointless suffering? The answer is obvious, as even the theist will insist. An omnipotent, omniscient being could have easily prevented the fawn from being horribly burned, or, given the burning, could have spared the fawn the intense suffering by quickly ending its life, rather than allowing the fawn to lie in terrible agony for several days. Since the fawn's intense suffering was preventable and, so far as we can see, pointless, doesn't it appear that premise (1) of the argument is true, that there do exist instances of intense suffering which an omnipotent, omniscient being could have prevented without thereby losing some greater good or permitting some evil equally bad or worse?

It must be acknowledged that the case of the fawn's apparently pointless suffering does not *prove* that (1) is true. For even though we cannot see how the fawn's suffering is required to obtain some greater good (or to prevent some equally bad or worse evil), it hardly follows that it is not so required. After all, we are often surprised by how things we thought to be unconnected turn out to be intimately connected. Perhaps, for all we know, there is some familiar good outweighing the fawn's suffering to which that suffering is connected in a way we do not see. Furthermore, there may well be unfamiliar goods, goods we haven't dreamed of, to which the fawn's suffering is inextricably connected. Indeed, it would seem to require something like omniscience on our part before we could lay claim to *knowing* that there is no greater good connected to the fawn's suffering in such a manner that an omnipotent, omniscient being could not have achieved that good without permitting that suffering or some evil equally bad or worse. So the case of the fawn's suffering surely does not enable us to *establish* the truth of (1).

The truth is that we are not in a position to prove that (1) is true. We cannot know with certainty that instances of suffering of the sort described in (1) do occur in our world. But it is one thing to *know* or *prove* that (1) is true and quite another thing to have *rational grounds* for believing (1) to be true. We are often in the position where in the light of our experience and knowledge it is rational to believe that a certain statement is true, even though we are not in a position to prove or to know with certainty that the statement is true. In the light of our past experience and knowledge it is, for example, very reasonable to believe that neither Goldwater nor McGovern will ever be elected President, but we are scarcely in the position of knowing with certainty that neither will ever be elected President. So, too, with (1), although we cannot know with certainty that it is true, it perhaps can be rationally supported, shown to be a rational belief.

Consider again the case of the fawn's suffering. Is it reasonable to believe that there is some greater good so intimately connected to that suffering that even an omnipotent, omniscient being could not have obtained that good without permitting that suffering or some evil at least as bad? It certainly does not appear reasonable to believe this. Nor does it seem reasonable to believe that there is some evil at least as bad as the fawn's suffering such that an omnipotent being simply could not have prevented it without permitting the fawn's suffering. But even if it should somehow be reasonable to believe either of these things of the fawn's suffering, we must then ask whether it is reasonable to believe either of these things of *all* the instances of seemingly pointless human and animal suffering that occur daily in our world. And surely the answer to this more general question must be no. It seems quite unlikely that *all* the instances of intense suffering occurring daily in our world are intimately related to the occurrence of greater goods or the prevention of evils at least as bad; and even more unlikely, should they somehow all be so related, that an omnipotent, omniscient being could not have achieved at least some of those goods (or prevented some of those evils) without permitting the instances of intense suffering that are supposedly related to them. In the light of our experience and knowledge of the variety and scale of human and animal suffering in our world, the idea that none of this suffering could have been prevented by an omnipotent being without thereby losing a greater good or permitting an evil at least as bad seems an extraordinary absurd idea, quite beyond our belief. It seems then that although we cannot *prove* that (1) is true, it is, nevertheless, altogether *reasonable* to believe that (1) is true, that (1) is a *rational* belief.

Returning now to our argument for atheism, we've seen that the second premise expresses a basic belief common to many theists and nontheists. We've also seen that our experience and knowledge of the variety and profusion of suffering in our world provides *rational support* for the first premise. Seeing that the conclusion, "There does not exist an omnipotent, omniscient, wholly good being" follows from these two premises, it does seem that we have *rational support* for atheism, that it is reasonable for us to believe that the theistic God does not exist.

The theist's defense. Can theism be rationally defended against the argument for atheism we have just examined? If it can, how might the theist best respond to that argument? Since the argument from (1) and (2) to (3) is valid, and since the theist, no less than the nontheist, is more than likely committed to (2), it's clear that the theist can reject this atheistic argument only by rejecting its first premise, the premise that states that there are instances of intense suffering which an omnipotent, omniscient being could have prevented without thereby losing some greater good or permitting some evil equally bad or worse. How, then, can the theist best respond to this premise and the considerations advanced in its support?

There are basically three responses a theist can make. First, he might argue not that (1) is false or probably false, but only that the reasoning given in support of it is in some way *defective*. He may do this either by arguing that the reasons given in support of (1) are in *themselves* insufficient to justify accepting (1), or by arguing that there are other things we know which, when taken in conjunction with these reasons, do not justify us in accepting (1). I suppose some theists would be content with this rather modest response to the basic argument for atheism. But given the validity of the basic argument and the theist's likely acceptance of (2), he is thereby committed to the view that (1) is false, not just that we have no good reason for accepting (1) as true. The second two responses are aimed at showing that it is reasonable to believe that (1) is false. Since the theist is committed to this view I shall focus the discussion on these two attempts, attempts which we can distinguish as "the direct attack" and "the indirect attack."

By a direct attack, I mean an attempt to reject (1) by pointing out goods, for example, to which suffering may well be connected, goods which an omnipotent, omniscient being could not achieve without permitting suffering. It is doubtful, however, that the direct attack can succeed. The theist may point out that some suffering leads to moral and spiritual development impossible without suffering. But it's reasonably clear that suffering often occurs in a degree far beyond what is required for character development. The theist may say that some suffering results from free choices of human beings and might be preventable only by preventing some measure of human freedom. But, again, it's clear that much intense suffering occurs not as a result of human free choices. The general difficulty with this direct attack on premise (1) is twofold. First, it cannot succeed, for the theist does not know what greater goods might be served, or evils prevented, by each instance of intense human or animal suffering. Second, the theist's own religious tradition usually maintains that in this life it is not given to us to know God's purpose in allowing particular instances of suffering. Hence, the direct attack against premise (1) cannot succeed and violates basic beliefs associated with theism.

The best procedure for the theist to follow in rejecting premise (1) is the indirect procedure. This procedure I shall call "the G. E. Moore shift," so-called in honor of the twentieth century philosopher, G. E. Moore, who used it to great effect in dealing with the arguments of the skeptics. Skeptical philosophers such as David Hume have advanced ingenious arguments to prove that no one can know of the existence of any material object. The premises of their arguments employ plausible principles, principles which many philosophers have tried to reject directly, but only with questionable success. Moore's procedure was altogether different. Instead of arguing directly against the premises of the skeptic's arguments, he simply noted that the premises implied, for example, that he [Moore] did not know of the existence of a pencil. Moore then proceeded indirectly against the skeptic's premises by arguing:

I do know that this pencil exists.
If the skeptic's principles are correct I cannot know of the existence of this pencil.
The skeptic's principles (at least one) must be incorrect.

Moore then noted that his argument is just as valid as the skeptic's, that both of their arguments contain the premise "If the skeptic's principles are correct Moore cannot know of the existence of this pencil," and concluded that the only way to choose between the two arguments (Moore's and the skeptic's) is by deciding which of the first premises it is more rational to believe—Moore's premise "I do know that this pencil exists" or the skeptic's premise asserting that his skeptical principles are correct. Moore concluded that his own first premise was the more rational of the two.[2]

Before we see how the theist may apply the G. E. Moore shift to the basic argument for atheism, we should note the general strategy of the shift. We're given an argument: p, q, therefore, r. Instead of arguing directly against p, another argument is constructed—not-r, q, therefore, not-p—which begins with the denial of the conclusion of the first argument, keeps its second premise, and ends with the denial of the first premise as its conclusion. Compare, for example, these two:
Compare, for example, these two:

I. p	II. not-r
q	q
r	not-p

It is a truth of logic that if I is valid II must be valid as well. Since the arguments are the same so far as the second premise is concerned, any choice between them must concern their respective first premises. To argue against the first premise (p) by constructing the counter argument II is to employ the G. E. Moore shift.

Applying the G. E. Moore shift against the first premise of the basic argument for atheism, the theist can argue as follows:

not-3. There exists an omnipotent, omniscient, wholly good being.
2. An omniscient, wholly good being would prevent the occurrence of any intense suffering
it could, unless it could not do so without thereby losing some greater good or permitting some evil equally bad or worse.

therefore,

not-1. It is not the case that there exist instances of intense suffering which an omnipotent, omniscient being could have prevented without thereby losing some greater good or permitting some evil equally bad or worse.

We now have two arguments: the basic argument for atheism from (1) and (2) to (3), and the theist's best response, the argument from (not-3) and (2) to (not-1). What the theist then says about (1) is that he has rational grounds for believing in the existence of the theistic God (not-3), accepts (2) as true, and sees that (not-1) follows from (not-3) and (2). He concludes, therefore, that he has rational grounds for rejecting (1). Having rational grounds for rejecting (1), the theist concludes that the basic argument for atheism is mistaken.

Varieties of atheism. We've had a look at a forceful argument for atheism and what seems to be the theist's best response to that argument. If one is persuaded by the argument for atheism, as I find myself to be, how might one best view the position of the theist? Of course, he will view the theist as having a false belief, just as the theist will view the atheist as having a false belief. But what position should the atheist take concerning the *rationality* of the theist's belief? There are three major positions an atheist might take, positions which we may think of as some varieties of atheism. First, the atheist may believe that no one is rationally justified in believing that the theistic God exists. Let us call this position "unfriendly atheism." Second, the atheist may hold no belief concerning whether any theist is or isn't rationally justified in believing that the theistic God exists. Let us call this view "indifferent atheism." Finally, the atheist may believe that some theists are rationally justified in believing that the theistic God exists. This view we shall call "friendly atheism." In this final part of the paper I propose to discuss and defend the position of friendly atheism.

If no one can be rationally justified in believing a false proposition then friendly atheism is a paradoxical, if not incoherent position. But surely the truth of a belief is not a necessary condition of someone's being rationally justified in having that belief. So in holding that someone is rationally justified in believing that the theistic God exists, the friendly atheist is not committed to thinking that the theist has a true belief. What he is committed to is that the theist has rational grounds for his belief, a belief the atheist rejects and is convinced he is rationally justified in rejecting. But is this possible? Can someone, like our friendly atheist, hold a belief, be convinced that he is rationally justified in holding that belief, and yet believe that someone else is equally justified in believing the opposite? Surely this is possible. Suppose your friends see you off on a flight to Hawaii. Hours after take-off they learn that your plane has gone down at sea. After a twenty-four hour search, no survivors have been found. Under these circumstances they are rationally justified in believing that you have perished. But it is hardly rational for you to believe this, as you bob up and down in your life vest, wondering why the search planes have failed to spot you. Indeed, to amuse yourself while awaiting your fate, you might very well reflect on the fact that your friends are rationally justified in believing that you are now dead, a proposition you disbelieve and are rationally justified in disbelieving. So, too, perhaps an atheist may be rationally justified in his atheistic belief and yet hold that some theists are rationally justified in believing just the opposite of what he believes.

What sort of grounds might a theist have for believing that God exists? Well, he might endeavor to justify his belief by appealing to one or more of the traditional arguments: Ontological, Cosmological, Teleological, Moral, etc. Second, he might appeal to certain aspects of religious experience, perhaps even his own religious experience. Third, he might try to justify theism as a plausible theory in terms of which we can account for a variety of phenomena. Although an atheist must hold that the theistic God does not exist, can he not also believe, and be justified in so believing, that some of these "justifications of theism" do actually rationally justify some theists in their belief that there exists a supremely good, omnipotent, omniscient being? It seems to me that he can.

If we think of the long history of theistic belief and the special situations in which people are sometimes placed, it is perhaps as absurd to think that no one was ever rationally justified in believing that the theistic God exists as it is to think that no one was ever justified in believing that human beings would never walk on the moon. But in suggesting that friendly atheism is preferable to unfriendly atheism, I don't mean to rest the case on what some human beings might reasonably have believed in the eleventh or thirteenth century. The more interesting question is whether some people in modern society, people who are aware of the usual grounds for belief and disbelief and are acquainted to some degree with modern science, are yet rationally justified in accepting theism. Friendly atheism is a significant position only if it answers this question in the affirmative.

It is not difficult for an atheist to be friendly when he has reason to believe that the theist could not reasonably be expected to be acquainted with the grounds for disbelief that he (the atheist) possesses. For then the atheist may take the view that some theists are rationally justified in holding to theism, but would not be so were they to be acquainted with the grounds for disbelief—those grounds being sufficient to tip the scale in favor of atheism when balanced against the reasons the theist has in support of his belief.

Friendly atheism becomes paradoxical, however, when the atheist contemplates believing that the theist has all the grounds for atheism that he, the atheist, has, and yet is rationally justified in maintaining his theistic belief. But even so excessively friendly a view as this perhaps can be held by the atheist if he also has some reason to think that the grounds for theism are not as telling as the theist is justified in taking them to be.

Conclusion. In this paper I've presented what I take to be a strong argument for atheism, pointed out what I think is the theist's best response to that argument, distinguished three positions an atheist might take concerning the rationality of theistic belief, and made some remarks in defense of the position called "friendly atheism." I'm aware that the central points of the paper are not likely to be warmly received by many philosophers. Philosophers who are atheists tend to be tough-minded—holding that there are no good reasons for supposing that theism is true. And theists tend either to reject the view that the existence of evil provides rational grounds for atheism or to hold that religious belief has nothing to do with reason and evidence at all. But such is the way of philosophy.

Notes

1. Some philosophers have contended that the existence of evil is *logically inconsistent* with the existence of the theistic God. No one, I think, has succeeded in

establishing such an extravagant claim. Indeed, granted incompatibilism, there is a fairly compelling argument for the view that the existence of evil is logically consistent with the existence of the theistic God. For a lucid statement of this argument see Alvin Plantinga, *God, Freedom, and Evil* (New York, 1974). There remains, however, what we may call the *evidential* form—as opposed to the *logical* form—of the problem of evil: the view that the variety and profusion of evil in our world, although perhaps not logically inconsistent with the existence of the theistic God, provides, nevertheless, *rational support* for atheism. In this paper I shall be concerned solely with the evidential form of the problem, the form of the problem which, I think, presents a rather severe difficulty for theism.

2. See, for example, the two chapters on Hume in G. E. Moore, *Some Main Problems of Philosophy* (London: Collier, 1953).

Discussion

1. Does the fawn's *apparently* pointless suffering give us reason to believe that the fawn's suffering *is* pointless? Why or why not?
2. Can you think of any goods which might result from the suffering of the fawn (which goods outweigh the badness of the fawn's pain)? If not, what follows?
3. Distinguish between the different varieties of atheism. Why does Rowe contend that "friendly atheism" is the only reasonable option? Do you agree with him? Why or why not?

Rowe's Argument from Particular Horrors
*Daniel Howard-Snyder**

Introduction. It is commonly thought that the evil and suffering in our world constitutes strong evidence for *atheism*, the thesis that no omnipotent, omniscient and
wholly good God exists. But exactly *how* is it strong evidence? And is it *strong
enough* to make it rational to believe there is no God?

Suppose God and evil are incompatible; then, since there clearly is evil, we
have enormously strong evidence for atheism. Very few philosophers today who
study our topic would endorse this argument, however. Why? Because it seems that
God and evil are, strictly speaking, compatible. We can think of various reasons
God might have to permit a fair bit of evil; and to the extent that we cannot think
of any reason for God to permit so much, we have no good grounds to think that
there *could not* be a justifying reason we do not know of.

Nevertheless, even if God and evil are compatible, and even if we can see how
God might be justified in permitting a good deal of evil and suffering, certain facts
about evil and suffering may constitute strong evidence for atheism, so strong that
it is rational to be an atheist—provided one has no equally good grounds to think
there is a God. This is William Rowe's thesis in his justly famous essay "The Problem of Evil and Some Varieties of Atheism".

The argument stated. In what follows, let's suppose—just to see what follows, or
perhaps because we really believe it's true—that there are no equally good grounds
for theism. With this supposition in place, let's turn to our title question: does evil
make it rational to be an atheist? Rowe answers "yes," and he gives a powerful argument for it. In its official form, it can be put as follows:

1. There are instances of intense suffering which God could have prevented
   without thereby losing some greater good or permitting some evil equally
   bad or worse.
2. God would prevent the occurrence of any intense suffering He could,
   unless He could not do so without thereby losing some greater good or
   permitting some evil equally bad or worse.
3. So, God does not exist.

What should we make of this argument? It is logically valid, i.e., the premises cannot all be true while the conclusion is false. But are all the premises true?

For the purposes of this paper, let's grant the second premise, although I don't
mean to give the impression that all is clear sailing here.[1] What about the first? It is

---

*Daniel Howard-Snyder is a professor of Philosophy at Seattle Pacific University.

equivalent to a claim that something of a certain sort does not exist, specifically this claim:

1. There is no greater good that would have been lost and no evil equally bad or worse that would have been permitted if God had prevented some instances of intense suffering.

In what follows, I will focus on this claim because it will allow us to see more easily what we must be committed to if we accept premise 1.

Rowe's argument for premise 1. Well, what should we make of premise 1? Rowe offers one particular instance of intense suffering that God could have prevented without thereby losing some greater good or permitting some equally bad or worse evil—the case of the fawn who is horribly burned in a forest fire, lying in agony for days before she dies, doubtlessly one of millions of such cases throughout history. In other essays, he points to other occurrences of especially horrible suffering. So Rowe initially supports premise 1 by pointing to certain cases of suffering, saying of *each one* that there is no greater good that would have been lost nor any equally bad or worse evil that would have been permitted if God had prevented it, that very occurrence of suffering. In effect, then, he draws up a list that begins like this:

1a. There is no greater good that would have been lost nor any other equally bad or worse evil that would have been permitted if God had prevented that fawn from being burned in that forest fire, or if He had prevented the fawn from lying in terrible agony for several days after being burned.
1b. There is no greater good that would have been lost nor any other equally bad or worse evil that would have been permitted if God had prevented Ashley Jones from being brutally raped and bludgeoned to death last September in Stanwood, Washington.[2]...

So Rowe supports premise 1 initially by a list of propositions like 1a and 1b. It will make things easier if we pretend that you and I have one list, *Our List of Pointless Evils*. A moment's reflection reveals that if all of the propositions on our list are true, then premise 1 is certainly true; indeed, if *just one* of them is true, then premise 1 is true.

An important question arises: *are* any of them true? Rowe briefly sketches his answer to this question:

So far as we can see, the fawn's intense suffering is pointless. For there does not appear to be any greater good such that the prevention of the fawn's suffering would require either the loss of that good or the occurrence of an evil equally bad or worse. Nor does there seem to be any equally bad or worse evil so connected to the fawn's suffering that it would have had to occur had the fawn's suffering been prevented. Could [God] have prevented the fawn's apparently pointless suffering? The answer is obvious, as even the theist will insist. [God] could have easily prevented the fawn from being horribly burned, or, given the burning, could have spared the fawn the intense suffering by quickly ending its life, rather than allowing the fawn to lie in terrible agony for several days. Since the fawn's intense suffering was preventable and, so far as we can see, pointless, doesn't it appear that premise (1) of the argument is true?

And similar things might be said of Ashley Jones. Consider the various candidates for greater goods that we know of, for example determining the sort of character one has, being of use to others, entering into and maintaining worthwhile relationships with our fellows and with God, seeing the hideousness that naturally follows from rejecting God and living on our own, sympathetically identifying with Christ's sufferings, and being punished for wrongdoing. (You may add any goods that you think should be listed here.) So far as we can see, none of these goods would have been lost or objectionably reduced if God had prevented Ashley's suffering and not permitted some other instance of comparable agony. On reflection, similar things can be said about the other goods mentioned above, and about their conjunction into one colossal good. Doesn't it seem, then, that Ashley's suffering was pointless, and therefore that premise 1 of Rowe's argument is true?

Here we have only considered the cases of Ashley Jones and the fawn. The other cases on our list must likewise be examined. Suppose we are able to say of each one what Rowe said of the fawn and what I suggested we should say about Ashley Jones: "So far as we can see, there is no greater good that would have been lost nor any other equally bad or worse evil that would have been permitted if God had prevented it." In that case, we can draw up a second list that exactly parallels our first list. It would start like this:

$1a_1$. So far as we can see, there is no greater good that would have been lost nor any other equally bad or worse evil that would have been permitted if God had prevented that fawn from being burned in that forest fire, or if He had prevented the fawn from lying in terrible agony for several days after being burned.

$1b_1$. So far as we can see, there is no greater good that would have been lost nor any other equally bad or worse evil that would have been permitted if God had prevented Ashley Jones from being brutally raped and bludgeoned to death last September in Stanwood, Washington....

And so on. Let's call the second list *Our Noseeum List* (pronounced, noh-see-um). It will become apparent below why I give it this name.

Now we're in a position to sum up our characterization of Rowe's initial defense of premise 1. It goes like this: none of the propositions on Our Noseeum List are false.[3] At least some of them make it highly likely that the corresponding propositions on Our List of Pointless Evils are true. If this last claim is correct, then premise 1 is highly likely to be true, and thus it is "altogether reasonable to believe" it. But *do* any of the items on Our Noseeum List make it highly likely that any of the corresponding items on Our List of Pointless Evils are true? More generally, is it really reasonable to infer that there is no greater good that would be lost on the grounds that, so far as we can tell, there is none? These are the questions that we must now answer. To get at them, let's pause to reflect on what *kind* of inference is involved here.

Rowe-style Noseeum Inferences. Suppose that, after rummaging around carefully in my fridge, I can't find a carton of milk. Naturally enough, I infer that there isn't one there. Or suppose that, on viewing a chess match between two novices, Kasparov says to himself, "So far as I can tell, there is no way for John to get out of check," and then infers that there is no way. These are what we might call *no-see-um inferences*: we don't see 'um, so they ain't there![4]

Notice four things about noseeum inferences. First, they have this basic shape: "So far as we can tell, there is no x; so, there is no x." Second, note that in each of the cases just mentioned, it is possible for the conclusion to be false even if the premise is true. Even though I rummaged through the fridge carefully and my vision is in tip-top shape, I could just simply miss the carton of milk. And even Kasparov can have an off day. Nevertheless—and this is the third point—in each case the argument is a strong one. Under certain conditions (about which I will say more shortly), our inability to see something makes it highly likely that there isn't anything of the sort we failed to see. Finally, it won't do to object to any particular noseeum inference that even if the premise is true the conclusion *might* be false. For *every* noseeum inference—even the strongest of them—is like that. When evaluating a particular noseeum inference, we can't just write it off with a casual, "Ah! But there *might* be an x we don't know of even if so far as we can tell there isn't one." That's true, but it's irrelevant to the strength of the inference.

Now, in effect, Rowe bids us to use at least some of the items on Our Noseeum List as a basis for believing some of the items on Our List of Pointless Evils, and this amounts to deploying some, perhaps several, noseeum inferences, like the inference from 1a₁ to 1a:

1a₁. So far as we can tell, there is no greater good that would have been lost if God had prevented that fawn from being burned in that forest fire, or from lying in terrible agony for several days afterwards.[5]

So, it is very likely that

1a. There is no such greater good.

Let us call this type of noseeum inference a *Rowe-style Noseeum Inference*. What should we make of this type of noseeum inference?

Obviously enough, many noseeum inferences are reasonable, like the ones mentioned at the beginning of this section. And just as obviously, many are not. For example, looking at my distant garden from my kitchen window, the fact that so far as I can tell, there are no slugs there hardly makes it likely that there are none. Likewise, a beginner viewing a chess match between Kasparov and Deep Blue would be ill-advised to reason: "I can't see any way for Deep Blue to get out of check; so, there is none." Or imagine us listening to the best physicists in the world discussing the mathematics used to describe quantum phenomena or the theory of general relativity. Presumably it would be unreasonable for us to infer that, since we can't comprehend or grasp what they are saying, there is nothing there to be grasped. The crucial question, then, is this: what distinguishes the reasonable noseeum inferences from the lousy ones?

Consider the cases already sketched. Notice that it is quite likely that I would see a milk jug in the fridge if one were there, and it is very likely that Kasparov would see a way out of check if there were one. That's because Kasparov and I have what it takes to discern the sorts of things in question. On the other hand, it is not very likely that I would see a slug in my garden even if there were one there, at least not from my kitchen window. Nor is it very likely that a beginner would be able to see a way out of check for Deep Blue even if there were one since strategy at the grandmaster level can be very complex. And the same goes for our comprehending exceedingly complex mathematics: even if what the physicists were talking about did make sense, it isn't very likely that we would be able to understand it.

We can distill these reflections in the following principle, which marks an important difference between reasonable and unreasonable noseeum inferences:

> A noseeum inference is reasonable only if it is reasonable to believe that we would very likely see (grasp, comprehend, understand) the item in question if it existed.

Applying this principle to Rowe-style Noseeum Inferences, we get the following result:

> The move from "So far as we can tell, there is no greater good ..." to it is very likely that "There is no such greater good" is reasonable only if it is reasonable to believe that *we would very likely see or comprehend a greater good, if there were one.*

Call the italicized portion *Rowe's Noseeum Assumption.*

Now we are in a position to raise a very important question: Is it reasonable to believe Rowe's Noseeum Assumption? Several arguments for Rowe's Noseeum Assumption have been given in the literature, and I have explained elsewhere why I think that those arguments fail.[6] Here I will simply offer reasons to think that it is not reasonable to believe Rowe's Noseeum Assumption.

Two strategies for assessing Rowe's Noseeum Assumption. I begin by distinguishing two strategies for assessing whether it is reasonable to believe Rowe's

Noseeum Assumption. We can get at them by way of analogy, comparing two questions.

First: is it highly likely that I would see a slug in my garden from the kitchen window if one were there? Not at all. I know that slugs are relatively small and I know that the unaided human eye is not suited to see such small things at a hundred feet; moreover, my garden is over an acre large and, per usual, it's overgrown. So we have superb reason to think that it is false that I would very likely see a slug in my garden even if one were there. Now, another question: is it highly likely that extra-terrestrial life forms would contact us if they existed? The only answer suitable here is "How should I know?" If there were extra-terrestrial life forms, how likely is it that some of them would be intelligent enough to consider contact? And of those intelligent enough, how many would care about it? And of those with the smarts and the desire, how likely is it that they would have the means at their disposal to try? And of those with the means, how likely is it that they would succeed? I haven't the foggiest idea how to answer any of these questions. I can't even begin to say with even the most minimal degree of confidence that the likelihood is low or middling or high. I just don't have enough to go on. In that case, I should be *in doubt* about how likely it is that extra-terrestrial life forms would contact us if they existed. I should be of two minds, neither for it, nor against it. I should just shrug my shoulders and say "I don't know. I'm in the dark on that score."

There are two points to see here. First, in each case it is *not reasonable to believe* that the proposition in question is highly likely to be true, although for different reasons. In the first case, it is not reasonable to believe it is highly likely that I would see a slug in the garden even if there were one there because it is reasonable to believe that the proposition is positively *false*—indeed, because the garden is large and overgrown and I am viewing it from quite a distance, I have good reason to believe it is very, very likely that I would *not* see a slug. In the second case, however, it is *not* reasonable to believe that the proposition in question is *false*. Rather, for the reasons mentioned, we have good reason to be *in doubt* about how likely it is that we would have been contacted by extra-terrestrials if there were any. Indeed, we don't even have enough to go on to make a rough guess. As a consequence—and here is the second, absolutely crucial point—*having good reason to be in doubt* about the matter is good enough reason all by itself to think that it is *not* reasonable to *believe* that we would probably have been contacted. For how could it be reasonable for us to believe something about which we have good reason to think we are utterly in the dark?

Now let's apply these points to Rowe's Noseeum Assumption. To assess the reasonableness of believing that we would very likely see a greater good if there were one, we might consider whether Rowe's Noseeum Assumption is *false*. In that case, we might try to think of reasons to believe that it is very likely that we would *not* see a greater good. We would then be treating Rowe's Noseeum Assumption as I treated the proposition that it is very likely that I would see a slug in my garden from the kitchen window. On the other hand, we might consider whether we should be *in doubt* about whether we would very likely see a greater good. This would be to treat Rowe's Noseeum Assumption as I treated the proposition that it is highly likely that extra-terrestrials would contact us if there were any. The crucial point to understand here is that even if *all* we have is good reason to be *in doubt* about whether it is highly likely that we would see a greater good, that is enough reason to deny that it is reasonable to believe Rowe's Noseeum Assumption.

Reasons to doubt Rowe's Noseeum Assumption. I suspect that it is not reasonable to believe Rowe's Noseeum Assumption. In what follows, I focus on reasons to be in doubt about it rather than reasons to think it is false. Why? Because the only reasons I can think of for believing that it is false presuppose that God has informed us that we should expect to be unable to discern His purposes in permitting particular horrors, which, of course, presupposes that there is a God. I don't want to presuppose that here. I want to show that even a *non*believer can have good reason to refrain from believing Rowe's Noseeum Assumption. So, what considerations might put us in doubt about whether it is reasonable to believe Rowe's Noseeum Assumption? Several have emerged in the literature. I have space for three.

Alston's analogies. The first consideration targets Rowe-style Noseeum Inferences directly. It says that such inferences involve two aspects which should make us wary of our ability to tell whether we would very likely see a greater good or a God-justifying reason if there were any.

First, a Rowe-style Noseeum Inference takes "the insights attainable by finite, fallible human beings as an adequate indication of what is available in the way of reasons to an omniscient, omnipotent being." But this is like supposing that when I am confronted with the activity or productions of a master in a field in which I have little expertise, it is reasonable for me to draw inferences about the quality of her work just because I "don't get it". I've taken a year of university physics. I'm faced with some theory about quantum phenomena and I can't make heads or tails of it. Certainly it is unreasonable for me to suppose it's likely that I'd be able to make sense of it. Similarly for other areas of expertise: painting, architectural design, chess, music, and so on.

Second, a Rowe-style Noseeum Inference "involves trying to determine whether there is a so-and-so in a territory the extent and composition of which is largely unknown to us." It is like someone who is culturally and geographically isolated supposing that if there were something on earth beyond their forest, they'd likely discern it. It is like a physicist supposing that if there were something beyond the temporal bounds of the universe, we'd probably know about it (where those bounds are the big bang and the final crunch).

All these analogies point in the same direction: we should be in doubt about whether we would very likely discern greater goods that would justify God's permission of particular horrors even if one were there.[7]

The progress argument. Knowledge has progressed in a variety of fields of enquiry, especially the physical sciences. The periodic discovery of previously unknown aspects of reality strongly suggests that there will be further progress of a similar sort. Since future progress implies present ignorance, it is very likely that there is much we are now ignorant of. Now, what we have to go on in charting the progress of the discovery of intrinsic goods by our ancestors is meager to say the least. Indeed, given the scant archeological evidence we have, and given paleontological evidence regarding the evolutionary development of the brain in *homo sapiens*, it would not be surprising at all that humans discovered various intrinsic goods over tens of thousands of years dotted by several millenia-long gaps in which nothing was discovered. Hence, given what we have to go on, it would not be surprising if there has been the sort of periodic progress that strongly suggests that there remain goods to be discovered. Thus it would not be surprising if there are *goods* of which we are ignorant, goods of which God—in His omniscience—would not be ignorant.

The argument from complexity. One thing Mozart's Violin Concerto No. 4, Ste. Michele's Cabernet Sauvignon (Reserve), and the best sorts of love have in common when compared to Chopsticks, cheap Gallo, and puppy love is that each illustrates the fact that the goodness of a state of affairs is sometimes greater, in part, because it is more complex. Now, since intense, undeserved suffering and horrific wickedness are so bad, it would take correspondingly greater goods to justify God's permitting such horrors. Hence, it would not be surprising if the greater goods involved in God's purposes possess a degree of complexity well beyond our grasp. It follows that it would not be surprising if there were *greater* goods outside our ken.

Of course, while complexity does not always adversely affect our ability to recognize value, it can and sometimes does. To defend this claim, I cannot show you a complex state of affairs whose value we fully recognize but whose complexity hinders such recognition. I must resort to more general considerations.

First, there is the general phenomenon of the complexity of something hindering our view of some important feature it has, e.g. the complexity of an argument hindering our ability to discern its validity, or the complexity of your opponent's strategy hindering your ability to discern that unless you move your knight to queen's side bishop 5, her next move is checkmate. But, more to the point, why can a child discern the literary merits of a comic book but not *Henry V* or *The Brothers Karamazov*? Why can a child clearly discern the aesthetic value of toffee but have a difficult time with alder-smoked Copper River sockeye served with pesto, lightly buttered asparagus *al dente*, fresh greens in a ginger vinegarette, and chilled chardonnay? Why can a child recognize the value of his friendship with his buddy next door but not the full value of his parents' mutual love? Surely because great works of literature, fine cuisine and adult love at its best involves much more than he is able to comprehend. And this is true of adults as well, as reflection on our progress in understanding the complexity of various things of value reveals. For example, periodically reflecting on the fabric of our relationships with those whom we love most and whose love we most cherish, we might well find strands and shades that when brought to full light permit us to see those love-relationships as more valuable than we had once thought. If the failure to grasp the more complicated aspects of our relationships can prevent a full appreciation of love's value, surely the failure to grasp the complexity of a state of affairs might well hinder us from discerning its goodness. Value is often veiled in complexity.

The three considerations presented here—Alston's Analogies, the Progress Argument, and the Argument from Complexity—*together* constitute good reasons to doubt whether it is highly likely that we would see a greater good if there were one. More specifically, they cumulatively constitute good reason to be in doubt about *each* of the instances of Rowe's Noseeum Assumption that we will have to believe reasonably if we are to move from *any* of the propositions on Our Noseeum List to any of the propositions on Our List of Pointless Evils. For example, here is one of the noseeum inferences that Rowe bids us to make in connecting Our Noseeum List to the corresponding items on Our List of Pointless Evils.

> $1a_1$. So far as we can tell, there is no greater good that would have been lost if God had prevented that fawn from being burned in the forest fire, or from lying in terrible agony for several days afterwards.

So, it is very likely that

> 1a. There is no such greater good.

We [have seen] that the move from "So far as I can tell, there is no greater good that would have been lost if God had prevented that fawn from being burned in the forest fire, or from lying in terrible agony for several days afterwards" to it is very likely that "There is no such greater good" is reasonable only if it is reasonable to believe that *we would very likely see or comprehend a greater good that would have been lost if God had prevented that instance of suffering.* The italicized portion is an instance of Rowe's Noseeum Assumption. We now see that Alston's Analogies, the Progress Argument, and the Argument from Complexity together constitute good reason to be in doubt about whether this instance of Rowe's Noseeum Assumption is true. And the same can be said for every other instance of Rowe's Noseeum Assumption that we would have to use if we were to move from *any* of the propositions on Our Noseeum List to the corresponding propositions on Our List of Pointless Evils.

So what? Three paragraphs before stating his argument, Rowe asks this question: "Is there an argument for atheism based on the existence of evil that may rationally justify someone in being an atheist?" He says the answer is "yes" and gives the argument we've been examining. As you might expect, Rowe's argument can rationally justify us in being atheists only if we are rationally justified in believing all of its premises. Unfortunately, his initial defense of premise 1 does *not* rationally justify us in believing premise 1. So if that's all we have to go on, we are *not* rationally justified in being atheists on the basis of Rowe's argument.

But what if some *other* defense of premise 1 works?[8] I suspect that any defense will not avoid the objections raised above. If all we have to go on is Rowe's initial defense, then we are not rationally justified in believing all of the premises of Rowe's argument; consequently, we are not rationally justified in being atheists on the basis of Rowe's argument. That strikes me as a point worth understanding, a point that fits snugly with our ignorance of whether there are any pointless evils. If the game is Let's Make An Argument That Rationally Justifies Us In Being Atheists, then doesn't this point seem like a winner?[9]

Notes

1. Michael Peterson and William Hasker deny premise 2 in *Evil and the Christian God* (Baker, 1982) and "The Necessity of Gratuitous Evil," *Faith and Philosophy* (1992), respectively. To see why their arguments fail, see my "Is Theism Compatible with Gratuitous Evil?," *American Philosophical Quarterly* (1999), co-authored with Frances Howard-Snyder. Peter van Inwagen, on the other hand, has sketched a fascinating objection in "The Magnitude, Duration, and Distribution of Evil: A Theodicy," *Philosophical Topics* 16 (1988), 167-68, and "The Problem of Evil, the Problem of Air, and the Problem of Silence," *Philosophical Perspectives* 5 (1991), 164, note 11. Both are collected in *God, Knowledge and Mystery* (Ithaca: Cornell University Press, 1995). In *God, Knowledge and Mystery*, pages 15-16 are particularly instructive. Also see "Reflections on the Chapters by Draper, Russell, and Gale," in ed. Daniel Howard-Snyder, *The Evidential Argument from Evil* (Indiana University Press, 1996), 234-235. Frances and I assess the merits of van Inwagen's objection in "Vagueness and the Compatibility of God and Gratuitous Evil" (forthcoming).
2. It is a useful exercise to come up with your own list of specific horrors that you think God would be able to prevent without thereby losing a greater good or permitting an equally bad or worse evil.
3. Richard Swinburne would challenge this claim. See *Providence and the Problem of Evil* (Oxford, 1998).
4. The noseeum lingo is Stephen Wykstra's. See "Rowe's Noseeum Arguments from Evil," in *The Evidential Argument from Evil*, 126-150.
5. I omit the phrase "nor any other equally bad or worse evil that would have been permitted" here and in what follows since it is not germane to my argument.
6. "The Argument from Inscrutable Evil," in *The Evidential Argument from Evil*, and "The Argument from Divine Hiddenness," *Canadian Journal of Philosophy* (1996).
7. William Alston, "Some (Temporarily) Final Thoughts on Evidential Arguments from Evil," 316- 319, in *The Evidential Argument from Evil*.
8. Rowe initially defends premise 1 by identifying some *particular* horrible instances of suffering and asserting of at least some of them that *they* are point-

less. In the penultimate paragraph of section I of his essay, he offers a different argument. Suppose it really is reasonable to believe that some greater good would have been lost if God had prevented the fawn's suffering, he says; indeed, we might suppose the same thing about the other horrors on our List of Pointless Evils. Of course, the particular horrors that we've identified are but a mere drop in the vast ocean of all the evil there is. And here an important point emerges: even if we cannot reasonably say of any *particular* horror on our list that *it* is pointless, it is reasonable to believe that no greater good would require God to permit *so much* evil—the vast quantity of horrific suffering and misery and wickedness that has stuffed terrestrial history and shows every sign of continuing unabated. Surely a being who is perfect in power and wisdom would not have to permit all of this enormous variety and profusion of intense human and animal suffering in order to achieve His purposes. Surely He could have prevented *some* of it without losing any greater good, *just some.* The idea that *none* of it could have been prevented by God without thereby losing a greater good seems an extraordinarily absurd idea, quite beyond our belief. In that case, at least *some instances of evil or other* are pointless, even if the instances on our List are not pointless and even if we can't say which instances are pointless.

The main thing to see about this second defense of premise 1 is that all of the worries about the initial defense arise for it as well. First, why suppose it is reasonable to believe that there is no greater good that would require God to permit so much horrible suffering in the world? Presumably because, so far as we can tell, there is no greater good that would require God to permit so much. So we have a new version of Rowe's Noseeum Assumption: we would very likely be able to see a greater good that would require God to permit *so much* horrible suffering, if there were one. Isn't it pretty clear that Alston's Analogies, the Progress Argument, and the Argument from Complexity jointly constitute just as good a reason to be in doubt about this new version of Rowe's Noseeum Assumption as they do its counterparts about particular horrors? If so, then the new defense of premise 1 is no better than the initial one. I leave it as homework to the reader to try to come up with a more promising option.

9. For useful reminders on an earlier draft of this essay, I thank William Rowe. I am indebted to William Alston and, especially, Stephen Wykstra for the main lines of thought I develop.

Discussion

1. What sort of initial plausibility would you apply to Rowe's Noseeum Inferences?

2. Consider Howard-Snyder's counter-examples to Rowe's Noseeum Inferences. Are they sufficiently powerful to overcome the initial plausibility of Rowe's Noseeum Inferences?

3. If Howard-Snyder's arguments are sound, what rational options are open with respect to belief in God? Are any closed off?
4. Can you come up with a defense of premise 1 that avoids Howard-Snyder's worries?

God and Human Suffering

Suggestions for Further Study

Adams, Marilyn McCord and Robert Merrihew, eds. *The Problem of Evil*. New York: Oxford University Press, 1990.

Clark, Kelly James. *When Faith is Not Enough*. Grand Rapids, MI: Eerdmans Publishing Company, 1997.

Gale, Richard. *On the Nature and Existence of God*. New York: Cambridge University Press, 1991.

Hick, John. *Evil and the God of Love*. New York: Harper & Row, 1978.

Howard-Snyder, Daniel, ed. *The Evidential Argument from Evil*. Bloomington and Indianapolis: University of Indiana Press, 1996.

Lewis, C. S. *The Problem of Pain*. New York: Macmillan, 1962.

Peterson, Michael, ed. *The Problem of Evil: Selected Readings*. Notre Dame: University of Notre Dame Press, 1992.

Plantinga, Alvin. *God, Freedom and Evil*. Grand Rapids, MI: Eerdmans Publishing Company, 1977.

Van Inwagen, Peter. *God, Knowledge and Mystery*. Ithaca: Cornell University Press, 1995.

Wolterstorff, Nicholas. *Lament for a Son*. Grand Rapids, MI: Eerdmans Publishing Company, 1987.

Part Four

Critiques of God

Introduction

~~~~

Critiques of God

Introduction. The title of this section is, of course, an exaggeration. If there is a God, a supremely perfect being, then he is beyond reproach. He is also, according to most Western religions, omnipotent, sovereign and righteous. So God stands above us ordering and judging our lives. God as so conceived is, therefore, a threat. So there is a reason to revolt against the moral tyranny and domineering sovereignty of God. Within Holy Writ itself passionate rebels like Job have questioned God's character and authority: "What are human beings that you make so much of them,/ that you set your mind on them,/ visit them every morning/ test them every moment?...Why have you made me your target?" (Job 7:17-20) God is a threat to human autonomy. In Friedrich Nietzsche's *Thus Spoke Zarathustra*, Zarathustra exclaims: "*If* there were gods, how could I endure not to be a god! Hence there are no gods."[1] And Jean-Paul Sartre seems to reject belief in God because of sovereignty's overpowering threat to human freedom.[2] So there is a rich tradition of critiques of God.

The essays in this section are critiques of a rather different sort. Each of the thinkers in this section assumes at the outset that God does not exist. Perhaps there is insufficient evidence to reasonably believe in God or perhaps there is evidence (say evil or science) but it is unfavorable to God's existence. In the 19th Century as science progressed, the explanatory need for God diminished. Natural processes were considered sufficient to account for the physical world. There was less and less need to call on God to explain natural phenomena. God was considered intellectually unnecessary. As belief in God declined among intellectuals, explanations of religious belief became increasingly naturalistic and suspicious. By "naturalistic" I mean without reference to any supernatural forces or entities. And by "suspicious" I mean skeptical of the noble or altruistic motives often (self-)attributed to religious believers.

Assuming that God is intellectually superfluous, these thinkers ask (at least) two questions: Given that God does not exist, how could belief in God have become so deeply entrenched in Western thought? What is the value or, better, disvalue of belief in God? Their criticism, therefore, is not so much of God as of belief in God.

The hermeneutics of suspicion. Karl Marx was an ethnic Jew in a Christian family. He abandoned any religious beliefs and made atheism the foundation of his philosophy. Marx's starting point is the 19th century working conditions of laborers. Due in part to the industrial revolution, workers were exploited with menial labor, low wages and long hours. Children often worked fifteen to eighteen hours per day and were given just enough food to sustain their existence so that they could continue working. Workers were treated as a commodity, according to the law of supply and demand: easily replaced workers (i.e., economically unvaluable people) could be paid little. Behind this exploition, Marx saw the ignoble forces of religion.

Marx came to believe that human beings create religion. Religion is, Marx contends, the opium of the masses: it is a painkiller which treats the symptoms while ignoring the disease—it dulls the pain of exploitation but it fails to redress the cause of pain and suffering. Religion arises because of legitimate needs but offers a false and illusory remedy. Marx also rejects religious belief because of the social atrocities that have been perpetuated in the name of God.

Friedrich Nietzsche was the son of a Lutheran pastor. He was educated in classics and, early on, theology. While studying at university, he moved decisively away from Christianity. Nietzsche's philosophy begins, first and foremost, with the death of God. Western society, nonetheless, continued to accept the trappings of Judeo-Christian morality without its metaphysical and theological underpinnings. With the foundation of theism dislodged, Nietzsche believed that Judeo-Christian morality would eventually crumble. If there is no God, then the following questions arise: where do Christianity, morality and guilt come from? What, if not God, is the source of good and evil? In answering these questions, Nietzsche looks not only at values themselves, but at the value behind the value. What weight, authority or power do values have? Are they life-affirming or life-denying? Are they destructive of what is most fundamentally human or are they creative and satisfying?

Nietzsche's work is a *genealogy* of morals, what he sometimes calls "a history of morals"—how do moralities arise, become approved and maintain their power? How is the history forgotten when moralities are charged with an allegedly transhistorical or transcendental legitimation and power? Nietzsche believes that there are two basic moralities: the Herd and Master Moralities. The Herd (or Slave) Morality is that of the weak, the feeble and the enslaved. Herd morality arose in the priestly cultures which denied desire and endorsed the weaknesses of the priest. The priestly morality developed out of fear and hatred of the master class. The impotent, unable to conquer their more worthy and physically powerful foes, sought "spiritual revenge." They made everything that was opposed to the master class "good." Aligning God with their cause, they endorsed the eternal damnation of everyone who violated their moral standards. Eternal damnation, the ultimate revenge, shows that Judeo-Christian morality is rooted not in love but in hatred and vengefulness. The Master Morality, on the other hand, affirms the virtues that arise from strength and nobility, such as pride, self-conquest, freedom, physical strength, vigorousness and domination.

Freud, like Nietzsche, looks for the value behind religious belief. Standing behind every human action is our natural narcissism—the drive for pleasure. Since the unfettered satisfaction of desires would create a chaos for human beings, we all join together for a measure of peace and security. But even within civilization our peace and security are threatened, this time by nature. By projecting human qualities and person-like entities onto the forces of nature, we attempt to "civilize" nature; we entreat those various powers as we might entreat various persons who would seek to wreak havoc.

The ultimate projection of human properties onto nature is the belief that the ultimate power is like a father. We wish God into existence—Freud coined the term "wish-fulfillment" to describe this phenomenon—and he hears our prayers: he can tame nature, help us accept our fate, and reward us for our sufferings. Narcissism creates gods: in God all of our desires are satisfied.

The Humanist Manifesto. "The Humanist Manifesto" is more an announcement than an argument. It is a clarion call to humanism—an anti-theistic philosophy which centers around humans. It begins with the "recognition" that science and economics have undermined religious belief; the progress of knowledge, the authors claim, has forced us in the direction of humanism. Since religions served the useful purpose of moral transformation, humanism must find a way of affirming significant human values in the absence of God.

To that end, humanism is presented in a positive light (not primarily in terms of what it opposes—traditional, metaphysical religion) through fifteen theses. The first four theses declare humanism's commitment to the natural world of which humans and their religions are natural products. While rejecting theism, deism, pantheism, and presumably any other metaphysically extravagant religious "-ism", they nonetheless affirm religion as "those actions, purposes, and experiences which are humanly significant." Religious humanism, therefore, seeks human flourishing in the here and now.

Notes

1. *Thus Spoke Zarathustra*, Walter Kaufmann, editor (New York: Penguin Books, 1954), p. 86.
2. I draw this inference from Sartre's play, "The Flies" from *No Exit and Three Other Plays* (New York: Alfred A. Knopf, Inc. 1948).

Chapter 14

❧

The Hermeneutics of Suspicion

The Opium of the Masses
*Karl Marx**

Man makes religion. For Germany *the criticism of religion* is in the main complete, and criticism of religion is the premise of all criticism.

The *profane* existence of error is discredited after its heavenly *oratio pro aris et focisa* [prayer for earth and home] has been disproved. Man, who looked for a superhuman being in the fantastic reality of heaven and found nothing there but the reflection of himself, will no longer be disposed to find but the semblance of himself, only an inhuman being, where he seeks and must seek his true reality.

The basis of irreligious criticism is: *Man makes religion*, religion does not make man. Religion is the self-consciousness and self-esteem of man who has either not yet found himself or has already lost himself again. But man is no abstract being encamped outside the world. Man is the world of man, the state, society. This state, this society, produce religion, an inverted world-consciousness, because they are an inverted world. Religion is the general theory of that world, its encyclopaedic compendium, its logic in a popular form, its spiritualistic *point d'honneur*, its enthusiasm, its moral sanction, its solemn complement, its universal source of consolation and justification. It is the *fantastic realisation* of the human essence because the human essence has no true reality. The struggle against religion is therefore indirectly a fight against the world of which religion is the spiritual aroma.

The opium of the masses. Religious distress is at the same time the *expression* of real distress and also the *protest* against real distress. Religion is the sigh of the oppressed creature, the heart of a heartless world, just as it is the spirit of spiritless conditions. It is the *opium* of the people.

To abolish religion as the *illusory* happiness of the people is to demand their *real* happiness. The demand to give up illusions about the existing state of affairs is *the demand to give up a state of affairs which needs illusions*. The criticism of religion is therefore *in embryo the criticism of the vale of tears*, the halo of which is religion.

---

*Karl Marx (1818-1883) was born in Prussia but did most of his writing in exile in England.

Criticism has torn up the imaginary flowers from the chain not so that man shall wear the unadorned, bleak chain but so that he will shake off the chain and pluck the living flower. The criticism of religion disillusions man to make him think and act and shape his reality like a man who has been disillusioned and has come to reason, so that he will revolve round himself and therefore round his true sun. Religion is only the illusory sun which revolves round man as long as he does not revolve round himself.

The task of history, therefore, once the *world beyond the truth* has disappeared, is to establish *the truth of this world*. The immediate task of philosophy, which is at the service of history, once the *holy form* of human self-estrangement has been unmasked, is to unmask self-estrangement in its unholy forms. Thus the criticism of heaven turns into the criticism of the earth, the criticism of religion into the criticism of law and the criticism of theology into the criticism of politics.

Critique of Christian morality. The social principles of Christianity have now had eighteen hundred years to develop and need no further development by Prussian consistorial councillors.

The social principles of Christianity justified the slavery of Antiquity, glorified the serfdom of the Middle Ages and equally know, when necessary, how to defend the oppression of the proletariat, although they make a pitiful face over it.

The social principles of Christianity preach the necessity of a ruling and an oppressed class, and all they have for the latter is the pious wish the former will be charitable.

The social principles of Christianity transfer the consistorial councillors' adjustment of all infamies to heaven and thus justify the further existence of those infamies on earth.

The social principles of Christianity declare all vile acts of the oppressors against the oppressed to be either the just punishment of original sin and other sins or trials that the Lord in his infinite wisdom imposes on those redeemed.

The social principles of Christianity preach cowardice, self-contempt, abasement, submission, dejection, in a word all the qualities of the *canaille* [rabble]; and the proletariat, not wishing to be treated as *canaille*, needs its courage, its self-feeling, its pride and its sense of independence more than its bread.

The social principles of Christianity are sneakish and the proletariat is revolutionary.

So much for the social principles of Christianity.

Discussion

1. Has the net effect of religious belief on history been positive or negative? Defend your answer.
2. Is it possible for religions that are committed to the heavenly realm to provide a stimulus for this-worldly social change?

Religion as Resentment

*Friedrich Nietzsche**

Preface, Section 3

Having a kind of scrupulousness peculiar to myself, which I do not readily acknowledge—inasmuch as it has reference to *morality*, to all that so far was known on earth, and celebrated as morality—a scrupulousness which arose in my life so prematurely, so uncalled-for, so irresistibly, so in contradiction to surroundings, age, precedent and ancestry, that I should almost be justified in calling it my *A priori*,—my curiosity as well as my suspicions had to be confronted, at an early date, by the question of *what origin* really are our Good and Evil?...

Fortunately, I learned betimes to separate theological from moral prejudices and to seek no longer *behind* the world for the origin of evil. A little historical and philological schooling, together with an inborn and delicate sense regarding psychological questions, changed my problem in a very short time into that other one: under what circumstances and conditions did man invent those valuations Good and Evil? *and what is their own specific value?* Did they retard or further human progress so far? Are they a sign of need, of impoverishment, of degeneration of life? Or is the reverse the case, do they point to the fullness, the strength, the will of life, its courage, its confidence, its future?...

Preface, Section 6

The problem of the *value* of sympathy and morality of sympathy (I am an opponent of shameful modern effeminacy of sentiment) seems, at first sight, to be something isolated,—a single interrogation-mark; but he who will pause here and will *learn* to question here, will fare even as I have fared: a vast, new prospect reveals itself to him, a possibility seizes upon him like some giddiness; every kind of distrust, suspicion, fear springs up; the faith in morality, in all morality, is shaken,—and finally, a new demand makes itself felt. Let us pronounce this *new demand*: we stand in need of a criticism of moral values; *the value of these values is first of all itself to be put in question*—and to this end a knowledge is necessary of the conditions and circumstances from which they grew and under which they developed and shifted in meaning (morality as effect, as symptom, as mask, as tartuffism [religious hypocrisy], as disease, as misunderstanding; but also, morality as cause, as remedy, as stimulant, as impediment, as poison),—a knowledge which hitherto was not existent, nay, not even desired. The *value* of these "values" was taken for granted, as a matter of fact, as being beyond all ... question. Never until now was there the least doubt or hesitation, to set down "the good man" as of higher value than "the evil man,"—of higher value in the sense of furtherance, utility,

---

*Nietzsche (1844-1900), a German philosopher who was trained in classical philology, taught briefly at the University of Basel and then devoted his life to writing.

prosperity as regards *man* in general (the future of man included). What if the reverse were true? What if in the "good one" also a symptom of decline were contained, and a danger, a seduction, a poison, a narcotic by which the present might live *at the expense of the future*? Perhaps more comfortably, less dangerously, but also in humbler style,—more meanly?

So that just morality were to blame, if a *highest mightiness and splendour* of the type of man—possible in itself—were never attained? And that, therefore, morality itself would be the danger of dangers?

First Essay, Section 2

All due deference, therefore, to the good spirits who may hold sway in these historians of morality! But I am sorry to say that they are certainly lacking in the *historical spirit*, that they have been, in fact, deserted by all the good spirits of history itself. They think, each and every one, according to an old usage of philosophers, *essentially* unhistorically; no doubt whatever! The botchery of their genealogy of morals becomes manifest right at the outset in the determination of the origin, of the concept and judgment "good." "Unselfish actions"—such is their decree—, "were originally praised and denominated 'good' by those to whom they were manifested, *i.e.* those to whom they were *useful*; afterwards, this origin of praise was *forgotten*, and unselfish actions, since they were always *accustomed* to be praised as good, were as a matter of course also felt as such,—as if, in themselves, they were something good." We see at once that this first derivation contains all the typical traits of English psychological idiosyncrasy,—we have "utility," "forgetting," "custom," and last of all "error," and all this as the basis of a valuation which hitherto formed the pride of superior man as being a kind of prerogative of man in general. This pride *must* be humbled, this valuation—devalued. Did they succeed in this?

Now in the first place it is clear to me, that the true and primitive home of the concept "good" was sought for and posited at the wrong place: the judgment "good" was *not* invented by those to whom goodness was shown! On the contrary, the "good," *i.e.* the noble, the powerful, the higher-situated, the high—minded, felt and regarded themselves and their acting as of first rank, in contradistinction to everything low, low-minded, mean and vulgar. Out of this *pathos of distance* they took for themselves the right of creating values, of coining names for these values. What had they to do with utility! In the case of such a spontaneous manifestation and ardent ebullition of highest rank-regulating and rank-differentiating valuations, the point-of-view of utility is as distant and out of place as possible; for in such things the feelings have arrived at a point diametrically opposite to that low degree of heat which is presupposed by every kind of arithmetical prudence, every utilitarian calculation,—and not momentarily, not for a single, exceptional hour, but permanently. The pathos of nobility and distance, as I said, the lasting and dominating, the integral and fundamental feeling of a higher dominating kind of man in contradistinction to a lower kind, to a "below"—*such* is the origin of the antithesis "good" and "bad." (The right of masters to confer names goes so far that we might venture to regard the origin of language itself as a manifestation of power on the part of rulers. They say: "This *is* such and such," they seal every thing and every happening with a sound, and by this act take it, as it were, into possession.) It follows from this derivation that the word "good" has *not* necessarily any connection with unselfish actions, as the superstition of these genealogists of morals would have it. On the contrary, it is only when a *decline* of aristocratic valuations sets in, that this antithesis "selfish" and "unselfish" forces itself with constantly increasing vividness upon the conscience of man,—it is, if I may express myself in my own way, the *herding instinct* which by means of this antithesis succeeds at last in finding expression (and in coining words). And even after this event, a long time elapses before this instinct prevails to such an extent that the moral valuation makes halt at and actually sticks to this antithesis....

First Essay, Section 7
The reader will have conjectured by this time, how readily the priestly manner of valuation will branch off from that of the chivalric-aristocratic caste and *develop* into the antithesis of it; which is especially prone to happen whenever the priest and the warrior-caste jealously oppose each other and fail to come to an agreement as to the prize. The chivalric-aristocratic valuations presuppose a powerful corporality, a vigorous, exuberant, ever-extravagant health, and all that is necessary for its preservation,—war, adventure, hunting, dancing, sports, and in general, all that involves strong, free and cheerful activity. The priestly aristocratic valuation has—as we have seen—other presuppositions: so much the worse it fares in case of war! The priests are, as is well known, the *worst enemies*—and why? Because they are the most impotent. From impotence in their case hatred grows into forms immense and dismal, the most spiritual and most poisonous forms. The greatest haters in history were, at all times, priests; and they were also the haters with the most *esprit*. Indeed, compared with the *esprit* of priestly vindictiveness, all the remaining intelligence is scarcely worth consideration. Human history would be an extremely stupid affair, but for the *esprit* brought into it by the impotent. Let us at once consider the greatest instance! All that has ever been accomplished on earth against the "noble," the "powerful," the "lords," the "mighty" is not worth speaking of, when compared with that which *the Jews* have done against them; the Jews, that priestly people, which finally succeeded in procuring satisfaction for itself from its enemies and conquerors only by a transvaluation of their values, *i.e.* an act of the keenest, *most spiritual vengeance*. Thus only it befitted a priestly people—the people of the most powerfully suppressed, priestly vindictiveness. It was the Jews who, with most frightfully consistent logic, dared to subvert the aristocratic equation of values (good = noble = powerful = beautiful = happy = beloved of God), and who, with the teeth of the profoundest hatred (the hatred of impotency), clung to their own valuation: "The wretched alone are the good; the poor, the impotent, the lowly alone are the good; only the sufferers, the needy, the sick, the ugly are pious; only they are godly; them alone blessedness awaits;—but ye, ye, the proud and potent,

ye are for aye and evermore the wicked, the cruel, the lustful, the insatiable, the godless; ye will also be, to all eternity, the unblessed, the cursed and the damned!"

It is known *who* has been the inheritor of this Jewish transvaluation.

In regard to the enormous initiative fatal, beyond all measure, which the Jews gave by this most fundamental declaration of war, I refer to the proposition which elsewhere presented itself to me (*Beyond Good and Evil*, aph. 195)—namely, that with the Jews *the slave-revolt in morality* begins: that revolt, which has a history of two thousand years behind it, and which today is only removed from our vision because it—has been victorious.

First Essay, Section 8

But this ye do not understand? Ye are blind to something which needed two thousand years ere it came to be triumphant? There is nothing in it surprising to me: all *long* things are hard to see, hard to survey. But *this* is the event: from the trunk of that tree of revenge and hatred, Jewish hatred—the deepest and sublimest hatred, *i.e.* a hatred which creates ideals and transforms values, and which never had its like upon earth—something equally incomparable grew up, a *new love*, the deepest and sublimest kind of love:—and, indeed, from what other trunk could it have grown?

Quite wrong it is, however, to suppose, that this love grew up as the true negation of that thirst of vengeance, as the antithesis of the Jewish hatred! No, the reverse is true! This love grew out of this trunk, as its crown,—as the crown of triumph, which spread its foliage ever farther and wider in clearest brightness and fullness of sunshine, and which with the same vitality strove upwards, as it were, in the realm of light and elevation and towards the goals of that hatred, towards victory, spoils, and seduction, with which the roots of that hatred penetrated ever more and more profoundly and eagerly into everything deep and evil. This Jesus of Nazareth, as the personified gospel of love, this saviour bringing blessedness and victory unto the poor, the sick, the sinners—did he not represent seduction in its most awful and irresistible form—the seduction and by-way to those same *Jewish* values and new ideals? Has not Israel, even by the round-about-way of this "redeemer," this seeming adversary and destroyer of Israel, attained the last goal of its sublime vindictiveness? Does it not belong to the secret black-art of truly *grand* politics of vengeance, of a vengeance far-seeing, underground, slowly-gripping and forereckoning, that Israel itself should deny and crucify before all the world the proper tool of its vengeance, as though it were something deadly inimical,—so that "all the world," namely all enemies of Israel, might quite unhesitatingly bite at this bait? And could, on the other hand, any still *more dangerous* bait be imagined, even with the utmost refinement of spirit? Could we conceive anything which, in influence seducing, intoxicating, narcotising, corrupting, might equal that symbol of the "sacred cross," that awful paradox of a "God on the cross," that mystery of an unfathomable, ultimate, extremest cruelty and self-crucifixion of God *for the salvation of man?*

Thus much is certain, that *sub hoc signo* [under this sign] Israel, with its vengeance and transvaluation of all values, has so far again and again triumphed over all other ideals, over all *nobler* ideals.

First Essay, Section 9

But, Sir, why still speak of *nobler* ideals? Let us submit to the facts: the folk have conquered—or the "slaves," or the "mob," or the "herd" or—call it what you will! If this has come about through the Jews, good! then never a people had a more world-historic mission. The "lords" are done away with; the morality of the common man has triumphed. This victory may at the same time be regarded as an act of blood-poisoning (it has jumbled the races together)—I shall not object. But, beyond a doubt, the intoxication *did succeed*. The redemption of mankind (from "the lords," to wit) is making excellent headway; everything judaïses, christianises or vulgarises in full view....

First Essay, Section 10

The slave-revolt in morality begins by *resentment* itself becoming creative and giving birth to values—the *resentment* of such beings, as real reaction, the reaction of deeds, is impossible to, and as nothing but an imaginary vengeance will serve to indemnify. Whereas, on the one hand, all noble morality takes its rise from a triumphant Yea-saying to one's self, slave-morality will, on the other hand, from the very beginning, say No to something "exterior," "different," "not—self"; *this* No being its creative deed. This reversion of the value-positing eye—this *necessary* glance outwards instead of backwards upon itself—is part of *resentment*. Slave-morality, in order to arise, needs, in the first place, an opposite and outer world; it needs, physiologically speaking, external irritants, in order to act at all;—its action is, throughout, reaction.

The reverse is true in the case of noble valuation. It acts and grows spontaneously. It only seeks for its antithesis in order to say, still more thankfully, still more rejoicingly, Yea to itself. Its negative concept "low," "mean," "bad," is merely a late-born and pale after-image in comparison with the positive fundamental concept of the noble valuation which is thoroughly saturated with life and passion, and says: "We, the noble, we, the good, we, the fair, we, the happy!"...

First Essay, Section 13

But to revert to our theme: the problem of the *other* origin of "good," of "good" as conceived by the man of resentment, calls for its settlement.

—That the lambs should bear a grudge to the big birds of prey, is nowise strange; but this is no reason for blaming the big birds of prey for picking up small lambs. And if the lambs say among themselves: "These rapacious birds are wicked; and he who is as little as possible of a bird of prey, but rather the opposite, *i.e.*, a lamb—should not he be good?" we cannot find fault with the establishment of such an ideal, though the birds of prey may make rather mocking eyes and say: *"We do* not bear at all a grudge to them, these good lambs, we even love them. Nothing is more delicious than a tender lamb." To demand of strength, that it should *not* manifest itself as strength, that it should *not* be a will to overpower, to subdue, to become master of, that it should *not* be a thirst for enemies, resistance, and triumphs, is as absurd as to demand of weakness that it should manifest itself as strength.... No wonder, therefore, if the suppressed and secretly glowing emotions, hatred and revenge, avail themselves of this belief and, in fact, support no belief with so much zeal as this, that the *strong are free* to be weak, and that a rapacious bird can, if it will, be a lamb. For in this way they appropriate in their minds the right of *imputing* to the bird of prey the fact that it is rapacious.

If the suppressed, the down-trodden and the wronged, prompted by the craft of impotence, say to themselves: "Let us be different from the bad, let us be good! and good are all those who wrong no one, who never violate, who never attack, who never retaliate, who entrust revenge to God, who, like us, live aloof from the world, who avoid all contact with evil, and who, altogether, demand little of life, as we do, the patient, the humble, the just"—this means, viewed coolly and unprejudicially, no more than: "We, the weak, are,—it is a fact—weak; it is well for us not to do anything, *for which we are not strong enough*." But this stern matter of fact, this meanest kind of prudence, shared even by insects (which occasionally simulate death, in order not to do "too much" in case of great danger), has, thanks to the trickery and self-imposition of impotence, clothed itself in the apparel of renouncing, silent, abiding virtue, as if the weakness of the weak one itself, *i.e.*, presumably his *being*, his action, his entire, unavoidable, inseparable reality—were a voluntary performance, a thing self-willed, self-chosen, a *deed*, a *desert*. To this kind of man, the *necessity* of the belief in an indifferent, free-willed "subject" is prompted by the instinct of self-preservation, self—assertion,—an instinct by which every falsehood uses to sanctify itself. The subject (or, speaking more popularly, the *soul*) has perhaps been, so far, the best religious tenet on earth, even for the reason that it made possible for the majority of mortals, the weak and oppressed of every description, that sublime self-defraudation of interpreting weakness itself as freedom, the fact of their being thus and thus as a *desert*.

First Essay, Section 14

Will some one look down and into the secret of the way in which *ideals are manufactured* on earth? Who has the courage to do so? Up! Here the view into this dark work-shop is open. Yet a moment, my good Sir Pry and Break-neck! Your eye must first get accustomed to this false and fickle light.

So! Enough! Now speak! What is going on below? Speak out, what you see, man of most dangerous curiosity! Now I am the listener.—

"I see nothing, I hear the more. It is a cautious, knavish, suppressed mumbling and muttering together in every nook and corner. It seems to me they lie. A sugared mildness cleaves to every sound. Weakness is to be falsified into *desert*, no doubt whatever—it is as you said."—

Go on!

"And impotence which requiteth not is falsified into 'goodness'; timorous meanness into 'humility'; submission to those whom one hates into 'obedience' (namely to one who they say commands this obedience; they call him God). The inoffensiveness of the 'weak one,' cowardice itself, in which he is rich, his standing at the door, his unavoidable necessity of waiting comes here by good names, such as 'patience'; they even call it *the cardinal virtue*. Not-to-be-able-to-take-revenge is called not-to-will-revenge, perhaps even forgiveness ('for *they* know not what they do; we alone know what *they* do'). They also talk of 'love for their enemies'—and sweat in doing so."

On!

"They are wretched, no doubt, all these mumblers and underground forgers, though warmly seated together. But they tell me that their wretchedness is a selection and distinction from God, that the dogs which are liked most are whipped, that their misery may, perhaps, also be a preparation, a trial, a schooling perhaps even more—something which at some time to come will be requited and paid back with immense interest in gold, no! in happiness. This they call blessedness."

On!

"Now they will have me understand, that not only they are better than the mighty, the lords of the earth, whose spittle they must lick (*not* from fear, no, not at all from fear! but because God commands to have respect for all authority)—that not only they *are* better, but are also, or certainly will be, 'better off' one day. But enough! enough! I cannot stand it any longer. Bad air! Bad air! This work-shop in which *ideals are manufactured*—methinks, it stinks from lying all over."

No! Yet a moment! You have not yet said anything of the masterpiece of these necromancers, who from every black prepare white, milk and innocence. Did you notice what the very acme of their *raffinement* [refinement] is,—their keenest, finest, subtlest, falsest artist manipulation? Mark well! These cellar-animals filled with hatred and revenge—what is it they are making just out of hatred and revenge? Have you ever heard such words? Would you believe, if trusting merely their words, that you are all among beings of resentment?

"I perceive, once again I open my ears (ah! ah! ah! and *shut* my nose). Now only I hear, what they were saying so often: 'We, the good, *we are the just*.' What they ask for, they do not call retribution, but 'the triumph of *justice*'; what they hate, is not their enemy, no! they hate '*wrong-doing*,' and 'ungodliness.' What they believe in, and hope for, is not the hope of revenge, the drunkenness of sweet revenge (—sweeter than honey, already Homer called it), but 'the victory of God, the just God, over the godless.' What remains for them to love on earth, is not their brethren in hatred, but their 'brethren in love,' as they say,—all the good and the just on earth."

And how do they call that which serves them as consolation in all the sufferings of life—their phantasmagoria of an anticipated future blessedness?

"What? Hear I right? They call it 'the final judgment,' the coming of *their* kingdom, of the 'kingdom of God!' *Meanwhile* they live 'in faith, in love, in hope.'"

Enough! Enough!

Discussion

1. Nietzsche is searching for the value behind values. Consider your moral values: what motives could lead you to cherish them? How is it possible for unrecognized motives to encourage the sustenance of these values?
2. If morality is not God-given, then it must have come from somewhere else. What is Nietzsche's explanation of the origin of Christian values? How satisfying is his explanation?
3. Nietzsche is often criticized for being nihilistic (denying all values). But he endorses knightly-aristocratic values. What are these values and what is the value behind these values?

The Future of an Illusion
*Sigmund Freud**

Threats to human existence. In what does the peculiar value of religious ideas lie?

We have spoken of the hostility to civilization which is produced by the pressure that civilization exercises, the renunciations of instinct which it demands. If on e imagines its prohibitions lifted—if, then, one may take any woman one pleases as a sexual object, if one may without hesitation kill one's rival for her love or anyone else who stands in one's way, if, too, one can carry off any of the other man's belongings without asking leave—how splendid, what a string of satisfactions one's life would be! True, one soon comes across the first difficulty: everyone else has exactly the same wishes as I have and will treat me with no more consideration than I treat him. And so in reality only one person could be made unrestrictedly happy by such a removal of the restrictions of civilization, and he would be a tyrant, a dictator, who had seized all the means to power. And even he would have every reason to wish that the others would observe at least one cultural commandment: 'thou shalt not kill'.

But how ungrateful, how short-sighted after all, to strive for the abolition of civilization! What would then remain would be a state of nature, and that would be far harder to bear. It is true that nature would not demand any restrictions of instinct from us, she would let us do as we liked; but she has her own particularly effective method of restricting us. She destroys us—coldly, cruelly, relentlessly, as it seems to us, and possibly through the very things that occasioned our satisfaction. It was precisely because of these dangers with which nature threatens us that we came together and created civilization, which is also, among other things, intended to make our communal life possible. For the principal task of civilization, its actual *raison d'etre* is to defend us against nature.

Civilization and consolation. We all know that in many ways civilization does this fairly well already, and clearly as time goes on it will do it much better. But no one is under the illusion that nature has already been vanquished; and few dare hope that she will ever be entirely subjected to man. There are the elements, which seem to mock at all human control: the earth, which quakes and is torn apart and buries all human life and its works; water, which deluges and drowns everything in a turmoil; storms, which blow everything before them; there are diseases, which we have only recently recognized as attacks by other organisms; and, finally there is the painful riddle of death, against which no medicine has yet been found, nor probably will be. With these forces nature rises up against us, majestic, cruel and inex-

---

*Sigmund Freud (1856-1939), considered the father of psychoanalysis, spent most of his life in Vienna.

orable; she brings to our mind once more our weakness and helplessness, which we thought to escape through the work of civilization. One of the few gratifying and exalting impressions which mankind can offer is when, in the face of an elemental catastrophe, it forgets the discordancies of its civilization and all its internal diffi-culties and animosities, and recalls the great common task of preserving itself against the superior power of nature.

For the individual, too, life is hard to bear, just as it is for mankind in general. The civilization in which he participates imposes some amount of privation on him, and other men bring him a measure of suffering, either in spite of the precepts of his civilization or because of its imperfections. To this are added the injuries which untamed nature—he calls it Fate—inflicts on him. One might suppose that this condition of things would result in a permanent state of anxious expectation in him and a severe injury to his natural narcissism. We know already how the individual reacts to the injuries which civilization and other men inflict on him: he develops a corresponding degree of resistance to the regulations of civilization and of hostility to it. But how does he defend himself against the superior powers of nature, of Fate, which threaten him as they threaten all the rest?

Civilization relieves him of this task, it performs it in the same way for all alike; and it is noteworthy that in this almost all civilizations act alike. Civilization does not call a halt in the task of defending man against nature, it merely pursues it by other means. The task is a manifold one. Man's self-regard, seriously menaced, calls for consolation; life and the universe must be robbed of their terrors; moreover his curiosity, moved, it is true, by the strongest practical interest, demands an answer.

Wish-fulfillment. A great deal is already gained with the first step: the humaniza-tion of nature. Impersonal forces and destinies cannot be approached; they remain eternally remote. But if the elements have passions that rage as they do in our own souls, if death itself is not something spontaneous but the violent act of an evil Will, if everywhere in nature there are Beings around us of a kind that we know in our own society, then we can breathe freely, can feel at home in the uncanny and can deal by psychical means with our senseless anxiety. We are still defenceless perhaps, but we are no longer helplessly paralysed; we can at least react. Perhaps, indeed, we are not even defenceless. We can apply the same methods against these violent supermen outside that we employ in our own society; we can try to adjure them, to appease them, to bribe them, and, by so influencing them, we may rob them of a part of their power. A replacement like this of natural science by psychology not only provides immediate relief, but also points the way to a further mastering of the situation.

For this situation is nothing new. It has an infantile prototype, of which it is in fact only the continuation. For once before one has found oneself in a similar state of helplessness: as a small child, in relation to one's parents. One had reason to fear them, and especially one's father, and yet one was sure of his protection against the dangers one knew. Thus it was natural to assimilate the two situations. Here, too, wishing played its part, as it does in dream-life. The sleeper may be seized with a presentiment of death, which threatens to place him in the grave. But the dream-work knows how to select a condition that will turn even that dreaded event into a wish-fulfillment.... In the same way, a man makes the forces of nature not simply into persons with whom he can associate as he would with his equals—that would not do justice to the overpowering impression which those forces make on him—but he gives them the character of a father. He turns them into gods, following in this, as I have tried to show, not only an infantile prototype but a phylogenetic one.

In the course of time the first observations were made of regularity and conformity to law in natural phenomena, and with this the forces of nature lost their human traits. But man's helplessness remains and along with it his longing for his father, and the gods. The gods retain their threefold task: they must exorcise the terrors of nature, they must reconcile men to the cruelty of Fate, particularly as it is shown in death, and they must compensate them for the sufferings and privations which a civilized life in common has imposed on them.

But within these functions there is a gradual displacement of accent. It was observed that the phenomena of nature developed automatically according to internal necessities. Without doubt the gods were the lords of nature; they had arranged it to be as it was and now they could leave it to itself. Only occasionally, in what are known as miracles, did they intervene in its course, as though to make it plain that they had relinquished nothing of their original sphere of power. As regards the apportioning of destinies, an unpleasant suspicion persisted that the perplexity and helplessness of the human race could not be remedied. It was here that the gods were most apt to fail. If they themselves created Fate, then their counsels must be deemed inscrutable. The notion dawned on the most gifted people of antiquity that Moira (Fate) stood above the gods and that the gods themselves had their own destinies. And the more autonomous nature became and the more the gods withdrew from it, the more earnestly were all expectations directed to the third function of the gods—the more did morality become their true domain. It now became the task of the gods to even out the defects and evils of civilization, to attend to the sufferings which men inflict on one another in their life together and to watch over the fulfillment of the precepts of civilization, which men obey so imperfectly. Those precepts themselves were credited with a divine origin; they were elevated beyond human society and were extended to nature and the universe.

The origin of gods. And thus a store of ideas is created, born from man's need to make his helplessness tolerable and built up from the material of memories of the helplessness of his own childhood and the childhood of the human race. It can clearly be seen that the possession of these ideas protects him in two directions—against the dangers of nature and Fate, and against the injuries that threaten him from human society itself. Here is the gist of the matter. Life in this world serves a higher purpose; no doubt it is not easy to guess what that purpose is, but it certainly signifies a perfecting of man's nature. It is probably the spiritual part of man, the soul, which in the course of time has so slowly and unwillingly detached itself from the body, that is the object of this elevation and exaltation. Everything that happens in this world is an expression of the intentions of an intelligence superior to us, which in the end, though its ways and byways are difficult to follow, orders everything for the best—that is, to make it enjoyable for us. Over each one of us there watches a benevolent Providence which is only seemingly stern and which will not suffer us to become a plaything of the over-mighty and pitiless forces of nature. Death itself is not extinction, is not a return to inorganic lifelessness, but the beginning of a new kind of existence which lies on the path of development to something higher. And, looking in the other direction, this view announces that the same moral laws which our civilizations have set up govern the whole universe as well, except that they are maintained by a supreme court of justice with incomparably more power and consistency. In the end all good is rewarded and all evil punished, if not actually in this form of life then in the later existences that begin after death. In this way all the terrors, the sufferings and the hardships of life are destined to be obliterated. Life after death, which continues life on earth just as the invisible part of the spectrum joins on to the visible part, brings us all the perfection that we may perhaps have missed here. And the superior wisdom which directs this course of things, the infinite goodness that expresses itself in it, the justice that achieves its aim in it—these are the attributes of the divine beings who also created us and the world as a whole, or rather, of the one divine being into which, in our civilization, all the gods of antiquity have been condensed....

Discussion

1. Is it surprising that the religious beliefs of most believers turn out to include just those things (powers or gods) that satisfy their deepest desires?
2. Suppose Freud was right in his understanding of the origin of religious belief. What is the relevance of Freud's claim to the truth of religious beliefs?
3. Try to use wish-fulfillment on Freud. Can you think of any deep desires that atheism would satisfy?

Chapter 15

Humanism

A Humanist Manifesto
by many authors, including Roy Wood Sellars and E. H. Wilson*

Introduction. The time has come for widespread recognition of the radical changes in religious beliefs throughout the modern world. The time is past for mere revision of traditional attitudes. Science and economic change have disrupted the old beliefs. Religions the world over are under the necessity of coming to terms with new conditions created by a vastly increased knowledge and experience. In every field of human activity, the vital movement is now in the direction of candid and explicit humanism. In order that religious humanism may be better understood we, the undersigned, desire to make certain affirmations which we believe the facts of our contemporary life demonstrate.

There is great danger of a final, and we believe fatal, identification of the word religion with doctrines and methods which have lost their significance and which are powerless to solve the problems of human living in the Twentieth Century. Religions have always been means for realizing the highest values of life. Their end has been accomplished through the interpretation of the total environing situation (theology or world view), the sense of values resulting therefrom (goal or ideal), and the technique (cult), established for realizing the satisfactory life. A change in any of these factors results in alteration of the outward forms of religion. This fact explains the changefulness of religions throughout the centuries. But through all changes religion itself remains constant in its quest for abiding values, an inseparable feature of human life.

Today man's larger understanding of the universe, his scientific achievements, and his deeper appreciation of brotherhood have created a situation which requires a new statement of the means and purposes of religion. Such a vital, fearless, and

---

*"The Manifesto is a product of many minds. It was designed to represent a developing point of view, not a new creed. The individuals whose signatures appear would, had they been writing individual statements, have stated the propositions in differing terms. The importance of the document is that more than thirty men have come to general agreement on matters of final concern and that these men are undoubtedly representative of a large number who are forging a new philosophy out of the materials of the modern world." — Raymond B. Bragg (1933)

frank religion capable of furnishing adequate social goals and personal satisfactions may appear to many people as a complete break with the past. While this age does owe a vast debt to the traditional religions, it is nonetheless obvious that any religion that can hope to be a synthesizing and dynamic force for today must be shaped for the needs of this age. To establish such a religion is a major necessity of the present. It is a responsibility which rests upon this generation.

Fifteen theses. We therefore affirm the following:

First: Religious humanists regard the universe as self-existing and not created.

Second: Humanism believes that man is a part of nature and that he has emerged as the result of a continuous process.

Third: Holding an organic view of life, humanists find that the traditional dualism of mind and body must be rejected.

Fourth: Humanism recognizes that man's religious culture and civilization, as clearly depicted by anthropology and history, are the product of a gradual development due to his interaction with his natural environment and with his social heritage. The individual born into a particular culture is largely molded by that culture.

Fifth: Humanism asserts that the nature of the universe depicted by modern science makes unacceptable any supernatural or cosmic guarantees of human values. Obviously humanism does not deny the possibility of realities as yet undiscovered, but it does insist that the way to determine the existence and value of any and all realities is by means of intelligent inquiry and by the assessment of their relation to human needs. Religion must formulate its hopes and plans in the light of the scientific spirit and method.

Sixth: We are convinced that the time has passed for theism, deism, modernism, and the several varieties of "new thought."

Seventh: Religion consists of those actions, purposes, and experiences which are humanly significant. Nothing human is alien to the religious. It includes labor, art, science, philosophy, love, friendship, recreation—all that is in its degree expressive of intelligently satisfying human living. The distinction between the sacred and the secular can no longer be maintained.

Eighth: Religious humanism considers the complete realization of human personality to be the end of man's life and seeks its development and fulfillment in the here and now. This is the explanation of the humanist's social passion.

Ninth: In place of the old attitudes involved in worship and prayer the humanist finds his religious emotions expressed in a heightened sense of personal life and in a cooperative effort to promote social well-being.

Tenth: It follows that there will be no uniquely religious emotions and attitudes of the kind hitherto associated with belief in the supernatural.

Eleventh: Man will learn to face the crises of life in terms of his knowledge of their naturalness and probability. Reasonable and manly attitudes will be fostered by education and supported by custom. We assume that humanism will take the path of social and mental hygiene and discourage sentimental and unreal hopes and wishful thinking.

Twelfth: Believing that religion must work increasingly for joy in living, religious humanists aim to foster the creative in man and to encourage achievements that add to the satisfactions of life.

Thirteenth: Religious humanism maintains that all associations and institutions exist for the fulfillment of human life. The intelligent evaluation, transformation, control, and direction of such associations and institutions with a view to the enhancement of human life is the purpose and program of humanism. Certainly religious institutions, their ritualistic forms, ecclesiastical methods, and communal activities must be reconstituted as rapidly as experience allows, in order to function effectively in the modern world.

Fourteenth: The humanists are firmly convinced that existing acquisitive and profit-motivated society has shown itself to be inadequate and that a radical change in methods, controls, and motives must be instituted. A socialized and cooperative economic order must be established to the end that the equitable distribution of the means of life be possible. The goal of humanism is a free and universal society in which people voluntarily and intelligently cooperate for the common good. Humanists demand a shared life in a shared world.

Fifteenth and last: We assert that humanism will: (a) affirm life rather than deny it; (b) seek to elicit the possibilities of life, not flee from it; and (c) endeavor to establish the conditions of a satisfactory life for all, not merely for the few. By this positive morale and intention humanism will be guided, and from this perspective and alignment the techniques and efforts of humanism will flow.

Conclusion. So stand the theses of religious humanism. Though we consider the religious forms and ideas of our fathers no longer adequate, the quest for the good life is still the central task for mankind. Man is at last becoming aware that he alone is responsible for the realization of the world of his dreams, that he has within himself the power for its achievement. He must set intelligence and will to the task.

Discussion

1. What do you think are the connections between science and traditional religion? Should we be as dismissive of traditional religion as these authors contend?
2. Defend the view that human values are meaningful in a world without God. What are some criticisms of this view?
3. Religions often avail themselves of powerful tools of moral transformation: religious and moral instruction, the power of small communities to create an ethos or expectation of righteousness, the Holy Spirit or some other "divine power", etc. What can the religious humanist offer human beings for moral transformation?

Critiques of God

Suggestions for Further Study

de Lubac, Henry. *The Drama of Atheist Humanism*. Cleveland: World Publishing Company, 1963.

Dupré, Louis. *The Philosophical Foundations of Marxism*. New York: Harcourt, Brace and World, 1966.

Kaufmann, Walter. *Nietzsche: Philosopher, Psychologist, Antichrist*. 3rd ed. New York: Random House, 1968.

Ricoeur, Paul. *Freud and Philosophy*. Trans. Denis Savage. New Haven: Yale University Press, 1970.

Rieff, Philip. *Freud: The Mind of a Moralist*. Garden City, NY: Doubleday, 1961.

Westphal, Merold. *Suspicion and Faith: The Religious Uses of Modern Atheism*. New York: Fordham University Press, 1998.

Part Five

Philosophical Theology

Introduction

❧

Philosophical Theology

Introduction. Most textbooks in the philosophy of religion contain a section on what are considered the traditional divine attributes of omnipotence, omniscience, immutability, aseity, perfect goodness and eternity; let us call the view that ascribes all of these properties to God *classical theism*. Omnipotence is the ability to do anything (with some qualifications as we shall see shortly). "Omniscience" means all-knowing and "immutability" means unchanging. God's aseity is usually attached to the doctrine of divine sovereignty—that everything depends upon God—and means that God does not depend on anything. "Perfect goodness" means that God is perfectly good, but it is difficult to say just exactly what that means! And "eternity" means that God is outside of, and therefore not bound by, time.

There is no reason that these particular attributes should merit more attention than any other divine attributes, although these attributes are at the center of a great many philosophical puzzles. Unfortunately, most non-philosophers find these puzzles sterile and unconnected with their religious concerns. The essays in this section will raise some of the problems of classical theism but through the medium of more existentially pressing concerns: the problems of divine suffering, prayer, hell, religious pluralism and feminist theology. These issues are not unrelated, as we shall see, to classical theism. We can, for example, raise the issue of divine immutability and eternity through a consideration of either divine suffering or prayer. We can approach God's omnipotence and omniscience through the problem of hell (or, as we have seen, through the problem of evil).

Many recent philosophers have seen fit to reject one or another of the divine attributes of classical theism. Arguments have been offered against divine eternity, immutability, omnipotence, foreknowledge, and even goodness. If all of the attributes the classical theist ascribes to God are rejected, one may wonder, of course, about just what is left that is distinctly *divine* in the nature of God. The essays in this section contain a cross-section of both classical theists and their critics.

Classical theism. Omniscience, omnipotence, immutability and eternity are a set of divine attributes that are considered necessary for a maximally perfect being. What is seen as necessary by some has been rejected by others as being too Greek. Early Judeo-Christian theology was more anthropomorphic, less abstruse and systematic than the subsequently developed theologies of Augustine, Anselm and Aquinas (or Maimonides for Jewish theology and Averroes and Avicenna for Muslim theology). Finding inspiration in the ideas of Plato, Aristotle and the neoplatonists, these thinkers wedded the philosophical systems of the Greeks with Biblical revelation. The resulting orthodoxy, classical theism, raised both problems and prospects for subsequent theorizing about the divine.

Omnipotence is, at first glance, a simple property: God can do anything. Many people have heard (and snickered at) the so-called paradox of omnipotence: can God create a stone so big that he cannot lift it? Various answers are "no" (a "stone that God cannot lift" is impossible and God can only do the logically possible) and "yes" (God *can* make a stone that he cannot lift and, being omnipotent, can lift it!). This paradox does raise a serious problem for omnipotence: can God do just anything? Is God limited by the logically impossible? And there are other concerns related to omnipotence: can God change the past or sin? Defining omnipotence is not nearly so simple as one might have at first thought.

Omniscience creates problems both in itself and in conjunction with other properties. If, for example, God is outside of time, can he know what time it is now? Since time is ever-changing, doesn't this sort of knowledge require that God be ever-changing (hence, creating a problem for immutability)? Omniscience of the foreknowledge variety generates a problem for belief in human freedom. If God infallibly knows whatever one will do before one does it, could one possibly be free? Freedom seems to include the ability to do otherwise (to be able to accept or refuse, say, that tempting piece of chocolate). But if God infallibly knows that you are going to accept that piece of chocolate, then you must do so. For, if you were not to choose that piece of chocolate, God would have had a false belief. But this, surely, is impossible. So you must, of necessity, do whatever God has already foreseen that you will do. So no one's actions are free. The most famous solution to this problem was offered by Boethius who appealed to divine eternity to solve the matter.[1]

As I said above, it is difficult to parse the definition of divine goodness. Theists believe in God's paternal care but must reconcile such care with the evils faced by his children. We would call no earthly father good if he could have prevented his children from suffering in, say, the holocaust but did not. In what sense was God good to the Ukrainians who were forced to starve under Stalin? In reply, theists often claim that God's ways are not our ways, but then the doctrine of divine goodness becomes an utter mystery. If God's ways are totally unlike human ways, then we could not possibly understand what it might mean for God to be good. The problem of divine goodness is raised to a fever pitch when it comes to the problem of the eternal suffering of the damned. How could a perfectly good being permit or perpetuate the eternal suffering of any of his creatures?

Since some of the properties of classical theism are entailed by other properties, there is a tight conceptual connection among all of the properties. For example, an immutable being must also be outside of time (for time, on some accounts, is the measure of change). Some thinkers contend that a perfectly good being must also be omniscient (to be good, one must know the good and how to maximize it); or, perhaps it goes the other way around, an omniscient being is perforce a perfectly good being. So the rejection of a single property might have ramifications for the entire set of properties endorsed by classical theism.

The suffering of God. The idea that God (the Father) could suffer was dismissed by the early Christian church as heresy. God, so it was believed, existed in a perfect state of uninterrupted, suffering-free bliss. God depends solely upon himself for his happiness and is sufficiently interesting and communal to satisfy himself. God need not, indeed could not, depend on his creatures for his well-being.

God's immutability, aseity, timelessness and, some claim, perfect goodness are all bound up in whether or not God can suffer. If God suffers with us, that is, upon the occasion of the suffering of his children, then God changes from a suffering-free condition (say prior to creation) to a suffering condition (say upon the fall of Adam or upon hearing the cries of his people in bondage in Egypt). If God were to change, then God would be in time. And if God were the kind of being whose well-being depended upon the well-being of his creatures, then God's aseity would be in jeopardy. On the other hand, how could God be loving, that is care for the welfare of his creatures, and remain in a state of bliss?

Johan Scotus Eriugena, John the Scot (who was Irish), defends the classical view of God and God's imperviousness to human woes. Scotus raises a particular problem for classical theism and its relation to divine love. If God is neither moved nor mover, neither actor nor acted upon, in what sense does God love his creatures? Scotus first makes a claim about language: we only speak of God's motion and action, and hence love, in metaphorical terms. Scotus then tries to cash out the metaphors in a less metaphorical manner which preserves both God's love and God's independence from his creatures. God loves his creatures not by acting upon them, nor by being affected by them, but by attracting them like a magnet attracts shards of iron.

Nicholas Wolterstorff locates the discussion of God's suffering within the broader context of happiness. The eudaemonistic ideal—that we are happiness-seekers—finds expression in the desire to remove all suffering and grief from our lives. To do so we must attach our loves, our *eros*, only to that which both fully satisfies and cannot be lost. For human beings that means attaching our eros to God and—here's the crucial point—for God it means exactly the same thing. God's eros is a longing for that which is fully adequate and cannot be lost—God's eros is for God himself. That means that God cannot love us in a manner which does not requite; God wills good things for his creatures (God is benevolent) but God's well-being does not depend on any (positive or negative) responses of his creatures.

Wolterstorff condemns this picture of the divine life as both unbliblical (many Jewish thinkers have made this point) and as incoherent. God embraces the world in suffering love—he cares enough for his creation to suffer with it.

Prayer. Prayer is a simple matter on the surface. Many people acquire the practice of prayer as early as they acquire language, and for the rest of their lives, they pray as naturally and unconsciously as they employ their native tongue. Prayer becomes part of the fabric of their lives in the same way that language does; so, if someone were to ask, "Why do you pray as you do?", they would return the same puzzled expression that the question "Why do you speak as you do?" would elicit. However, as soon as one begins to respond to the former question, one enters a large and complicated labyrinth of ideas that mingle in and around the core of theological thought. One's ideas about prayer have significant ramifications for one's beliefs about God's power, knowledge, goodness, and agency, the nature of causal relations, and human freedom. All of these ideas are interrelated; one's views on one of these ideas will significantly affect one's views on the others. Those who haven't thought much about prayer may find, upon reflection, that their spontaneous practice of prayer is inconsistent with their beliefs on these related ideas.

There have been at least two significant attempts to systematize these ideas into a coherent package. Classical theism, defended here by Thomas Aquinas, held that because it was impossible to move an immutable God with requests, prayer was meant for the edification of human beings. There are many different modes of prayer, including thanksgiving, praise, worship, intercession, petition, and repentance, but they can all be summed up in the following way. Prayer is a discipline which humans practice in order to develop appropriate attitudes towards God. When we bring praise to God in prayer we are acknowledging his awesome power and his tender love, which naturally gives birth to joy and thanksgiving in us. When we bring a sin to God in prayer, we are acknowledging our depravity before God, which cultivates the appropriate feelings of guilt and repentance. When we bring a request to God in prayer, we are acknowledging our utter dependence on God, which enables us in turn to strive more diligently to perform his will with humility.

Recent thinkers have suggested that prayer is meant to establish a relation between God and humans, a relation that affects both members. Eleonore Stump, a classical theist, brings together the relational and the edificational views of prayer in her essay. Petitionary prayer, according to Stump, is precisely what is necessary for God to establish a good relationship with human beings. If God were to give us everything we need without asking, we would get spoiled and be ungrateful. And if God did not permit his creatures to communicate with him through prayer, we might despair. Prayer keeps human beings at the right distance from God, neither too close nor too distant, for a good relationship.

Is there a hell? The problem of evil as traditionally framed is minor in comparison to the eternal suffering of the damned. No finite, earthly suffering could create a problem as big as an eternity of suffering, especially if the suffering is as severe as indicated in most holy writ.

In "Universalism, Hell and the Fate of the Ignorant," Stephen Davis takes on the formidable task of defending the doctrine of hell. After criticizing the doctrine of universalism (that all people will eventually end up in heaven), Davis defines and defends his understanding of the doctrine of separationism—that some people will be separated from divine grace forever. His defense is partly biblical—he is part of the Christian tradition that accepts the authority of scripture. And his defense is partly philosophical—paying heed to philosophical consequences of free will, justice and grace.

Marilyn McCord Adams finds the problems related to the traditional doctrine of hell insurmountable. Adams' critique of hell and corresponding defense of universalism trade on notions of divine goodness and finite human agency. Adams believes that God is good to people as individuals, wishing to create a life for each person that is good (to them) on the whole. Eternal suffering, of course, would prevent God from being good to persons. Adams also defends an Irenaean view of human persons: human beings are not created perfect (contra Augustine) but are finite in both moral and intellectual capacities. Our inability to conceive of the consequences of our actions diminishes our moral responsibility for those actions. Eternal punishment of such impaired creatures would be disproportionate to the "crime." Intriguingly, Adams defends a cognitive role for feelings in making judgments about the doctrine of hell.

Religious pluralism. I live in the midwest of the United States of America. Many Dutch immigrants settled here, most of whom are in the Protestant tradition of John Calvin. There are many Latinos in my town, the vast majority of whom are Roman Catholics. If I were to go to different cities, I would find a connection between religious beliefs and socio-ethnic background. People of this ethnic background, in this neighborhood, who migrated from that part of the world are Jewish or Muslim or Christian or Hindu or Buddhist. If I were teaching philosophy of religion in Saudi Arabia, my students would just as certainly believe that Allah is God and Mohammed is his prophet as my predominantly Christian students believe that Jesus is God. The problems of religious pluralism loom large: who's to say who's right and who's wrong in matters religious? Isn't a claim to exclusive truth on the part of religious practitioners arrogant and unjustifiable? Is religion simply a matter of socio-historical accident?

The leading defender of religious pluralism, the belief that there are many, equally valid paths to God, is John Hick. Hick divides the territory into three options: *religious exclusivism*: that there is only one path to God (say Hinduism or Islam); *religious inclusivism*: there is only one path to God but people can take it without knowing it (there might be "anonymous" Christians or Jews); and *religious pluralism*: the claim that there are many paths all leading to ... to what? It is difficult to say because each religion postulates a different goal for life: nirvana, God (in the Judeo-Christian-Muslim sense), Brahman, the ground of being, non-being, the Tao, etc. Hick claims that each religion is equally successful at salvation-trans-formation-fulfillment. So, at the level of practice, each religion is roughly equal. But it is at the cognitive level that Hick is revisionary. Following Kant, Hick believes that each religion is an expression of the ultimate *as humanly experienced* but not the ultimate *as it is in itself*. One's socio-cultural background shapes the experience of the divine or ultimate reality. The divine reality exceeds one's puny cognitive and linguistic grasp. But, since each religion is equally efficacious at salvation, the essence of religion is left unimpaired; the essence of religion, according to Hick, is to move us from self-centeredness to "reality-centeredness."

Peter van Inwagen is, to put it mildly, an enthusiastic critic of religious plural-ism.[2] He paints a picture of the world as viewed by pluralists and seeks to erase it. Van Inwagen's critique is partly just a summary of his Christian beliefs which entails that other religions are theologically and salvifically deficient. This "scandal of particularity" may sound arrogant so van Inwagen faces these charges straight-away. Suppose that, in fact, Christianity (or Islam or Judaism) *is* the only way to God; shouldn't its practitioners, to the best of their ability, both defend and prop-agate their beliefs? Van Inwagen also notes the similarities between political and religious beliefs. Political beliefs are often mutually exclusive and are seldom reject-ed simply because of their holders' socio-cultural backgrounds. And van Inwagen puts the shoe of arrogance on the pluralist's foot: the pluralist is making a claim about reality and our abilities to grasp it; in so doing she is claiming that everyone who disagrees with her—every Muslim, Buddhist or Christian who makes a claim about divine reality—is wrong. Van Inwagen concludes with a defense of the role of the Church which is salvifically generous.

Feminist theology. A new attack on classical theism has been leveled by feminist thinkers who see an oppressive patriarchy inherent in certain concepts of the divine. Patriarchy is particularly evident in the religions of the Judeo-Christian-Muslim holy writ which seems to root oppression of women in the very nature of God. Indeed, in calling God "Father," there is a privileging of things male. The idea of God as distant, unaffected, benevolent (but lacking eros for his creatures), etc. fits better with the view of God as the unconcerned, stoic father-figure who reigns but doesn't relate. This view has been exacerbated by the divine right of kings—again, the privileging of male authority figures who rule at a great physical and emotional distance from their subjects. And finally, all religious authority on heav-en and on earth has been granted to priests—males who have special access to the divine. Feminist philosophy of religion is a call for freedom from an oppressive patriarchy and all of the defective doctrines which enshrine it.

Patricia Altenbernd Johnson heeds Alvin Plantinga's advice to do philosophy from a Christian perspective. However, she takes her task as doing Christian phi-losophy without the patriarchy which may be embedded in the very conceptual scheme of typical Christian philosophy. Drawing upon the work of Elizabeth

Schussler-Fiorenza, Johnson begins with a biblical deconstruction of patriarchy. She also rejects the exclusive use of masculine names of God because names are symbols that limit the reality they point to. Especially in patriarchal societies negative associations of, for example, "Father" limit our conception of God. These misconceptions can be partly alleviated by expanding our symbols of the sacred to include feminine names and imagery. Johnson develops a philosophy of religion from the perspective of God as Mother.

Notes

1. Boethius, *The Consolation of Philosophy*, Book V (New York: Viking, 1987).
2. For those inclined to believe that the character of philosophers plays a role in the development of their philosophies, there are curious asymmetries between Hick and van Inwagen. Hick was formerly an orthodox Christian who "converted" to an anti-incarnational Christianity (mostly due to the pressures of pluralism). Van Inwagen was not raised in a Christian home and was an adult convert to Christianity.

Chapter 16

Does God Suffer?

Divine Impassibility
*Johan Scotus Eriugena**

The problem raised. If action and reception of action, as we have said, are predicated of God not truly, i.e., not properly, it follows that He neither moves nor is moved; for to move is to act and to be moved is to be acted upon. Then, too, if He neither acts nor is acted upon, how can He be said to love everything and to be loved by everything made by Him? Love is a certain motion of one acting, and being loved is a motion of one being acted upon.... If God loves what He has made, He surely is seen to be moved, for He is moved by His own love. Also, if He is loved by whatever can love, whether or not they know what they love, isn't it obvious that He moves? Of course, the love of His beauty moves them. I cannot see by myself, therefore, how, in order to prevent His appearing to act and be acted upon, He can be said neither to move nor to be moved. I therefore beg you to solve this knotty problem....

Expressing the inexpressible. If the names of essences, substances, or accidents are attributed to God not truly, but by a certain necessity of expressing the Ineffable Nature, doesn't it necessarily follow that neither can the verbs which signify the motions of essences, substances, and accidents be predicated properly of God who, by the incomprehensible and ineffable excellence of His nature, surpasses all essence, substance, accident, motion (both active and passive), and whatever is said and understood, or not said and understood about such things, and yet is present in them? For example, if God is metaphorically called Love, although He is More Than Love and surpasses all love, why would He not similarly be said to love, although He surpasses all motion of love since He aspires to nothing besides Himself, since He alone is all in all? Similarly, if He is described as acting and Actor, doing and Doer, not properly but by a kind of metaphor, why should the same kind of figure of speech not predicate that He acts and does, is acted upon and has

---

*Johan Scotus Eriugena (810-?) was perhaps the greatest Christian philosopher from the time of Augustine (fifth century) to the time of Anselm (eleventh century).

something done to Him? I believe that we must have a similar understanding about the other verbs which signify the motions of all changeable creation, whether those motions are natural, unnatural, intellectual, rational, irrational, corporeal, incorporeal, local, temporal, straight, oblique, angular, circular, or spherical....

God cannot be acted upon. There is no question about reception of action, for I both believe and understand that God is wholly impassive. By *passivity* I mean being acted upon," the opposite of action. Who would dare to say or believe, much less understand, that God is subject to being acted upon when He is Creator, not creature? A long time ago we concluded that when God is said to be acted upon, the expression is obviously figurative....

The problem of divine impassibility and love. I wish that you would tell me more plainly, though, to make me see clearly that when I hear that God loves or is loved, I should understand simply His nature without any motion of lover or beloved. When I am convinced on this point, I won't have any hesitation when I read or hear that He wishes or desires and is desired, cherishes and is cherished, sees and is seen, longs and is longed for, and also moves and is moved. All of these must be grasped by one and the same concept. Just as will, love, affection, vision, longing, and motion, when predicated of Him, implant one and the same idea within us; so the verbs, whether active, passive, or intransitive and whatever their mood have no difference of meaning, in my opinion.

The solution. You are quite right. First, then, hear this definition of love: "Love is the connection and bond by which the whole universe is joined together with ineffable friendship and insoluble unity." It can also be defined as "the natural motion of all things in motion, and the end and resting place beyond which no motion of created things advances." St. Dionysius openly assents to these definitions in his "Amatory Hymns" when he says: "Let us understand love, whether we are speaking of the divine, angelic, intellectual, spiritual, or natural kind, as a unifying and blending power which moves higher things to forethought for the lower, joins equals in a reciprocal bond of communion, and turns the lowest and subordinate toward their betters, placed above them." In the same work he says: "Since we have arranged in order the many loves from the one, let us now join them all together again and gather them from the many into a single, combined love, the father of them all. First let us draw them together into the two universal powers of love, over which complete dominion and primacy are held by the immeasurable Cause of all love, which transcends all things. Toward It universal love reaches out in accordance with the nature of each and every existing thing."... God is deservedly called "Love", therefore, since He is the use of all love and is diffused through everything and gathers everything together, and revolves toward Himself with an ineffable motion of return, and limits the motions of love in all creation in Himself. The very diffusion of Divine Nature into everything in and from It is said to love everything, not that It really is diffused in any way (for It lacks all motion and fills everything at the same time), but that It diffuses and moves the sight of the rational mind through everything (since It is the cause of the mind's diffusion and motion) to search out and find It and, insofar as possible, to understand that It fills all things in order that they may have being; and that, as though by a pacifying bond of universal love, It collects and inseparably comprehends everything in an inseparable unity which is Itself. God is likewise said to be loved by all things that are from Him, not because He is acted upon by them in any way (for He alone is incapable of being acted upon), but because they all long for Him, and His beauty attracts all things to itself. He alone is truly lovable, because He alone is the highest and the true Goodness and Beauty. Indeed, everything in creatures which is understood as truly good, beautiful, and lovable is Himself. As there is nothing essentially good besides Him alone, so there is nothing essentially beautiful or lovable besides Him.

Just as a magnet by its natural power attracts iron near it without moving itself to do so, and without being acted upon by the iron which it attracts, so the Cause of all things leads everything from It back to Itself without any motion of Its own, but by the sole power of Its beauty.

Discussion

1. Describe the God of Johan Scotus. Is this being worthy of worship? Why or why not?
2. What problems does Scotus's view of God raise for God's relationship with his creatures?
3. What is Scotus's view of divine love? Do you think it covers all of the essential aspects of love?

Suffering Love

*Nicholas Wolterstorff**

My heart grew sombre with grief, and wherever I looked I saw only death. My own country became a torment and my own home a grotesque abode of misery. All that we had done together was now a grim ordeal without him. My eyes watched everywhere for him, but he was not there to be seen. I hated all the places we had known together, because he was not in them and they could no longer whisper to me, "Here he comes!." as they would have done had he been alive but absent for a while.... My soul was a burden, bruised and bleeding. It was tired of the man who carried it, but I found no place to set it down to rest. (Augustine, *Confessions* IV, 4; IV, 7)[1]

Confessions. It is in passages such as this, where he exposes to full view the grief which overwhelmed him upon the death of his dear friend from Tagaste, that Augustine is at his most appealing to us in the twentieth century. We are attracted both by the intensity of his love and grief, and by his willingness to expose that grief to his friends and the readers of his *Confessions*. To any who may have experienced torments similar to those Augustine here describes, the passage also has the mysteriously balming quality of expressing with delicate precision the grief they themselves have felt. All the places and all the objects that once whispered "Here he comes" or "Here she comes" have lost their voice and fallen achingly mute.

It is a rough jolt, to discover that at those very points in his life where we find Augustine most appealing, he, from the time of his conversion onward, found himself thoroughly disgusting. His reason for exposing his grief was to share with his readers his confession to God of the senselessness and sinfulness of a love so intense for a being so fragile that its destruction could cause such grief. "Why do I talk of these things?" he asks. And he answers, "It is time to confess, not to question!" (*Confessions* IV, 6).

In the years between the death of his friend and the death of his mother Augustine embraced the Christian faith. That embrace made his response to his mother's death very different from that to his friend's. "I closed her eyes," he says, "and a great wave of sorrow surged into my heart. It would have overflowed in tears if I had not made a strong effort of will and stemmed the flow, so that the tears dried in my eyes...." (*Confessions* IX, 12) On that earlier occasion, tears and "tears alone were sweet to him, for in his heart's desire they had taken the place of his friend" (*Confessions* IV, 4). In his reminiscences he asked why that was so, "why tears are sweet to the sorrowful." "How ... can it be that there is sweetness in the fruit we pluck from the bitter crop of life, in the mourning and the tears, the wailing and the sighs?" (*Confessions* IV, 5) But now, on the occasion of his mother's death, he "fought against the wave of sorrow" (*Confessions* IX, 12).

---

*Nicholas Wolterstorff is the Noah Porter Professor of Philosophical Theology at Yale University.

His struggle for self-control was not successful. He reports that after the burial, as he lay in bed thinking of his devoted mother, "the tears which I had been holding back streamed down, and I let them flow as freely as they would, making of them a pillow for my heart. On them it rested...." (*Confessions* IX, 12) So now, he says to God, "I make you my confession.... Let any man read it who will.... And if he finds that I sinned by weeping for my mother, even if only for a fraction of an hour, let him not mock at me ... but weep himself, if his charity is great. Let him weep for my sins to you...." (*Confessions* IX, 12) The sin for which Augustine wants the person of charity to weep, however, is not so much the sin of weeping over the death of his mother as the sin of which that weeping was a sign. I was, says Augustine, "guilty of too much worldly affection."

Obviously there is a mentality coming to expression here which is profoundly foreign to us. In our own day there are still those who hold back tears—usually because they think it unbecoming to cry, seldom because they think it sinful. But rare is the person who believes that even to feel grief upon the death of a friend or one's mother is to have been guilty of too much worldly affection. The mentality expressed not only shapes Augustine's view of the proper place of sorrow and suffering in human life; it also contributes to his conviction that in God there is no sorrow or suffering. God's life is a life free of sorrow—indeed, a life free of upsetting emotions in general, a life free of passions, a life of apathy, untouched by suffering, characterized only by steady bliss....

The eudaemonistic ideal. But why would anyone who placed himself in the Christian tradition think of God's life as that of non-suffering apathy? The identity of that tradition is determined (in part) by the adherence of its members, in one way or another, to the scriptures of the Old and New Testaments. And even those who read while running cannot fail to notice that God is there pictured as one who sufferingly experiences his world and therefore grieves. What was it, then, that led the tradition to "bracket" this dimension of the biblical picture of God?...

We cannot do better than begin with Augustine. But we would be ill-advised to move at once to what Augustine said about emotions and suffering in the life of God. For it was true of Augustine, as it was of most others in the tradition, that his reflections on the place of emotions and suffering in God's life were merely a component within his more comprehensive reflections on the place of emotions and suffering in the ideal life of persons generally—divine and human together. We must try, then, to grasp that totality. Let us begin with what Augustine says about the proper place of emotions and suffering in human experience.

Augustine frames his thought within the eudaemonistic [happiness] tradition of antiquity. We are all in search of happiness—by which Augustine and the other ancients did not mean a life in which happiness outweighs grief and ennui but a life from which grief and ennui have been cast out—a life of uninterrupted bliss. Furthermore, Augustine aligns himself with the Platonic tradition in his conviction that one's love, one's *eros*, is the fundamental determinant of one's happiness.

Augustine never imagined that a human being could root out *eros* from his existence. Incomplete beings that we are, we inescapably long for fulfillment. The challenge, accordingly, is to choose objects for one's love such that happiness ensues.

Now it was as obvious to Augustine as it is to all of us that grief ensues when that which we love is destroyed or dies, or is altered in such a way that we no longer find it lovable. Says he, in reflecting on his grief upon the death of his friend, "I lived in misery like every man whose soul is tethered by the love of things that cannot last and then is agonized to lose them.... The grief I felt for the loss of my friend had struck so easily into my inmost heart simply because I had poured out my soul upon him, like water upon sand, loving a man who was mortal as though he were never to die" (*Confessions* IV, 6; IV, 8). The cure is to detach one's love from such objects and to attach it to something immutable and indestructible. For Augustine, the only candidate was God. "Blessed are those who love you, O God.... No one can lose you ... unless he forsakes you" (*Confessions* IV, 9).... If it is happiness and rest for your soul that you desire—and who does not?—then fix your love on the eternal immutable God....

Stoicism. Prominent in the ethical philosophy of middle and late antiquity were discussions over the proper place of emotions in life. In those discussions, the Stoic view was famous. Augustine, in *The City of God*,[2] participates in those discussions by staking out his own position on the proper place of emotions in the life of the godly person in opposition to the Stoic position.

Now the Stoics did not say that in the ideal life there would be no emotional coloring to one's experience. They insisted, on the contrary, that in such a life there would be various non-perturbing emotions which they called *eupatheidi*. They regularly cited three of these: Joy, wishfulness, and caution. Their thought was that the ideal life, the happy life, is the life of the wise person—of the person who, by virtue of directing his life by reason, is a person whose character and intentions are morally virtuous. To make it clear that, in their judgment, the only thing good in itself is moral good, they typically refused even to *call* anything else "good." Certain other things are, at best, *preferable*. The wise person, then, *will* rejoice over the moral status he has attained, will wish for the continuation of that status, and will be watchful for what threatens it.

The Stoics went on to say, though, that the sage would be without *pathos*, without passion. He would be *apathés*, apathetic. His condition would be that of *apatheia*—apathy, impassibility, passionlessness. What did they mean?...

It is clear that the classic Stoics thought [all emotional disturbances—with fear, grief, and ecstasy as prime examples—are passions]. One grieves, they would have said, only over what one evaluates as evil; but the sage, finding no trace of moral evil in himself, has nothing over which to grieve. So too, one fears what one evaluates as an evil threatening; but for the sage, who is steady in virtue, there are no threatening evils. And one goes into ecstasy over something that happens to come one's way which one evaluates as good. But for the sage, there are no goods which just happen to come his way; that which is the only thing good for him, namely, his own moral character, is entirely of his own making. It was, thus, the contention of the classic Stoics that as a matter of fact the upsetting emotions are all passions, and will, on that account, have no place in the life of the wise person. The true sage experiences no emotional disturbances....

We have been speaking of the place of the passions in the life of the imperfectly godly person in this imperfect world of ours. But, we must be reminded that Augustine also points us away from life in this world to a perfected life in a perfected world—a life not earned or achieved but granted. In that life there will be no such emotional disturbances as grief and fear. For that will be a life of uninterrupted bliss; and "who that is affected by fear or grief can be called absolutely blessed?" Even "when these affections are well regulated, and according to God's will, they are peculiar to this life, not to that future life we look for" (*City of God* XIV, 9). Augustine's argument, as we have seen, is not the Stoic argument that the passions are always based on false evaluations; they are not. His argument is that having emotions always involves *being overcome,* and that the pain embedded within such emotions as grief and fear is incompatible with full happiness. Grief and fear are not as such incompatible with *reason.* They are as such incompatible with *eudaemonia.* Hence the abolition of those passions from our lives will not occur by way of illumination as to the true nature of things. It will occur by way of removal from our existence of that which it is appropriate to fear or grieve over.

So our perfected existence will exhibit not only *eros* attached entirely to God, but apathy. For attachment to God and detachment from world, we struggle here and now. For *apathy,* we merely long, in the meanwhile fearing and grieving over the evil worth fearing and grieving over. Struggle and longing, aiming and hoping, pull apart in the Augustinian universe. It is not, though.... a feelingless apathy for which we long. We long for a life of joy and bliss....

Divine impassibility. And now the eternal life of God, as understood by Augustine, can be very simply described: God's life satisfies the eudaemonistic ideal implicit in all that has preceded. God's life is through and through blissful. Thus God too is free of negative *pathe.* Of *Mitleiden* [sympathy] with those who are suffering, God feels nothing, as also he feels no pain over the shortfall of godliness in his errant creatures. His state is *apatheia*—an *apatheia* characterized positively by the steady non-perturbing state of joy. God dwells eternally in blissful non-suffering *apatheia.* Nothing that happens in the world alters his blissful unperturbed serenity. Certainly God is not oblivious to the world. There is in him a steady disposition of benevolence toward his human creatures. But this disposition to act benevolently proceeds on its uninterrupted successful course whatever transpires in the world.

In sum, the Augustinian God turns out to be remarkably like the Stoic sage: devoid of passions, unfamiliar with longing, foreign to suffering, dwelling in steady bliss, exhibiting to others only benevolence....

Augustine does indeed make clear that in one important respect God's life is not to be identified with our eudaemonistic ideal. In humanity's perfected existence *eros* is fixed steadily on God. God, in contrast, has no *eros*. Since there is in him no lack, he does not reach out to what would fulfill him. God reaches out exclusively in the mode of benevolence, not in the mode of *eros*....

Are we to say, then, that in his picture of God as dwelling in blissful non-suffering apathy Augustine shows that, whatever be the qualifications he wishes to make for human beings, he still embraces the late antique, Stoic notion of what constitutes perfect existence? Is that the bottom line? Yes, I think we must indeed say this—not only for Augustine but for the tradition in general. Shaped as they were by the philosophical traditions of late antiquity, it was inconceivable to the church fathers that God's existence should be anything other than perfect and that ideal existence should be anything other than blissful....

It is possible, however, to be struck by quite a different aspect of the picture; namely, God remains blissfully unperturbed while humanity drowns in misery. When looked at in this way the picture's look is startlingly reversed, from the compelling to the grotesque. It is this grotesque look of the picture which has forcefully been called to our attention by various contemporary thinkers as they have launched an attack on the traditional picture of the apathetic God....

Suffering love. Does God sufferingly experience what transpires in the world? The tradition said that he does not. The moderns say that he does—specifically, that he sufferingly experiences our suffering. Both parties agree that God loves the world. But the tradition held that God loves only in the mode of benevolence; it proposed construing all the biblical passages in the light of that conviction. The moderns insist that God's love includes love in the mode of sympathy. The moderns paint in attractive colors a moral ideal which is an alternative to that of the tradition, and point to various biblical passages speaking of God's suffering love—passages which the tradition, for centuries, has construed in its own way. The tradition, for its part, offered essentially two lines of defense. It argued that the attribution of emotions and suffering to God was incompatible with God's unconditionedness[3].... And second, it offered a pair of what it took to be obvious truths: that suffering is incompatible with ideal existence, and that God's existence is immutably ideal....

How can we advance from here? Perhaps by looking more intently than we have thus far at that claim of the tradition that God's love consists exclusively of benevolence. Benevolence in God was understood as his steady disposition to do good to his creatures. And since as long as there are creatures—no matter what their condition—there is scope for God's exercise of that disposition, and since his exercise of that disposition is never frustrated, God endlessly takes joy in this dimension of himself. He does not take joy—let us carefully note—in his awareness of the condition of his creatures. He does not delight in beholding the creaturely good that he has brought about. If that were the case, his joy would be conditional on the state of things other than himself. What God joyfully experiences is simply his own exercise of benevolence. God's awareness of our plunge into sin and suffering causes him no disturbance; his awareness of the arrival of his perfected kingdom will likewise give him no joy. For no matter what the state of the world, there is room for God's successful exercise of his steady disposition to do good; and it is in *that* exercise that he finds delight.

An analogue which comes to mind is that of a professional healthcare specialist. Perhaps when first she entered her profession she was disturbed by the pain and limping and death she saw. But that is now over. Now she is neither perturbed nor delighted by the condition of the people that she sees. What gives her delight is just her inner awareness of her own well-doing. And always she finds scope for well-doing—so long, of course, as she has clients. To those who are healthy she gives reassuring advice on health maintenance. To those who are ill she dispenses medicine and surgery. But it makes no difference to her whether or not her advice maintains the health of the healthy and whether or not her proffered concoctions and cuttings cure the illness of the ill. What makes a difference is just her steadiness in well-doing; in this and in this alone she finds her delight. If it falls within her competence she will, of course, cooperate in pursuing the elimination of smallpox; that is doing good. But should the news arrive of its elimination, she will not join the party; she has all along been celebrating the only thing she finds worth celebrating—namely, her own well-doing. She is a Stoic sage in the modern world.

I dare say that most of us find such a person thoroughly repugnant; that shows how far we are from the mentality of many of the intellectuals in the world of late antiquity. But beyond giving vent to our feelings of repugnance, let us consider whether the picture I have drawn is even coherent. Though this person neither rejoices nor suffers over anything in the condition of her patients, nonetheless she rejoices in her own doing of good. But what then does she take as *good*? What does she *value*? The health of her patients, one would suppose. Why otherwise would she give advice to the one on how to maintain his health, and chemicals to the other to recover his, and all the while rejoice, on account of thus acting, in her own doing of good? But if she does indeed value the health of her patients, then perforce she will also be glad over its presence and disturbed by its absence (when she knows about these). Yet we have pictured her as neither happy nor disturbed by anything other than her own well-doing. Have we not described what cannot be?

Perhaps in his description of moral action that great Stoic philosopher of the modern world, Immanuel Kant, can be of help to us here. In the moral dimension of our existence, the only thing good in itself is a good will, said Kant. Yet, of course, the moral person will do such things as act to advance the health of others. Insofar as she acts morally, however, she does not do so because her awareness of health in people gives her delight and her awareness of illness proves disturbing. She may indeed be so constituted that she does thus value health and sickness in others and act thereon. But that is no moral credit to her. To be moral she must act not out of delight over health nor out of disturbance over illness but out of duty. She must act on some rule specifying what one ought to do in her sort of situation—a rule to which, by following, she accords "respect." That is what it is to value good will: to act out of respect for the moral law rather than out of one's natural likings and dislikings, rejoicings and grievings. And the moral person is the person who, wherever relevant, thus values the goodness of her will. Her valuing of that will mean, when her will is in fact good, that she will delight therein. But if she acts out of a desire to delight in having a good will, that too is not moral action; she must act out of respect for the moral law.

Suppose then that our health-care specialist values the goodness of her will and acts thereon by dutifully seeking to advance the health of her patients—delighting in thus acting. She may or may not also value the health of her patients, being disturbed by its absence and delighted by its presence. But if she does not in that way value her patients' health, that does not in any way militate against her delighting in her own well-doing.

We have here, then, a way of understanding how it can be that God delights in his doing good to human beings without either delighting in, or being disturbed by, the human condition. God acts out of duty. Thus acting, he values his own good will without valuing anything in his creation. If we interpret God's benevolence as his acting out of duty, then the traditional picture becomes coherent.

But of course it buys this coherence at great price. For to think thus of God is to produce conflict at a very deep level indeed with the Christian scriptures. These tell us that it is not out of duty but out of love that God blesses us, not out of obligation but out of grace that he delivers us. To construe God's love as purely benevolence and to construe his benevolence along Kantian-Stoic lines as his acting out of duty, is to be left without God's love.

So we are back with the model in which God values things other than his own good will—values positively some of the events and conditions in his creation, and values negatively others. To act out of love toward something other than oneself is to value that thing and certain states of that thing. And on this point it matters not whether the love be erotic or agapic. If one rejects the duty-model of God's action, then the biblical speech about God's prizing of justice and shalom in his creation will have to be taken at face value and not construed as meaning that God has a duty to work for justice and shalom....

I come then to this conclusion: The fact that the biblical writers speak of God as rejoicing and suffering over the state of the creation is not a superficial eliminable feature of their speech. It expresses themes deeply embedded in the biblical vision. God's love for his world is a rejoicing and suffering love. The picture of God as a Stoic sage, ever blissful and nonsuffering, is in deep conflict with the biblical picture.

But are we entitled to say that it is a *suffering* love, someone may ask—a love prompted by a *suffering* awareness of what goes on in the world. An unhappy awareness, Yes; but does it reach all the way to suffering?

What the Christian story says is that God the Father, out of love for humanity, delivered his only begotten Son to the suffering and abandonment and death of the cross. In the light of that, I think it grotesque to suggest that God's valuing of our human predicament was so mildly negative as to cause him no suffering....

Conclusion. In closing let me observe that if we agree that God both sufferingly and joyfully experiences this world of ours and of his, then at once there comes to mind a question which the tradition never asked; namely what in it causes him joy? And then at once there also comes to mind a vision of the relation between *our* suffering and joy and *God's* suffering and joy.... What comes to mind now is the vision of *aligning ourselves* with God's suffering and with his joy: of delighting over that which is such that his awareness of our delight gives him delight and of suffering over that which is such that his awareness of our suffering causes him suffering....

To some of the things of this world one can pay the tribute of recognizing in them worth sufficient to merit a love which plunges into suffering upon their destruction. In one's love one can say a "Yes" to the worth of persons or things and in one's suffering a "No" to their destruction. To friends and relatives one can pay the tribute of loving them enough to suffer upon their death. To justice among one's people one can pay the tribute of loving it enough to suffer upon its tyrannical denial. To the delights of music and voice and birdsong one can pay the tribute of loving them enough to suffer upon going deaf. One can pay to persons and things the existential triumph of suffering love.... Suffering is an essential element in that mode of life which says not only "No" to the misery of our world but "Yes" to its glories.

[This] is a better way [to go]. For it is in line with God's sufferings and God's joys. Instead of loving only God we will love what God loves, including God. For it is in the presence of justice and shalom among his human creatures that God delights, as it is for the full realization of justice and shalom in his perfected Kingdom that he works....

Notes

1. Translated by R. S. Pine-Coffin (Harmondsworth, Middlesex: Penguin Books, 1961). All my citations from the *Confessions* will be from this translation.
2. Augustine, *The City of God*, trans. Marcus Dods (New York: Random House, 1950). My citations will be from this edition.
3. In an omitted section, Wolterstorff rejects this argument.

Discussion

1. Which view of God—suffering or impassible—is more useful when one is suffering? Defend your view.
2. The Bible speaks of a suffering God. But it also speaks of a jealous God and a God who forgets. Where does one draw the line in attributing human properties to God?

3. Wolterstorff suggests that there are practical advantages (i.e., the pursuit of justice and shalom) that result from his conception of God. How could classical theism ground such a pursuit?

Chapter 17

Prayer

Whether It Is Becoming to Pray?

Thomas Aquinas *

Objections to Aquinas's view. *Objection* I. It would seem that it is unbecoming to pray. Prayer seems to be necessary in order that we may make our needs known to the person to whom we pray. But according to Matth. vi. 32, *Your Father knoweth that you have need of all these things.* Therefore it is not becoming to pray to God.

Obj. 2. Further, by prayer we bend the mind of the person to whom we pray, so that he may do what is asked of him. But God's mind is unchangeable and inflexible, according to I Kings xv. 29, *But the Triumpher in Israel will not spare, and will not be moved to repentance.* Therefore it is not fitting that we should pray to God.

Obj. 3. Further, it is more liberal to give to one that asks not, than to one who asks, because, according to Seneca (*De Benefic.* ii. 1), *nothing is bought more dearly than what is bought with prayers.* But God is supremely liberal. Therefore it would seem unbecoming to pray to God.

Aquinas's view. *On the contrary,* It is written (Luke xviii.1): *We ought always to pray, and not to faint.*

I answer that, Among the ancients there was a threefold error concerning prayer. Some held that human affairs are not ruled by Divine providence; whence it would follow that it is useless to pray and to worship God at all: of these it is written (Malach. iii. 14): *You have said: He laboreth in vain that serveth God.* Another opinion held that all things, even in human affairs, happen of necessity, whether by reason of the unchangeableness of Divine providence, or through the compelling influence of the stars, or on account of the connection of causes: and this opinion also excluded the utility of prayer. There was a third opinion of those who held that human affairs are indeed ruled by Divine providence, and that they do not happen of necessity; yet they deemed the disposition of Divine providence to be changeable, and that it is changed by prayers and other things pertaining to the worship of God. All these opinions were disproved in the First Part [of this work]. Where-

---

*Thomas Aquinas (1224-1274) was a monk who taught at the University of Paris.

fore it behooves us so to account for the utility of prayer as neither to impose necessity on human affairs subject to Divine providence, nor to imply changeableness on the part of the Divine disposition.

In order to throw light on this question we must consider that Divine providence disposes not only what effects shall take place, but also from what causes and in what order these effects shall proceed. Now among other causes human acts are the causes of certain effects. Wherefore it must be that men do certain actions, not that thereby they may change the Divine disposition, but that by those actions they may achieve certain effects according to the order of the Divine disposition: and the same is to be said of natural causes. And so is it with regard to prayer. For we pray not that we may change the Divine disposition, but that we may impetrate that which God has disposed to be fulfilled by our prayers, in other words *that by asking, men may deserve to receive what Almighty God from eternity has disposed to give* as Gregory says (*Dial.* i. 8).

Aquinas answers the objections. *Reply Obj*. 1. We need to pray to God, not in order to make known to Him our needs or desires but that we ourselves may be reminded of the necessity of having recourse to God's help in these matters.

Reply Obj. 2. As stated above, our motive in praying is, not that we may change the Divine disposition, but that, by our prayers we may obtain what God has appointed.

Reply Obj. 3. God bestows many things on us out of His liberality, even without our asking for them: but that He wishes to bestow certain things on us at our asking, is for the sake of our good, namely, that we may acquire confidence in having recourse to God, and that we may recognize in Him the Author of our goods. Hence Chrysostom says: *Think what happiness is granted thee, what honor bestowed on thee, when thou conversest with God in prayer, when thou talkest with Christ, when thou askest what thou wilt, whatever thou desirest.*

Discussion

1. From this brief selection, what can be learned about Aquinas's view of God?
2. What problems do divine immutability, providence and goodness create for prayer?
3. Since it is impossible for humans to have any effect upon God, prayer must affect the person praying. How, according to Aquinas, does prayer affect the person praying? Are these benefits adequate?

Petitionary Prayer

Eleonore Stump *

Introduction. Ordinary Christian believers of every period have in general taken prayer to be fundamentally a request made of God for something specific believed to be good by the one praying. The technical name for such prayer is "impetration"; I am going to refer to it by the more familiar designation "petitionary prayer." There are, of course, many important kinds of prayer which are not requests; for example, most of what is sometimes called "the higher sort of prayer"—praise, adoration, thanksgiving—does not consist in requests and is not included under petitionary prayer. But basic, common petitionary prayer poses problems that do not arise in connection with the more contemplative varieties of prayer, and it is petitionary prayer with its special problems that I want to examine in this paper.

... I want to ... concentrate on just one problem. It is, I think, the problem stemming from petitionary prayer which has most often occurred to ordinary Christian believers from the Patristic period to the present....

Put roughly and succinctly, the problem comes to this: is a belief in the efficacy and usefulness of petitionary prayer consistent with a belief in an omniscient, omnipotent, perfectly good God? It is, therefore, a problem only on certain assumptions drawn from an ordinary, orthodox, traditional view of God and of petitionary prayer. If one thinks, for example, as D. Z. Philipps does,[1] that all "real" petitionary prayer is reducible to the petition "Thy will be done," then the problem I want to discuss evaporates. And if one thinks of God as the unknowable, nondenumerable, ultimate reality, which is not an entity at all, as Keith Ward does,[2] the problem I am interested in does not even arise. The cases which concern me in this paper are those in which someone praying a petitionary prayer makes a specific request freely (at least in his own view) of an omniscient, omnipotent, perfectly good God, conceived of in the traditional orthodox way. I am specifying that the prayers are made freely because I want to discuss this problem on the assumption that man has free will and that not everything is predetermined. I am making this assumption, first because I want to examine the problem of petitionary prayer as it arises for ordinary Christian believers, and I think their understanding of the problem typically includes the assumption that man has free will, and secondly because adopting the opposite view enormously complicates the attempt to understand and justify petitionary prayer. If all things are predetermined—and worse, if they are all predetermined by the omnipotent and omniscient God to whom one is praying—it is much harder to conceive of a satisfactory justification for petitionary prayer. One consequence of my making this assumption is that I will not be drawing on important traditional Protestant accounts of prayer such as those given by Calvin

---

*Eleonore Stump is the Robert J. Henle Professor of Philosophy at St. Louis University.

and Luther, for instance, since while they may be thoughtful, interesting accounts, they assume God's complete determination of everything....

The general problem. We can, I think, generalize these arguments to all petitionary prayer by means of a variation on the argument from evil against God's existence. (The argument that follows does not seem to me to be an acceptable one, but it is the sort of argument that underlies the objections to petitionary prayer which I have been presenting. I will say something about what I think are the flaws in this argument later in the paper.)

(1) A perfectly good being never makes the world worse than it would otherwise be if he can avoid doing so.

The phrase "than it would otherwise be" here should be construed as "than the world would have been had he not brought about or omitted to bring about some state of affairs." In other words, a perfectly good being never makes the world, in virtue of what he himself does or omits to do, worse than it would have been had he not done or omitted to do something or other. *Mutatis mutandis* [changing equals for equals], the same remarks apply to "than it would otherwise be" in (4) and (7) below.

(2) An omniscient and omnipotent being can avoid doing anything which it is not logically necessary for him to do.

∴ (3) An omniscient, omnipotent, perfectly good being never makes the world worse than it would otherwise be unless it is logically necessary for him to do so. (1, 2)

(4) A perfectly good being always makes the world better than it would otherwise be if he can do so.

(5) An omniscient and omnipotent being can do anything which it is not logically impossible for him to do.

∴ (6) An omniscient, omnipotent, perfectly good being always makes the world better than it would otherwise be unless it is logically impossible for him to do so. (4, 5)

(7) It is never logically necessary for an omniscient, omnipotent, perfectly good being to make the world worse than it would otherwise be; it is never logically impossible for an omniscient, omnipotent, perfectly good being to make the world better than it would otherwise be.

∴ (8) An omniscient, omnipotent, perfectly good being never makes the world worse than it would otherwise be and always makes the world better than it would otherwise be. (3, 6, 7).

This subconclusion implies that unless the world is infinitely improvable, either the world is or will be absolutely perfect or there is no omniscient, omnipotent, perfectly good being. In other words, (8) with the addition of a pair of premisses—

(i) The world is not infinitely improvable

and

(ii) It is not the case that the world is or will be absolutely perfect (i.e., there is and always will be evil in the world)—

implies the conclusion of the argument from evil. That is not a surprising result since this argument is dependent on the argument from evil.

(9) What is requested in every petitionary prayer is or results in a state of affairs the realization of which would make the world either worse or better than it would otherwise be (that is, than it would have been had that state of affairs not been realized)....

∴ (10) If what is requested in a petitionary prayer is or results in a state of affairs the realization of which would make the world worse than it would otherwise be, an omniscient, omnipotent, perfectly good being will not fulfill that request. (8)

∴ (11) If what is requested in a petitionary prayer is or results in a state of affairs the realization of which would make the world better than it would otherwise be, an omniscient, omnipotent, perfectly good being will bring about that state of affairs even if no prayer for its realization has been made (8)....

∴ (12) Petitionary prayer effects no change. (9, 10, 11)

There is, of course, a sense in which the offering of a prayer is itself a new state of affairs and accompanies or results in natural, psychological changes in the one praying, but step (12) ought to be understood as saying that no prayer is itself efficacious in causing a change of the sort it was designed to cause. An argument which might be thought to apply here, invalidating the inference to the conclusion (13), is that prayer need not effect any change in order to be considered efficacious, provided the offering of the prayer itself is a sufficient reason in God's view for God's fulfillment of the prayer. In other words, if, for certain reasons apart from consideration of a prayer for a state of affairs *S*, God has determined to bring about *S*, a prayer for *S* may still be considered to be efficacious if and only if God would have brought about *S* just in response to the prayer for *S*. But I think that even if this view is correct, it does not in fact invalidate the inference to (13)....

∴ (13) Petitionary prayer is pointless. (12)

The basic strategy of this argument is an attempt to show that there is an inconsistency between God's goodness and the efficacy of petitionary prayer; but it is possible to begin with other divine attributes and make a case for a similar inconsistency, so that we can have other, very different arguments to the same conclusion, namely, that petitionary prayer is pointless. Perhaps the most formidable of such alternative arguments is the one based on God's immutability, an argument the strategy of which can be roughly summarized in this way. Before a certain petitionary prayer is made, it is the case either that God will bring about the state of affairs requested in the prayer or that he will not bring it about. He cannot have left the matter open since doing so would imply a subsequent change in him and he is immutable. Either way, since he is immutable, the prayer itself can effect no change in the state of affairs and hence is pointless. Even leaving aside problems of foreknowledge and free will to which this argument (or attempted objections to it) may give rise, I think that orthodox theology will find no real threat in the argument because of the doctrine of God's eternality. However problematic that doctrine may be in itself, it undercuts arguments such as this one because it maintains God's atemporality. My thirteen-step argument against petitionary prayer is, then, not the only argument rejecting petitionary prayer on theistic principles, but it (or some argument along the same lines) does, I think, make the strongest case against petitionary prayer, given Christian doctrine....

Friendship and prayer. Judaeo-Christian concepts of God commonly represent God as loving mankind and wanting to be loved by men in return. Such anthropomorphic talk is in sharp contrast to the more sophisticated-sounding language of the Hellenized and scholastic arguments considered so far. But a certain sort of anthropomorphism is as much a part of Christianity as is Thomas's "perfect being theology," and it, too, builds on intricate philosophical analysis, beginning perhaps with Boethuis's attempt in *Contra Eutychen et Nestorium* to explain what it means to say of something that it is a person. So to say that God loves men and wants to be loved in return is to say something that has a place in philosophical theology and is indispensable to Christian doctrine. Throughout the Old and New Testaments, the type of loving relationship wanted between man and God is represented by various images, for example, sometimes as the relationship between husband and wife, sometimes as that between father and child. And sometimes (in the Gospel of John, for instance) it is also represented as the relationship between true friends.[3] But if the relationship between God and human beings is to be one which at least sometimes can be accurately represented as the love of true friendship, then there is a problem for both parties to the relationship, because plainly it will not be easy for there to be friendship between an omniscient, omnipotent, perfectly good person and a fallible, finite, imperfect person. The troubles of generating and maintaining friendship in such a case are surely the perfect paradigms of which the troubles of friendship between a Rockefeller child and a slum child are just pale copies. Whatever other troubles there are for friendship in these cases, there are at least two dangers for the disadvantaged or inferior member of the pair. First, he can be so overcome by the advantages or superiority of his "friend" that he becomes simply a shadowy reflection of the other's personality, a slavish follower who slowly loses all sense of his own tastes and desires and will. Some people, of course, believe that just this sort of attitude towards God is what Christianity wants and gets from the best of its adherents; but I think that such a belief goes counter to the spirit of the Gospels, for example, and I don't think that it can be found even in such intense mystics as St. Teresa and St. John of the Cross. Secondly, in addition to the danger of becoming completely dominated, there is the danger of becoming spoiled in the way that members of a royal family in a ruling house are subject to. Because of the power at their disposal in virtue of their connections, they often become tyrannical, willful, indolent, self-indulgent, and the like. The greater the discrepancy in status and condition between the two friends, the greater the danger of even inadvertently overwhelming and oppressing or overwhelming and spoiling the lesser member of the pair; and if he is overwhelmed in either of these ways, the result will be replacement of whatever kind of friendship there might have been with one or another sort of using. Either the superior member of the pair will use the lesser as his lackey, or the lesser will use the superior as his personal power source. To put it succinctly, then, if God wants some kind of true friendship with men, he will have to find a way of guarding against both kinds of overwhelming.

It might occur to someone to think that even if we assume the view that God wants friendship between himself and human beings, it does not follow that he will have any of the problems just sketched, because he is omnipotent. If he wants friendship of this sort with men, one might suppose, let him just will it and it will be his. I do not want to stop here to argue against this view in detail, but I do want just to suggest that there is reason for thinking it to be incoherent, at least on the assumption of free will adopted at the beginning of this paper, because it is hard to see how God could bring about such a friendship magically, by means of his omnipotence, and yet permit the people involved to have free will. If he could do so, he could make a person freely love him in the right sort of way, and it does not seem reasonable to think he could do so. On the face of it, then, omnipotence alone does not do away with the two dangers for friendship that I sketched above. But the institution of petitionary prayer, I think, can be understood as a safeguard against these dangers.

It is easiest to argue that petitionary prayer serves such a function in the case of a man who prays for himself. In praying for himself, he makes an explicit request for help, and thereby he acknowledges a need or a desire and his dependence on God for satisfying that need or desire. If he gets what he prayed for, he will be in a position to attribute his good fortune to God's doing and to be grateful to God for what God has given him. If we add the undeniable uncertainty of his getting what he prays for, then we will have safeguards against what I will call (for lack of a better phrase) overwhelming spoiling. These conditions make the act of asking a safeguard against tyrannical and self-indulgent pride, even if the one praying thinks of himself grandly as having God on his side.

We can see how the asking guards against the second danger, of oppressive overwhelming, if we look for a moment at the function of roughly similar asking for help when both the one asking and the one asked are human beings. Suppose a teacher sees that one of his students is avoiding writing a paper and is thereby storing up trouble for himself at the end of the term. And suppose the student *asks* the teacher for extra help in organizing working time and scheduling the various parts of the work. In that case I think the teacher can without any problem give the student what he needs, provided, of course, that the teacher is willing to do as much for any other student, and so on. But suppose, on the other hand, that the student does not ask the teacher for help and that the teacher instead calls the student at home and simply presents him with the help he needs in scheduling and discipline. The teacher's proposals in that case are more than likely to strike the student as meddling interference, and he is likely to respond with more or less polite variations on "Who asked you?" and "Mind your own business." Those responses, I think, are healthy and just. If the student were having ordinary difficulties getting his work done and yet docilely and submissively accepted the teacher's unrequested scheduling of his time, he would have taken the first step in the direction of unhealthy passivity towards his teacher. And if he and his teacher developed that sort of relationship, he could end by becoming a lackey-like reflection of his teacher. Bestowing at least some benefits only in response to requests for them is a safeguard against such an outcome when the members of the relationship are not equally balanced.

It becomes much harder to argue for this defense of prayer as soon as the complexity of the case is increased even just a little. Take, for example, Monica's praying for her son Augustine. There is nothing in Monica's praying for Augustine which shows that *Augustine* recognizes that *he* has a need for God's help or that he will be grateful if God gives him what *Monica* prays for. Nor is it plain that *Monica's* asking shields Augustine from oppressive overwhelming by God. So it seems as if the previous arguments fail in this case. But consider again the case in which a teacher sees that a student of his could use help but does not feel that he can legitimately volunteer his help unasked. Suppose that John, a friend of that student, comes to see the teacher and says, "I don't know if you've noticed, but Jim is having trouble getting to his term paper. And unless he gets help, I think he won't do it at all and will be in danger of flunking the course." If the teacher now goes to help Jim and is rudely or politely asked "What right have you got to interfere?", he'll say, "Well, in fact, your friend came to me and *asked* me to help." And if John is asked the same question, he will probably reply, "But I'm your friend; I had to do *something*." I think, then, that because John asks the teacher, the teacher is in a position to help with less risk of oppressive meddling than before. Obviously, he cannot go very far without incurring that risk as fully as before; and perhaps the most he can do if he wants to avoid oppressive meddling is to try to elicit from *Jim* in genuinely uncoercive ways a request for help. And, of course, I chose Monica and Augustine to introduce this case because, as Augustine tells it in the *Confessions*, God responded to Monica's fervent and continued prayers for Augustine's salvation by arranging the circumstances of Augustine's life in such a way that finally Augustine himself freely asked God for salvation.

One might perhaps think that there is something superfluous and absurd in God's working through the intermediary of prayer in this way. If Jim's friend can justify his interference on the grounds that he is Jim's friend and has to do *something*, God can dispense with this sort of petitionary prayer, too. He can give aid unasked on the grounds that he is the *creator* and has to do something. But suppose that Jim and John are only acquaintances who have discussed nothing more than their schoolwork; and suppose that John, by overhearing Jim's phone conversations, has come to believe that all Jim's academic troubles are just symptoms of problems he is having with his parents. If John asks the teacher to help Jim with his personal problems, and if the teacher begins even a delicate attempt to do so by saying that John asked him to do so, he and John could both properly be told to mind their own business. It is not the *status* of his relationship or even the depth of his care and compassion for Jim which puts John in a position to defend himself by saying "But I'm your friend." What protects John against the charge of oppressive meddling is rather the degree to which Jim has freely, willingly, shared his life and thoughts and feelings with John. So John's line of defense against the charge of oppressive meddling can be attributed to God only if the person God is to aid has willingly shared his thoughts and feelings and the like with God. But it is hard to imagine anyone putting himself in such a relation to a person he believes to be omnipotent and good without his also *asking* for whatever help he needs.

Even if the argument can be made out so far, one might be inclined to think that it will not be sufficient to show the compatibility of God's goodness with the practice of petitionary prayer. If one supposes that God brought Augustine to Christianity in response to Monica's prayers, what is one to say about Augustine's fate if Monica had not prayed for him? And what does this view commit one to maintain about people who neither pray for themselves nor are prayed for? It looks as if an orthodox Christian who accepts the argument about petitionary prayer so far will be committed to a picture of this sort. God is analogous to a human father with two very different children. Both Old and New Testaments depict God as doing many good things for men without being asked to do so, and this human father, too, does unrequested good things for both his children. But one child, who is healthy and normal, with healthy normal relations to his father, makes frequent requests of the father which the father responds to and in virtue of which he bestows benefits on the child. The other child is selectively blind, deaf, dumb, and suffering from whatever other maladies are necessary to make it plausible that he does not even know he has a father. Now either there are some benefits that the father will never bestow unless and until he is asked; and in that case he will do less for his defective child, who surely has more need of his help than does the healthy child. Or, on the other hand, he will bestow all his benefits unasked on the defective child, and then he seems to make a mockery of his practice with the normal child of bestowing some benefits only in response to requests—he is, after all, willing to bestow the same benefits without being asked. So it seems that we are still left with the problem we started with: either God is not perfectly good or the practice of petitionary prayer is pointless. But suppose the father always meets the defective child's needs and desires even though the child never comes to know of the existence of his father. The child knows only that he is always taken care of, and when he needs something, he gets what he needs. It seems to me intuitively clear that such a practice runs a great risk, at least, of making the defective child willful and tyrannical. But even if the defective child is not in danger of being made worse in some respects in this situation, still it seems plain that he would be better off if the father could manage to put the child in a position to know his father and to frame a request for what he wants. So I think a good father will fulfill the child's needs unasked; but I think that he can do so without making a mockery of his practice of bestowing benefits in response to requests only if putting the child in a position to make requests is among his first concerns.

And as for the question whether God would have saved Augustine without Monica's prayers, I think that there is intermediate ground between the assertion that Monica's prayers are necessary to Augustine's salvation, which seems to impugn God's goodness, and the claim that they are altogether without effect, which undercuts petitionary prayer. It is possible, for example, to argue that God would have saved Augustine without Monica's prayers but not in the same amount of time or not by the same process or not with the same effect. Augustine, for instance, might have been converted to Christianity but not in such a way as to become one of its most powerful authorities for centuries.

With all this, I have still looked only at cases that are easy for my position; when we turn to something like a prayer for Guatemala after the earthquake ... it is much harder to know what to say. And perhaps it is simply too hard to come up with a reasonable solution here because we need more work on the problem of evil. Why would a good God permit the occurrence of earthquakes in the first place? Do the reasons for his permitting the earthquake affect his afterwards helping the country involved? Our inclination is surely to say that a good God must *in any case* help the earthquake victims, so that in this instance at any rate it is pointless to pray. But plainly we also have strong inclinations to say that a good God must in any case prevent earthquakes in populated areas. And since orthodox Christianity is committed to distrusting these latter inclinations, it is at least at sea about the former ones. Without more work on the problem of evil, it is hard to know what to say about the difference prayer might make in this sort of case.

.... Now suppose it is true that God would bring about his kingdom on earth even if an individual Christian such as Jimmy Carter did not pray for it. It does not follow in this case, however, that the prayer in question is pointless and makes no difference. Suppose no one prayed for the advent of God's kingdom on earth or felt a need or desire for those millennial times strongly enough to pray for them. It seems unreasonable to think that God could bring about his earthly kingdom under those conditions, or if he could, that it would be the state of affairs just described, in which earth is populated by people who *freely* love God. And if so, then making [such] requests ... resembles other, more ordinary activities in which only the effort of a whole group is sufficient to achieve the desired result. One man can't put out a forest fire, but if everyone in the vicinity of a forest fire realized that fact and on that basis decided not to try, the fire would rage out of control. So ... too, it seems possible to justify petitionary prayer without impugning God's goodness.

Summary, review and conclusion. Obviously, the account I have given is just a preliminary sketch for the full development of this solution, and a good deal more work needs to be done on the problem. Nonetheless, I think that this account is on the right track and that there is a workable solution to the problem of petitionary prayer which can be summarized in this way. God must work through the intermediary of prayer, rather than doing everything on his own initiative, for man's sake. Prayer acts as a kind of buffer between man and God. By safeguarding the weaker member of the relation from the dangers of overwhelming domination and overwhelming spoiling, it helps to promote and preserve a close relationship between an omniscient, omnipotent, perfectly good person and a fallible, finite, imperfect person. There is, of course, something counter-intuitive in this notion that prayer acts as a buffer; prayer of all sorts is commonly and I think correctly said to have as one of its main functions the production of closeness between man and God. But not just any sort of closeness will result in friendship, and promoting the appropriate sort of closeness will require inhibiting or preventing inappropriate sorts of closeness, so that a relationship of friendship depends on the maintenance of both closeness and distance between the two friends. And while I do not mean to denigrate the importance of prayer in producing and preserving the appropriate sort of closeness, I think the problem of petitionary prayer at issue here is best solved by focusing on the distance necessary for friendship and the function of petitionary prayer in maintaining that distance.

As for the argument against prayer which I laid out at the start of the paper, it seems to me that the flaw lies in step (7), that it is never logically necessary for God to make the world worse than it would otherwise be and never logically impossible for him to make the world better than it would otherwise be. To take a specific example from among those discussed so far, orthodox Christianity is committed to claiming that the advent of God's kingdom on earth, in which all people freely love God, would make the world better than it would otherwise be. But I think that it is not possible for God to *make* the world better in this way, because I think it is not possible for him to *make* men *freely* do anything. And in general, if it is arguable that God's doing good things just in virtue of men's requests protects men from the dangers described and preserves them in the right relationship to God, then it is not the case that it is always logically possible for God to make the world better and never logically necessary for him to make the world worse than it would otherwise be. If men do not always pray for all the good things they might and ought to pray for, then in some cases either God will not bring about some good thing or he will do so but at the expense of the good wrought and preserved by petitionary prayer.

It should be plain that there is nothing in this analysis of prayer which *requires* that God fulfil every prayer; asking God for something is not in itself a sufficient condition for God's doing what he is asked. Christian writings are full of examples of prayers which are not answered, and there are painful cases of unanswered prayer in which the one praying must be tempted more to the belief that God is his implacable enemy than to the sentimental-seeming belief that God is his friend. This paper proposes no answer for these difficulties. They require a long, hard, careful look at the problem of evil, and that falls just outside the scope of this paper....

Notes

1.   [D.Z. Phillips] *The Concept of Prayer* (New York, 1966), pp. 112 ff.
2.   [Richard Swinburne] *The Concept of God* (New York, 1974), pp. 62, 101, 111, and 185.
3.   See especially John 15: 12-15.

Discussion

1.   Show how the traditional doctrine of immutability or omniscience might raise a similar problem for petitionary prayer as does divine goodness.
2.   Stump's defense of petitionary prayer relies on our intuitions concerning friendship, particularly friendship among non-equals. How does prayer affect the proper relationship between God and humans? Does Stump's account square with your intuitions about friendship?
3.   Stump's defense of petitionary prayer focuses more (but not exclusively) on the proper relationship between humans and God than on the effect of prayer on future states of affairs. Does this adequately separate her view from a view that she intends to criticize—that the effect of prayer is solely on the one praying and not on future states of affairs?

Chapter 18

~~~~

Is There a Hell?

Universalism, Hell, and the Fate of the Ignorant
*Stephen T. Davis**

Introduction. Christianity traditionally teaches that at least some people, after death, live eternally apart from God. Let us call those who believe this doctrine *separationists*, because they hold that these people are eternally separated both from God and from the people who are with God. Some Christians, on the other hand, espouse the quite different doctrine known as *universalism*. Universalists believe that all human beings will ultimately live eternally with God, i.e., that no one will be eternally condemned.

... Though I am sympathetic with the intentions of those who espouse universalism, I am not a universalist myself, and will argue against the doctrine in this paper. What I will do here is: (1) state the strongest doctrine of universalism...; (2) present the strongest arguments in favor of it...; (3) reply to these arguments from a separationist standpoint; and (4) make a case for separationism....

Universalism. Let me now sketch what I take to be a strong doctrine of universalism: God does indeed hate sin and does indeed judge sinners. But God's judgment is always therapeutic; it is designed to bring people to repentance. Thus God's wrath is an integral part of God's loving strategy for reconciling people to God. Some are reconciled to God in this life; some die unreconciled. But God continues to love even those who die apart from God, and to work for their reconciliation. If there is a hell, it exists only for a time, i.e., until the last recalcitrant sinner decides to say yes to God. It is *possible* that hell will exist forever because it is possible some will deny God forever. But after death, God has unlimited time, arguments, and resources to convince people to repent. God will not force anyone into the kingdom; the freedom of God's creatures is always respected. But because of the winsomeness of God's love, we can be sure that God will emerge victorious and that all persons will eventually be reconciled to God. We are all sinners and deserve punishment, but God's love is so great and God's grace so attractive that eventually all

---

*Stephen T. Davis is Professor of Philosophy at Clarement McKenna College.

persons will be reconciled to God. This, then, is what I take to be a strong version of universalism. Now, what about the arguments in favor? Let me mention five of them.

(1) *The Bible implies that universalism is true.* Many universalists are quite prepared to admit that their doctrine is not taught in the Bible and indeed that separationism seems much more clearly taught. Nevertheless, they do typically argue that universalism is at least implied or suggested in various texts. First, it can be pointed out that many texts show that it is God's intention that everyone be reconciled to God. Second, it can be shown that the work of God's grace in Christ was designed for the salvation of everyone. Third, texts can be cited in which God's total victory is proclaimed and in which it is said that everything will ultimately be reconciled to God. Finally, there are texts which seem to the universalists explicitly to predict that all will eventually be reconciled to God.[1]...

(2) *How can God's purposes be frustrated?* Universalists sometimes argue as follows: eternal sin and eternal punishment would obviously frustrate God's intention that no one be eternally lost. But if God is truly sovereign, how can any divine intention be frustrated? If separationism is true, some will eternally resist God and it follows that God is at least a partial failure. Surely if God is omnipotent nothing can eternally frustrate the divine aims; if it is God's aim that all be rescued, all *will* be rescued.

(3) *How can a just God condemn people to eternal torment?* Universalists frequently argue that no one deserves *eternal* punishment. Perhaps terrible sinners deserve to suffer terribly for a terribly long time. But surely sin should be punished according to its gravity; why do they deserve to suffer for an *infinitely* long time? They certainly do not cause anyone else (or even God) *eternal* sorrow or pain. Suppose we decide that some tyrant, say Nero, deserves to suffer a year in hell for every person he ever killed, injured, treated unfairly, insulted, or even inconvenienced. Suppose further that on this criterion he deserves to suffer for 20,000 years. The problem, however, is that once he has served this sentence he will not have made even the slightest dent in eternity. According to separationism, he must suffer forever. Is this just? It does not seem so. (And this is not even to speak of more run-of-the-mill sinners who perhaps never cause anyone serious harm.)

(4) *How can the Blessed experience joy in heaven if friends and loved ones are in hell?* Obviously (so universalists will argue), they can't. People can only know joy and happiness in heaven if everyone else is or eventually will be there too. If the Blessed are to experience joy in heaven, as Christian tradition says they are, universalism must be true.

(5) *What about the fate of those who die in ignorance of Christ?* Christianity has traditionally taught that salvation is to be found only in Christ. Jesus is reported as having claimed this very thing: "I am the way, and the truth, and the life; No one comes to the Father but by me" (John 14:6). And this claim seems to dovetail well with standard Christian notions about sin and salvation: there is nothing we can do to save ourselves; all our efforts at self-improvement fail; all we can do is trust in

God as revealed in Christ; those who do not know God as revealed in Christ are condemned. And surely—so universalists argue—the traditional notion is unfair. It is not right to condemn to hell those who die in ignorance of Christ.

Suppose there was a woman named Oohku who lived from 370-320 B.C. in the interior of Borneo. Obviously, she never heard of Jesus Christ or the Judeo-Christian God; she was never baptized, nor did she ever make any institutional or psychological commitment to Christ or to the Christian church. She *couldn't* have done these things; she was simply born in the wrong place and at the wrong time. Is it right for God to condemn this woman to eternal hell just because she was never able to come to God through Christ? Of course not. The only way Ookhu can be treated fairly by God is if universalism is true. God is just and loving; thus, universalism is true.

Critique of universalism. These are the best arguments for universalism that I can think of. We now need to see how separationists will handle them and defend their own doctrine.

Let us begin with the biblical argument of the universalist. The first thing to notice is that separationists like me do not deny that God desires the salvation of all persons and that Christ's atoning work was designed to rescue everyone. Accordingly, the texts cited under these headings ... do not tell against separationism. As to the texts that emphasize God's total victory and which seem to universalists to predict universal salvation, the separationist replies that this is not their proper interpretation. To affirm that God is ultimately victorious over all enemies and that God's authority will one day be universally recognized is one thing, and will be agreed on by all Christians. But to say that every person will eventually be reconciled to God is quite another, and can only be based on a surprisingly literalistic interpretation of such terms as "all," "all things," "every knee," and "the world" in the passages cited. It is odd that universalists, who typically protest against literalistic interpretations of the many texts that seem to teach separationism (see below), appear themselves to adopt a kind of literalism here. They need to approach the passages cited with a bit more hermeneutical subtlety; they need to ask (especially in the light of other texts—again, see below) whether this is what these passages really mean.

Furthermore, the fact that these "universalistic passages" appear in many of the same texts in which separationism seems clearly taught ought to make us doubt that universalists interpret them correctly....

Furthermore, separationists can produce a biblical argument of their own, one which is much more compelling. For the reality of hell—and even of eternal hell[2]—*is* spoken of often in the New Testament, and seems inextricably tied to such major themes in New Testament theology as God, sin, judgment, atonement, and reconciliation. Thus it would seem that the introduction of universalism would require severe changes at various other points in the traditional Christian scheme of salvation.... In fact, if there is no hell it is hard to see, in New Testament terms, why there would be any need for atonement or a savior from sin.... Furthermore, it seems methodologically odd for a person both to deny the reality of eternal hell and (because of biblical teaching and Christian tradition) affirm the reality of heaven. For both seem to stand on an equally firm exegetical and traditional foundation. It is clear that for most universalists, exegetical considerations are outweighed by philosophical ones.

My reply to the biblical argument of the universalist, then, is as follows. It is true that when read in a certain way, a few New Testament and especially Pauline texts might lead one toward universalism. But a careful look shows that not even those texts actually imply universalism. Furthermore, biblically oriented Christians believe that problematical passages on any topic are to be interpreted in the light of the testimony of the whole of scripture, and universalism—so I have argued—is inconsistent with that testimony.

Let me confess that I would deeply like universalism to be true. Like all Christians, I would find it wonderfully comforting to believe that all people will be citizens of the kingdom of God, and certain thorny intellectual problems, especially the problem of evil, might be easier to solve if universalism were true. But as a matter of theological method, we cannot affirm a doctrine just because we would like it to be true. The fact is that separationism is taught in the Bible and that the so-called "universalistic passages" do not imply universalism. That is enough for me; that is why I am a separationist. Philosophical and theological arguments over what God should do are outweighed by the teaching of Scripture. God has revealed to us a doctrine of eternal judgment; we had best accept it. That God has not also revealed to us how to reconcile this doctrine with our understanding of God's love creates a theological problem which we must do our best to solve.

Separationism. I will now briefly sketch the separationist doctrine I believe in and am prepared to defend. It differs from some traditional theological accounts at two points: (1) For exegetical reasons I do not believe people in hell suffer horrible fiery agony; and (2) while I believe hell in some sense can be spoken of as punishment, I do not believe it is a place where God, so to speak, gets even with those who deny God. It is not primarily a place of retribution.

We know little about hell. Much of what the New Testament says is dearly metaphorical or symbolic. For example, the New Testament uses the metaphor of fire to convey the suffering of people in hell. But this need not mean that condemned people actually suffer the pain of burns. Mark 9:48 describes hell as a place where "the worm does not die" and "the fire is not quenched." Why take the second literally and not the first? I would say both are metaphors of the eternality of hell. The parable of the rich man and Lazarus in Luke 16:19-31 has been taken by some interpreters as a picture of the after-life, but this does not seem sensible. It is a parable, i.e., a made-up story designed to convey a certain religious message. Furthermore, it is difficult to imagine that heaven and hell could be separated by a "great chasm" which cannot be crossed but across which communication can take place. There are many biblical metaphors for hell, e.g., everlasting fire, bottomless pit, outer darkness, place of weeping and gnashing of teeth, place of no rest, place where the uttermost farthing must be paid.[3] None, I would argue, is a literal description.

Hell is a place of separation from God. Not total separation, of course—that would mean hell would not exist. Furthermore, the biblical tradition denies that anything or anyone can ever be totally separated from God.... But hell is separation from God as the source of true love, joy, peace, and light. It is not a place of agony, torment, torture, and utter horror (here I am opposing the lurid and even sadistic pictures of hell envisioned by some Christian thinkers). But there is no deep or ultimate joy there and I believe its citizens are largely miserable. To be apart from the source of love, joy, peace, and light is to live miserably.

A defense of separationism. *Why are the damned in hell?* I have already ruled out retribution or any notion of God's "getting even" with them.[4] To put it radically, I believe they are in hell because they choose to be in hell; no one is sent to hell against his or her will. Sadly, some people choose to live their lives apart from God, harden their hearts, and will continue to do so after death; some will doubtless do so forever. For such people, living in God's presence might well seem worse than living in God's absence. Allowing them to live forever in hell is simply God's continuing to grant them the freedom that they enjoyed in this life to say yes or no to God. I nevertheless suspect that people in hell are deeply remorseful. Can people both freely choose hell over heaven, knowing they would be unable to endure heaven, but still be full of remorse that they cannot happily choose heaven? I believe this is quite possible.

Is the existence of hell consistent with God's love and power? Yes, it is. Some Christians try to justify the existence of hell by speaking of it as the "natural consequence" of a life of sin. I accept the notion that hell is the natural consequence of a life of sin (and it is in this sense that hell is a punishment). But this in itself does not justify God in sending people to hell, for it does not justify the divinely-ordained laws of natural necessity that make hell sin's natural consequence. I claim, then, that the people who are in hell are there because they freely choose it, i.e., freely choose not to live in God's presence. If so, then hell can be an expression not only of divine justice but of divine love.

Response to philosophical objections to separationism. I have been replying to the biblical argument of the universalist. Now I must comment on the others.

How can God's purposes be frustrated? I agree that God desires the salvation of everyone; thus separationism implies that at least one of God's desires is not satisfied: some people will be lost. How can this be, if God is sovereign? The answer is that God created us as free agents; God gave us the ability to say yes or no to God. One of the risks God ran in so doing was precisely that God's purposes *would* be frustrated, and this, sadly, is exactly what has happened. God's will is flaunted whenever anyone sins. It is just not true that "God's will is always done."... Furthermore, it seems that sovereignty entails only *the power* to impose one's will, not the actual imposition of it.

How can a just God condemn someone to eternal torment? In the first place, as already noted, I believe the citizens of hell are there because they freely choose to be there; they have hardened their hearts and would be unable to endure heaven. Unless one bows to God and makes the divine will one's own, heaven is too much to bear and one chooses hell. Thus, as I noted, it is not only just but loving that God allows them to live forever in hell. Second, hell may have the effect on many of strengthening their resolve never to repent; sin may voluntarily continue; and if it is right for evil-doers to experience the consequences of the evil deeds they do here and now, this will be true of the evil deeds they do after death. Third, Christians believe their salvation is a matter of grace alone; we deserve to be condemned, but out of love rather than sheer justice God forgives us and reconciles us to God. The notion of grace, then, is at the heart of the Christian good news. God loves us though we are unlovable; God accepts us though we are unacceptable. But the thing to notice here is that if separationism is inconsistent with God's love, i.e., if a loving God cannot condemn anyone to hell, then our salvation (i.e., our rescue from hell) is no longer a matter of grace; it becomes a matter of our justly being freed from a penalty we don't really deserve. In the end, universalism overturns the Christian notion of grace.

How can the Blessed be joyous if friends and loved ones are in hell? I do not know an adequate answer to this question. I expect that if I knew enough about heaven I would know the answer, but I know little about heaven. The problem is perhaps less acute for me than for those separationists who believe hell is a place of permanent torture. If I am right, the Blessed need not worry that loved ones are in agony and are allowed to hope (see below) that God's love can even yet achieve a reconciliation. But there is still the question how, say, a wife can experience joy and happiness in heaven while her beloved husband is in hell. And that is the question I am unable to answer satisfactorily. It would seem to be unjust for God to allow the wrong choices of the damned—i.e., their rejection of God—to ruin the joy of the Blessed, who have chosen to love God. But how God brings it about that the Blessed experience the joy of the presence of God despite the absence of others, I do not know.

The fate of the ignorant. What about the fate of those who die in ignorance of Christ? The main point to note here is that the Bible does not speak in any connected or clear way on this question. Biblical Christians must take seriously those exclusivistic sayings of Jesus and the New Testament writers ... that create for us this problem. As an orthodox Christian, then, I do believe that salvation is to be found only in Christ. If any person at any time in this life or the next is ever reconciled to God, it is because of the saving work of Jesus Christ. His life, death, and resurrection made it possible. If I am somehow to be reconciled to God, if our imaginary friend Oohku is somehow to be reconciled to God, it is only through Christ that it happens.[5]

Some Christians have taken to heart the Bible's exclusivistic sayings and have concluded that people like Oohku must be lost, that their eternal destiny is hell. But this is to confuse the claim that the Bible is authoritative on matters of faith and practice with the claim that the Bible authoritatively tells us everything we might want to know about Christian faith and practice. It doesn't; I believe the Bible tells us enough so that we can read it, be convicted of sin, and learn how to come to God through Christ. But it does not answer all the questions we might want to ask it and it certainly does not say or imply that those who die in ignorance of Christ are lost. The Bible simply does not in any direct or thorough way address itself to the precise issue of the fate of people like Oohku. The Bible tells us what we *need* to know, not all that we might *want* to know.

What then must the separationist say about the fate of those who die in ignorance of Christ? Again, there is no clear or connected teaching in the Bible on this question; what we find are some vague and unformulated hints which can perhaps guide us but which cannot be used to justify a dogmatic position.... I am quite convinced that this much is true—God can indeed make us in any way God pleases and we have no authority over God to challenge this decision. But this by itself does not answer the question of the fate of those who die in ignorance of Christ....

[Let me make] a theological conjecture: that there are ways those who are ignorant of Christ can be reconciled to God through Christ. In other words, if redemption is to be found only in Christ, and if the atoning work of Christ was intended for all people, and if God is loving and just, then it seems sensible to suppose that it must be causally possible for all people, wherever or whenever they live or however ignorant they are, to come to God through Christ. (I would like to stress that this is a conjecture, not a dogma or a teaching or even a firm belief.)... As long as it is recognized that these are conjectures without systematic or clear biblical warrant, we might even suggest that Christ has the power to save human beings *wherever* they are, even in hell. I recognize some will resist this suggestion. It is one thing—they will say—to suggest that the ignorant after death receive a chance (their first) to respond positively to the gospel. But it is quite another to suggest that those who have been condemned receive *other* chances to respond positively. But a question must be asked here: Is it possible that there are persons who would respond positively to God's love after death even though they have not responded positively to it before death? I believe this is possible. In fact, one reason for this latest conjecture is the observation that some who hear the gospel, hear it in such a way that they are psychologically unable to respond positively. Perhaps they heard the gospel for the first and only time from a fool or a bigot or a scoundrel. Or perhaps they were caused to be prejudiced against Christianity by skeptical parents or teachers. Whatever the reason, I believe it would be unjust of God to condemn those who did indeed hear the good news but were unable to respond positively. This is why I suggest that even in hell, people can be rescued.

Conclusion. Does this bring in universalism by the back door? Certainly not. I have little doubt some will say no to God eternally (the Bible predicts this, in fact), nor do I see any need for a "second chance" for those who have freely and knowingly chosen in this life to live apart from God. Perhaps God never gives up on people, but some folk seem to have hardened their heart to such a degree that they will never repent. For such people, hell as separation from God exists forever, just as it exists for them now. But perhaps some who die in ignorance of Christ will hear the good news, repent, and be rescued. Perhaps even some citizens of hell will do so too. Again, the key word is *perhaps*. We have no ground to dogmatize here. I do not think we know the fate of those who die in ignorance of Christ. All I am sure of is that God's scheme for the salvation of human beings will turn out to have been just, perhaps in ways we cannot now understand.

Notes

1. First point: see Romans 11:32; I Timothy 2:4-6; II Peter 3:9. Second point: II Corinthians 5:14, 15; Titus 2:11; Hebrews 2:9; 1 John 2.2. Third point: see I Corinthians 15:22; cf. 23-28; II Corinthians 5:19; Colossians 1:19. Fourth point: see Romans 5:18; Philippians 2:9-11; John 1:29; 3:17; 12:32, 47.
2. See Mark 9:43-50; Matthew 25:41, 46; II Thessalonians 1:7-9; Jude 6; Revelation 14:11; 19:3; 20:10.
3. Respectively: Matthew 25:41, Revelation 9:2, Matthew. 8:12, Matthew. 8:12, Revelation 14:11, Matthew 5:26.
4. It must be admitted that there are New Testament texts that can be taken to imply that hell is an act of vengeance or retribution on sinners. See Matthew 5:22, 29; 8:12; 10. 15; II Thessalonians 1:6-9; Hebrews 2:2-3; 10:28-31; II Peter 2:4-9; 12-13. Some even seem to suggest degrees of punishment corresponding to degrees of guilt. See Matthew 11:22-24; Luke 12:47-48; 20:47.
5. A suggestion also perhaps made (in literary form) by C.S. Lewis in *The Great Divorce* (New York: Macmillan, 1957), 120-24.

Discussion

1. Distinguish separationism from universalism. List some reasons in favor of each view. Now list some reasons in opposition to each view.
2. Davis theorizes about the doctrine of hell from within the Christian tradition. Has he adequately defended separationism, given the constraints of his tradition?
3. In the previous question, "constraints" suggests "unfair limitations"—how could the boundaries set by one's religious tradition be understood positively?

The Problem of Hell: A Problem of Evil for Christians

*Marilyn McCord Adams**

The problem. Since the 1950s, syllabi in analytic philosophy of religion have given the problem of evil pride of place. So-called atheologians have advanced as an argument against the existence of God the alleged logical incompossibility of the statements

(I) God exists, and is essentially omnipotent, omniscient, and perfectly good

and

(II) Evil exists....

My own view is that hell....

(III) Some created persons will be consigned to hell forever....

poses the principal problem of evil for Christians....
My purpose here is to engage the problem of hell at two levels: a theoretical level, concerning the logical compossibility of (I) and (III); and a pragmatic level, concerning whether or not a God who condemned some of His creatures to hell could be a logically appropriate object of standard Christian worship. My own verdict is no secret: statement (III) should be rejected in favor of a doctrine of universal salvation.

Theoretical Dimension. The argument for the logical incompossibility of (I) with (III), mimics that for (I) with (II):

(1) If God existed and were omnipotent, He would be able to avoid (III).
(2) If God existed and were omniscient, He would know how to avoid (III).
(3) If God existed and were perfectly good, He would want to avoid (III).
(4) Therefore, if (I), not (III).

Obviously, the soundness of this argument depends on the construals given to the attribute terms and to 'hell'.... For example, the Gospel according to Matthew speaks in vivid imagery of the disobedient and unfaithful being "cast into outer darkness" where there is "weeping and gnashing of teeth" (Matt. 13:42, 50; 22:13) or being thrown into the "unquenchable fire" "prepared for the devil and all his angels" (Matt. 13:42, 50; 18:8-9; 22:13; cf. 3:10). Cashing the metaphors, it says of Judas that it would have been better for him never to have been born (Matt. 26:24)....

---

*Marilyn McCord Adams is Professor of Medieval Theology and Philosophy at Yale University.

Premiss (1) is true because an omnipotent creator could altogether refrain from making any persons or could annihilate created persons any time He chose; either way, He could falsify (III). Again, many traditional theologians (e.g., Augustine, Duns Scotus, Ockham, Calvin) have understood divine sovereignty over creation—both nature and soteriology [doctrine of salvation]—to mean that nothing (certainly not creatures' rights) binds God as to what soteriological scheme (if any) He establishes. For example, God could have had a policy of not preserving human persons in existence after death, or He could have legislated temporary reform school followed by life in a utopian environment for all sinners. In these, and many other ways, God could avoid (III), and such was within His power.

Likewise, (3) would be true if "perfectly good" is construed along the lines of person-relative goodness:

'God is good to a created person p' iff 'God guarantees to p a life that is a great good to p on the whole, and one in which p's participation in deep and horrendous evils (if any) is defeated within the context of p's life',

where

'Evil is horrendous' iff 'Participation in e by p (either as a victim or a perpetrator) gives everyone *prima facie* reason to believe that p's life cannot— given its inclusion of e—be a great good to p on the whole'.

The traditional hell is a paradigm horror, one which offers not merely prima facie but conclusive reason to believe that the life of the damned cannot be a great good to them on the whole. Any person who suffers eternal punishment in the traditional hell will, on the contrary, be one within whose life good is engulfed and/or defeated by evils.

For all we know, however, (3) may be false if divine goodness is evaluated in relation to God's role as producer of global goods. It is at least epistemically possible that (III) be true of a world that exhibits maximum variety with maximum unity or of a very good world that displays the best balance of moral good over moral evil.... And in general, it is epistemically possible that the world have a maximally good overall order and still include the horrors of damnation for some created persons. Aquinas rationalizes this conclusion when he explains that since the purpose of creation is to show forth God's goodness, some must be damned to manifest his justice and others saved to advertise His mercy.[1]

Pragmatic implications. The pragmatic consequences of reconciling (I) with (III) by restricting divine goodness to its global dimension are severe.... [T]his assumption makes human life a bad bet. Consider (adapting John Rawls's device) persons in a preoriginal position, surveying possible worlds containing managers of varying power, wisdom, and character, and subjects with diverse fates. The subjects are to answer, from behind a veil of ignorance as to which position they would occupy, the question whether they would willingly enter a given world as a human being. Reason would, I submit, render a negative verdict already for worlds whose omniscient and omnipotent manager permits antemortem horrors that remain undefeated within the context of the human participant's life and a fortiori for worlds some or most of whose human occupants suffer eternal torment....

Free will and the problem of hell. Many Christians ... [mount] a kind of free-will defense; they claim that God has done a good thing in making incompatibilist free creatures. Like any good governor or parent, He has established a set of general conditional decrees, specifying sanctions and rewards for various sorts of free actions. His preference ("antecedent" or "perfect" will) is that everyone should be saved, but He has given us scope to work out our own destinies. Damnation would never happen but for the errant action of incompatibilist free creatures within the framework of divine regulations. It is not something God *does*, but rather allows; it is neither God's means, nor His end, but a middle-known but unintended side effect of the order He has created. Thus, (3) is true only regarding God's antecedent but not His all-things-considered preferences, and the incompossibility argument ... fails....

Divine justice and the ontological gap. I merely join the consensus of the great medieval and reformation theologians in recognizing that God and creatures are *ontologically incommensurate*. God is a being a greater than which cannot be conceived, the infinite being, in relation to which finite creatures are "almost nothing." Drawing on social analogies, Anselm contends that God is so far above, so different in kind from us, as not to be enmeshed in merely human networks of mutual rights and obligations; God is not the kind of thing that could be obligated to creatures in any way. Duns Scotus concurs, reasoning that God has no obligation to love creatures, because although the finite *goodness* of each provides *a* reason to love it, the fact of its *finitude* means that this reason is always defeasible, indeed negligible, almost nothing in comparison with the reason divine goodness has to love itself. Their conclusion from this ontological disproportion is that God will not be *unjust to* created persons no matter what He does.

Finite temporal agency versus eternal destiny.... More recently, I have concentrated on the incommensuration between horrendous evils and human life and agency. For, on the one hand, *horrors have a power to defeat positive meaning disproportionate to their extension in the space-time worm of an individual's life*. And, on the other, *horrors are incommensurate with human cognitive capacities*. For (i) the human capacity to cause horrors unavoidably exceeds our ability to experience them. Many examples make this clear as to quantity: for example, on the traditional doctrine of the fall, Adam experiences one individual's worth of ignorance and difficulty, but his sin brought it on his many descendants; Hitler organized a holocaust of millions; small numbers of government leaders, scientists, and military personnel brought about the atomic explosions over Hiroshima and Nagasaki. Likewise for quality, it is probably true that, for example, a childless male soldier cannot experience anything like enough to the suffering of a mother whose child is murdered before her eyes. But (ii) where suffering is concerned, conceivability follows capacity to experience, in such a way that we cannot adequately conceive of what we cannot experience. Just as a blind person's color concepts are deficient because lack of acquaintance deprives him or her of the capacity for imaginative representation of colors despite lots of abstract descriptive knowledge about them, so lack of experience deprives an agent of the capacity empathetically to enter in to what it would be like to suffer this or that harm, despite more or less detailed abstract descriptive knowledge about such suffering. To these observations, I add the claim (iii) that agent responsibility is diminished in proportion to his or her unavoidable inability to conceive of the relevant dimensions of the action and its consequences, and I draw the conclusion that human agents cannot be fully responsible for the horrendous consequences of their actions.

Returning to the problem of hell, I maintain that damnation is a horror that exceeds our conceptual powers. For even if we could experience for a finite period of time some aspect of hell's torments (e.g., the burning of the fire, deep depression, or consuming hatred) or heaven's bliss (e.g., St. Teresa's joyful glimpse of the Godhead), we are unavoidably unable to experience their cumulative effect in advance and so unable more than superficially to appreciate what is involved in either. It follows that human agents are unavoidably unable to exercise their free choice with fully open eyes....

Finite agency in the region of the divine. It may be objected that the ontological incommensuration between God and creatures redounds another way, however. For Anselm pointed out that the badness of sin is to be measured not simply in terms of what the creature is or does but in terms of the creature's relation to God, a being a greater/more worthy of honor, respect, and esteem than which cannot be conceived. Since God is infinitely worthy of honor, any offense against God is immeasurably indecent and hence infinitely culpable. Even if every created *harm* we caused were finite, at the very worst the ruin of finite created lives, Anselm's principle shows how we have the capacity to cause infinite *offense*. Any and every sin would turn out to be a horrendous evil. And if eternal torment for the creature is incommensurate with human agency taken in itself, it does not adequately measure the offensiveness of one small look contrary to God's will. Eternal torment is merely the closest approximation that creatures can make to experiencing the just punishment.

My reply is that it is not "fair" ... to put created agency (even if we think of its starting in utopian Eden with ideal competence of its kind) into a position where the consequences of its exercise are so disproportionate to its acts. Suppose the powers that be threaten a nuclear holocaust if I do not always put my pencil down no more than one inch from the paper on which I am writing. Although it is within my power to meet such a demand, such disproportionate consequences put my pencil-placing actions under unnatural strain. Although in some sense I *can* comply, I am also in some sense *bound* to "slip up" sooner or later. Hence, the demand is unreasonable, the responsibility too hard for me to bear....

I do not say that were God to create persons with the intention of condemning to hell any who fail to honor him appropriately, he would be unjust in the sense (a) of violating his (nonexistent) obligations to them (us). I do claim that such punishment would be *unusual*, because acting in the region of the divine levels out the differences among created act types (e.g., between peeking out at prayers and torturing babies). Moreover, God would be "unfair" ... and hence cruel in setting created persons conditions relative to which not only were they (we) unlikely to succeed, but also their (our) lives were as a consequence more apt than not to have all positive meaning swallowed up by horrendous evil.

The idol of human agency. Where soteriology is concerned, Christians have traditionally disagreed about human nature along two parameters. First, some hold that human nature was created in ideal condition and placed in a utopian environment: i.e., that *ab initio* humans had enough cognitive and emotional maturity to grasp and accurately apply relevant normative principles, while (on the occasion of their choice) their exercise of these abilities was unobstructed by unruly passions or external determinants of any kind. Others maintain, on the contrary, that humans are created immature and grow to adult competence through a messy developmental process. Second, where salvation is concerned, some take the human race collectively while others consider humans individualistically. According to the Augustinian doctrine of the fall, Adam and Eve began as ideal agents in utopian Eden. The consequence of their sin is not only individual but collective: agency impaired by "ignorance" (clouded moral judgment) and "difficulty" (undisciplined emotions), which passes from the first parents to the whole family of their descendants. In his earlier works, Augustine insists that despite such inherited handicaps, the reprobate still bring damnation on themselves, because God has offered help sufficient to win the difficult struggle through faith in Christ. In later anti-Pelagian works, Augustine abandons the idea that God confers on each fallen human grace sufficient for salvation; he concedes that damnation is the consequence of such divine omissions and Adam's original free choice to sin. Nevertheless, the damned deserve no pity, because the family collectively brought it on themselves through Adam's free choice of will.[2]...

In my judgment, the arguments from incommensuration ... hold even where ideal human nature is concerned. For my own part, I reject the notion of a historical fall and read Genesis 2-3 the Irenaean way, as about the childhood of the human race. I deny not only that we human beings do have, but also that we ever had, ideal agency....

By contrast, a realistic picture of human agency should recognize the following: (a) We human beings start life ignorant, weak and helpless, psychologically so lacking in a self-concept as to be incapable of choice. (b) We learn to "construct" a picture of the world, ourselves, and other people only with difficulty over a long period of time and under the extensive influence of other non-ideal choosers. (c) Human development is the interactive product of human nature and its environment, and from early on we humans are confronted with problems that we cannot adequately grasp or cope with, and in response to which we mount (without fully conscious calculation) inefficient adaptational strategies. (d) Yet, the human psyche forms habits in such a way that these reactive patterns, based as they are on a child's inaccurate view of the world and its strategic options, become entrenched in the individual's personality. (e) Typically, the habits are unconsciously "acted out" for years, causing much suffering to self and others before (if ever) they are recognized and undone through a difficult and painful process of therapy and/or spiritual formation. (f) Having thus begun *immature,* we arrive at adulthood in a state of *impaired freedom,* as our childhood adaptational strategies continue to distort our perceptions and behavior. (g) We adults with impaired freedom are responsible for our choices, actions, and even the character molded by our unconscious adaptational strategies, in the sense that we are the *agent causes* of them. (h) Our assessments of moral responsibility, praise, and blame cannot afford to take this impairment into account, because we are not as humans capable of organizing and regulating ourselves in that fine-tuned a way. And so, except for the most severe cases of impairment, we continue to hold ourselves *responsible to one another.*

Taking these estimates of human nature to heart, I draw two conclusions: first, that such impaired adult human agency is no more competent to be entrusted with its (individual or collective) eternal destiny than two-year-old agency is to be allowed choices that could result in its death or physical impairment; and second, that the fact that the choices of such impaired agents come between the divine creator of the environment and their infernal outcome no more reduces divine responsibility for the damnation than two-year-old agency reduces the responsibility of the adult caretaker. Suppose, for example, that a parent introduces a two-year-old child into a room filled with gas that is safe to breathe but will explode if ignited. Assume further that the room contains a stove with brightly colored knobs, which if turned will light the burners and ignite the gas. If the parent warns the child not to turn the knobs and leaves, whereupon the child turns the knobs and blows itself up, surely the child is at most marginally to blame, even if it knew enough to obey the parent, while the parent is both primarily responsible and highly culpable....

Once again, my further conclusion is not that God would (like the parent ...) be culpable if He were to insert humans into a situation in which their eternal destiny depended on their exercise of impaired agency, for I deny that God has any obligations to creatures (see section 2.2.1). Rather, God (like the parent ...) would bear primary responsibility for any tragic outcomes, and God would be cruel to create human beings in a world with combinations of obstacles and opportunities such as are found in the actual world and govern us under a scheme according to which whether or not we go to the traditional hell depends on how we exercise our impaired adult agency in this life—cruel, by virtue of imposing horrendous consequences on our all-too-likely failures....

The hermeneutics of charity. When authorities seem to say things that are inconsistent or unreasonable, our first move is, not to cut off, but to twist the wax nose a bit, so that without crediting the troublesome pronouncements taken literally, we can "make something" of them by finding some deeper and more palatable truths which (we may claim) they were attempting to express. In this spirit, some agree that the notion of hell as an eternal torture chamber, as a punitive consequence for not accepting Christ, is not compatible with any tolerable understanding of divine goodness. That is, if 'hell' is understood the traditional way, then they construe 'perfectly good' in such a way as to render true the statement:

3. If God existed and were perfectly good, he would want to avoid (III).

Rather than abandon the doctrine of hell altogether, they modify or reinterpret it as some other fate involving permanent exclusion from heaven.

Hell as leaving people to the natural consequences of their choices. On [a] politico-legal model, the relation between a person's sinning to the end and his or her suffering eternal punishment is extrinsic and contingent (as is that between speeding and paying a monetary fine). Other philosophers think there is a better chance of construing (III) in such a way as to be compatible with (I) if one discovers an intrinsic connection between the created persons' choices and their postmortem punishments or deprivations. Thus, Richard Swinburne maintains that "heaven is not a reward for good behavior" but "a home for good people."[3] He insists on the high value not only of created free agency but also of the autonomy of created persons to determine their own destinies. Noting psychological commonplaces about how patterns of choice build habits of thinking, wanting, valuing, and doing, and the more entrenched the habit, the harder it is to break, Swinburne reckons such habits may become so entrenched as to be unbreakable. For a person may so thoroughly blind himself or herself to what is really worth going for, that she or he can no longer see or rationally choose it. Since heaven is a society organized around the things that are really worth wanting, being, and doing, people locked into their vices could not enjoy it there.

Swinburne is less interested in (III) than in

(III') Some persons that God creates are permanently excluded from heaven.

He is willing to recognize "various possible fates for those who have finally rejected the good": (i) "they might cease to exist after death"; (ii) "they might cease to exist after suffering some limited amount of physical pain as part of the punishment for their wickedness"; or (iii) "they might continue to exist forever pursuing trivial pursuits." In Swinburne's estimation, "the crucial point is that it is compatible with the goodness of God that he should allow a man to put himself beyond possibility of salvation, because it is indeed compatible with the goodness of God that he should allow a man to choose the sort of person he will be," even where these decisions have eternal consequences.

Likewise, dismissing literal construals of Matthew 25:41-46 and Luke 16:19-26 as "a crude and simplistic account of the doctrine of hell,"[4] Eleonore Stump turns to Dante, who understands the fundamental awfulness of hell in terms of eternal deprivation of union with God. Stump takes Dante's "graphic images" at theological face value and suggests that the latter is fully compatible with a Limbo of beautiful physical surroundings "in which the noblest and wisest of the ancients discuss philosophy." Moreover, in the more punitive regions of hell, external tortures are not suffered the way they would be in this world but serve rather as outward and visible signs of inner psychological states—afflictions which are nevertheless compatible with long and leisurely intellectual discussions. So far as the problem of hell is concerned, Stump maintains, "Everlasting life in hell is the ultimate evil which can befall a person in this world; but the torments of hell are *the natural* conditions of some persons, and God can spare such persons those pains only by depriving them of their nature or their existence. And it is arguable that, of the alternatives open to God, maintaining such persons in existence and as human is the best." In other words, when 'hell' in (III) is thus reinterpreted, Stump finds the logical compossibility of (I) with (III) defensible.

Once again, my principal complaint about these approaches centers on their understanding of human nature. Swinburne and Stump/Dante begin by taking human psychology very seriously: that entrenched habits of character, established tastes, and concomitant states of inner conflict are *naturally* consequent upon sinful patterns of choice is supposed to explain the *intrinsic* connection between the sinner's earthly behavior and his or her exclusion from heaven and/ or consignment to hell. By contrast, their estimates of the *natural* effects of vice over the very (i.e., eternally) long run leave human psychology far behind. For vice is a psychospiritual disorder. Just as running a machine contrary to its design leads, sooner rather than later, to premature breakdown, so also persistent psychological disorders caricature and produce breakdowns even in the medium run of twenty to seventy years. My own view resonates with C. S. Lewis's suggestion in *The Problem of Pain*,[5] that vice in the soul preserved beyond three score and ten brings about a total dismantling of personality, to the torment of which this-worldly schizophrenia and depression are but the faintest approximations. A fortiori excluded is the notion that persons with characters unfit for heaven might continue forever philosophizing, delivering eloquent speeches, or engaging in trivial pursuits. Likewise, either union with God is the natural human telos, in which case we cannot both eternally lack it and yet continue to enjoy this-worldly pleasures forever; or it is not, because we are personal animals and unending life is not a natural but a supernatural endowment. For God to prolong life eternally while denying access to the only good that could keep us eternally interested would likewise eventually produce unbearable misery. In short, I think that the Swinburne/Stump/Dante suggestion that God might keep created persons in existence forever but abandon them to the consequences of their sinful choices collapses into the more traditional doctrine of hell, when such consequences are calculated from a realistic appraisal of human psychology.

Annihilation by the creator? Among others, Swinburne mentions the option of replacing (III) with

> (III") Some created persons who die with characters unfit for heaven will be annihilated, either at death or after the Judgment.

Nor is this suggestion without ancient precedent: the non-canonical apocalyptic work, I Enoch, predicts that after the Judgment, the wicked will suffer for a while until they wither away.... [T]his move has the advantage of avoiding the claim that God has subjected created persons to cruel and/or unusual punishment by extending their life span into an eternity of horrendous suffering.

True to my Suarezian bias, I reject it, on the ground that it involves an uncharitable estimate of divine wisdom, goodness, and power. St. Anselm reasons that omnipotent, all-wise goodness would do the hard as well as the easy. For God, it is easy to make good from the good; what is more remarkable, it is no effort for Him to make good out of nothing. For Him, the real challenge would be to make good out of evil; so He must be able to do that. Moreover, St. Anselm argued that it is unfitting to omnipotent wisdom either to change its mind or to fail in what it attempts.[6] I agree both ways. To me, it is a better theological bargain to hold the mystery that God will not give up on the wicked, will eventually somehow be able to turn them to good, than to swallow the tragic idea that created persons, finite and dependent though we are, are able ultimately and finally to defeat our Creator's purpose, the mystery of transworld final impenitence ending in the Creator's destroying His own creation....

The pragmatics of universalism. Surprisingly many religiously serious people reject the doctrine of universal salvation, on the pragmatic ground that it leads to moral and religious laxity. Withdraw the threat, and they doubt whether others—perhaps even they themselves—would sustain the motivation for moral diligence and religious observance.

My pastoral experience suggests, on the contrary, that the disproportionate threat of hell ... produces despair that masquerades as skepticism, rebellion, and unbelief. If your father threatens to kill you if you disobey him, you may cower in terrorized submission, but you may also (reasonably) run away from home. My brand of universalism offers all the advantages of Augustine's and Calvin's *sola gratia* approaches (like them, it makes our salvation utterly gratuitous and dependent on God's surprising and loving interest in us) and then some (because it gives everyone reason to hope and to be sincerely thankful for his or her life).

The relevance of feelings. [Defenders of hell often] do not enter at any length into how bad horrendous sufferings are.... [They] imply that those who are offended [by the doctrine of eternal torment] will be motivated by understandable feelings, which are nevertheless not relevant to a rational consideration of the subject.

I want to close with a contrary methodological contention...: namely, that feelings are highly relevant to the problem of evil and to the problem of hell, because they are one source of information about how bad something is for a person. To be sure, they are not an infallible source. Certainly they are not always an articulate source. But they are *a* source. Where questions of value are concerned, reason is not an infallible source either. That is why so-called value calculations in abstraction from feelings can strike us as "cold" or "callous". I do not believe we have any infallible faculties at all. But our best shot at valuations will come from the collaboration of feelings and reason, the latter articulating the former, the former giving data to the latter.

Personally, I am appalled at [the] valuations of defenders of eternal torment, at levels too deep for words (although I have already said many). I invite anyone who agrees with [them]—that the saved can in good conscience let their happiness be unaffected by the plight of the damned because the destruction of the latter is self-willed—to spend a week visiting patients who are dying of emphysema or of the advanced effects of alcoholism, to listen with sympathetic presence, to enter into their point of view on their lives, to face their pain and despair. Then ask whether one could in good conscience dismiss their suffering with, "Oh well, they brought it on themselves!"[7]

I do not think this is sentimental. Other than experiencing such sufferings in our own persons, such sympathetic entering into the position of another is the best way we have to tell what it would be like to be that person and suffer as they do, the best data we can get on how bad it would be to suffer that way. Nor is my thesis especially new. It is but an extension of the old Augustinian-Platonist point, that where values are concerned, what and how well you see depends not simply on how well you think, but on what and how well you love (a point to which Swinburne seems otherwise sympathetic). I borrow a point from Charles Hartshorne[8] when I suggest that sensitivity, sympathetic interaction, is an aspect of such loving, one that rightfully affects our judgment in ways we should not ignore.

Notes

1. Thomas Aquinas, *Summa theologica* I, q. 23, a. 5, ad 3.
2. These views are presented in Augustine, *De libero arbitrio*. Corpus Scriptorum Ecclesiasticorum Latinorum, vol. 74. (Vindobonae: Hoelder-Pichler-Tempsky,

1956), passim. And Augustine, *De gratia et libero arbitrio* (A.D. 426), and Augustine, *De correptione et gratia* (A.D. 426 or 427).

3. All quotations from Swinburne in this section are from Richard Swinburne, "A Theodicy of Heaven and Hell," in *The Existence and Nature of God*, ed. Alfred Freddoso (Notre Dame, Indiana: University of Notre Dame Press, 1983), 37-54.
4. All of the Stump quotations in this section are from Eleonore Stump, "The Problem of Evil," *Faith and Philosophy* 4 (1985): 392-423.
5. C.S. Lewis, *The Problem of Pain* (New York: Macmillan, 1979), pp. 124-26.
6. St. Anselm, *Proslogion*, chap. ix; *Sancti Anselmi: Opera Omnia*: 6 vols., ed. F.S. Schmitt (Edinburgh: Thomas Nelson, 1946-61); Schmitt I, 108. St. Anselm *Cur Deus homo* II, chap. IV; Schmitt II, 99; cf. *Proslogion*, chap. vii; Schmitt I, 105-6.
7. William Lane Craig, "No Other Name," *Faith and Philosophy* 6, 1989, pp. 183-185.
8. Charles Hartshorne, *The Divine Relativity* (New Haven: Yale University Press, 1948, 1964), chap. 3, 116-58.

Discussion

1. Consider Adams's definition of God's goodness. Do you think divine goodness entails such consideration for his (human) creatures? Why or why not? What do you think is a more adequate conception of divine goodness?
2. Defend either the Augustinian or the Irenaean view of human nature. Relate your view of human beings to your view of divine goodness (keeping the traditional doctrine of hell in mind).
3. Suppose you accept the Augustinian view of human nature and the traditional doctrine of hell but also reject the belief that God will ensure that the lives of his creatures will be a great good on the whole. If you had been consulted, would you have consented to being created under such circumstances? That is, does this combination of views make life a bad bet?
4. What role, if any, should feelings play in our understanding of God and his relations with his creatures?

Chapter 19

~~~

Religious Pluralism

The Philosophy of Religious Pluralism
John Hick *

The lamps are different, but the Light is the same.
(Jalalu'l-Din Rumi [13th century])

The need for such an hypothesis. I have argued that it is rational on the part of those who experience religiously to believe and to live on this basis. And I have further argued that, in so believing, they are making an affirmation about the nature of reality which will, if it is substantially true, be developed, corrected and enlarged in the course of future experience. They are thus making genuine assertions and are making them on appropriate and acceptable grounds. If there were only one religious tradition, so that all religious experience and belief had the same intentional object, an epistemology of religion could come to rest at this point. But in fact there are a number of different such traditions and families of traditions witnessing to many different personal deities and nonpersonal ultimates.

To recall the theistic range first, the history of religions sets before us innumerable gods, differently named and often with different characteristics....What are we to say, from a religious point of view, about all these gods? Do we say that they exist? And what would it be for a named god, say Balder, with his distinctive characteristics, to exist? In any straightforward sense it would at least seem to involve there being a consciousness, answering to this name, in addition to all the millions of human consciousnesses. Are we then to say that for each name in our directory of gods there is an additional consciousness, with the further attributes specified in the description of that particular deity? In most cases this would be theoretically possible since in most cases the gods are explicitly or implicitly finite beings whose powers and spheres of operation are at least approximately known; and many of them could coexist without contradiction. On the other hand the gods of the monotheistic faiths are thought of in each case as the one and only God, so that it is impossible for there to be more than one instantiation of this concept. It is thus

---

*John Hick is Emeritus Professor of Philosophy at Claremont Graduate School and University of Birmingham.

not feasible to say that all the named gods, and particularly not all the most important ones, exist—at any rate not in any simple and straightforward sense.

Further, in addition to the witness of theistic religion to this multiplicity of personal deities there are yet other major forms of thought and experience which point to non-personal ultimates: Brahman, the Dharmakaya, Nirvana, Sunyata, the Tao.... But if the ultimate Reality is the blissful, universal consciousness of Brahman, which at the core of our own being we all are, how can it also be the emptiness, non-being, void of Sunyata? And again, how could it also be the Tao, as the principle of cosmic order, and again, the Dharmakaya or the eternal Buddha-nature? And if it is any of these, how can it be a personal deity? Surely these reported ultimates, personal and non-personal, are mutually exclusive. Must not any final reality either be personal, with the nonpersonal aspect of divinity being secondary, or be impersonal, with the worship of personal deities representing a lower level of religious consciousness, destined to be left behind in the state of final enlightenment?

The naturalistic response is to see all these systems of belief as factually false although perhaps as expressing the archetypal daydreams of the human mind whereby it has distracted itself from the harsh problems of life. From this point of view the luxuriant variety and the mutual incompatibility of these conceptions of the ultimate, and of the modes of experience which they inform, demonstrates that they are "such stuff as dreams are made on." However ... it is entirely reasonable for the religious person, experiencing life in relation to the transcendent—whether encountered beyond oneself or in the depths of one's own being—, to believe in the reality of that which is thus, apparently, experienced. Having reached that conclusion one cannot dismiss the realm of religious experience and belief as illusory, even though its internal plurality and diversity must preclude any simple and straightforward account of it.

Nor can we reasonably claim that our own form of religious experience, together with that of the tradition of which we are a part, is veridical whilst the others are not. We can of course claim this; and indeed virtually every religious tradition has done so, regarding alternative forms of religion either as false or as confused and inferior versions of itself. But the kind of rational justification ... for treating one's own form of religious experience as a cognitive response—though always a complexly conditioned one—to a divine reality must (as we have already noted) apply equally to the religious experience of others. In acknowledging this we are obeying the intellectual Golden Rule of granting to others a premise on which we rely ourselves. Persons living within other traditions, then, are equally justified in trusting their own distinctive religious experience and in forming their beliefs on the basis of it. For the only reason for treating one's tradition differently from others is the very human, but not very cogent, reason that it is one's own!...

Having, then, rejected ... the sceptical view that religious experience is *in toto* delusory, and the dogmatic view that it is all delusory except that of one's own tradition, I propose to explore the third possibility that the great post-axial faiths constitute different ways of experiencing, conceiving and living in relation to an ultimate divine Reality which transcends all our varied visions of it.

The real in itself and as humanly experienced. In discussing ... problems of terminology I opted—partly as a matter of personal linguistic taste—for "the Real" (in preference to "the Ultimate," "Ultimate Reality," "the One" or whatever) as a term by which to refer to the postulated ground of the different forms of religious experience. We now have to distinguish between the Real *an sich* [in itself] and the Real as variously experienced-and-thought by different human communities. In each of the great traditions a distinction has been drawn, though with varying degrees of emphasis, between the Real (thought of as God, Brahman, the Dharmakaya ...) in itself and the Real as manifested within the intellectual and experiential purview of that tradition....

In one form or another such a distinction is required by the thought that God, Brahman, the Dharmakaya, is unlimited and therefore may not be equated without remainder with anything that can be humanly experienced and defined. Unlimitedness, or infinity, is a negative concept, the denial of limitation. That this denial must be made of the Ultimate is a basic assumption of all the great traditions. It is a natural and reasonable assumption: for an ultimate that is limited in some mode would be limited by something other than itself, and this would entail its non-ultimacy. And with the assumption of the unlimitedness of God, Brahman, the Dharmakaya, goes the equally natural and reasonable assumption that the Ultimate, in its unlimitedness exceeds all positive characterisations in human thought and language....

Using this distinction between the Real *an sich* and the Real as humanly thought-and-experienced I want to explore the pluralistic hypothesis that the great world faiths embody different perceptions and conceptions of, and correspondingly different responses to, the Real from within the major variant ways of being human; and that within each of them the transformation of human existence from self-centredness to Reality-centredness is taking place. These traditions are accordingly to be regarded as alternative soteriological "spaces" within which, or "ways" along which, men and women can find salvation/liberation/ultimate fulfilment.

Kant's epistemological model. In developing this thesis our chief philosophical resource will be one of Kant's most basic epistemological insights, namely that the mind actively interprets sensory information in terms of concepts, so that the environment as we consciously perceive and inhabit it is our familiar three-dimensional world of objects interacting in space.

... Kant's later much more detailed development of the theme is particularly helpful because he went on to distinguish explicitly between an entity as it is in itself and as it appears in perception. For the realisation that the world, as we consciously perceive it, is partly our own construction leads directly to a differentiation between the world *an sich* unperceived by anyone, and the world as it appears to, that is as it is perceived by, us.[1] The distinction plays a major part in Kant's thought. He points out that since the properties of something as experienced "depend upon the mode of intuition of the subject, this object as appearance is to be distinguished from itself as object in itself" (*Crit. Pure Reason*, B69 1958, 88). And so Kant distinguished between noumenon and phenomenon, or between a *Ding an sich* [thing in itself] and that thing as it appears to human consciousness.... In this strand of Kant's thought—not the only strand, but the one which I am seeking to press into service in the epistemology of religion—the noumenal world exists independently of our perception of it and the phenomenal world is that same world as it appears to our human consciousness. The world as it appears is thus entirely real.... Analogously, I want to say that the noumenal Real is experienced and thought by different human mentalities, forming and formed by different religious traditions, as the range of gods and absolutes which the phenomenology of religion reports. And these divine *personae* and metaphysical *impersonae*, as I shall call them, are not illusory but are empirically, that is experientially, real as authentic manifestations of the Real.

... In the religious case there are two fundamental circumstances: first, the postulated presence of the Real to the human life of which it is the ground; and second, the cognitive structure of our consciousness, with its capacity to respond to the meaning or character of our environment, including its religious meaning or character. In terms of information theory, we are speaking of the transmission of information from a transcendent source to the human mind/brain and its transformation by the mind/brain into conscious experience.... The "presence" of the Real consists in the availability, from a transcendent source, of information that the human mind/brain is capable of transforming into what we call religious experience. And, as in the case of our awareness of the physical world, the environing divine reality is brought to consciousness in terms of certain basic concepts or categories. These are, first, the concept of God, or of the Real as personal, which presides over the various theistic forms of religious experience; and second, the concept of the Absolute, or of the Real as non-personal, which presides over its various non-theistic forms.[2]

... On this view our various religious languages—Buddhist, Christian, Muslim, Hindu ... —each refer to a divine phenomenon or configuration of divine phenomena. When we speak of a personal God, with moral attributes and purposes, or when we speak of the non-personal Absolute, Brahman, or of the Dharmakaya, we are speaking of the Real as humanly experienced: that is, as phenomenon.

The Relation between the Real *an sich* and its *personae* and *impersonae*. It follows from this distinction between the Real as it is in itself and as it is thought and experienced through our religious concepts that we cannot apply to the Real *an sich* the characteristics encountered in its *personae* and *impersonae*. Thus it cannot be said to be one or many, person or thing, substance or process, good or evil, purposive or non-purposive. None of the concrete descriptions that apply within the realm of human experience can apply literally to the unexperiencable ground of that realm. For whereas the phenomenal world is structured by our own conceptual frameworks, its noumenal ground is not. We cannot even speak of this as a thing or an entity.... However we can make certain purely formal statements about the postulated Real in itself. The most famous instance in western religious discourse of such a formal statement is Anselm's definition of God as that than which no greater can be conceived. This formula refers to the ultimate divine reality without attributing to it any concrete characteristics. And in this purely formal mode we can say of the postulated Real *an sich* that it is the noumenal ground of the encountered gods and experienced absolutes witnessed to by the religious traditions.

There are at least two thought-models in terms of which we can conceive of the relationship between the Real *an sich* and its *personae* and *impersonae*. One is that of noumenon and phenomena, which enables us to say that the noumenal Real is such as to be authentically experienced as a range of both theistic and non-theistic phenomena. On this basis we cannot, as we have seen, say that the Real *an sich* has the characteristics displayed by its manifestations, such as (in the case of the heavenly Father) love and justice or (in the case of Brahman) consciousness and bliss. But it is nevertheless the noumenal ground of these characteristics. In so far as the heavenly Father and Brahman are two authentic manifestations of the Real, the love and justice of the one and the consciousness and bliss of the other are aspects of the Real as manifested within human experience. As the noumenal ground of these and other modes of experience, and yet transcending all of them, the Real is so rich in content that it can only be finitely experienced in the various partial and inadequate ways which the history of religions describes.

The other model is the more familiar one in western thought of analogical predication, classically expounded by Aquinas. According to him we can say that God is, for example, good—not in the sense in which we say of a human being that he or she is good, nor on the other hand in a totally unrelated sense, but in the sense that there is in the divine nature a quality that is limitlessly superior and yet at the same time analogous to human goodness. But Aquinas was emphatic that we cannot know what the divine super-analogue of goodness is like: "we cannot grasp what God is, but only what He is not and how other things are related to Him" (*Summa contra Gentiles*, 1:30:4—Pegis 1955, 141). Further, the divine attributes which are distinguished in human thought and given such names as love, justice, knowledge, power, are identical in God. For "God ... as considered in Himself, is altogether one and simple, yet our intellect knows Him according to diverse conceptions because it cannot see Him as He is in Himself."[3] When we take these two doctrines together and apply them to the Real we see that, whilst there is a noumenal ground for the phenomenal divine attributes, this does not enable us to trace each attribute separately upwards into the Godhead or the Real. They represent the Real as both reflected and refracted within human thought and experience. But nevertheless the Real is the ultimate ground or source of those qualities which characterise each divine *personae* and *impersonae* insofar as these are authentic phenomenal manifestations of the Real.

This relationship between the ultimate noumenon and its multiple phenomenal appearances, or between the limitless transcendent reality and our many partial human images of it, makes possible mythological speech about the Real. I define a myth as a story or statement which is not literally true but which tends to evoke an appropriate dispositional attitude to its subject-matter. Thus the truth of a myth is a practical truthfulness: a true myth is one which rightly relates us to a reality about which we cannot speak in non-mythological terms. For we exist inescapably in relation to the Real, and in all that we do and undergo we are inevitably having to do with it in and through our neighbours and our world. Our attitudes and actions are accordingly appropriate or inappropriate not only in relation to our physical and social environments but also in relation to our ultimate environment. And true religious myths are accordingly those that evoke in us attitudes and modes of behaviour which are appropriate to our situation in relation to the Real....

But what is it for human attitudes, behaviours, patterns of life to be appropriate or inappropriate within this ultimate situation? It is for the *persona* or *impersona* in relation to which we live to be an authentic manifestation of the Real and for our practical response to be appropriate to that manifestation. To the extent that a *persona* or *impersona* is in soteriological alignment with the Real, an appropriate response to that deity or absolute is an appropriate response to the Real. It need not however be the only such response for other phenomenal manifestations of the Real within other human traditions evoke other responses which may be equally appropriate.... [T]he "truthfulness" of each tradition is shown by its soteriological effectiveness. But what the traditions severally regard as ultimates are different and therefore cannot be all truly ultimate. They can however be different manifestations of the truly Ultimate within different streams of human thought-and-experience—hence the postulation of the Real *an sich* as the simplest way of accounting for the data....

But if the Real in itself is experienced, why postulate such an unknown and unknowable *Ding an sich*? The answer is that the divine noumenon is a necessary postulate of the pluralistic religious life of humanity. For within each tradition we regard as real the object of our worship or contemplation. If, as I have already argued, it is also proper to regard as real the objects of worship or contemplation within the other traditions, we are led to postulate the Real *an sich* as the presupposition of the veridical character of this range of forms of religious experience. Without this postulate we should be left with a plurality of *personae* and *impersonae* each of which is claimed to be the Ultimate, but no one of which alone can be. We should have either to regard all the reported experiences as illusory or else return to the confessional position in which we affirm the authenticity of our own stream of religious experience whilst dismissing as illusory those occurring within other traditions. But for those to whom neither of these options seems realistic the pluralistic affirmation becomes inevitable, and with it the postulation of the Real *an sich* which is variously experienced and thought as the range of divine phenomena described by the history of religion....

Notes

1. And also as it may appear to creatures with different cognitive equipment from our own. Kant was conscious that he was investigating the specifically *human* forms and categories of perception (*Critique of Pure Reason*, B59).
2. The term "Absolute" seems to be the best that we have, even though it is not ideal for the purpose, being more naturally applied to some non-personal manifestations of the Real than to others. It is more naturally applicable, e.g., to Brahman than to Nirvana...
3. *Summa Theologica*, part I, Q. 13, art. 12—Pegis, Anton C. (ed.), *Basic Writings of St. Thomas Aquinas* (New York: Random House, 1945), I:133.

Discussion

1. There is a rather dizzying array of religious beliefs on offer. What is your attitude toward the various religions?
2. Hick sympathetically accepts the religious experience of religious believers of virtually every tradition. On what grounds is this acceptance justified? Is Hick justified in his affirmation of all of these religious experiences?
3. What is the difference between the Real *an sich* and the Real as humanly experienced? If you (as a religious believer) were to accept that you had no knowledge of the Real *an sich*, what affect would that have on your religious beliefs and practices?

Non Est Hick

*Peter van Inwagen** *

Religious pluralism. There is a currently very popular picture of what are called "the World Religions" that looks to me a lot like those puzzle pictures from my childhood. The picture is done in prose, rather than in pen and ink outline. I shall have to provide you with a copy of it if I am to proceed with this essay, ...

There are a number of entities called "religions"; the most important among them are called the "World Religions," with or without capitals. The world religions are the religions that appear in the history books, and appear not merely as footnotes or as clues to "what the Assyrians were like" or evidences of "the beginnings of cosmological speculation." The world religions are important topics of historical inquiry in their own right. Each of them, in fact, has a history of its own; the majority of them have founders and can be said to have begun at fairly definite dates. The list of world religions must include at least the following: Buddhism, Christianity, Confucianism, Hinduism, Islam, Judaism, and Taoism. But other religions are plausible candidates for inclusion in the list.... It is the division of humanity into the adherents of the various world religions (of course, many people practice a tribal religion or belong to some syncretistic [the often uncritical attempt to unite diverse religious traditions] cult or have no religion at all) that is the primary datum of all responsible thinking about religion. Comparative studies of the world religions have shown that each of these religions is a species of a genus and that they have important common characteristics that belong to no other human social institutions. There are, of course, differences as well as similarities among the world religions, and some might think that there were grave differences, or even outright inconsistencies.... It might be thought, moreover, that these apparent inconsistencies among the world religions were not matters of the surface. It might be thought that each of them pertained to the very root and essence of the religions involved.

It cannot be denied that the apparent inconsistencies exist. What can be denied is that they have anything to do with "the root and essence" of the world religions. Each of the world religions is a response to a single divine reality. The responses are *different*, of course; no one could dispute that. The world religions are different because they arose and developed under different climatic, geographical, cultural, economic, historical, and social circumstances....

The divine reality that each of the world religions responds to is in an important sense beyond the reach of human thought and language. Therefore, any attempt to conceptualize this reality, to describe it in words, to reduce it to formulas, must be woefully inadequate. And when we reflect on the fact that all our religious

---

*Peter van Inwagen is the John Cardinal O'Hara Professor of Philosophy at University of Notre Dame.

conceptualizations, descriptions, and formulations are reflections of local and temporary conditions of human social and economic organization, we are led irresistibly to the conclusion that the letter of the creed of any particular religion cannot possibly be an expression of the essence of the divine reality toward which that religion is directed. What we can hope to see over the next couple of hundred years—as each of the great world religions becomes more and more separated from the conditions and the geographical area in which it arose, and as the earth becomes more and more a single "global village"—is a sloughing off of many of the inessential elements of the world religions. And we may hope that among these discarded inessentials will be those particular elements that at present divide the world religions. It may be that each will retain much of its own characteristic language and sacred narrative and imagery. Indeed, one hopes that this will happen, for diversity that does not produce division is a good thing. But it is to be hoped that the great religions will "converge" to the point at which the differences between them are not incompatibilities—not even apparent incompatibilities. We may look forward to the day when a sincere seeker after the divine may (depending on the momentary circumstances of his or her life) move back and forth among the world religions as easily and consistently as the late-twentieth-century American Protestant who attends a Presbyterian church in California and a Methodist church after moving to North Carolina.

... There is a lot more that I might have included. I might, for example, have said something more about the sense in which each of the great world religions is supposed to be a response to the divine. (I might have included the idea that the aim of each of the world religions is to lead humanity to salvation, and that the real essence of salvation is a move from self-centeredness to "reality-centeredness.") I might have said something about the "credentials" that each of the world religions can produce to support its claim to be a response to the divine reality. (I might have included the idea that the hallmark of a religion that is truly a response to a divine reality is its capacity for "saint production," its capacity to produce people who have left self-centeredness behind and become reality-centered.) But one must make an end somewhere.

Christian belief. Now what am I to do with this picture?... I will present a sort of model or theory of "religion" that is intended to provide a perspective from which the traditional, orthodox Christian can view such topics as "the world religions," "the scandal of particularity," and "religious pluralism." I do not expect this theory to recommend itself to anyone who is not a traditional, orthodox Christian.

There is, to begin with, a God. That is, there is an infinite, perfect, self-existent person, a unique and necessarily unique bearer of these attributes. It may be, as many great Christians have said, that the language of personality can be applied to this being only analogically.... But even if the language of personality can be applied to God only analogically, it is the only language we Christians have been given and the only language we have. It is not open to us to talk of God only in the impersonal terms appropriate to a discussion of Brahman or the Dialectic of History or the Absolute Idea or Being-as-Such or the *Elan vital* or the Force.... This is the meaning of Genesis 11:26-17—it is because we are made in the image of God and after His likeness that we can properly apply to Him terms that apply to human beings.

This God, although He is the only thing that is self-existent, is not the only thing that exists. But all other things that exist exist only because He has made them.... Moreover, He did not produce the world of created things and then allow it to go its own way. Even He could not do that, for it is intrinsically impossible for anything to exist apart from Him ... even for the briefest moment. He sustains all other things in existence, and if He were to withdraw His sustaining power from any being—a soap bubble or a cosmos or an archangel—it would, of absolute, metaphysical necessity, immediately cease to exist. And He does not confine His interactions with the created beings to sustaining them in existence. He is, as we learn from St. John, love; He loves His creatures and, because of this love, governs the world they inhabit providentially.

Among His creatures are human beings, who were, as we have said, made in His image. They were made for a purpose. They have, as the Shorter Catechism of the Church of Scotland says, a "chief end": to glorify God and to enjoy Him forever. This end or purpose implies both free will and the ability to know God....

Unfortunately, the first human beings, having tasted and enjoyed God, did not persist in their original felicity.... They turned away from God ... and ruined themselves. In fact, they ruined not only themselves but their posterity, for the separation from God that they achieved was somehow hereditary. This turning away from God and its consequences are known as the Fall....

Each of us is at birth the product of two factors: the original plan of a wise and providential Creator and the changes that chance—different in the case of every individual—has introduced into the original perfection that came from the Creator's hand. The effects of these changes are ... moral and intellectual and aesthetic and spiritual....

What is more relevant to our present concerns is our "spiritual endowments"—that is, the degree to which the spiritual endowment that was a part of the Creator's plan for each individual has managed to survive the Fall. We have said that human beings were made to be intimately aware of God.... I expect that this awareness was somehow connected with the subject's ordinary sensory awareness of physical objects (which endure and move and have their being in God). I expect that the way in which I am aware of the "invisible" thoughts and emotions of others through their faces and voices provides some sort of analogy. I expect that the way the natural world looked to unfallen humanity and the way it looks to me are as similar and as different as the way a page of Chinese calligraphy looks to a literate Chinese and to me. But whatever the nature of our primordial awareness of God, we have largely lost it. Perhaps, however, none of us has lost it entirely, or only a very few of us have. And it may be that this awareness is present in various people in varying degrees....

It is because a capacity to be aware of God is present in people in varying degrees that people are more religious or less religious—or at any rate this is one reason among others for the varying degrees of engagement with religion exhibited by various people. It is because there are people in whom the capacity to be aware of God is relatively intact ... that there are great religious leaders and doctors and saints—or, again, this is one reason among others. And these people are not confined to any particular geographical area or to any historical period. This statement is, of course, consistent with the statement that it is only in certain social and cultural milieux that they will flourish spiritually or have any effect upon history....

The world religions, insofar as they have any reality at all ... are human creations. That is, they are the work of human beings, and their existence and properties are not a part of God's plan for the world. Other examples of human creations that are similar to religions in that they are in some sense composed of human beings would be: the Roman Empire, Scotland, the Children's Crusade, Aunt Lillian's sewing circle, the Comintern, the Vienna Circle, the Gestapo, the American Academy of Religion, Tokyo, fauvism, the Palestine Liberation Organization, the *New York Times*, and the National Aeronautics and Space Administration.

The existence and properties of the institutions in this list are due to chance and to the interplay of a wide variety of "climatic, geographical, cultural, economic, historical, and social circumstances" that it is the business of the social sciences to identify and map. When I say that they are "not a part of God's plan for the world," I am assuming that there *are* things in the world that are not a part of God's plan for the world. As to the individual items in the list, I am assuming that given that there is anything that is not a part of God's plan for the world—it is fairly evident that none of these things is. Perhaps some will disagree with me about particular cases. And even if no one disagrees, it may be that we are all wrong. God's ways are mysterious, and I do not claim to be privy to them. I am proceeding only by such dim lights as I have. Nothing in the sequel really depends on whether the *New York Times* or the Vienna Circle is a part of God's plan for the world: the items listed are meant only to be suggestive examples. But I should make it clear that in saying that these institutions are not parts of God's plan for the world, I do not mean to deny that God may make use of them in carrying out His plan—as I may make pedagogical use of various physical objects that happen, independently of my plans and my will, to be among the fixtures of a lecture room in which I am giving a lecture on perception. Indeed, I would suppose that God makes *constant* use of human institutions, human individuals, animals, inanimate objects, and transient psychological phenomena in His moment-to-moment shepherding of His creatures toward the fulfilment of His plan.

Like the *New York Times* and the Vienna Circle, the world religions have arisen amid the turmoil of the fallen world by chance and have developed and grown and acquired their peculiar characteristics partly by chance and partly by the interplay of the factors that a completed social science would understand. In the case of the world religions, however, a third factor is present, one that can hardly be supposed to have been involved in the development of the *Times* and the Vienna Circle: their growth and properties are affected by the innate awareness of God (both within their "ordinary" members and within their founders and great teachers) that is still present, in varying degrees, throughout fallen humanity. It is also possible—and we might make the same point about any things that exist in this present darkness— that the world religions have been partly shaped by God so that they may be instruments of His purpose. (If this is so, it does not follow that there is some *common* purpose that they serve. For all I know, God may have shaped Islam partly to be a reproach to a complacent Christendom, and it may be that no other religion has this purpose.)...

There are, I suggest, two and only two things that are in any sense composed of human beings and are both God's creations and a part of His plan for the world. These are His people Israel and the Catholic Church.

By Israel I mean a *people*. I mean those descendants of Jacob who are the heirs of the promises made to Abraham. It was to this people, and not to a religion called Judaism, that the Law was given.... It was not "Judaism" whom David ruled and who heard the prophets, but a people.

By the Catholic Church I mean a certain *thing*.... It was this thing that was created by the Holy Spirit on the day of Pentecost, of which Jesus Christ is the head and cornerstone, which has charge of the good news about Jesus Christ and the sacraments of Baptism and the Eucharist, which is specifically mentioned in the Creeds. There are, we believe, both a visible and an invisible Church....

It will be noted that my characterization of Israel and the Catholic Church has been in terms of God's action in history. If God has not acted in history, these things do not exist. If God has not spoken of old by the prophets, then Israel does not exist. If He has not spoken in these last days by a Son, then the Catholic Church does not exist....

May it not be that all the world's religions are instruments of God's salvation? May it not be that Islam and Buddhism are not merely accidental instruments of salvation, as literally anything under the sun may be, but intended instruments, spiritual equals of the Catholic Church?

I have no way to prove that this is false. If I had, I should be living not by faith but by sight. I can say only this: if that suggestion were true, then the Bible and the Creeds and all of Jewish and Christian history (as Jews and Christians tell the story) are illusions. The teachings of the Church are quite plain on the point that the Church is a unique instrument by which Christ and the Holy Spirit are working (and the Father is working through them) to bring us to the Father. And the teachings of the Church are quite plain on a second point: While the genesis and purpose of the Church belong to eternity, it has been given to us temporal creatures in time. (How else could it be given to us?) It was given to us through events that happened in Palestine in the first century of our era, and all possibility of our salvation depends on those events and on the Church's bringing us into the right relation with them....

The scandal of particularity. I will devote the remainder of this essay to an investigation of a difficulty that people sometimes feel in connection with the idea of the uniqueness of the Church. If I understand the phrase, this difficulty is what is sometimes referred to as "the scandal of particularity." Is there not something arrogant about the Church's claim to be unique? The odd thing is, the idea of there being such a scandal seems to make no sense at all.

Most of us have probably heard the old anti-Semitic quatrain, "How odd / Of God / To choose / The Jews." In addition to being morally rather nasty, this verse makes no sense at all. It presupposes that the Jews are "the chosen people" in the following sense: They were *about* somewhere, and God examined the various peoples of the world and, from among them, chose the Jews. But that is not how things went. The only thing that God chose in that sense was Abraham and his household—who were not yet "the Jews." God's people are a *product* of that choice. In a very straightforward sense, God did not choose, but made, or, one might even say, *forged*, Israel. The Hebrew scriptures are the story of that terrible forging ("for it is a terrible thing I will do with you").

If the Jews claim the distinction of being the one people among all the peoples of the world that God has made, do they call down a charge of scandal upon themselves? No, indeed. One can understand why it would be scandalous if the Jews claimed that God had chosen them from among all the peoples of the earth because of their excellent qualities, if they claimed to have bested all the other peoples of the earth in a contest for God's favour.... But that is not the story the Jews tell.

In a similar way, if the Catholic Church claims to be the unique instrument of salvation, there is no scandal. The United States and the Soviet Union and many other things have invented themselves, but the Church did not invent herself. The Church is God's creation, and what makes her the unique instrument of His salvation is no more the achievement of her members than the splendor and bounty of the earth are the achievements of her inhabitants. Those features of the Church that are the work of human beings (like those features of the earth that are the work of human beings) are mere details added to God's design. And those details, like all the other works of human hands, contain good, bad, and indifferent things, hopelessly intermingled.

"Well, isn't it fortunate for you that you just happen to be a member of this 'unique instrument of salvation.' I suppose you realize that if you had been raised among Muslims, you would make similar claims for Islam?" Yes, it is fortunate for me, very fortunate indeed. And I concede that if I and some child born in Cairo or Mecca had been exchanged in our cradles, very likely I should be a devout Muslim. (I'm not so sure about the other child, however. I was not raised a Christian.) But what is supposed to follow from this observation? If certain people claim to be the members of a body that is the unique instrument of God's salvation, who is supposed to defend their claim? Those who are not members of that body? It should be noted, moreover, that this style of argument (whatever its merits) can hardly be confined to religion. Consider politics. As is the case with religious options, a multitude of political options faces the citizens of any modern nation.... Tell the Marxist or the liberal or the Burkean conservative that if only he had been raised in Nazi Germany he would probably have belonged to the Hitler Youth, and he will answer that he is well aware of this elementary fact, and ask what your point is. No one I know of supposes that the undoubted fact that one's adherence to a system of political thought and action is conditioned by one's upbringing is a reason for doubting that the political system one favors is—if not the uniquely "correct" one—clearly and markedly superior to its available rivals. And yet any argument to show that the Church's belief in her own uniqueness was arrogant would apply a fortiori to this almost universally held belief about politics. The members of the Church can, as I have remarked, take no pride in her unique relation to God, for that relation is His doing and not theirs. But the superiority of one's own political party to all others must be due to the superiority of the knowledge, intelligence, wisdom, courage, and goodness of one and one's colleagues to the knowledge, intelligence, wisdom, courage, and goodness collectively embodied in any other political party.

While we are on the topic of arrogance, I must say that if I am to be charged with arrogance, it had better not be by the authors of the picture of the world religions that I outlined at the beginning of this essay. Any of *them* that flings a charge of arrogance at me is going to find himself surrounded by a lot of broken domestic glass. I may believe that everything that the Muslim believes that is inconsistent with what I believe is false. But then so does everyone who accepts the law of the excluded middle or the principle of noncontradiction. What I do *not* do is to inform the Muslim that every tenet of Islam that is inconsistent with Buddhism is not really essential to Islam. (Nor do I believe in my heart of hearts that every tenet of Islam that is inconsistent with the beliefs of late twentieth-century middle-class Anglo-American professors is not really essential to Islam.) Despite the fact that I reserve the right to believe things that are not believed by Muslims, I leave it to the Muslims to decide what is and what is not essential to Islam.

"But why should membership in the unique instrument of God's salvation depend upon accidents of birth? Isn't that rather unfair to those born at the wrong time and place to belong to it? Wouldn't God's unique instrument of salvation, if there were one, be universally available?"

This is a serious question. Before I answer it, let me remove a red herring. It is not necessary for Christians to believe that there is no salvation outside the *visible* Church. I do not know how widespread this belief has been in the past, but it is certainly not widespread today.... Nor do very many Christians believe that those who died before the creation of the Church are denied salvation.... The medieval legend of the Harrowing of Hell may be without any actual basis in the Apostles' Creed, but it testifies to the popularity of the belief that Christ's salvation is offered to those who died before His Incarnation.

So much for the red herring. Now for the serious question.... I take the only sure condition of damnation in which Christian belief is involved to be the following: Anyone who has accepted Christian belief and rejects it and rejects it still at the moment of his death—and rejects it with a clear mind, and not when maddened by pain or grief or terror—is damned.... What provision God makes for those who have never heard the Christian message, or who have heard it only in some distorted and falsifying form, I do not know. That is God's business and not ours. Our business is to see that as many as possible do hear the Christian message, and do not hear it in a distorted and falsifying form. (But I do know that one of the things that may keep a person from hearing the Good News in its right form is the presuppositions of his native culture and religion. A Christian of our culture may know the words that a missionary has spoken to, say, a Buddhist who thereafter remains a Buddhist; he will not necessarily know what the Buddhist has heard. I do not know, but I suspect, that many people in our own culture who are, formally, apostate Christians may never have heard the Christian message in its right form. I certainly hope so, and the statements that many apostate Christians make about the content of the Christian message encourage me in this hope.)

The way for a Christian to look at the saving power of the Church is, I believe, like this: The Church is like an invading army that, having established a bridgehead in occupied territory, moves on into the interior, consolidating its gains as it goes. All those who do not consciously and deliberately cast in their lot with the retreating enemy and flee with him to his final refuge will be liberated—even those who, misled by enemy propaganda, fear and mistrust the advancing army of liberation.

If an army establishes a bridgehead, it must establish it at some particular place. "And why in Palestine?" Because that's where Israel was. "And why did God choose to locate His people there rather than in India or China?" Well, it would have to be *somewhere*. Why *not* there? The question borders on the absurd, although it has been pointed out that Palestine is approximately at the center of the great Euro-Afro-Asian supercontinent. Why did the Allied armies land in Normandy? No doubt Eisenhower and Montgomery had their reasons. But if a skeptical Norman farmer or Resistance fighter had heard rumors of the Allied landing, and had asked "Why *here*?" you wouldn't have to know the reasons the Allied commanders had for choosing the Normandy beaches to answer him. It would suffice to point out that the same question could be raised about any reported landing site by those who happened to be in its vicinity, and that the question therefore raised no doubts about the veracity of the rumor.

"But why should our salvation be accomplished by the institution of something that can be compared to an invading army?" I have no idea, although I am glad that God has chosen a method that allows some of His servants the inestimable (and entirely unearned) honor of being His co-workers in bringing salvation to others. Perhaps there was no other way. Perhaps there were lots of other ways, but this one recommended itself to the divine wisdom for reasons that surpass human understanding. Or perhaps the reasons are ones we could understand but that it would not, at present, be profitable for us to know ("What is that to thee? Follow thou Me."). But I am sure of one thing. Anyone who believes in God, in a being of literally infinite knowledge and power and wisdom, and who believes that human beings require salvation, and who thinks he can see that God would not have used such a method to procure our salvation, has a very high opinion of his own powers of *a priori* reason.

Conclusion. If we are Christians we must believe that salvation has not come to humanity through Confucius or Gautama or Mohammed. We must believe that the salvation of humanity began with events that were quite unrelated to the lives and teachings of these men. We must believe that it began when some women standing outside a tomb were told, "He is not here." Perhaps there is some authority who has discovered good reasons for thinking that these central Christian beliefs are false. If so, it is not John Hick.

Discussion

1. Van Inwagen defends his particularist beliefs from the perspective of his Christian commitments. How might a Buddhist, Hindu, Taoist, Jew or Muslim approach this topic?
2. Particularists are often accused of arrogance. How would you define "arrogance"? Does it apply to particularists? Has van Inwagen adequately rebutted the accusation?

Chapter 20

~~~

Feminist Theology

Feminist Christian Philosophy?

Patricia Altenbernd Johnson *

Advice to Christian philosophers. Seven years ago Alvin Plantinga offered some Advice to Christian Philosophers.[1] He suggested that, within the philosophical community in which we, as Christians, find ourselves, we need to display more autonomy, more integrity, and more boldness. My aim is to offer some further, but related advice. Christian philosophers would do well to heed the voices of feminist philosophers both within and outside of the Christian community. If our philosophy is an "expression of deep and fundamental perspectives, ways of viewing ourselves and the world and God" (Plantinga, p. 271), then we must constantly examine those perspectives in order better to articulate them and to understand how those perspectives relate to our thought and our action. In this paper, I will set out the hermeneutical structure of the task that Plantinga recommends for Christian philosophers and show how the voices of feminism contribute to this task....

The hermeneutical stance of the Christian philosopher. Plantinga's advice helps us understand our stance as Christian philosophers in relation to the wider philosophical community. He tells us the story of a young woman (Christian in her religious commitments) who goes to college and discovers that "philosophy is the subject for her" (p. 254). As an undergraduate she learns how philosophy is currently practiced. She goes to grad-school and learns even more fully the standards and assumptions that guide contemporary philosophical thought. She learns these parameters well. She respects her mentors, and she is inclined to think that departure from these parameters is "at best marginally respectable" (p. 255). Plantinga suggests that as time goes on this young philosopher—now a professional—may "note certain tensions between her Christian belief and her way of practicing philosophy" (p. 256). She may become so concerned about these tensions that she tries to put the two together, "to harmonize them" (p. 256). Plantinga's advice to her is that she is misdirected in doing this. What she should do instead is allow her

---

*Patricia Altenbernd Johnson is Professor of Philosophy at University of Dayton.

sense of tension to help her critique the presuppositions of current philosophy. Moreover, she should listen to her own voice and be emboldened to set aside the philosophical parameters of her mentors, to reject their presuppositions and begin from within her own context. She must recognize that all philosophy is engaged, is committed to a definite presuppositional stance, and she must have the Christian courage to follow through on her own engagement.

I find this story compelling for a number of reasons. It describes the hermeneutical process of my own philosophical development in a simple and direct manner. It speaks to me as a religious person who loves philosophy and who is schooled within contemporary philosophical parameters. Moreover, it recognizes the philosophical voice of women.

The hermeneutical process depicted by this story is one that can be called a "hermeneutic of transformation".... It is a [hermeneutical] process that uncovers and critiques the presuppositions of our fundamental interpretive stances. It then provides us with a transformed framework for further interpreting our basic experiences and texts. This hermeneutical process involves four steps or stages.

(1) Contemporary philosophical hermeneutics has shown us that all understanding is engaged and has a presuppositional structure. Entering into any specific discipline or role requires that we take on certain presuppositions, that we become engaged in certain ways.

Usually we do not reflect on those presuppositions. We learn them as part of standing within a particular role or discipline. We do this from at least the time we begin to learn language. We learn to speak and conceptualize in a particular language long before we ever reflect on the implications of the structure of that language. Indeed, a person can speak a language for all of her or his life and never reflect on the structure of the language.

(2) Sometimes, as was the case with the young philosopher in Plantinga's account, something from our experience leads us to sense a tension between the commitments in one area of our life and those in another area,... for example in our religious life, make us suspicious of our commitments in another area, for example in our philosophical activity. Often it is the experience of exclusion or of trivialization of something that our experience tells us is important that leads us to our suspicions.... This has certainly been the case for the Christian in contemporary philosophy. The experience of the importance of spiritual life or religious community has led us to be suspicious of any philosophy that excludes these.

(3) The first response to our suspicions is usually to try to harmonize the commitments that we experience in tension. Our understanding changes and we ask for changes in the discipline or role, but we try not to abandon the presuppositions, the engagements, of the areas that are in tension....

(4) While in some cases it may be possible to retain two sets of presuppositions, harmonizing them to eliminate the tensions, in many cases the suspicion raised leads us to reject certain presuppositions and so to transform a discipline or role. Plantinga advises us to listen to our experience as Christians and to be bold

enough to philosophize out of that experience rather than to try to accommodate our thought to the parameters of others. Indeed, he advises us that we need not be concerned with trying to convince these others of the legitimacy or importance of our presuppositional structure. We are to do philosophy as Christians. We might say that he suggests that transformation takes place through action....

If we recognize this hermeneutical process as one that we have gone through in our experience as Christians and as philosophers, then we must also recognize the importance of examining the presuppositional structure of our present philosophical engagement. We must listen to the voices of those who, while sharing our Christian commitments, raise suspicions about the nature of our presuppositional structure. It is the voices of women I would urge us to hear today: women who stand commitedly within the Christian community and within the philosophical community, women who raise suspicions out of the experience of lack of agency (exclusion) and silencing (trivialization), and women who speak out of their own experiences of what it means to be bold.

Their suspicion is that patriarchy is deeply embedded in the presuppositional structure of Christianity and so also of any philosophy that accepts unquestioningly this presuppositional structure. Their task, if they are to take Plantinga seriously, is to do Christian philosophy while rejecting patriarchy—to do feminist Christian philosophy. Those who make this attempt are cautioned as to its impossibility by two groups, both claiming that Christianity cannot abandon the presupposition of patriarchy. One group shares the experience of being a woman in a Christian society. They say: Abandon the Christian community. As long as you stay within it you are subject to tyranny and will succumb to patriarchy. This is like the advice that most of us have probably received that we should abandon philosophy so as not to destroy our faith. Others, who share the commitment to Christianity, say that God has ordained patriarchal presuppositions. To be Christian requires the acceptance of those presuppositions. This is not unlike the advice to leave our faith behind when we do philosophy. I would like to repeat Plantinga's advice and suggest that we have integrity and be bold. Let us do feminist Christian philosophy.

I want to suggest some of what this may mean for how we, as Christians, are to view ourselves, name and symbolize the sacred, and conceptualize the work of God in the world.

Visibility, voice, and the discipleship of equals. We are aware of gendered language and the way that such language has served to render women invisible. Since experience is so important to the hermeneutic process that I am following, it is still important to remind us of that experience. I grew up speaking the language "properly" using "man" and "he" as generic words. Like most women in our society, I became quite competent at hermeneutics, the art of interpretation, before I had any idea as to what the art was. I learned when these words meant male only and when they included me, and I became quite skilled in these interpretive moves. Like the young philosopher, I was so involved in the joy of what I was learning that I did not experience tensions. An awareness of those tensions came upon me slowly. But I still remember the day that I really understood how this language rendered women invisible. I was with colleagues (all male—and all reasonable people) and we were discussing our curriculum in relation to students' future needs. The pronouns were all male, and the word "guy" occurred frequently. As I listened to my colleagues, it hit me that even though half of their students were women, they really saw only the men. Their language revealed women as invisible.

Women also experience themselves as silenced. In the history of the Christian church, women have been told that their role is to be silent, at least about issues of any theological or social importance. If they do have something to say, it is better to have it spoken by a man. The male voice lends authority. While we may dismiss these ideas as part of the distant past, the experience of women today is often one of being silenced. Recent studies still indicate that women are often not heard. When an idea, already voiced by a woman, is put forward by a male voice, it becomes viewed as significant.

Other studies confirm this experience.[2] They show that children learn parameters from the language of their culture. Girls quickly come to exclude certain possibilities from their futures when the words and images they have for these possibilities are male.... Women [often] experience themselves as silent beings. And so I would urge you to listen to the voices of women who reflect on their experience of invisibility and silence and who develop in their Christian faith a critique of patriarchy that challenges us to rethink our anthropology. Elizabeth Schüssler Fiorenza is one of these voices.[3]

Fiorenza recognizes that women experience invisibility and silence within Christianity, but she also maintains that women find positive experiences within biblical religion; there is a source of strength and boldness.... In order to do the reconceptualization necessary to address this oppression, she sets out a feminist critical hermeneutics that stresses the importance of identifying, acknowledging, and taking responsibility for our theoretical presuppositions. This activity is particularly important as we reflect on the Jesus tradition and scriptures. While her work is primarily theological, it is important to our work as philosophers because it examines and critiques the biblical and theological presuppositions that often go unexamined in our work....

One presupposition that many readings of the Jesus movement perpetuate is that women were excluded from the new community that Jesus formed. The image of the disciples is of a band of itinerant men who had left family (including wives) and home behind them to live a radical ethos ... that those left at home did not live. This radical ethos is identified especially by the abandonment of traditional family relations.... Fiorenza concludes that it is clear that Jesus did not respect patriarchal family bonds. Moreover, it would be a misreading "to claim that such a radical a-familial ethos is asked only of the male wandering charismatics" (p. 146) and not also of female disciples.

Fiorenza takes a further step in the interpretation that Jesus advocated a community of equal discipleship by looking at those texts where Jesus discusses the constitution of his true family. These texts (Mark 10:29-30 and 3:31-35) mention brothers, sisters, and mothers, but no fathers.... She concludes: "The discipleship community abolishes the claims of the patriarchal family and constitutes a new familial community, one that does not include fathers in its circle" (p. 147).

Certainly this does not mean that men who participated in the procreation of children were not part of the community. But that the word "father" is not used is significant.... The term "father" is not to be used to justify patriarchal relationships in the community. Reserving the term for God is intended "precisely to reject all such claims, powers, and structures" (p. 150). "Thus liberation from patriarchal structures is not only explicitly articulated by Jesus but is in fact at the heart of proclamation" (p. 151).

From her work Fiorenza proposes to draw strength for women in overcoming sexism and prejudice, especially that encountered within religion. But there are equally important implications to be drawn for Christian philosophy. If we acknowledge our roots in biblical tradition as important presuppositions to our work, then we must also acknowledge as part of our anthropological and political commitments the community of equality and the overcoming of patriarchy. More particularly, we must be committed to the visibility of women as women and be bold enough to follow out the implications of that commitment. If the name "Father" was to be reserved for God, but has been usurped by men within the family and within the church to perpetuate patriarchal structure, then how do we name God?

Naming the sacred. In his insightful and formative work on symbols, Paul Tillich shows why we must be wary of identifying our symbols of the sacred, the ultimate, with the fullness of such a reality.[4] Symbols point beyond themselves to the reality that they symbolize. But they also participate in that reality. It becomes easy for us to mistake that participation for the fullness of the reality. Our symbol may limit that which is symbolized and may even lead us to understand that which is symbolized in a fundamentally incorrect manner. This incorrect understanding can have destructive consequences for the religious community.

In a patriarchal society, it is very easy to slip into such problems when we use the word "Father" as a primary symbol for the sacred. While some fathers in our society take on work that has traditionally been the task of mothers, it is still the case that the title "Father" is used only of men and connotes patriarchal authority. Our concept of Father may include love, but it also includes a sense of distance and ultimate control. If we call the sacred "Father," then our image of the sacred includes these characteristics. If we limit the symbols we use of the sacred to the point that this is one of the few allowable symbols and we combine that symbol with those of Lord and Master, we define the sacred in a very limited and potentially destructive manner. The symbol serves to limit the possibility of other aspects of the sacred being present to us.

Religious feminists have addressed this problem by suggesting that we need a wide range of names for the sacred. Many do not totally reject "Father" as a way of naming the sacred, but suggest that also making use of other names will better enable us to experience the fullness of the sacred. Rosemary Ruether suggests that using the name "God/ess" would help us overcome the dualism of nature and spirit....

Letty Russell reminds us that we need not go outside of the Christian biblical and ecclesiastical traditions to find other names for God.[5] She points to the image of God as servant.... God is described as analogous to a female bird protecting her young.... And finally, she reminds us that there is biblical precedent for naming God "mother" and "wife" (Ps. 51; Deut. 32:18; Isa. 46:3, 51:1, 49:14-15; Ps. 131:2). The name "mother" seems particularly important for helping in overcoming the continued power of patriarchal structures in Christian society....

Certainly, as Tillich has cautioned, every symbol for the sacred has its limitations. The limitations of the image of father have clearly been to reinforce patriarchy and thus to alienate at least some humans from the divine. The symbol of mother will also have its limitations. But anticipation of these limitations should not prevent us from incorporating the power of this symbol into our Christian imagery.

Maternal work, maternal thinking, and Mother-God. In the context of this paper, I can neither set out nor develop all of the implications of incorporating the image of Mother-God into Christian symbolism and thus into the presuppositions of Christian philosophy arising out of the image of Mother-God. Since most of those working in Christian philosophy are men, many of whom identify with the name "father," I wish to stress that these suggestions are not intended to set mother against father. They are intended to lead to further reflection on the implications of including the image of mother.

There are many feminist philosophers who are reflecting on the epistemological and ethical implications of the work of mothering. These reflections come from a wide range of feminist perspectives. Sara Ruddick's recent book, *Maternal Thinking*,[6] is not particularly aimed at the Christian community and does not discuss the issue of God language. I will, however, present aspects of her work showing how these contribute to the discussion of what it means to speak of Mother-God.

Ruddick begins her analysis from the perspective that she terms "practicalism." She explains: "From the practicalist view, thinking arises from and is tested against practices. Practices are collective human activities distinguished by the aims that identify them and by the consequent demands made on practitioners committed to those aims"(pp. 13-14). It is from within the context of our practice that we raise questions, judge these questions to be sensible, determine criteria of truth and falsity, and determine what will count as evidence. In other words, practice and thinking are radically interconnected. Her contention is that the maternal practice gives rise to maternal thinking. She acknowledges that mothers as individuals are diverse and shaped by many practices. She focuses on the demands that all mothers must face and the disciplined reflection that arises out of the attempts to meet those demands. She ... does not restrict the activity of mothering to women. Men also perform maternal labor. She does think that mothering is far more often the work of women than of men [and] that we should be careful not to gloss over the labor of carrying and giving birth which only women do. In order not to conceal women's role she emphasizes the importance of retaining the word "maternal" rather than using "parental."

I find her work helpful to the task of thinking about the image of Mother-God. If God is our mother, then we are imaging Mother-God as carrying out certain practices and as thinking in ways similar to humans who carry out these practices.

She suggests that maternal practice is founded on giving birth.... Ruddick identifies three demands that all mothers face that are correlated with three sorts of maternal practice. The demands are for preservation, growth, and social acceptability. The work required is that of preservative love, nurturance, and training. Ruddick does not idealize the role of mother in her analysis. She uses stories that emphasize that the practice of mothering is a struggle, sometimes even a struggle against our own violence. Yet, she believes that out of this practice and struggle certain cognitive capacities can and do arise. Reflecting on these helps us better to understand what it means to be a mother.

The first demand, that for preservation, requires the mother to develop "cognitive capacities and virtues of protective control" (p. 71). One capacity that mothers often develop is what Ruddick calls the scrutinizing gaze. Children must be watched, but not watched too closely. It is not that mothers relinquish control. They come to think about it differently. Often because of desire to resort either to domination or passivity, mothers can come to recognize the patience required in order to exhibit appropriate control. If children are to survive they must be protected, and yet they must learn to deal with their world, both social and natural. The practice of mothering tends to lead to the development of an ability to identify danger and to deal with it, not always by eliminating that danger, but by helping the child to deal with the danger. Sometimes that means helping the child to die.

Christian philosophers may be able to use this notion of the scrutinizing gaze of Mother-God in reflections on theodicy. If the preservative love of Mother-God is of this sort, then we should not be expected to be protected from all evil. On the other hand, we should expect a hopeful and supportive presence to help us face and cope with our lives. If God's power is not so much that of total control as of helping us deal with the real dangers of our existence, then the concern of theodicy may be to show how a caring Mother-God helps us to confront and cope with the real dangers and griefs of our lives. The expectation is not that Mother-God will prevent all evil. Rather, the power of Mother-God is to help us preserve ourselves so that we may grow and flourish. I am not suggesting that this image will solve the problems of reconciling a good God with the existence of evil. Like human mothers, Mother-God may be experienced as destructive rather than preservative. That the image contributes to the complexity of the issue should not count against its significance.

The second demand that Ruddick identifies is for growth. This demand results in the development of ways of thinking that help the mother and child grow and change. Ruddick identifies storytelling as one of these cognitive practices.... To tell a child a story is to help that child incorporate change into an ongoing unity. It is to help the child and the mother to share a history.

Thinking of Mother-God as storyteller seems very compatible with the image of God as presented in Christian scriptures and traditions. The stories presented there tell of a *Heilsgeschichte*, a history of the presence and activity of the divine in and with human history. The notion of Mother-God can augment this tradition. The contribution of this aspect of maternal work to Christian philosophy may be to direct us to focus more on narrative and the use of narrative in legitimating philosophical as well as religious presuppositions.

The third demand, that for social acceptance, requires the work of training. Ruddick describes training as a work of conscience. The work of training is to help "a child to be the kind of person whom others can accept and whom the mothers themselves can actively appreciate" (p. 104). Again, mothers must struggle against the tendency to dominate. There are many pressures placed on mothers, many of whom are quite young, to have well-behaved children. I remember well the pressure on me to toilet train my son. One person claimed that all of her children were trained by nine months—so mine should be too. A mother is pushed to examine her own conscience as she tries to give guidance to her children. Perhaps the child could be trained at nine months, but what sort of power would that require and what sort of relation would it establish? The work of training requires the mother to trust herself and to be sensitive to the spirit of her child. Ruddick suggests that when this practice is developed at its best, mother becomes more trustworthy so that the child can be trustworthy. Moreover, the child comes to recognize that when trust breaks down, as it inevitably does, it is proper to protest.

If Mother-God is our trainer, our guide in coming to conscience, then she is one who is our help in the ongoing struggle to develop our human goodness and trust. We look to her not as a source of all answers or as a dominating rule to be obeyed. She is a help, a guide, a refuge. She recognizes that the work of conscience is a struggle, ongoing and often difficult. For Christian philosophy, this image might contribute to discussions of a soul-making theodicy. For example, this image of God supports John Hick's claim that it would be contradictory to conceive of a God as creating human beings such "that they could be guaranteed freely to respond" to God "in authentic faith and love and worship."[7]

The image of Mother-God as part of the ongoing development of conscience may also contribute to process theology. Reflecting on how human parents change when they both trust and are trusted by their children could contribute to the process claim that God is, at least in one respect, changing. Such reflection could also provide a way of understanding God as both changing and unchanging. The mothering person may be very trustworthy to begin with, but in concretely exhibiting that characteristic, by being self-reflective about trustworthiness, and by being trusted by a child, may be said to be more trustworthy. So also, Mother-God might be said to be trustworthy and yet to become more trustworthy in the process of divine-human relationships. Indeed, the image of Mother-God may be better received by process theology than by other forms of Christian theology because process thought is already inclined to be open to changing images of God as well as to a changing God.

Conclusion. There is much more work going on in feminist religious and philosophical thought. Most of it remains to be incorporated into the work of Christian philosophy. What I have touched on in this paper only gives some suggestions for a beginning. In Alvin Plantinga's advice, with which I began, he warned us to be "wary about assimilating or accepting presently popular philosophical ideas and procedures" (p. 271). Some of you may be wary of developing feminist Christian philosophy, thinking that you are assimilating that which comes from outside the tradition. I have chosen to look primarily at thinkers who show us the basis of feminist work from within the Christian tradition. Reflecting on their work leads me to conclude that the autonomy, integrity, and boldness that Plantinga called for is advanced by the work of feminists. In particular, the integration of the name "Mother" for the sacred may help us relate to God in ways that enable us to develop these very virtues and thereby strengthen Christian philosophy.

Notes

1. Plantinga, Alvin. "Advice to Christian Philosophers," *Faith and Philosophy*, volume 1, number 3 (1984), pp. 253-271.
2. Vetterling-Braggin, Mary. *Sexist Language* (New York: Littlefield, Adams, 1981); and Baron, Dennis. *Grammar and Gender* (New Haven: Yale University Press, 1986).
3. Fiorenza, Elizabeth Schüssler. *In Memory of Her. A Feminist Theological Reconstruction of Christian Origins* (New York: Crossroad, 1989).
4. Tillich, Paul. *Dynamics of Faith* (New York: Harper and Row, 1957).
5. Russell, Letty M. *Human Liberation in a Feminist Perspective—A Theology* (Philadelphia: Westminster, 1974).
6. Ruddick, Sara. *Maternal Thinking: Toward a Politics of Peace* (Boston: Beacon, 1989).
7. John Hick. *Evil and the God of Love* (London: Collins, 1970), 311.

Discussion

1. Reflect on Johnson's affirmation of Plantinga's contention that philosophy is a reflection of one's deep and fundamental commitments about the world and

God. Does Plantinga's contention seem right or does philosophy seem more like a purely rational, unprejudiced search for the truth?

2. Do the writings of the world's religions have the flexibility to accomodate feminist theorizing? Why or why not? (You might try to look at this from Johnson's own Christian tradition.)

3. Suppose you hold a traditional, patriarchial view of God. How would it change if you followed Johnson's advice? Would that change be positive or negative?

Philosophical Theology

Suggestions for Further Study

Byrne, Peter. *Prolegomena to Religious Pluralism: Reference and Realism in Religion.* New York: St. Martin's Press, 1995.

Clark, Kelly James. *Our Knowledge of God: Essays on Natural and Philosophical Theology.* Dordrecht: Kluwer Academic Publishers, 1992.

Creel, Richard. *Divine Impassibility.* Cambridge: Cambridge University Press, 1986.

Davis, Stephen. *Logic and the Nature of God.* Grand Rapids, MI: Eerdmans Publishing Company, 1983.

Hamnett, Ian, ed. *Religious Pluralism and Unbelief.* New York: Routledge, 1990.

Kenny, Anthony. *The God of the Philosophers.* Oxford:Clarendon Press, 1979.

Kvanvig, Jonathan. *The Problem of Hell.* New York: Oxford University Press, 1993.

Morris, Thomas, ed. *The Concept of God.* Oxford: Oxford University Press, 1987.

Pinnock, Clark et. al. *The Openness of God.* Downers Grove: InterVarsity Press, 1994.

Quinn, Philip and Charles Taliaferro, eds. *A Companion to Philosophy of Religion.* Oxford: Basil Blackwell, 1997.

Schüssler Fiorenza, Elizabeth. *In Memory of Her: A Feminist Theological Reconstruction of Christian Origins.* New York: Crossroad, 1985.

Soelle, Dorothy. *The Strength of the Weak: Toward a Christian Feminine Identity.* Trans. R. Kimber and R. Kimber. Philadelphia: Westminster Press, 1984.

Swinburne, Richard. *The Coherence of Theism.* Oxford: Clarendon Press, 1977.

Part Six

Asian Philosophy of Religion

Introduction

~~~

Asian Philosophy of Religion

Introduction. For most Westerners, Asian religions are an utter mystery; we know almost nothing about them, and the little we do know seems bizarre to us. What seems strange, of course, is in the eye of the beholder. No doubt Western religions seem foreign, perhaps bizarre, to someone raised in Burma, for example, or China. There are, you will soon learn, some remarkable affinities between Eastern and Western religions. Both types of religions, for example, find the overweening self to be one of the primary obstacles to attaining human fulfillment. Some forms of Eastern religions embrace a deity that is not unlike the god of the Judeo-Christian-Islamic traditions. East and West share many common ethical beliefs. And the disparate traditions often view suffering as redemptive.

And yet there are differences, deep differences. Eastern religions come in non-theistic, anti-theistic and pantheistic forms. Some endorse reincarnation while others restrict human life to our earthly three score and ten. Some deify nature while others deify the Nothing. So there are differences.

In this section I have chosen to focus on three Asian religions—Hinduism, Buddhism and Taoism. The selections include primary texts from the ancient sources of these religions. I also include contemporary philosophers who have reflected on their own traditions. The primary texts provide the data for reflection so that the contemporary philosophers provide philosophy *of* religion. Due to the brevity of these introductions I can only make the most general and cursory of remarks. Students are invited to explore these religions on their own.

The sources. It would be difficult to define Hinduism so that it characterized all of the diverse Hindu traditions from ancient times. Perhaps the only shared doctrines among Hindus are the acceptance of the Vedic writings as revelatory and belief in reincarnation. Theologically, Hindus hold remarkably disparate beliefs: some Hindus believe in a personal god while other Hindus are atheists. I have selected portions of the Hindu writings that raise significant philosophical issues: the nature of both humans and ultimate reality.

The Vedic scripture called "the Upanishads," written (perhaps) between 800 and 300 B.C., influenced both Hinduism and Buddhism. The Upanishads are the most philosophically rich of the Vedic writings. They discuss the nature of *Brahman* (the universal soul or power which sustains the universe) and the identity of *atman* (the eternal and innermost soul of each individual) with Brahman.

Human happiness is secured, according to the Upanishads, when one clearly perceives the Real. When one becomes fully aware that atman is Brahman and that everything is one, one can be liberated from the prison of the ego and desire. The self, human desire and the world of multiplicity are all opaque obstacles to the clear perception of the Unity which is the Truth. The ultimate reality, Brahman, is one and the goal of human life is to seek, amidst the dizzying multiplicity of the shadowlands that we perceive with our senses, and find Brahman. Brahman manifests itself as atman in people. Therefore, atman and Brahman are one: "So that I may see your blessed Self / Even that very Self am I!"

Buddhism, an offshoot of Hinduism, follows the philosophy of Gautama Buddha whose ideas are intended to liberate us from our enslavement to suffering. The principle cause of our suffering is our attachment to our enduring self. Freedom from self liberates one from the illusory world of perception and impermanence and frees us from the endless cycle of suffering and rebirth.

The Buddha is said to have attained enlightenment while seated for three nights under the Bohdi tree. During the first and second watches of the night, he becomes aware that he is responsible for the deeds of his past lives and that, because of their deeds, humans are born and reborn according to their karma. During the watch of the third night, he learns the Four Noble Truths.

The Four Noble Truths are listed as follows. (1) There is suffering and this suffering includes birth, sickness and death. (2) Suffering has a cause: clinging to desire, especially for further existence. (3) Suffering will end when one lets go of one's desires. (4) There is a way to end suffering: The Noble Eightfold Path which includes wisdom, morality and concentration.

Buddhist philosophy of religion. Buddhists are often accused of being irrational, even embracing contradictory beliefs. The doctrine of ineffability holds that ultimate reality cannot be expressed in words (and, therefore, cannot be understood). Matilal rejects a radical understanding of ineffability—that the content of mystical experience cannot be expressed *at all*. Matilal is concerned with the contradiction involved in believing in Ultimate Reality while having no understanding of it. How can mystics speak of the unspeakable? How can one believe in something that one simply does not understand? How can one love a beauty queen that one has not seen? Matilal discusses several common expressions of the Buddhist doctrine of ineffability. (1) The *via negativa* (the way of negation—we can only speak of what Ultimate Reality is *not*). (2) Affirming contradictory attributes or predicates of the Ultimate Reality. (3) The use of metaphor and rhetoric to indicate or point to reality without actually touching it. While there is some evidence that the Buddha may have held a radical doctrine of ineffability, Matilal marshalls evidence to the contrary. Matilal opposes the mystical irrationalism inherent in the radical ineffability doctrine. He affirms the Nyaya-Vaisesika thesis: (a) If anything is or exists, it is, in principle, knowable and nameable, and (b) Whatever is knowable is also nameable or expressible in language. Matilal does not deny that Ultimate Reality transcends or goes beyond our ability to describe and understand it, but he rejects the this-worldly denial of the mystics who so eagerly embrace their undescribable nether-worlds.

If Matilal is concerned to educate our mistaken beliefs in the irrationality of Buddhism, Conze is concerned to educate our mistaken beliefs in the foreignness of Buddhism. Indeed, Conze shows some of the many parallels between Buddhist thought and Western philosophy. The first parallel he draws is between Buddhism and Greek skepticism, especially the skepticism of Sextus Empiricus. The second parallel is between Buddhists and the other-worldly, wisdom-seeking mystics. The final parallel is between Buddhism and the monism [the view that reality is one] of, say, Parmenides. Since reality presents itself as a many, monists downgrade our perceptual knowledge. Truth is of what Is and what Is is an unchanging unity.

Taoism. Lao Tzu is the alleged author of *Tao Te Ching*, the most important document of Taoism (pronounced "dow-ism"). The first portion of the *Tao Te Ching*, the Tao, explicates the notion of the Tao. "Tao" is typically translated "way" and is the nameless source of the universe. The Tao is a natural force that flows through all of life. It is neither personal nor good but produces the universe through yin and yang—the pair of opposites that are, respectively, evil and good, dark and light, female and male, submissive and dominant. All change in the universe is mediated through the opposition of yin and yang. Taoism is generally considered a nature religion; indeed, because it is so thoroughly naturalistic, many deny that it is a religion at all.

Most of the portions of *Tao Te Ching* that I have chosen discuss the nature of the Tao. Although the Tao is nameless, Lao Tzu nonetheless talks about it. The Tao is eternal, the origin of heaven and earth, the mysterious female, above the gods, great (and small), transcendent and like water.

The second portion of the *Tao Te Ching* is the Te which describes how life is lived when ordered according to the Tao, or the flow of nature. The goal of human existence is the development of virtue which is accomplished through *wu wei* which means "inaction." Although *wu wei* seems to suggests surrender and withdrawal from action, it is generally taken to imply that actions should be done naturally, with little expense of energy and with little effort. Go with the stream of Tao, don't resist it, and let the Tao do the work. There are three jewels or character traits which should be sought: compassion (which leads to courage); moderation (which permits generosity) and humility (which fosters leadership).

Given its naturalistic bent, in what sense is Taoism religious? T'ang Chün-I contends that there are indeed spiritual values embraced by Taoism. The values that

Taoism endorses—quiescence and tranquility—are transcendent in the sense that they transcend the grasping of worldly things. The (positive) values can be attained (negatively) by turning away from our ordinary way of living. The difficulty of turning away from the world toward the "Divine Nothing" is clear: how does one discern the Nothing? The wisdom of the Tao is to find the Nothing from the emptiness out of which things come and into which things return. This natural order or way of all things is the Tao and finds expression in the teachings of Lao Tzu and Chuang Tzu. Lao Tzu sees the Nothing in everything and, in tolerance, embraces all things gladly. Since all things come from the Nothing, including mind, the Taoist sage views everything as neither good nor bad. Chuang Tzu advised taking spiritual flight from, rising above, the things of the world. This heavenly traveller focusses more on the Tao, the way of transformation of all things, and in so doing attains spiritual liberation.

Chapter 21

The Sources

The Upanishads

Isha Upanishad

All this is full. All that is full.
From fullness, fullness comes.
When fullness is taken from fullness,
Fullness still remains.

O M *shanti [peace] shanti shanti*

The Lord is enshrined in the hearts of all.
The Lord is the supreme Reality.
Rejoice in him through renunciation.
Covet nothing. All belongs to the Lord....

Those who deny the Self are born again
Blind to the Self, enveloped in darkness,
Utterly devoid of love for the Lord.

The Self is one. Ever still, the Self is
Swifter than thought, swifter than the senses.
Though motionless, he outruns all pursuit.
Without the Self, never could life exist....

Those who see all creatures in themselves
And themselves in all creatures know no fear.
Those who see all creatures in themselves
And themselves in all creatures know no grief.
How can the multiplicity of life
Delude the one who sees its unity?

The Self is everywhere. Bright is the Self,
Indivisible, untouched by sin, wise,
Immanent and transcendent. He it is
Who holds the cosmos together.

In dark night live those for whom
The world without alone is real; in night
Darker still, for whom the world within
Alone is real. The first leads to a life
Of action, the second to a life of meditation.
But those who combine action with meditation
Cross the sea of death through action
And enter into immortality
Through the practice of meditation.
So have we heard from the wise.

In dark night live those for whom the Lord
Is transcendent only; in night darker still,
For whom he is immanent only.
But those for whom he is transcendent
And immanent cross the sea of death
With the immanent and enter into
Immortality with the transcendent.
So have we heard from the wise.

The face of truth is hidden by your orb
Of gold, O sun. May you remove your orb
So that I, who adore the true, may see
The glory of truth. O nourishing sun,
Solitary traveler, controller,
Source of life for all creatures, spread your light
And subdue your dazzling splendor
So that I may see your blessed Self.
Even that very Self am I!

May my life merge in the Immortal
When my body is reduced to ashes.
O mind, meditate on the eternal Brahman.
Remember the deeds of the past.
Remember, O mind, remember.

O god of fire, lead us by the good path
To eternal joy. You know all our deeds.
Deliver us from evil, we who bow
And pray again and again.

O M *shanti shanti shanti*

The Kena Upanishad

[I]

The student inquires:
"Who makes my mind think?
Who fills my body with vitality?
Who causes my tongue to speak? Who is that
Invisible one who sees through my eyes
And hears through my ears?"

The teacher replies:
"The Self is the ear of the ear,
The eye of the eye, the mind of the mind,
The word of words, and the life of life.
Rising above the senses and the mind
And renouncing separate existence,
The wise realize the deathless Self.

"Him our eyes cannot see, nor words express;
He cannot be grasped even by the mind.
We do not know, we cannot understand,
Because he is different from the known
And he is different from the unknown.
Thus have we heard from the illumined ones.

"That which makes the tongue speak but cannot be
Spoken by the tongue, know that as the Self.
This Self is not someone other than you.

"That which makes the mind think but cannot be
Thought by the mind, that is the Self indeed.
This Self is not someone other than you.

"That which makes the eye see but cannot be
Seen by the eye, that is the Self indeed.
This Self is not someone other than you.

"That which makes the ear hear but cannot be
Heard by the ear, that is the Self indeed.
This Self is not someone other than you.

"That which makes you draw breath but cannot be
Drawn by your breath, that is the Self indeed.
This self is not someone other than you."

[II]

THE TEACHER

If you think, "I know the Self," you know not.
All you can see is his external form.
Continue, therefore, your meditation.

THE STUDENT

I do not think I know the Self, nor can
I say I know him not.

THE TEACHER

There is only one way to know the Self,
And that is to realize him yourself.
The ignorant think the Self can be known
By the intellect, but the illumined
Know he is beyond the duality
Of the knower and the known.

The Self is realized in a higher state
Of consciousness when you have broken through
The wrong identification that you are
The body, subject to birth and death.
To be the Self is to go beyond death.

Realize the Self, the shining goal of life!
If you do not, there is only darkness.
See the Self in all, and go beyond death.

The Katha Upanishad Part I, 3

In the secret cave of the heart, two are seated
By life's fountain. The separate ego
Drinks of the sweet and bitter stuff,
Liking the sweet, disliking the bitter,
While the supreme Self drinks sweet and bitter
Neither liking this nor disliking that.
The ego gropes in darkness, while the Self
Lives in light. So declare the illumined sages
And the householders who worship
The sacred fire in the name of the Lord.

May we light the fire of Nachiketa
That burns out the ego and enables us
To pass from fearful fragmentation
To fearless fullness in the changeless whole.

Know the Self as lord of the chariot,
The body as the chariot itself,
The discriminating intellect as charioteer,
And the mind as reins.
The senses, say the wise, are the horses;
Selfish desires are the roads they travel.
When the Self is confused with the body,
Mind, and senses, they point out, he seems
To enjoy pleasure and suffer sorrow.

When one lacks discrimination
And his mind is undisciplined, the senses
Run hither and thither like wild horses.
But they obey the rein like trained horses
When one has discrimination and has made
The mind one-pointed. Those who lack
Discrimination, with little control
Over their thoughts and far from pure,
Reach not the pure state of immortality
But wander from death to death; but those
Who have discrimination, with a still mind
And a pure heart, reach journey's end,
Never again to fall into the jaws of death.
With a discriminating intellect
As charioteer and a trained mind as reins,

They attain the supreme goal of life
To be united with the Lord of Love.

The senses derive from objects of sense-perception,
Sense objects from mind, mind from intellect,
And intellect from ego;
Ego from undifferentiated consciousness,
And consciousness from Brahman.
Brahman is the first cause and last refuge.
Brahman, the hidden Self in everyone
Does not shine forth. He is revealed only
To those who keep their mind one-pointed
On the Lord of Love and thus develop
A superconscious manner of knowing.
Meditation enables them to go
Deeper and deeper into consciousness,
From the world of words to the world of thoughts,
Then beyond thoughts to wisdom in the Self....

The supreme Self is beyond name and form,
Beyond the senses, inexhaustible,
Without beginning, without end, beyond
Time, space, and causality, eternal,
Immutable. Those who realize the Self
Are forever free from the jaws of death.

The wise, who gain experiential knowledge
Of this timeless tale of Nachiketa,
Narrated by Death, attain the glory
Of living in spiritual awareness.
Those who, full of devotion, recite this
Supreme mystery at a spiritual
Gathering, are fit for eternal life.
They are indeed fit for eternal life.

Part II, 3

The Tree of Eternity has its roots above
And its branches on earth below.
Its pure root is Brahman the immortal
From whom all the worlds draw their life, and whom
None can transcend. For this Self is supreme!

The cosmos comes forth from Brahman and moves
In him. With his power it reverberates
Like thunder crashing in the sky. Those who realize him
Pass beyond the sway of death....

If one fails to realize Brahman in this life
Before the physical sheath is shed,
He must again put on a body
In the world of embodied creatures....

Knowing the senses to be separate
From the Self, and the sense experience
To be fleeting, the wise grieve no more.
Above the senses is the mind,
Above the mind is the intellect,
Above that is the ego, and above the ego
Is the unmanifested Cause.
And beyond is Brahman, omnipresent,
Attributeless. Realizing him one is released
From the cycle of birth and death.

He is formless, and can never be seen
With these two eyes. But he reveals himself
In the heart made pure through meditation
And sense-restraint. Realizing him one is released
From the cycle of birth and death.

When the five senses are stilled, when the mind
Is stilled, when the intellect is stilled,
That is called the highest state by the wise.
They say yoga is this complete stillness
In which one enters the unitive state,
Never to become separate again.
If one is not established in this state,
The sense of unity will come and go.

The unitive state cannot be attained
Through words or thoughts or through the eye.
How can it be attained except through one
Who is established in this state himself?

There are two selves, the separate ego
And the indivisible Atman. When

One rises above *I* and *me* and *mine*,
The Atman is revealed as one's real Self.
When all desires that surge in the heart
Are renounced, the mortal becomes immortal.
When all the knots that strangle the heart
Are loosened, the mortal becomes immortal.
This sums up the teaching of the scriptures.

The Mundaka Upanishad
Part III, 1

Like two golden birds perched on the selfsame tree,
Intimate friends, the ego and the Self
Dwell in the same body. The former eats
The sweet and sour fruits of the tree of life
While the latter looks on in detachment.

As long as we think we are the ego,
We feel attached and fall into sorrow.
But realize that you are the Self, the Lord
Of life, and you will be freed from sorrow.
When you realize that you are the Self,
Supreme source of light, supreme source of love,
You transcend the duality of life
And enter into the unitive state....

By truth, meditation, and self-control
One can enter into this state of joy
And see the Self shining in a pure heart.

Truth is victorious, never untruth.
Truth is the way; truth is the goal of life,
Reached by sages who are free from self-will.

The effulgent Self, who is beyond thought,
Shines in the greatest, shines in the smallest,
Shines in the farthest, shines in the nearest,
Shines in the secret chamber of the heart.

Beyond the reach of the senses is he,
But not beyond the reach of a mind stilled
Through the practice of deep meditation.

Beyond the reach of words and works is he,
But not beyond the reach of a pure heart
Freed from the sway of the senses....

O M *shanti shanti shanti*

Discussion

1. What do these texts teach about Brahman? Atman?
2. In what does understanding of Reality consist?
3. How is liberation attained (and what are we liberated from)?

The Life of the Buddha

The search for enlightenment. Seeing all this, he was pleased and thought: "From what I have seen in my dreams, it will not be long now before I attain highest knowledge."...

Now Indra, Brahma, and the other gods, knowing the thoughts of the bodhisattva, approached him and said:.. "Get up, get up, well-minded one! Leave this place and set out into the world! Upon reaching omniscience, you will save all beings."

The bodhisattva replied: "Do you not see, Indra? I am trapped in a net like the king of beasts. The city of Kapila is completely surrounded by a great many troops, with lots of horses, elephants, chariots, and very capable men bearing bows, swords, and scimitars...."

Indra said: "Good sir, recall your former vow, and the past Buddha Dipampkara's prediction, that having abandoned this world that is afflicted by suffering, you would wander forth from your home. We gods will arrange it so that you will be able to dwell in the forest this very day, free from all hindrances."

Hearing this, the bodhisattva was very pleased. Then Indra, Lord of the gods and causer of sleepiness, gave orders to Pancika, the great yaksa general: "My friend, bring on sleep, and the bodhisattva will come down from his palace!" So he brought on sleep, and the bodhisattva came out.

Then as had been prearranged by Indra, the bodhisattva came across his attendant Chandaka, and saw that Chandaka had succumbed to a deep sleep. With some effort, he managed to rouse him and spoke to him this verse:

"Ho! Chanda! Get up, and from the stable,
quickly fetch me Kanthaka,
that jewel of a horse;
I am determined to set out for the forest of asceticism
which previous Buddhas enjoyed
and which brings satisfaction to sages...."

Then the bodhisattva, seeing that the king of horses, Kanthaka, stood ready,... mounted him, and with Chandaka holding on behind, he flew up into the air. This was out of the bodhisattva's bodhisattva-power, as well as out of the divine power of the gods.

And because of the departure of the bodhisattva, the divinities who inhabited the harem of the palace began to cry, and the tears of those crying divinities began to fall onto the earth....

Then the bodhisattva, turning his whole body around to the right like an elephant, considered the following matter: "This for me is the last night on which I will have lain with a woman." And he further reflected: "I will depart through the eastern gate; were I to go out through another gate, my father, the king, would be upset that I, as prince, did not come to see him and take my leave at this final moment." Therefore he went and gazed upon King Suddhodana, who was sleeping soundly. He circumambulated him and said: "Father, I am leaving not out of lack of respect, not out of lack of reverence, but for no other reason than that I wish to liberate the world, which is afflicted by old age and death, from the fear of the suffering that comes with old age and death...."

Then, surrounded by several hundreds of thousands of deities headed by Indra and Brahma, the bodhisattva crossed over to the other side.... And, unsheathing his sword, which was like a blue lotus, he cut off his hairknot and threw it very high into the air. It was taken by Indra, king of the gods, and received with great honor by the deities in his heaven, who instituted a Festival of the Hairknot....

Enlightenment. Then, having received some grass from the grass-cutter Svastika, the bodhisattva approached the foot of the Bodhi Tree, by the road pointed out to him by the gods. Getting there, he prepared a broad, nicely arranged, firmly established seat of grass.... And mounting this adamantine throne, he sat down with his legs crossed like a sleeping snake-king's coils. Holding his body upright and fixing his mind in front of him, he resolved: "I will not uncross my legs until the destruction of defilements has been attained."...

And in the first watch of the night, he inclined his mind toward achieving firsthand knowledge of the field of supernatural powers,... and he set himself to the task of remembering, in a firsthand way, his former births.... He recalled his many various previous existences: one birth, two, three, four,... ten, twenty, thirty, forty, fifty, a thousand,... many thousands,... many hundreds of thousands....

And in the second watch of the night, he inclined his mind to achieving firsthand knowledge of the transmigration of beings from one existence to another. With his pure divine eye transcending human sight, he saw beings dying and being reborn, of good caste and bad, low and high, in good rebirths [and] unfortunate ones.... They were wandering in samsara [the process of death and rebirth which is marked by suffering] according to the evil inclinations of their sensual desires, birth, and ignorance....

Then in the third watch of the night, he declared his intention to achieve direct perception of the destruction of evil inclinations, and disciplining himself and persevering, he meditated on the dharmas [the fundamental truths] that are conducive to enlightenment.... And he truly realized: "This is the Noble Truth of Suffering; this is the Origination of Suffering; this is the Cessation of Suffering; this is the Noble Truth of the Way leading to the Cessation of Suffering." Knowing that and seeing that, he was then released from thoughts inclined to sensual desire, he was released from thoughts inclined to rebirth, he was released from thoughts inclined to ignorance. And released, he had a realization of his liberation: "Destroyed is my birth; consumed is my striving; done is what had to be done; I will not be born into another existence!" Thus the Blessed One attained to the highest enlightenment....

The four noble truths. Thus have I heard: Once, when the Blessed One was dwelling in Benares, at the Deer Park in Rsivadana he spoke of the "Fortunate Five," the group of elders who were his first disciples.

"Monks," he said, "for one who has wandered forth, there are two extremes. What two? On the one hand, there is attachment to sensual pleasures; this is vulgar, common, ignoble, purposeless, not conducive to a chaste and studious life, to disgust with the world, to aversion from passion, to cessation, monkhood, enlightenment, or nirvana. On the other hand, there is addiction to exhausting the self through asceticism, this is suffering, ignoble, and purposeless. Monks, for one who has wandered forth, these are the two extremes. Staying with the Tathagata's Noble Doctrine and Disciple, away from both of these extremes, is the middle course, fully realized, bringing about insight, and conducive to tranquillity, disgust with the world, aversion from passion, cessation, monkhood, enlightenment, and nirvana.

"Furthermore, monks, there are Four Noble Truths. What four? The Noble Truth of suffering, the Noble Truth of the origination of suffering, the Noble Truth of the cessation of suffering, and the Noble Truth of the way leading to the cessation of suffering.

Birth is suffering, old age is suffering, sickness is suffering, death is suffering. Involvement with what is unpleasant is suffering. Separation from what is pleasant is suffering. Also, not getting what one wants and strives for is suffering. And form is suffering, feeling is suffering, perception is suffering, karmic constituents are suffering, consciousness is suffering; in sum, these five agglomerations, which are the basis of clinging to existence, are suffering. This, monks, is the Noble Truth of suffering.

"And what is the Noble Truth of the origination of suffering? It is the thirst for further existence, which comes along with pleasure and passion and brings passing enjoyment here and there. This, monks, is the Noble Truth of the origination of suffering.

"And what is the Noble Truth of the cessation of suffering? It is this: the destruction without remainder of this very thirst for further existence, which comes along with pleasure and passion, bringing passing enjoyment here and there. It is without passion. It is cessation, forsaking, abandoning, renunciation. This, monks, is the Noble Truth of the cessation of suffering.

"And what is the Noble Truth of the way leading to the cessation of suffering? Just this: the Eightfold Noble Path, consisting of right views, right intention, right effort, right action, right livelihood, right speech, right mindfulness, right meditation. This, monks, is the Noble Truth of the way leading to the cessation of suffering.

"'This is suffering.... This is the origination of suffering.... This is the cessation of suffering.... This is the way that leads to the cessation of suffering': monks, from these basic mental realizations, according to doctrines that were not handed down from previous teachers, there were produced in me knowledge, insight, understanding, enlightenment, intelligence, and wisdom; illumination became manifest.

"'This Noble Truth of suffering is to be thoroughly known.... This origination of suffering is to be given up.... This Noble Truth of the cessation of suffering is to be realized. This Noble Truth of the way leading to the cessation of suffering is to be cultivated': monks, from this basic mental realization, according to doctrines that were not handed down from previous teachers, there were produced in me knowledge, insight, understanding, enlightenment, intelligence, and wisdom; illumination became manifest.

"'This Noble Truth of suffering has come to be known thoroughly.... This origination of suffering has been given up.... This Noble Truth of the cessation of suffering has been realized. This Noble Truth of the way leading to the cessation of suffering has been actualized': monks, from this basic mental realization, according to doctrines that were not handed down from previous teachers, there were produced in me knowledge, insight, understanding, enlightenment, intelligence, and wisdom; illumination became manifest.

"And monks, as long as I did not perceive, with right wisdom, these Four Noble Truths as they are, thrice-turned and in their twelve aspects, I could not claim to have fully attained unsurpassed complete enlightenment, nor would there be produced knowledge in me, nor would I have realized certain emancipation of the mind. But since, monks, I did perceive, with right wisdom, these Four Noble Truths as they are, thrice-turned and in their twelve aspects, I know I have fully attained unsurpassed complete enlightenment. Knowledge was produced in me, and I did realize certain emancipation of the mind, liberation through wisdom."

Thus the Buddha spoke while he was residing in Benares, at the Deer Park in Rsivadana. And hearing this explanation, the Venerable Ajnata Kaundinya's understanding was awakened, and he attained the perfectly pure, pristine, unstained Dharma-eye into the nature of things....

Discussion

1. What insights does the Buddha gain during the different watches of the night? How do they liberate him (and from what)?
2. What would your life be like if your adhered to the Four Noble Truths?
3. There is some dispute over whether or not the Buddha actually existed. What impact would it have on these teachings if he did not exist?

≈≈≈

Chapter 22

Buddhist Philosophy of Religion

Mysticism and Reality: Ineffability

Bimal K. Matilal[*]

Wherefrom words turn back,
Along with the mind, without reaching
The bliss of Brahman, (but) he who knows
Fears nothing at any time.
        (2.4)[1]

Introduction. This is how the Taittirīya Upanishad describes the bliss of Brahman as something indescribable in words. An echo of the same idea is found in the Katha Upanishad: 5.14:

"This is it"—thus they recognize
The highest happiness that is ineffable.[2]

The point is that the peak experience in Brahman realization, the supreme joy or happiness, is something that cannot be put into words. The mystical consciousness is an ecstatic feeling that is ineffable....

The closest notion to mystical states in early Buddhism would be the talk of mental states developed in what is called *bhāvanā* "meditation." Usually there are two types of meditation mentioned in the Buddhist canons, *samatha* (or *samādhi)* and *vipassanā* (or *vipaśyanā*). The first kind was prevalent in India before the time of the Buddha. The second kind was what the Buddha was supposed to have discovered. The first kind leads through extreme mental concentration to the highest mystical states such as the mind conforming to the sphere of Infinite Space, the sphere of Nothingness, or the sphere of Neither perception Nor non-perception. But all these mystical states, according to the Buddha, are conditioned by the mind. They are not "unconditioned" (*a-saṃskṛta*), and not Truth. Nirvāṇa is Truth because nirvāṇa is unconditioned....

---

[*]Bimal Krishna Matilal (1935-1991) taught at the University of Toronto and Oxford University.

It is clear.... that the Buddha regarded all mystic states developed through the form of meditation called *samatha* as mind-conditioned. They did not give to the Buddha insight into the Ultimate Reality. He practiced them and found that these mystic states were "mere happy living in this existence" and "peaceful living, but nothing more."[3]

The Buddha is said to have discovered and preached the second type of meditation called *vipassanā*, which gives *Insight* into the real nature of things leading to the complete liberation of mind—to the realization of the Ultimate Truth, Nirvāṇa.... Since these [mystical] states are said to be mind-conditioned, they cannot be regarded as beyond linguistic expression or ineffable. For it is conceded in Buddhism that whatever is mind-conditioned is also expressible in language. Even the nirvāṇa consciousness is not clearly stated to be ineffable in early Buddhism. It is only claimed to be an insight— the deepest insight into the nature of things. What is, however, claimed to be beyond verbal knowledge or language in Buddhism, particularly in different forms of Mahāyāna Buddhism, is the so-called Ultimate Reality or *Tattva*....

A serious formulation of the ineffability of mysticism would concern the ineffability of the "content" of mystical experience rather than the mystical experience itself. In other words, it is about the alleged ineffability of what we may call the ultimate reality, what true mystics assert to have experienced, although it may be named differently by different mystics, God, Brahman, Śūnyatā or Suchness....

Ineffability. Let us now attend to the problem of the ineffability of the Ultimate Reality, the supposed "content" of a true mystical experience. I shall try first to give the traditional Indian formulation of the "Ineffability" doctrine—a philosophically, i.e., epistemologically, oriented doctrine, which is found primarily in Mahāyāna Buddhism and monistic Vedānta. A critique of this doctrine will be given at the end. Let us start with an imaginary dialogue between a mystic and a non-mystic:

MYSTIC: The true reality, the Essence, the Absolute, the pure Existence, the pure Consciousness, Emptiness, that is what I call the Ultimate Reality.

NON-MYSTIC: If you only would tell me somewhat plainly, what that means: the Ultimate Reality.

M: That I shall never succeed in doing. The plainest talk would be that it cannot be talked about. Is it not good enough for you?

N: It is not sober enough for me. Could it not be that there you have fallen into some kind of lofty rhapsodizing? Besides, you do talk about it when you call it the Ultimate Reality, and hence you would be able to indicate what it is you are talking about.

M: The problem is that I cannot actually say anything except uttering that phrase "the Ultimate Reality." One must try to think of that to which this phrase points, that to which it can only point but which it cannot actually say.

N: What is a phrase for if it cannot *say* anything, if through it one cannot understand?

M: It is an innate difficulty, or a defect, of our language that it cannot express what you are asking me to express....

The above imaginary dialogue may very well have taken place between a Buddhist and a Naiyāyika in the Indian tradition. Whether the Buddha himself supported the ineffability doctrine or not, is not known. Evidence is not available to prove the point. But it is true that the Buddha was responsible for mobilizing what may be called a thorough-going "de-personalization" of the philosophic language or discourse. Thus, he rejected terms like "soul," "self," "person," or "living being" (*ātman, pudgala, jīva* or *sattva*) as not meaning anything.... The Ultimate Reality cannot be described or expressed in words or language. The Ultimate Reality is beyond the realm of language, is ineffable. Words cannot express it although they may indicate it through indirection. Thus, any linguistic discourse on the Ultimate Reality should be understood in this indirect sense.... The *Laṅkāvatāra-sūtra* expresses the same position with a nice simile: (The Buddha says:)

> Just as a king or merchant (at first) attracts his children with the help of beautiful clay animals for play, and then (at the right time) presents them with real animals, I attract similarly my disciples with various shadow characteristics of the dharmas, and then instruct them (when the right time comes) the *bhū takoṭi*, which is to be experienced by each of them personally.[4]

This is the general Mahāyāna Buddhist position about the Ultimate Reality....

We have on the other hand a curious dialogue in *Majjhima Nikāya*. II. 32, which seems to ridicule indirectly the "ineffability" doctrine. I quote the dialogue below:

> Buddha: What, Udayi, is your teacher's teaching?
> Udayi: Our teacher's teaching is that this is the highest colour, this is the highest colour.
> B: What is that colour?
> U: That colour than which there is no other colour which is higher or better, is the highest colour.
> B. What is that colour than which there is no colour higher or better?
> U: That colour than which there is no other colour which is higher or better, is the highest colour.
> B. You say that the highest colour is that than which there is no other colour, which is higher or better. But you do not specify that colour. It is like a person saying, "I like and am in love with the 'beauty queen' of this country."...

One can remove "colour" from the above and substitute "bliss" in its place, and then *the highest bliss*—the goal of mystical experience—can be similarly criticized *à la* Buddha. In other words, one can say that the Buddha in the above dialogue does not come out in favour of the "ineffability" doctrine, i.e., ineffability of the ultimate goal of mystical experience. The Buddha seems to have been critical of such a doctrine. To consider the highest bliss or highest state of consciousness as the goal of mystical experience without *specifying* that state in words, is like being in love with the beauty queen of a country without having seen her at all!

Since the Ultimate is ineffable, silence would be the best way to teach it or instruct it. This need not be taken as a joke, for the Mahāyāna Buddhist asserted such a position quite seriously. A verse ascribed to Nāgārjuna runs thus:

> . Not a word was uttered by you. O Master, and (yet) all the disciples were refreshed (satisfied) by the *dharma*-shower.[5]...

In the Mahāyāna tradition, we find various formulations of the "ineffability" doctrine.... The *tathatā* or reality is repeatedly described in the Mahāyāna sūtras as *anakṣara* "without letters or words," ie., ineffable. In the *Laṅkāvatāra* the Buddha is said to be saying:

> But the "Ultimate Reality," O Mahāmati, is experienced by each enlightened individual and it is not within the domain of speech and conceptualization. Thus, conceptual construction does not express the Ultimate Reality.[6]...

Ineffability and talk of Ultimate Reality. We have seen thus different formulations of the "ineffability" doctrine in the Indian tradition. One thing is, however, common to all of them. They all do not feel that they should refrain from talking about the "ineffable" Ultimate Reality. In fact, this is no ground for embarrassment for them. First, they agree, all discourses about the Ultimate Reality are provisional. Besides, they all contend that such a discourse has a soteriological purpose to serve. There are indirect discourses by which people should be convinced. In other words, they all agree that their religious or philosophical discourse is only a game, but a worthwhile game or play leading to a goal. They even try to devise different acceptable means by which this GAME—i.e., their religio-philosophical discourse about the ineffable Ultimate Reality—should be effectively conducted. Broadly speaking, they resort to *three* such means. I shall describe them individually.

The first of these three methods is what is generally known as the method *via negativa*. This method in the Indian tradition goes as far back as Yājñavalkya in the *Bṛhadāraṇyaka* Upanishad, where the oft-quoted doctrine "*neti, neti*" ("not this, not that") was first propounded (III. 9.26).[7] Gauḍapāda commented on this doctrine as follows (*Āgamaśāstra*)

> The scripture, "This is not, this is not," denies whatever is explained (about the Ultimate Reality), and thus reveals the truth that nothing originates, for (otherwise) origination would be incomprehensible.[8]

Stated in simple language, the method consists in this: Although we cannot ascribe any predicate to the Ultimate Reality, we might very well say what the Ultimate Reality is not....

The second method used by the upholders of the "ineffability" doctrine consists in bestowing contradictory attributes or predicates on the Ultimate Reality. This method is widely in use by the mystics of all countries and of all ages. To begin with, the early Upanishadic thinkers of India were champions of this method.

It moves, It moves not.
It is far, and It is near.
It is within all this,
And It is outside of all (*Īśa*, 5).

What that is, know as Being and Non-being
As the object of desire, higher than understanding,
As what is the best of creatures.... (*Muṇḍaka* 2.2.1)[9]

Now we come to discuss the third method used by the mystics to convince us about the ineffability of the Ultimate Reality. This method consists in the use of metaphor and rhetoric to convey the notion of ineffability. In the Sanskrit tradition of philosophical semantics, a very important place has been assigned to what is called *lakṣaṇā* "indication" (= the *indicative* function of the word) by which the word gets an indirect or secondary meaning.... Roughly speaking, "indication" *lakṣaṇā* means this. A word has usually a conventionally accepted meaning in isolation, which we can call its *direct* meaning. But sometimes, in a given context, the direct meaning of the same word may not fit in. That is, a combined, acceptable meaning of the phrase or sentence in question cannot be derived from the direct meanings of the individual component words. In such cases, we resort to an *indicated* meaning, a metaphorical meaning, of some particular word or words in order to derive a combined, acceptable meaning of the phrase or sentence in question. Most Sanskrit semanticists say that the word has a second power or function called "indication" *lakṣaṇā* which gives its *indicated* meaning under such conditions. But this is not all. The rule of the language requires that the indicated or metaphorical meaning must be related in some way or other with the primary or direct meaning of the word in question.

An example from the English language will make our point clear. We often say, "the chair speaks" or "the House unanimously agrees," but obviously we do not mean that an actual chair speaks. We can say following the convention of the Sanskrit semanticist that the *indicated* or secondary meanings in these contexts are the Chairman for "the chair" and members of the House for "the House." Note also that "the chair" means the Chairman who is related to the chair, and not just any man in the street. Similarly there is a definite relation between the members of the House and the House itself. Thus, even the indicated meaning of a word cannot depend simply on the whim of the speaker.

Philosophers like Madhusūdana Sarasvatī use this device of "indication" *lakṣaṇā* to defend their position on the ineffability of the Ultimate Reality in the following manner: Words like "the Ultimate Reality," "Brahman" and "Ānanda" (and one can add "Śūnyatā," "Tathatā" and "Bhūtakoṭi" of Mahāyāna Buddhism) are used by the mystics to *mean* the Ultimate Reality only through indication. In other words, they can only point to what the Ultimate reality is, instead of *expressing* it directly. This pointing is done indirectly.

The Indian mystics explain this method sometimes by a popular example of showing or pointing at a very dimly lighted star in the sky called Arundhatī. It is almost impossible to point to this particular star in the vast sky. But one may proceed as follows: Arundhatī is situated beside a bright star which is one of the seven stars in the constellation called the Ursa Major ("the Seven Saints" in Indian terminology). This bright star is the sixth star in the constellation, which is named by the Indians as Vasiṣṭha (in Indian mythology, Vasiṣṭha and Arundhatī are names of husband and wife—a sage and his wife who figure in the Rāmāyana). One may thus say: Look at that Ursa Major (or the Great Bear), and then look at that sixth star there, and then you can see Arundhatī by its side. In other words, it is not a direct ostentation but an indirect pointing. The so-called words for the Ultimate Reality mentioned above can point, in the same manner, to it through indirection.

The matter, however, is not so simple. For the words do not really function as pointers. They express or mean something in a given context. The Indian mystics resort to the theory of *lakṣaṇā* or "indicative function" of words in order to get out of the quandary created by the notion of ineffability. But this position can hardly be defended on the acceptable theory of meaning. Remember that even the *indicative* function does not allow us to derive any meaning from a word according to our whims. In other words, it is not a license like that of Humpty Dumpty in Lewis Carroll's *Alice's Adventures Through the Looking Glass*. We may recall what Humpty Dumpty said to Alice:

> "When *I* use a word," Humpty Dumpty said in rather scornful tone, "it means just what I choose it to mean—neither more nor less." "The question is," said Alice, "whether you *can* make words mean different things." "The question is," said Humpty Dumpty, "which is to be master—that is all."

We may very well ask, as Alice did, whether the mystic *can* make a word mean, even through indirection, what he chooses it to mean, i.e., his Ultimate Reality or the ineffable. Remember that even to derive an *indicated* meaning of a word to fit a given context we have to follow certain rules of idioms of the language. "The chair" in "the chair speaks" cannot mean just any odd unrelated thing in the world. It means "the Chairman" who is related to the primary meaning, the chair. Besides, the indicated meaning is sought after only when the direct meaning or primary meaning is understood but fails to give a combined meaning of the entire expression, "the chair speaks."

Critique of ineffability. Thus, we may ask: what are the direct meanings of such expressions like "Brahman," "Suchness," "Highest Bliss" and "the Ultimate Reality"? If they mean the goal of all mystic paths, the Ultimate Reality, through indication or indirection, what do they mean directly?... Now, to fulfil the condition of *indication*, the mystic has to show that his Ultimate Reality is related in some definite way to these direct meanings of the above expressions—meanings that are, as far as we know, denizens of the Platonic world. Just as the indicated meaning, the Chairman, is derived from "the chair" on the basis of an existent relationship between the chair and the Chairman, the mystic will similarly have to specify a relationship between his Ultimate Reality—the ineffable Ultimate Reality—and the "shadow" meanings of the above expressions. What could be this relation that the mystic supposes to exist between the Ultimate Reality and the direct meanings of the above expressions? In hindsight and not entirely facetiously one may remark that unless we reduce our everyday world into a shadow play, we cannot make any good sense of the mystic's justification of the ineffability doctrine on the basis of the theory of *lakṣaṇā* "indication."

This brings us to our more fundamental criticism of mysticism and its ineffability doctrine. In the Indian tradition, the Nyāya-Vaiśeṣika school has been strongly opposed to mysticism and its ineffability doctrine. The fundamental thesis of the Nyāya-Vaiśeṣika school can be stated as a combination of the following two propositions:

(a) If anything is or exists, it is, in principle, knowable, and nameable.
(b) Whatever is knowable is also nameable or expressible in language....

It is clear that the Nyāya-Vaiśeṣika thesis is a good antidote to mysticism and the ineffability doctrine. It should also remove the modern (overwhelmingly Western) misunderstanding that Indian philosophy is invariably mystical. The business of most classical philosophers of India was solid and down-to-the-earth philosophic argumentation, not creation of mystical illusion or poetic description of mystical experiences. Even the ineffability doctrine was defended and criticized by both proponents and opponents with serious and sophisticated reasonings. It is unfortunate that in a modern discussion of Indian or Oriental mysticism, these texts usually go unnoticed or unrecognized. Thus, any book today which purports to be about mysticism and Indian thought generally represents Indian philosophy as a heterogenous congeries of primitive religion, dogmas, pantheisms and bizarre animisms. But this only perpetuates the illusion about Indian mysticism.

If the Ultimate Reality is claimed to be accessible only to the mystical experience and no other accredited means of knowledge is of any help, then I do not see how such an Ultimate Reality can be expressible in language in order to be communicable to others. To avoid the quandary, the Buddhist (specially of the Diṅnāga school) makes a further claim that the mystical experience is another means of knowledge—an accredited means like perception (*pratyakṣa*). It is in fact said to be a special kind of perceptual experience....

Since the validity of the mystical experience itself is in question here, neither accumulation of millions of cases of such experience nor corroboration of one such experience by another can take us very far by way of establishing its validity. For, any psychologist can tell that there is a general pattern or agreement among the dream experiences of different people living under similar conditions. But certainly that cannot prove the reality of dream objects. Corroboration in cases of mystical experiences would very much be like what the Indian critics call the case of a blind man guiding another blind man. Thus, the status of the Ultimate Reality revealed in some "mystical experiences" is very dubious because such an experience can hardly be claimed to be knowledge. For no other means of knowledge, except the mystical experience itself (whose validity is under consideration), can establish its existence. Thus, the attempt to even *indirectly* describe the Ultimate Reality with the help of negation or negative properties or with metaphors and indicated meaning loses its significance....To say that I teach the highest or ultimate colour (see before for such a dialogue of the Buddha with Udayi) or the Ultimate Reality, is like saying that I am in love with the Beauty Queen of this country when I do not know or have never seen that Beauty Queen!

Mysticism and therefore the ineffability doctrine, in most cases, though probably not in all cases, are sustained and supported by a belief—a religious belief, to all intents and purposes—in "A Separate Reality." This "separate" reality is claimed sometimes to be the Ultimate Reality that is beyond or behind the ordinary everyday world. Fascination for such "a separate reality" is widespread throughout the ages....

Whether such a "separate" reality exists or not, we cannot tell. And the mystic cannot prove it either. It does not exist, at least, in the same way the world around us exists. There are certainly many *separate ways* of seeing or looking at things and the world around us. It should also be admitted that part of the way of our *seeing* the world is considerably conditioned by our culture, training, up-bringing and society. And different ways of *seeing* the world are results of different internalized conceptual apparatus. But if the mystic is trying to make only this point through his ineffability doctrine, it would be a trivial point. Of course, if a person is religiously and mystically inclined he can see religious and mystical significance in everything around him. Much in the same way, an artist sees artistic significance in everyday objects.

Implied in the notion of the Ultimate Reality or a supersensible world as well as in the claim that such a world is more REAL or even more VALUABLE than the ordinary world, is a theory that regards the material and external world as unreal and dream-like, as not final but a mere appearance. Most mystics reinforce this theory about the illusory nature of this world by asserting their belief in the position that reality is one and indivisible, and that multiplicity or diversity is only an appearance. It is true that unity is a concept against which we understand the multiplicity of this visible world, just as invisibility is a concept against which we understand the visibility of this world. But if, for this reason, we assign the highest reality or ultimacy to unity over multiplicity, should we then be justified in assigning ultimacy or finality to invisibility over visibility?

The pertinent question is: Why is multiplicity of plurality (ie., the world) not to be regarded as real? The mystic answers: Because it does not make sense. Why? The mystic, e.g., the Buddhist, answers (*Laṅkāvatārasūtra*, 2.173, 2.163):

> Its nature cannot be ascertained by our discriminating intellect (by dialectical process of reasoning). Things collapse into nothing as we analyze them with reasoning.[10]

Udayana, the Naiyāyika, has sarcastically remarked of the so-called analytical or dialectical argument of the Buddhist, as follows:

> Your criticism of the multiplicity and the status of the phenomenal world in order to expose its unreality (emptiness) is like the argument of someone possessed by a spirit.[11]

Udayana then goes on to cite a humorous argument as an example: Suppose a man (who is apparently possessed by a ghost) sees an elephant standing near the courthouse and starts wondering about it: what could this dark thing be? He "discovers" four alternative possibilities. It could be "solidified" darkness, or a rain-cloud, or just a "friend," or only a "shadow" of a thing lying on the ground. The first two alternatives are suggested for the obvious similarity of appearance. The third alternative is suggested because the ancient teacher, Kauṭilya, defined a "friend" as someone who waits for you at the courthouse (or at the cremation ground). The fourth alternative is a humorous illustration of confusing the shadow for the real thing and the thing for the shadow. Then this man proceeds to reject all these four alternatives with his so-called dialectical reasoning and concludes:

> I, therefore, conclude that there is no such *thing* that I see out there (it is only my imagination)!

After citing this argument, Udayana asks:

> By such reasonings shall we consider that the existence of the elephant has been refuted? Or, shall we say that another who is equally possessed by a ghost (or obsessed) is doing better, for he says, "What it is, it is," without committing himself to the existence of an elephant.[12] (p. 231)

Apart from sarcasm, I think Udayana here points up to a very valid and genuine difficulty inherent in the so-called dialectical arguments of the mystic and idealist philosophers who try to prove the hollowness of the phenomenal world. It is true that sometimes with a dialectical argument we can demolish a theory or proposition about the world.... Udayana suggests that by such pseudo-arguments the mystic might persuade himself to believe in one of the two alternatives: (a) The outside world is unreal and dream-like, and (b) The outside world is what it is....

It is true that sometimes, in the light of certain overwhelming experiences or in a peculiar state of mind, we feel that many things in this world are meaningless, senseless and phantom-like. But this cannot constitute an over-all rejection of everything real and material in the world unless we are in a psychotic condition. It is also true that sometimes for someone who is undergoing unspeakable pain and suffering it is worthwhile to tell him to think that pain is unreal and the world where such pain exists and fear of pain exists is unreal. But that is a physician's privilege (or the privilege of the Buddha, the great physician) to comfort his patient, and not certainly a tested view of reality. Such a doctrine can have a value only in context, just as drugs and anaesthesia have values in removing painful feelings. But this cannot be taken to be a valid, or the ultimate, description of Reality....

Conclusion. Finally, if the moral of the mystic's ineffability doctrine is that our comprehension or experience always outruns our language or linguistic capacities, then such a doctrine can be highly educational. It might challenge us to clarify, modify and reorganize our ordinary experience and understanding of the world. It might warn us against being dogmatic in our comprehension of reality or against our having a complacent attitude about many things that we do not know. For although human knowledge (and science) is progressing everyday, there are many more things that we still do not know about the world around us. The progress of knowledge must be maintained and kept going. Complacence destroys this progress. Thus, we should be wary of complacence. But if the moral to be derived from mysticism is that the world around us is unreal, shadowy and phantom-like, or that the initial undifferentiated, uncategorized consciousness that we all experience at our birth or at our infantile stage is what is ultimately real and most valuable because it is blissful, then we will find ourselves some day back where we started—primitive human society or the Garden of Eden before our eating of the tree of knowledge.

Notes

1. Taittirya Upanishad, *Thirteen Principal Upanishads*, trans. R.E. Hume (Oxford: Oxford University Press, 1921) 285.
2. Katha Upanishad, *Ekādasópaniṣadaḥ*, ed. V.S. Sastri (Delhi: B. Notilal, 1966).
3. Rahula, W. *What the Buddha Taught* (London: Gordon Fraser, 1959) 68.
4. *Laṅkāvatāra-sūtra*, ed. P.L. Vaidya (Darbhanga: Mithila Institute, 1963) 37.
5. Tucci, G. "The Hymn to the Incomparable One," *Journal of the Royal Asiatic Society*, New Series 27 (1932): 314.
6. Vaidya 37.
7. *Bṛhadāranyaka* Upanishad, ed. S. Sastri *et al.* (Poona: Anandasrama, 1911).

8. Gauḍapāda, *Āgamaśāstra*, ed. V. Bhattracharya (Calcutta: University of Calcutta, 1943).
9. Hume.
10. Vaidya.
11. Udayana, *Atmatattvaviveka*, ed. D. Sastri (Benares: Chwokhamba, 1940) 230f.
12. Udayana, 231.

Discussion

1. Consider your stereotypes of Eastern religion. Which of those stereotypes does Matilal reject?
2. Matilal claims that successful indicative language is parasitic upon the direct or primary use of language. Does this claim refute the notion of ineffability? Why or why not?
3. How are Matilal's ways of arguing (as an Indian philosopher) alike or different from some of the Judeo-Christian philosophers' ways of arguing (those that you have already read in this collection)?

Buddhist Philosophy and Its European Parallels
*Edward Conze**

Introduction. The search for philosophical parallels is fraught with pit-falls. Some parallels are fruitful and significant, others incidental and fortuitous....

As for my interpretation of the basic principles of Buddhism, I have recently given it in some detail in *Buddhist Thought in India.*[1]... I will briefly sum them up so that the reader can see what kind of "Buddhism" I compare with European philosophy.

Buddhism. The basic teaching of the Buddha can be expressed in one sentence: The conditioned world as it appears to us is fundamentally and irreparably undesirable, and salvation can be found only through escape to the Unconditioned, also called "Nirvāṇa" Everything else is elaboration.

All conditioned things are marred by having three "marks," i.e., by being impermanent, "ill," and "alien to our true self." Much thought has gone into determining the full meaning of those marks. "Ill," for instance, comprises not only pain and suffering, but also the unease which is nowadays known as "existential anxiety".... Human beings fret against a world which is impermanent, ill, and not-self and are not content to live in it, because they believe that in the core of their own being they are eternal, at ease, and in full control of everything. This alienation of our empirical personality from our true being ... within us is brought about by "craving."

If we want to return to our original state of purity, we must first regenerate ourselves by developing five cardinal virtues, of which wisdom is the last and most important. After these virtues have sufficiently matured, we can slowly attempt a break-through to the Unconditioned, which, through the three doors of deliverance, i.e., Emptiness, the Signless, and the Wishless, leads to Nirvāṇa, which is a state in which the self has become extinct, in which none of this world is any longer extant, and which therefore transcends all words and concepts.

This is all quite simple to understand, though at times hard to believe. It is very much complicated, however, by being combined with an ontological theory of "Dharma" which requires a tremendous intellectual effort. This theory distinguishes three levels of reality: [1] the one and single Dharma, which is the ultimate and unconditioned reality of Nirvāṇa; [2] a multiplicity of dharmas, or momentary and impersonal events, which, though illusory compared with the one single Dharma, are more real than the things around us; and [3] the things of the common-sense world, which are mere verbal constructions, in that they are combinations of dharmas held together by words. The Buddhist "dharma-theory" is unique, and has no exact equivalent anywhere else.

---

*Edward Conze (1904-1979) taught at the Universities of Oxford, London and Wisconsin.

So much for the tenets of what I call "archaic Buddhism."... The further elaboration of these ideas led to two distinct schools, i.e., the "scholastic Hīnayāna" and the "Mahāyāna," which, contrary to what is often said, did not significantly conflict in their doctrines but merely diverged in their range of interest. The "scholastic Hīnayāna" concentrated on the conditioned dharmas, systematized their classification, defined more precisely their particular attributes and general marks, and worked out the relations pertaining among them. The creative contributions of the Mahāyāna, on the other hand, almost exclusively concern the Unconditioned. In particular, the notion of "Emptiness," which in "archaic" Buddhism had been one of the avenues to Nirvāṇa, was now immensely enriched.... The result is a "monistic" ontology which shows many analogies to European metaphysical systems of the same type, while the descriptions of the bafflement experienced by the intellect when confronted with this one and unique Absolute resemble the position of the Greek skeptics in many ways.

Contra modern European philosophy.... Buddhist thinkers made a number of tacit assumptions which are explicitly rejected by modern European philosophers. The first, common to nearly all Indian, as distinct from European, "scientific," thought treats the experiences of Yoga as the chief raw material for philosophical reflection.

Secondly, all "perennial" (as against "modern") philosophers, agree on the hierarchical structure of the universe, as shown in (a) the distinction of a "triple world" and (b) of degrees of "reality," and (c) the establishment of a hierarchy of insights dependent on spiritual maturity.

Thirdly, all religious (as against a-religious) philosophies (a) use "numinous" as distinct from "profane" terms, and (b) treat revelation as the ultimate source of all valid knowledge....

The cornerstone of my interpretation of Buddhism is the conviction shared by nearly everyone, that it is essentially a doctrine of salvation, and that all its philosophical statements are subordinate to its soteriological purpose. This implies, not only that many philosophical problems are dismissed as idle speculations, but that each and every proposition must be considered in reference to its spiritual intention and as a formulation of meditational experiences acquired in the course of the process of winning salvation....

Perennial vs. sciential philosophy. What, then, is the relation of these Buddhist teachings to European philosophy? From the outset, I must admit that I do not believe in a clear-cut distinction between "Eastern" and "Western" mentality. Until about 1450, as branches of the same "perennial philosophy," Indian and European philosophers disagreed less among themselves than with many of the later developments of European philosophy.

The "perennial philosophy" is in this context defined as a doctrine which holds [1] that as far as worth-while knowledge is concerned not all men are equal, but that there is a hierarchy of persons, some of whom, through what they are, can know much more than others; [2] that there is a hierarchy also of the levels of reality, some of which are more "real," because more exalted than others; and [3] that the wise men of old have found a "wisdom" which is true, although it has no "empirical" basis in observations which can be made by everyone and everybody; and that in fact there is a rare and unordinary faculty in some of us by which we can attain direct contact with actual reality—through the *prajñā* [wisdom, understanding of the true nature of reality] of the Buddhists, the logos of Parmenides, the sophia of Aristotle and others, Spinoza's *amor dei intellectualis* [intellectual love of God], Hegel's *Vernunft* [reason], and so on; and [4] that true teaching is based on an authority which legitimizes itself by the exemplary life and charismatic quality of its exponents.

Within the perennial philosophy Indian thought is marked off by two special features: [1] the reliance on yoga as providing the basic raw material of worthwhile experience, and [2] the implicit belief in karma and rebirth. Yoga, of course, has its counterpart in the West in the spiritual and ecstatic practices of contemplatives, and belief in reincarnation is nearly world-wide, though rare among philosophers accorded academic recognition....

In the West, a large number of philosophers discarded the basic presuppositions of the "perennial philosophy," and developed by contrast what for want of a better term we may call a "sciential" philosophy. That has the following features: [1] Natural science, particularly that dealing with inorganic matter, has a cognitive value, tells us about the actual structure of the universe, and provides the other branches of knowledge with an ideal standard in that they are the more "scientific" the more they are capable of mathematical formulation and the more they rely on repeatable and publicly verified observations. [2] Man is the highest of beings known to science, and his power and convenience should be promoted at all costs. [3] Spiritual and magical forces cannot influence events, and life after death may be disregarded, because unproven by scientific methods. [4] In consequence, "life" means "man's" life in this world, and the task is to ameliorate this life by a social "technique" in harmony with the "welfare" or "will" of "the people."

Buddhists must view all these tenets with the utmost distaste. "Sciential" philosophy is an ideology which corresponds to a technological civilization. It arises in its purity only to the extent that its social substratum has freed itself from all pre-industrial influences, and in the end it must lead to the elimination of even the last traces of what could properly be called "philosophy" in the original sense of "love of wisdom."

For centuries it existed only blended with elements from the traditional "perennial" philosophy. As philosophies, both the "perennial" and the "sciential" systems possess some degree of intellectuality, and up to a point they both use reasoning. But ... they differ in that the first is motivated by man's spiritual needs, and aims at his salvation from the world and its ways, whereas the second is motivated by his utilitarian needs, aims at his conquest of the world, and is therefore greatly concerned with the natural and social sciences.

Between the two extremes there are, of course, numerous intermediary stages. They depend to some extent on the quality of the spirituality behind them, which is very high, say, in Buddhism, slightly lower in Plato and Aristotle, and still quite marked in such men as Spinoza, Leibniz, Berkeley, Kant, Goethe, Hegel, and Bergson. The general trend, however, has been a continuous loss of spiritual substance between 1450 and 1960, based on an increasing forgetfulness of age-old traditions, an increasing unawareness of spiritual practices, and an increasing indifference to the spiritual life by the classes which dominate society.

Leaving aside the relative merits of the "perennial" and the "sciential" approaches to philosophy, all I want to establish at present is their mutual incompatibility, which is borne out by their mutual hostility. Our "sciential" philosophers are well aware of this. We need only peruse the writings of empiricists, logical positivists, and linguistic analysts, and it will become obvious that the animosity displayed toward a philosopher is almost a measure of his spirituality. And, in a way, the moderns are quite right. For "perennial" and "sciential" philosophies represent two qualitatively different kinds of thinking which have almost nothing in common, except perhaps for a certain degree of respect for rationality. Our contemporaries continually assure us that the spiritual philosophers of the past are not "philosophers" at all, but dreamers, mystics, poets, and so on. All we can conclude from this is that the word "philosophy" is being used in two quite disparate senses: [1] as the pursuit of "wisdom," and [2] as a "rigorous" academic exercise without much ostensible purpose.

The "wisdom" meant here is compounded of knowledge and a "good life".... It is not easy to see how such words could be used of "philosophy" in the second sense.

Having stated the general principles on which the comparison of Buddhist and European thought must be based, I now speak of the only three currents of European philosophy which can significantly be compared with Buddhism, i.e., the Greek Skeptics, the wisdom-seeking mystics, and the monists and dialecticians.

The Greek skeptics. The European system nearest to the Mādhyamikas is that of the Greek Skeptics.... They also agree in that the history of skepticism exhibits the same tendency to deviate into a purely theoretical intellectualism which has continually threatened the integrity of Buddhist thought. Greek Skepticism went through four stages, which R. G. Bury[2] has called the practical, the critical, the dialectical, and the empirical. The parallel with Buddhism is closest in the first stage, i.e., with Pyrrho (360-275 B.C.). In the last, with Sextus Empiricus (A.D. 160-210), it is barely perceptible. Indeed, taking the later developments as his norm, Bury can affirm that Pyrrho "was probably not at all a full-blown Sceptic, but rather a moralist of an austere and ascetic type who cultivated insensibility to externals and superiority to environment." It was only in the New Academy, with

Arcesilas (315-241 B.C.), that Skepticism "ceased to be purely practical and became mainly theoretical."... In fact, when we read Sextus Empiricus, we find that, although some of the original message has remained intact, it has been overlaid by a vast technical apparatus accumulated over five centuries and by numerous concessions to common sense. The bulk of Sextus' work is parasitical on the dogmatic philosophers, and seems to be motivated more by disputatiousness and the desire to score debating points than by a positive interest in mental repose. In many ways his attitude resembles that of the later Buddhist logicians.

At the time of Cicero, halfway between Pyrrho and Sextus Empiricus, this loss of spiritual earnestness had not gone quite so far. Some of the statements which Cicero makes in his *Academica*,[3] on behalf of or in response to the Skeptics, are indeed strikingly similar to the teachings of the Mādhyamikas and other later Buddhists. The Skeptics were people who "sanctioned nothing as proved".... "All those things you talk about are hidden, closely concealed (*occultata*) and enfolded in thick clouds of darkness, so that no human intellect has sufficiently powerful sight to be able to penetrate to heaven and get inside the earth." Though "it is possibly the case that when exposed and uncovered they change their character,"... the Skeptics "have a habit of concealing ... their opinion, and do not usually disclose it to any one except those that had lived with them right up to old age."... They hold that "nothing can be perceived," or grasped.... and the "wise man will restrain all acts of assent".... There is also a reference to the "perversity".... of seeing the non-real as real, and to arguments against the senses, which are said to be "full of darkness," and against "everything that is approved in common experience." And, as though he had read the Prajñāpāramitā, an opponent points out that "as for wisdom herself, if she does not know whether she is wisdom or not, how in the first place will she make good her claim to the name of wisdom? Next, how will she venture with confidence to plan or execute any undertaking when there will be nothing certain for her to act upon?"

The mystics. Secondly, there is a close similarity with those ascetic, other-worldly, and "mystical" thinkers who assigned a decisive importance to "spiritual experience." They are represented by four main trends: (a) First, there are the Wisdom speculations of the Near East between 200 B.C. and A.D. 300. Their conception of *chochma* [wisdom, Hebrew] and *sophia* [wisdom, Greek] is closely analogous to that of *prajñā*, and some of the similarities are really quite startling. (b) Next, the kindred Gnostic and Neo-Platonic modes of thought, especially the later Neo-Platonists ... and also their Christian form in Origenes and in Dionysius Areopagita, who in some passages of his Mystical Theology gives what may well be called a Christian version of the Heart Sutra. (c) Thirdly, there are the great mystics of the thirteenth and fourteenth centuries, such as Meister Eckhart, Ruysbroeck, and Suso. Their kinship with Buddhism has been noted so often that I can be quite brief. Ruysbroeck says of the "God-seeing man" that "his spirit is undifferentiated and without distinction, and therefore feels nothing without the unity."

Among Western contemplatives, *śūnyatā* [emptiness] corresponds to the "desert of the Godhead," to Ruysbroeck's "idle emptiness," to Eckhart's still wilderness where no one is at home, to the "naked orison," the "naked intent stretching unto God," which becomes possible with entire self-surrender, and also to the fathomless abyss of Ruysbroeck and Tauler. This "abyss" is wholeheartedly welcomed by those steeped in self-negation and self-naughting....

The Theologia Germanica[4] (ca, 1425), as is well known, contains many formulations with a distinctly Buddhist flavor. The most striking similarity lies, of course, in the constant emphasis on "I-hood and selfhood," on "I, me, and mine" as the source of all alienation from true reality, and on the need to undo that "blindness and folly." But this is not all. On re-reading the book I have been astounded to find how close it is in so many ways to Buddhist mentality, in spite of its author's "cautious limitation of his speculations to what is compatible with the Church," and some minor concessions to theism, especially in the later parts.... [T]his is true of what is said about the Godhead (= Nirvāṇa), the "deified man" (=the bodhisattva[5]), activated by both "cognition" and a "love" wherein "there neither is nor can remain any I, Me, Mine, Thou, Thine, and the like."...

(d) Toward the end of the seventeenth century, shortly after Galileo, European mysticism of this type lost its intellectual distinction, and faded away into the "Quietism" of Molinos and Mme. Guyon. In the aftermath of the French revolution, many of the basic laws of the spiritual life were rediscovered by great poets who were also fine thinkers, such as Blake, Shelley, Wordsworth, and Coleridge in England. Though often vitiated by a fatal rift between theory and practice, their thought offers many parallels to Buddhist thinking.

To this generation of rebels against the Goddess of Reason belonged Arthur Schopenhauer, whose thought, partly under Indian influence, exhibits numerous, and almost miraculous, coincidences with the basic tenets of Buddhist philosophy.... As he himself said, Schopenhauer continued the triple tradition of "quietism, i.e. the giving up of all willing, asceticism, i.e. intentional mortification of one's own will, and mysticism, i.e. consciousness of the identity of one's own inner being with that of all beings, or with the kernel of the world."[6] He shows that life in the world is meaningless, essentially suffering, and bound to disappoint the hope that our desires might be fulfilled. He attributes this suffering to "the will to live," which is the equivalent of *tṛṣṇā* [desire or craving], and which "involves us in a delusion." He looks for salvation from this world by way of a "denial of the will to live," which is a "consequence of the dawning of better knowledge," and by an asceticism and self-renunciation exemplified in "the lives of saints, penitents, *samanas* [recluses], *sannyasins* [ascetics], and so on." We may add his atheism, his denial of an immaterial, substantially unchanging, soul, his belief in reincarnation, his stress on compassion as the basis of morality, his indifference to the "achievements" or "rhythm" of human history, as well as his insight into impermanence and into the reasons why Nirvāṇa can be described only negatively, and yet it is not nothing.

[Schopenhauer, however,] fails to appreciate the importance of disciplined meditation. Educated non-Catholic Germans of the nineteenth century were quite unfamiliar with the tradition of spiritual contemplation. On the other hand, for relaxation they habitually visited art galleries and went for walks in the countryside. It is no wonder, therefore, that Schopenhauer sees the foretaste of "the exalted peace" of Nirvāṇa, not in trances, but in "pure esthetic contemplation." Although the contemplation of beauty has some analogy to the conditions prevailing in trance, it is on the whole an undisciplined faculty, and its results are rather fleeting and have little power to transmute the personality. In this respect, the German bourgeois town-dweller was a lesser man than the Indian man in the forest.

The monists. Furthermore, Buddhism has a distinct affinity with the "monistic" traditions of European thought. The Eleatic emphasis on the One implied devaluation, depreciation, and at times even rejection of the plural and multiple world. However they may phrase it, all monistic systems are in tune with the feeling which Shelley formulated in the famous verse:

> Life, like a dome of many-coloured glass
> Stains the white radiance of eternity
> Until death tramples it to fragments.

Parmenides (ca. 480 B.C., nearly the Buddha's contemporary) and his successors assume a radical difference between appearance and reality, between surface and depth, between what we see (*phainomena*) and what we can only think (*noumena*), between opinion and truth. For Parmenides, opinion ... is derived from the senses, which are deceptive and the basis of false information. Truth is derived from the *logos*, which has for its object Being (that which is and has no other attributes but to be). Being is, non-being is not; and that which Is can never not be, either now or later (as in change). Nothing that Is can either arise or perish.

All monistic systems are remarkably uniform, and they are all equally beset by at least four unavoidable difficulties. They must, first of all, try to guard against the misunderstanding that the One might be a datum within the world, or a part of the conglomeration. Both East and West acutely felt the difficulties of finding an adequate verbal expression for the essentially transcendent and elusive reality of the One, and both made many attempts to circumvent them by the use of paradoxes, absurdities, contradictions, tautologies, riddles, negations, and other devices.

Secondly, the monists must attempt to maintain the simplicity of the One by redefining the meaning of predication in regard to it. In this context, scholastic philosophers explained that God *is* each of his predicates, whereas creatures *have* them, and that the predicates of God are not different from one another, since otherwise he would not be simple. "The absolute essence is not in one respect different from what it is in another; what it is, it is in the totality of its being."[7] Everything plural is itself and in addition something else, and only the completely free can be itself pure and simple.

A third problem concerns the relation between the One and Being. The old Eleatic school, which flourished between 540 and 300 B.C., identifies the two.... Plotinus describes the One expressly as "beyond being"; [and] Meister Eckhart ... said that "in the Kingdom of Heaven all is in all, all is one, and all is ours." Pure Being, as the most general, becomes the richest of all terms; and Hegel, again, treats "being" as the initial and minimal definition of the Absolute, which is later enriched by many further "attributes." The *Theologia Germanica* says that "he who finds satisfaction in God, his satisfaction is the One, and is all in the One. And he to whom the One is not all and all not the One, and to Whom something and nothing are not one and the same, cannot find satisfaction in God." The Buddhist non-dual One was in the same way by many devices transferred beyond all logical categories.

And, fourthly, monists must come to some decision on the status of appearance. It may well be that not all of them have, like most Buddhists, regarded appearance as a mere illusion, and it is probably true that "there is never any suggestion in Plotinus that all things except the One are illusions or fleeting appearances." But this is a distinction without much of a difference, because also in the Plotinian system the sensory and material world has an extremely low degree of reality, and is afflicted by a great loss of the original reality, near its point of extinction. In the same way, in the Hegelian system the natural world is a state of estrangement from the Absolute Spirit. In Eckhart, "all creatures, insofar as they are creatures, as they are in themselves,... are not even an illusion, but they are a pure nothing."...

The background of all "monistic" views is a religious contempt for the world of ordinary experience, for that which is not One or not He who Is. That world is held to be unsatisfactory—partly emotionally as a source of suffering, and partly logically as self-contradictory, and as therefore either non-existing or unable to abide in the state in which it is.[8]

Notes

1. *Buddhist Thought in India* (London: George Allen & Unwin Ltd., 1962).
2. R.G. Bury, trans., *Sextus Empiricus*, 4 vols. Vol. I, *Outlines of Pyrrhonism* (New York: G. P. Putnam's Sons, 1933). The following quotations are from pp. xxx, xxxii, xxxiii.
3. Cicero, *De Natura Deorum; Academica*, H. Rackham, ed. and trans. (Cambridge: Harvard University Press, 1961).
4. New York: Pantheon Books, Inc., 1949. London: Gollancz, 1950. This is the translation of S. Winkworth, revised by W. Trask, on the basis of J. Bernhart's translation into modern German: *Theologia Germanica* (New York: Pantheon Books, 1949).

5. 'Bodhisattva' refers to anyone who has vowed to become a Buddha. Until that goal has been attained, such persons must compassionately serve others.
6. E.F.J. Payne, trans., *The World as Will and Representation*, 2 vols. (Indian Hills, Colorado: The Falcon's Wing Press, 1958), p. 613. Vol. II., Vol. II, p. 608., Vol. II chap. 38, Bk. I, par. 3; Bk. III, par. 33, Vol. II, pp. 608, 612.
7. Plotinus, *Enneads*, VI. viii. 10.
8. It may be objected that the comparison of all this with Buddhism applies more to the "monistic" Mahāyāna than to the "pluralistic" Hīnayāna theories. But the difference should not be overstressed. As the Theravāda had a latent idealism and an implicit bias toward a mentalistic interpretation of physical reality,... so it teaches also the one Dharma side by side with the multiple dharmas....

Discussion

1. Consider the distinction between "perennial" and "sciential" philosophy. Which most closely captures your view of knowledge and reality?
2. Does Buddhism (or do any of its European counterparts) provide a live alternative to twentieth-century Western materialism and the emptiness that it seems to create in its adherents?
3. How are your own deepest beliefs and commitments like and unlike Buddhist ideas?

Chapter 23

Taoism

The Tao Te Ching
*Lao Tzu**

1.

The Tao that can be followed is not the eternal Tao.
The name that can be named is not the eternal name.
The nameless is the origin of heaven and earth
While naming is the origin of the myriad things.
Therefore, always desireless, you see the mystery
Ever desiring, you see the manifestations.
These two are the same—
When they appear they are named differently.

Their sameness is the mystery,
Mystery within mystery;

The door to all marvels.

4.

The Tao is so vast that when you use it, something is always left.
How deep it is!
It seems to be the ancestor of the myriad things.
It blunts sharpness
Untangles knots
Softens the glare
Unifies with the mundane.
It is so full!
It seems to have remainder.

---

*Lao Tzu, if he really existed, was born around 600 B.C.E. in Honan province in China.

It is the child of I-don't-know-who.
And prior to the primeval Lord-on-high.

6.

The valley spirit never dies.
It is called "the mysterious female."
The opening of the mysterious female
Is called "the root of Heaven and Earth."
Continuous, seeming to remain.

Use it without exertion.

14.

Look for it, it cannot be seen.
It is called the distant.
Listen for it, it cannot be heard.
It is called the rare.
Reach for it, it cannot be gotten.
It is called the subtle.
These three ultimately cannot be fathomed.
Therefore they join to become one.

Its top is not bright;
Its bottom is not dark;
Existing continuously, it cannot be named and it returns to no-thingness.

Thus, it is called the formless form,
The image of no-thing.
This is called the most obscure.

Go to meet it, you cannot see its face.
Follow it, you cannot see its back.

By holding to the ancient Tao
You can manage present existence
And know the primordial beginning.

This is called the very beginning thread of the Tao.

16.

Effect emptiness to the extreme.
Keep stillness whole.
Myriad things act in concert.
I therefore watch their return.
All things flourish and each returns to its root.

Returning to the root is called quietude.
Quietude is called returning to life.
Return to life is called constant.
Knowing this constant is called illumination.
Acting arbitrarily without knowing the constant is harmful.
Knowing the constant is receptivity, which is impartial.

Impartiality is kingship.
Kingship is Heaven.
Heaven is Tao
Tao is eternal.

Though you lose the body, you do not die.

21.

The form of great virtue is something that only the Tao can follow.
The Tao as a "thing" is only vague and obscure.
How obscure! How vague! In it there is form.
How vague! How obscure! In it are things.
How deep! How dark! In it there is an essence.

The essence is so real—therein is belief.

From the present to antiquity, its name has never left it, so we can examine all origins.
How do I know the form of all origins?

By this.

24.

Standing on tiptoe, you are unsteady.
Straddle-legged, you cannot go.
If you show yourself, you will not be seen.

If you affirm yourself, you will not shine.
If you boast, you will have no merit.
If you promote yourself, you will have no success.

Those who abide in the Tao call these

Leftover food and wasted action
And all things dislike them.

Therefore the person of the Tao does not act like this.

25.

There is something that is perfect in its disorder
Which is born before Heaven and Earth.

So silent and desolate! It establishes itself without renewal.
Functions universally without lapse.
We can regard it as the Mother of Everything.

I don't know its name.

Hence, when forced to name it, I call it "Tao."
When forced to categorize it, I call it "great."

Greatness entails transcendence.
Transcendence entails going-far.
Going-far entails return.

Hence, Tao is great, Heaven is great, the Earth is great
And the human is also great.

Within our realm there are four greatnesses and the human being is one of them.

Human beings follow the Earth.
Earth follows Heaven
Heaven follows the Tao
The Tao follows the way things are.

34.

The Tao is like a great flooding river. How can it be directed to the left or right?
The myriad things rely on it for their life but do not distinguish it.

It brings to completion but cannot be said to exist.
It clothes and feeds all things without lording over them.

It is always desireless, so we call it "the small."
The myriad things return to it and it doesn't exact lordship
Thus it can be called "great."
Till the end, it does not regard itself as Great.

Therefore it actualizes its greatness.

40.

Return is the motion of the Tao.
Softening is its function.
All things in the cosmos arise from being.
Being arises from non-being.

42.

The Tao produces one, one produces two.
The two produce the three and the three produce all things.
All things submit to yin and embrace yang.
They soften their energy to achieve harmony....

43.

The softest thing in the world
Will overcome the hardest.
Non-being can enter where there is no space.
Therefore I know the benefit of unattached action.
The wordless teaching and unattached action

Are rarely seen.

51.

Tao gives birth to it,
Virtue rears it,
Materiality shapes it,
Activity perfects it.
Therefore, there are none of the myriad things who do not venerate the Tao or esteem its virtue.
This veneration of the Tao and esteeming of its virtue is something they do naturally, without being forced.

Therefore, Tao gives birth.
Its virtue rears, develops, raises, adjusts and disciplines,
Nourishes, covers and protects,
Produces but does not possess,
Acts without expectation,
Leads without forcing.

This is called "Mysterious Virtue."

Discussion

1. The Tao is like water. What are some of the properties or effects of water? What insights does this reflection give into the Tao?
2. How is the Tao like or unlike the God of Abraham, Isaac and Jacob?
3. If you were to order your life according to the Tao, how would it be different?

Spiritual Values in Taoism

*T'ang Chün-I**

Introduction. Taoist ideas about spiritual life were usually expounded as in contrast with the life of worldly man. Such names as "real man," "Heavenly man," "spirit-man" or "divine man", "perfect man," and "sage-man" were used by Taoist philosophers to differentiate their ideal man from the worldly man.

Taoist philosophers, who looked aloof at everything here, felt some fatigue in worldly affairs and sought spiritual quiescence and tranquillity, and then, withdrawing their minds from worldly things, were men who had a transcendent mentality. Taoist philosophers usually thought and spoke about their ideals of human life negatively, unlike the Confucians, who usually thought and spoke positively. Lao Tzu (sixth century B.C.) taught men to be weak, soft, quiet, and foolish, instead of strong, hard, active, and wise. Chuang Tzu (399-295? B.C.) taught man not to seek reputation, honor, or social success, to forget himself and be indifferent to worldly gain and loss, happiness and misery, and life and death. They taught people to live a way of life which is neither driven by instinctive desires nor motivated by calculation, forgetting worldly benefits. So, the value of their ideal life is quite beyond the category of the satisfaction of natural desires and utilitarian value.... But what is the spiritual value of this kind of life, which seems purely negative and from which we can derive nothing?

The answer is twofold. First, the Taoist ideal of life has its positive side. Second, this positive value of life can be realized by living in a negative way. I shall begin with the latter point.

Positive through negative life. The reason the positive value of life can be realized by living in a negative way is very simple. If our ordinary way of living is considered of no value or of disvalue, then not living in this way is a positive value. For example, if the toil of the whole day is considered to be disvalue, is not rest itself a positive value? The important thing is that the negating of disvalue should be presented to the spiritual subject. If the negating of disvalue is presented to a spiritual subject, the value of the negating itself is positively presented to the spiritual subject, immanently exists in the subject, and becomes positive spiritual value. So, when I am not seeking worldly wealth, reputation, and honor, which are considered to be of disvalue, the very quiescence and tranquillity in my non-seeking can be presented to my spiritual self as full of positive value (just as rest after a day of toil can be presented as of positive value).

If we understand this clearly, then we know there are as many kinds of values experienced by the men who want to transcend worldly things as by men who cling

---

*T'ang Chün-I was one of the founders of New Asia College, which is now part of The Chinese University of Hong Kong.

to worldly things. The sense of tranquillity and quiescence of the men who transcend worldly things successfully seems homogeneously extended. Yet, under this homogeneous extension, the heterogeneous worldly things are transcended co-extensively. So, the spiritual content of the life of the man who transcends worldly things is as full as the life of the worldly man, the difference being that all worldly things are transcended and superseded in his mind. From this point we may proceed to the reason many Eastern and Western mystics who see the transcendent world as Divine Nothing estimate the value of the Divine Nothing as higher than everything, full of everything that has been superseded, and as a Divine All-Being.

The wisdom of Nothing. The problem of all mystics, who want to transcend worldly things, is that the deep quiescence or tranquillity of the spirit is not easily preserved, and the Divine Nothing is not easily revealed. So, it may be easily concluded that, without faith in a transcendent savior who descends from above to help us ascend to the transcendent world, we can never raise ourselves. However, in Oriental religious and metaphysical thought there is an idea which is most important: that it is not necessary for us to have faith in a transcendent savior to help us transcend the mundane world. Instead, we may have wisdom to see that worldly things are themselves sunk down and have no power to disturb our tranquillity and quiescence of mind and that the world is itself a place where something like the Divine Nothing reveals itself. This is the wisdom of Nothing in Taoist philosophy.

This wisdom is very simple in essence. It is the realization that any worldly thing begins in or comes from "where it is not," or "Nothing," through a process of transformation or change, and ends at or goes back to "where it is not." Then, "beginning and ending in Nothing" is the general nature of all things and the Great Way, or *Tao*, where all things pass through. This idea is based primarily on our everyday experience. Everybody agrees, at least from the point of view of phenomena, that the future is what has not "yet been" and is now nothing, and that the present, which was the future and becomes the past, may be said to come from Nothing and go to Nothing. If we know deeply that everything comes from Nothing and goes back to Nothing, then all things may be taken as involved in a Great Nothing,[1] or as floating out from the Great Nothing, only to sink into it again. Then not anything can really constitute bondage or disturb our spirit. When its very nature of "shall-be-sinking" is really presented to me in the immediate present, it is already nothing and has no effect as a disturbance or bondage for me even now.

The teaching of Lao Tzu. The two great founders of Taoist philosophy, Lao Tzu and Chuang Tzu both present the wisdom of Nothing in metaphysics as the theoretical basis for the development of the spiritual life of tranquillity and quiescence so as to achieve an actual transcendence over worldly things. This is the negative side of their teachings. On the positive side, there are differences in their teachings on the spiritual life.

When Lao Tzu thought about the relation of worldly things to the "Nothing," he usually thought that worldly things were involved and contained in the Nothing. The ideal spiritual life, corresponding to this metaphysical vision, is identified in our mind or spirit with the Nothing and is free from all the limitations of finite particular worldly things. Thus we can comprehend and embrace all things without partiality. When this kind of mind is used in political philosophy, it is the mind of a sage-king, which has no special reaction to any particular thing, but is glad to see all things and actions of all people well done, and embraces all people as his children. This kind of mind is mild, kind, soft, as broad as Heaven or the Void, always wishing for all things to go their own way, and tolerating them, following them, and never interfering with them. This is the first aspect of Lao Tzu's teaching, which has cultivated the virtue of tolerance and broad-mindedness in the Chinese people, and has provided Chinese government with the political ideals of non-interference with the people, concession to the will of the people, and so on.

In the second aspect of Lao Tzu's teaching, the mind, which is identified with Nothing and is as broad as Heaven or the Void, may simply contemplate the "coming and going," "birth and death," and "prosperity and decay" of all things without affection or mercy. It is the mind of a spectator of the universe. It is neither morally bad nor morally good, and maintains ethical neutrality. The metaphysical truth is thus presented to this mind with a kind of intellectual value.

In the third aspect of Lao Tzu's teaching, the mind, which knows that what is prosperous shall decay, that what is strong shall become weak, and that what is born shall die, can generalize all these into a principle: Everything moves in a curve which represents the natural law of all things. According to this principle, when a thing reaches the top of the curve it is destined to fall. Therefore, if we do not want to be a victim of this natural law, the only way is never to progress to the top of the curve, or, when we approach the top, to go back to the beginning of the curve again, for then the top of the curve will always be in our purview, but we shall never arrive there, and so we shall never fall. So, Lao Tzu taught us to go backward, to learn the way of the child or the female, and to be humble and modest, in order to preserve our vitality and other powers to prevent falling down. This is the utilitarian aspect of Lao Tzu's philosophy, which is neither morally good nor morally bad and may not include any spiritual value to be realized by this kind of mind.

The teachings of Chuang Tzu. In contrast with Lao Tzu, when Chuang Tzu thought about the things of the world, he did not hold that all things are contained in the Great Nothing, but paid more attention to the great process of incessant change or transformation of all things in the Infinite Heaven. In this process, all definite forms and colors of things come into being and pass away. So, this process can also be taken as a great change or transformation of a great ether or air, which is itself formless and colorless, being combined with non-being. Since Chuang Tzu paid more attention to the process of transformation in the universe, his view of human life placed more emphasis on the spiritual transformation of human life itself. If one wants to be a real man or a man of Heaven, free from one's past habits or ordinary self, one ought to live a life of spiritual flight, or spiritual wandering, through the process of the infinite transformations in the universe. He should also take all things as equals when they are presented and enjoyed by one's spirit, yet without judging them as good or bad from one's partial, personal point of view. In its flight or wandering in the universe, one's spirit sees everything with empathy and takes the myriad forms as the forms of things which it encounters, yet without attachment to any one, and lets the forms successfully be taken and then left. When the form of anything is left, then nothing remains and nothing needs to be remembered. When the form of anything is being taken, it is absolutely new, just as the world which is present to the new-born child or new-born animal is preceded by nothing, and, as we may not expect anything from it, is followed by nothing. It is immediately presented and enjoyed, as if it were floating in an infinite Void or Heaven as its background. This is the way of life of the real man, the man of Heaven, or the spirit-man of Chuang Tzu. Therefore, the word "spirit" (shen), which originally meant an invisible spirit which existed objectively, was used by Chuang Tzu as the name of the spiritual mood or activity of the spirit-man which extends his spirit beyond the limitation of the universe. He used "shen-yü" (literally, spirit-meeting) as the term for the way of the ideal man when he encounters anything immediately with empathy for the moment, without attachment.

Conclusion. From the above, we may conclude that the spirit of Chuang Tzu's way of life is more aesthetic than Lao Tzu's way of life, and therefore can appreciate with empathy the beauties of all things or the "beauty of Heaven and Earth," as he called it. Yet, this kind of beauty does not consist simply in the forms of things. As every form exists in the process of "transformation of ether or air," so the most beautiful forms should never be clear-cut and should be permeated by the flow of ether and become ethereal forms. As the forms pass through the ether and return, they create rhythms. Ethereal rhythm (ch'i-yün) is a key term of Chinese aesthetics; it has the Infinite Void or Heaven as its background. It permeates the whole universe charged with life.

Notes

1. Taoist philosophers used the word "wu" which does not actually have the same meaning as "nothing." "Wu" means nothing or non-being in phenomena but may not mean nothing or non-being in reality. We use the phrase "Great Nothing" here as the translation of the word "wu" to indicate that it is like nothing in the phenomenal world, yet it may be something in reality.

Discussion

1. In what sense is Taoism a religion?

2. How does Taoism compare to Christianity, Islam or Judaism as religions?
3. If everything comes from and returns to the Divine Nothing, what sorts of value should we attach to existent things? What should our attitude be towards life between the two Nothings?

Asian Philosophy of Religion

Suggestions for Further Study

Burke, T. Patrick. *The Major Religions*. Oxford: Basil Blackwell, 1995.

Conze, Edward. *Buddhism: Its Essence and Development*. New York: Harper Torch-books, 1975.

Corless, Roger. *The Vision of Buddhism: The Space Under the Tree*. New York: Paragon House, 1989.

Griffiths, Paul. *On Being Buddha: The Classical Doctrine of Buddhahood*. Albany: State University of New York Press, 1994.

Hiriyanna, Mysore. *The Essentials of Indian Philosophy*. London: Allen and Unwin, 1951.

Klostermaier, Klaus. *A Survey of Hinduism*. Albany: State University of New York Press, 1989.

Lott, Eric. *Vedantic Approaches to God*. London: Macmillan, 1980.

Moore, Charles, ed. *The Chinese Mind: Essentials of Chinese Philosophy and Culture*. Honolulu: University of Hawaii Press, 1967.

Perett, R. W. *Indian Philosophy of Religion*. Dordrecht: Kluwer Academic Publishers, 1989.

Rhadhakrishnan, Sarvepalli. *Eastern Religions and Western Thought*. New York: Oxford University Press, 1959.

Sharma, Arvind. *A Hindu Perspective on the Philosophy of Religion*. New York: St. Martin's Press, 1990.